STARS,
THE FILM READER

Stars, The Film Reader brings together key writings and new perspectives on stars and stardom in cinema, addressing questions of production, labor, and circulation, and examining neglected areas of study such as the avant-garde star, the non-American stars, and the question of ethnicity.

Grouped in thematic sections, each with an introduction by the editors, the articles explore key issues and developments in the study of stardom, providing a comprehensive overview of stardom across the world and in different genres and media.

Lucy Fischer is a Professor of Film Studies and English at the University of Pittsburgh where she serves as Director of the Film Studies Program. She is the author of *Designing Women: Art Deco, Cinema and the Female Form* (Columbia University Press, 2003), *Sunrise* (British Film Institute, 1998), *Cinematernity: Film, Motherhood, Genre* (Princeton University Press, 1996), and *Imitation of Life* (Rutgers University Press, 1991).

Marcia Landy is Distinguished Service Professor of English and Film Studies at the University of Pittsburgh. Her publications include *The Historical Film: History and Memory in Media* (Rutgers University Press, 2000), *Italian Film* (Cambridge University Press, 2000), *Cinematic Uses of the Past* (University of Minnesota Press, 1996), and *British Genres: Cinema and Society 1930–1960* (Princeton University Press, 1991).

In Focus: Routledge Film Readers
Series Editors: Steven Cohan (Syracuse University) and Ina Rae Hark (University of South Carolina)

The In Focus series of readers is a comprehensive resource for students on film and cinema studies courses. The series explores the innovations of film studies while highlighting the vital connection of debates to other academic fields and to studies of other media. The readers bring together key articles on a major topic in film studies, from marketing to Hollywood comedy, identifying the central issues, exploring how and why scholars have approached it in specific ways, and tracing continuities of thought among scholars. Each reader opens with an introductory essay setting the debates in their academic context, explaining the topic's historical and theoretical importance, and surveying and critiquing its development in film studies.

Exhibition, The Film Reader
Edited by Ina Rae Hark

Experimental Cinema, The Film Reader
Edited by Wheeler Winston Dixton and Gwendolyn Audrey Foster

Hollywood Comedians, The Film Reader
Edited by Frank Krutnik

Hollywood Musicals, The Film Reader
Edited by Steven Cohan

Horror, The Film Reader
Edited by Mark Jancovich

Movie Music, The Film Reader
Edited by Kay Dickinson

Stars, The Film Reader
Edited by Lucy Fischer and Marcia Landy

Forthcoming Titles:

Marketing, The Film Reader
Edited by Justin Wyatt

Reception, The Film Reader
Edited by Barbara Klinger

STARS,
THE FILM READER

Edited by Lucy Fischer
and Marcia Landy

Routledge
Taylor & Francis Group

NEW YORK AND LONDON

First published 2004
in the USA and Canada
by Routledge
29 West 35th Street, New York, NY 10001

Simultaneously published
by Routledge
11 New Fetter Lane, London EC4P 4EE

Routledge is an imprint of the Taylor & Francis Group

Selection and editorial matter © 2004 Lucy Fischer and Marcia Landy
Individual chapters © copyright holders

Designed and typeset in Novarese and Scala Sans
by Keystroke, Jacaranda Lodge, Wolverhampton
Printed and bound in Great Britain
by The Cromwell Press, Trowbridge, Wiltshire

Library of Congress Cataloging in Publication Data
    Stars: the film reader/edited by Marcia Landy and Lucy Fisher.
       p. cm. – (In focus–Routledge film readers)
    1. Motion picture actors and actresses–Biography. I. Fischer, Lucy.
    II. Landy, Marcia, 1931– III. Series.
    PN1998.2.S715 2004
    791.4302′8′0922–dc22   2003023806

British Library Cataloguing in Publication Data
A catalogue record for this book is available from the British Library

ISBN 0–415–27892–9 (hbk)
ISBN 0–415–27893–7 (pbk)

For our shared history in the Film Studies Program at the University of Pittsburgh

Contents

PART FOUR: RACE AND ETHNICITY AND THE AMERICAN STAR 163

PART FIVE: THE NETWORK TELEVISION STAR 229

Illustrations

Figures

Tables

Contributors

Tim Bergfelder is Senior Lecturer in Film Studies at the University of Southampton, United Kingdom. He has published on aspects of German, British, and European cinema history in various journals and edited collections. He is co-editor (with Erica Carter and Deniz Göktörk) of *The German Cinema Book* (British Film Institute, 2002), and author of a monograph on European co-productions and popular German film genres of the 1960s, *International Adventures* (forthcoming).

Sarah Berry is the author of *Screen Style: Fashion and Femininity in 1930s Hollywood* (University of Minnesota Press). She writes on film, media, and cultural studies and designs interactive multimedia. She teaches film studies at Portland State University in Portland, Oregon.

Danae Clark is Associate Professor of Media Studies in the Department of Communication at the University of Pittsburgh. She is author of the book *Negotiating Hollywood: The Cultural Politics of Actors' Labor* (University of Minnesota Press, 1995) and has published articles in such film journals as *Camera Obscura* and *Journal of Film and Video*.

Wheeler Winston Dixon is the James Ryan endowed Professor of Film Studies, Professor of English at the University of Nebraska, Lincoln, Series Editor for the State University of New York Press Cultural Studies in Cinema/Video, and Editor-in-Chief of the *Quarterly Review of Film and Video*. His most recent books are *The Second Century of Cinema: The Past and Future of the Moving Image* (State University of New York Press, 2000) and *Film Genre 2000: New Critical Essays* (State University of New York Press, 2000) and *Collected Interviews: Voices from 20th Century Cinema* (Southern Illinois University Press, 2001). Forthcoming are *Straight: Constructions of Heterosexuality in the Cinema* (State University of New York Press); and *Experimental Cinema, The Film Reader* (Routledge), co-edited with Gwendolyn Audrey Foster.

Richard Dyer teaches Film Studies at the University of Warwick. His numerous books include: *Stars* (BFI, 1979); *Gays and Film* (Zoetrope, 1984); *Heavenly Bodies: Film Stars and Society* (St. Martin's Press, 1986); *Now You See It: Studies on Lesbian and Gay Film* (Routledge, 1990); *Matter of Images: Essays on Representations* (Routledge, 1993); *White* (Routledge, 1997); and *The Culture of Queers* (Routledge, 2002).

Lucy Fischer is a Professor of Film Studies and English at the University of Pittsburgh where she serves as Director of the Film Studies Program. She is the author of: *Jacques Tati* (G.K. Hall, 1983), *Shot/Countershot: Film Tradition and Women's Cinema* (Princeton, 1989), *Imitation of Life* (Rutgers University Press, 1991), *Cinematernity: Film, Motherhood, Genre* (Princeton University Press, 1996), *Sunrise* (British Film Institute, 1998) and *Designing Women: Cinema, Art Deco, and the Female Form* (Columbia University Press, 2003).

Stephen Gundle is Reader in Italian Cultural History at Royal Holloway, University of London. He is the author of *Between Hollywood and Moscow: The Italian Communists and the Challenge of Mass Culture, 1943–91* (Duke University Press, 2000) and co-editor of *The New Italian Republic: From the Fall of the Berlin Wall to Berlusconi* (Routledge, 1995). He has written many articles on Italian stars and other aspects of Italian culture and history.

Dan M. Harries is Senior Lecturer in Film and Visual Culture at Middlesex University, London. He is the author of *Film Parody* (BFI, 2000) and editor of *The New Media Book* (BFI, 2002). Formerly Director of Online Media at the American Film Institute in Los Angeles and creator of CineMedia.org (the Internet's largest film and media directory), his current research interests include intertexuality, online spectatorship, and digital culture.

Ian C. Jarvie is a Professor of Philosophy and Film at York University, Canada. His latest publications include a study of Hollywood abroad: *Hollywood's Overseas Campaign* (Cambridge University Press, 1992); and research on effects: *Children and the Movies* (Cambridge University Press, 1996).

Kathleen Rowe Karlyn teaches Film Studies at the University of Oregon. She is the author of the award-winning book, *The Unruly Woman: Gender and the Genres of Laughter* (University of Texas Press, 1995), and her work on feminism and genre has appeared in numerous film journals and anthologies. Her current research examines the family romance in recent American cinema in the context of teen girl culture, the men's movement, and the popular discourse of incest.

Marcia Landy is Distinguished Service Professor of English/Film Studies at the University of Pittsburgh. Her books include *Fascism in Film: The Italian Commercial Cinema,1929–1943* (Princeton University Press, 1992); *Imitations of Life: A Reader on Film and Television Melodrama* (Wayne State University Press, 1991); *British Genres: Cinema and Society, 1930–1960* (Princeton University Press, 1991); *Film, Politics, and Gramsci* (University of Minnesota Press, 1994); *Queen Christina* (with Amy Villarejo, British Film Institute, 1995); *Cinematic Uses of the Past* (University of Minnesota Press, 1997); *The Folklore of Consensus* (SUNY Press, 1998); *Italian Film* (Cambridge University Press, 2000); and *The Historical Film: History and Memory in Media* (Rutgers University Press, 2000). She is currently at work on a book entitled, *Monty Python's Flying Circus and Unholy Television*.

Kwai-Cheung Lo is currently teaching in the Humanities Program and English Department at Hong Kong Baptist University. His research interests include English minor literature, Asian American literature, East–West comparative studies, Trans-Chinese cultural studies, literary theory, film studies, psychoanalysis and creative writing. His book on Hong Kong transnational popular culture and cinema is forthcoming from the University of Illinois Press.

Gloria-Jean Masciarotte teaches film at Rhode Island School of Design. In addition to her scholarly work, she is also a freelance journalist contributing political and cultural essays to a variety of magazines and newspapers. She co-wrote the screenplay for *What Faroki Taught*, the award-winning documentary selection of the Whitney Biennial 2000. Masciarotte is currently working on a collection of essays, *Memoirs of Feminist Girlhood: Riding the Second Wave*.

Maria Pramaggiore is an Associate Professor of Film Studies at North Carolina State University. She has published essays on feminist performance art, bisexuality and cinema, and contemporary Irish film. Her current projects include *Identifying Others: Irish and African-American Film Since* 1980 and a book on Neil Jordan and the Irish gothic.

M. Madhava Prasad is a Fellow at the Centre for the Study of Culture and Society in Bangalore, India. In addition to his book, *Hindi Cinema*, he has published numerous articles, the most recent of which is "Signs of Ideological re-form in Two Recent Films: Toward Real Subsumption" (in *Making Meaning in Indian Cinema* (Oxford University Press, 2000)).

Paul Smith is a Professor of Cultural Studies and English at George Mason University and a Professor of Media Studies at the University of Sussex. His recent works include *Millennial Dreams: Contemporary Culture and Capital in the North* (Verso, 1997), *Boys: Masculinity in Contemporary Culture* (Westview Press, 1996), and *The Enigmatic Body: Essays on the Arts*, ed. Paul Smith (Cambridge University Press, 1995).

Acknowledgments

The authors wish to acknowledge the support and assistance of the following individuals at the University of Pittsburgh: David Bartholomae, Chair, English; Andrea Campbell, Film Studies; Carol Mysliwiec, English; Robert Mitchell, Center for Instructional Development and Distance Learning; and the following graduate student assistants in the Department of English: Louise Malakoff, Jessica Mesman, Allana Sleeth, Kirstin Strayer, and Ben Feldman. We would also like to thank the editors of the Film Reader series with whom it has been a pleasure to work. Steven Cohan and Ina Rae Hark. Finally, we are indebted to the following people at Routledge: Rebecca Barden, Helen Faulkner, Lesley Riddle, Richard Willis and, especially, copy editor, Liz Dawn.

Danae Clark, "The Subject of Acting," from *Negotiating Hollywood: The Cultural Politics of Actors' Labor* (Minneapolis: University of Minnesota Press, 1995), pp. 18–36, 131–133.

Lucy Fischer, an earlier version of "*Marlene*: Modernity, Mortality, and the Biopic" appeared in *Biography: An Interdisciplinary Quarterly* 23 (1) (Winter 2000): 193–211.

Paul Smith, "Action Movie Hysteria, or Eastwood Bound," from *Differences: A Journal of Feminist Critical Studies* 1 (3) (1989): 88–107. © 1989, Indiana University Press.

Tim Bergfelder, "Negotiating Exoticism: Hollywood, Film Europe and the Cultural Reception of Anna May Wong," from *"Film Europe" and "Film America": Cinema, Commerce and Cultural Exchange 1920–1939*, edited by Andrew Higson and Richard Maltby (University of Exeter Press, 1999), pp. 302–324.

Stephen Gundle, "Sophia Loren, Italian Icon," *Historical Journal of Film, Radio and Television* 15 (3) (1995): 367–385. The journal's web site is: http://www.tandf.co.uk

Kwai-Cheung Lo, "Muscles and Subjectivity: A Short History of the Masculine Body in Hong Kong Popular Culture," from *Camera Obscura* 39 (1995): 105–125. © 1995, Indiana University Press. All rights reserved. Reproduced with permission from Duke University Press.

Maria Pramaggiore, "Performance and Persona in the U.S. Avant-Garde: The Case of Maya Deren," from *Cinema Journal* 36 (2) (1997): 17–40. © 1997 by the University of Texas Press. All rights reserved.

Dan M. Harries, "Camping with Lady Divine: Star Persona and Parody," *Quarterly Review of Film and Video* 12 (1990): 13–22. © 1990 by Taylor & Francis Ltd.

Ian C. Jarvie, "Stars and Ethnicity: Hollywood and the United States, 1932–51," from *Unspeakable Images: Ethnicity and the American Cinema*, edited by Lester D. Friedman. © 1991 by Board of Trustees. Used with permission of the University of Illinois Press. This essay appears in abridged form in this volume.

Sarah Berry, "Hollywood Exoticism," from *Screen Style* (Minneapolis: University of Minnesota Press, 2000), pp. 94–141. This essay appears in abridged form in this volume.

Richard Dyer, "Paul Robeson: Crossing Over," from *Heavenly Bodies: Film Stars and Society*, 1987, by permission of the author. This essay appears in abridged form in this volume.

Marcia Landy, "Mario Lanza and the 'fourth world'," from *Keyframes: Popular Cinema and Culture Studies*, edited by Matthew Tinkcom and Amy Villarejo (London: Routledge, 2001), pp. 242–258.

Kathleen Rowe Karlyn, "Roseanne: Unruly Woman as Domestic Goddess," was first published in *Screen*, 31 (4) (1990): 408–419 and appeared later in *The Unruly Woman: Gender and Genres of Laughter* (Austin: University of Texas Press, 1995), pp. 50–91. The latter version appears in abridged form in this volume.

Gloria-Jean Masciarotte, "C'mon Girl: Oprah Winfrey and the Discourse of Feminine Talk," from *Genders* 11 (1991): 89–110. © 1991, University of Texas Press. This essay appears in abridged form in this volume.

Wheeler Winston Dixon, "The Moving Image in Crisis," *Disaster and Memory: Celebrity Culture and the Crisis of Hollywood* (New York: Columbia University Press, 1999), pp. 1–19.

Stars,
The Film Reader

General Introduction: Back Story

The intense focus in cultural and cinema studies on the subject of stardom, which began in the 1970s with the revaluation of popular culture, continues unabated. Over the years, studies of the star phenomenon have confronted the genealogy of stardom and its situation within modes of film production, circulation, and exhibition. Star studies have been sensitive to the economic and political determinants of a system that relies on the physical character and "personality" of a figure to circulate value in terms of labor, profit, and social meaning. Especially productive have been studies that have sought to account for the continuing fascination the star exerts within the context of genre production. Here, studies of melodrama, in particular, have offered a fertile field in which to examine connections between the star's on-screen persona and off-screen life as invented by publicity operations. Moreover, the link between the star's image and screen roles has been intimately tied to questions of the national imaginary, of how the star embodies and also alters characteristics associated with questions of political identity, value, and attitude. In sum, these studies are emblematic of the ongoing, albeit changing, power exerted by the phenomenon of stardom, a force largely identified with Hollywood and its imitation on a transnational scale. What accounts for the enduring dimensions of the star persona? What explains changes in the phenomenon of stardom? What justifies yet another star study?

Now is a propitious moment to confront these questions. Rather than diminishing, the star phenomenon seems to be ever expanding and assuming new forms. It has moved beyond the cinema to include television. It has leaped beyond the screen into the political arena. It has enlisted ever new recruits into fandom based on shifting demographics of gender and generation. Witness the pre-teen girls who model their physical appearance, couture, and demeanor on that of Britney Spears. Or at the other end of the age spectrum, consider how certain male stars (Sean Connery, Clint Eastwood) enjoy a spectacular longevity, allowing their audiences to grow old with them. If fandom continually expands, so do conceptions of stardom. Think, for example, about the instant celebrity of anonymous reality show contestants (e.g. from *Survivor*) who get immediate cameo appearances on prestigious talk shows. Or observe the performers who instantly "jump track" from TV commercials to entertainment shows: a young man whose only current claim to fame is a Dell computer ad supposedly has a sitcom "in development" based on his alleged persona. These events raise questions about what constitutes the "threshold" for stardom, about the connections between stardom and celebrity, and about the trajectory of the "star" persona. If stardom, these days, is easy to come by, it is almost impossible to lose. A recent *New York Times*[1] article chronicles how "has-beens" perennially stay in the limelight: boxing matches take place between Paula Jones and Tonya Harding and game shows are populated with yesteryear's child actors. The insatiable, content-hungry global television apparatus ensures the introduction of new celebrities as well as the resurrection of the old.

Thus, the phenomenon of stardom today would seem to have no limits, but it is also, paradoxically, in crisis. While the career of male actors seems infinite, the half-life of actresses is often quite finite in both the U.S. and internationally. The careers of performers like Jean Moreau or Sophia Loren are exceptional; those of Melanie Griffith, Jessica Lange, and Demi Moore, the rule. But a major challenge to traditional conceptions of the star is now mounted by computer animation. In 2001 a film entitled *Final Fantasy: The Spirits Within* was produced in which no "real" actors appeared. Instead, the drama's cast was completely synthesized (in a manner that resembled live-action and not animation). As Roger Ebert said, with some irony: "the [film's] space soldier Gray Edwards [.] looks so much like Ben Affleck that I wonder if royalties were involved." In the same vein, 2002 brought the release of *Simone*, a film about a producer who creates a digital replacement for his star when the real actress temperamentally walks off the set.

Thus, we might ask: Is screen acting (already a virtual performance by dint of its removal from pro-filmic space) now on its way to being entirely dematerialized? At the same time that digitized stars are being created, actual ones (once living but now dead) are being revivified. For example, a television commercial appeared a few years back that re-animated the image of Fred Astaire – now dancing with a vacuum cleaner instead of a human partner. Word has it that technicians are poised to re-situate such star personalities in new dramatic films by manipulating images culled from their cinematic oeuvre. Surely, this technological development must lead the media critic to ask: What is the Work of the Star in the Age of Digital Reproduction? If stardom continues to live on, what will be the effect on it of such new technologies? Finally, we might inquire: What can we learn about the cultural character and impact of the star phenomenon through an examination of the historical narratives that have described its emergence, its systemic character, its producers, its modes of circulation, its transformations, and its reception? For, the star system is not only the product of the film industry, it is also the creation of scholarly and popular writing about it.

Here, it is important to note that, at the birth of cinema, the star system did not exist, though the focus on the exceptional individual as a projection of social, sexual, and class aspirations, desires, and failures was deeply embedded in Western cultural conceptions of individualism. Such singular figures had functioned in a number of high cultural and popular venues – and the elevation of the artist to a position of prominence and adulation had been a feature of theater, opera, and painting. The new medium of cinema did not immediately foreground the singularity of the performer. Initially viewers came to the movies without knowing what they would see, just for the thrill of a spectacle – be it an exotic shot of the Pyramids, a frightening view of an approaching train, an image of royalty (such as King Umberto and Queen Margarita of Italy walking in their garden), or a mundane glimpse of workers leaving a factory.

As movie-going became more common in the early years of the twentieth century, and as films became more reliant on existing popular narratives, audiences were attracted to shows by the genre of the product (a historical spectacle, an adaptation of a "classic," a comedy), by the recurrent character featured in the narrative (Fantomas, Cretinetti, or Pauline) or by the name of the company producing the film (Pathé, Cines, or Lubin). In the U.S., it was not until the 1910s that the names of the performers were even featured; one of the first was Florence Lawrence, the "Biograph Girl." With the burgeoning careers of such actors as Mary Pickford, Douglas Fairbanks, Tom Mix, and Charlie Chaplin, a full-fledged American star system was born. In the case of early European cinema, however, the situation was different. The name of the performer played an important role in the selection of narratives and the wooing of audiences. With cinema closely tied to the theater and the music hall, such comedic figures as André Deed and Max Linder were among its most popular early stars. Moreover, high culture figures like Sarah Bernhardt and Eleonora Duse appeared in early movies as did Francesca Bertini, an enduring Italian melodramatic diva of the period.

The early 1910s saw the worldwide consolidation of the multi-reel feature-length film. The international popularity of Italian historical movies was particularly influential in this regard, including *The Taking of Rome* (1905), *The Last Days of Pompei* (1907), *The Fall of Troy* (1911), *Quo Vadis* (1913) and *Cabiria* (1914). These works are credited with influencing D. W. Griffith in his move to make such early features as *Judith of Bethulia* (1914). Similarly, the Italian phenomenon of "divismo" and its role in the development of the star system has been obscured by the intense focus on the Hollywood cinema, but it has much to teach us about the constituent material and cultural elements of stardom. The "diva" or star not only became a major economic determinant of the success of a film but, according to critics, expressed a number of cultural values concerning femininity and masculinity, class position, life style, and national identity. In the annals of star studies, only now are critics beginning to move beyond a fixation on Hollywood to recognize transnational influences on the conceptions of stardom.

From the 1910s through the 1940s, film critics largely approached stardom from a "fan" perspective, composing paeans to beloved actors (in newspaper reviews, journalistic articles, and movie magazine essays). With the early 1960s came longer and more erudite studies such as Edgar Morin's *The Stars*, published in France in the first year of the decade. As he declares in his opening sentence: "Throughout an immense part of the world, for an overwhelming proportion of the film industry, the movies revolve around a kind of solar performer appropriately called a star" (5). Although Morin admits that there are precedents in the theater for this occurrence, he counters: "A stage actor has never become a star to this degree, has never been able to play so important a role within and beyond the spectacle . . . The movies have invented and revealed the star" (8). Morin's observations address several key features of the cinematic apparatus: its connection to other artistic forms and its unique presentation of the actor. If Morin is correct that the movies have "invented" stardom, we must now ask: How has film studies "invented" its analysis?

In truth, a consideration of this subject involves confronting a series of specific topics and approaches that have characterized the literature on stardom from the 1960s to the present. The most prevalent form of writing on the issue has been that of *biography*. Not only is this mode the one with which the public has become most familiar, but it is the one most relevant to questions of publicity – a product of the star system itself. Furthermore, biography is a genre that reaps high profits for the publishing industry – a business that is always on the lookout for popular subjects. Rather than abating in the age of television, biography has usurped its performers as well, inviting scholars and popular writers to extend the genre into a new medium. Most of these biographies are heavily saturated with the codes of melodrama, often turning the star's life and career into a narrative that rivals the visual texts in which he or she may have appeared. Hence the style and structure of these volumes privilege tales of personal and social struggle, of intense, even excessive, emotional conflict. In constructing these biographies, writers have not only considered a particular actor but have created a "star text" through weaving a fabric that encompasses both the individual's on- and off-screen lives. Certain performers are more "suitable" for this form of narrative: those whose lives have been tinged with scandal, or those who have met early and tragic deaths – ideally both. Another important ingredient in the selection of candidates for star biographies has been the actor's involvement with dominant figures of his or her time – from politics, high finance, or international high society (e.g. Orson Welles's friendship with Nelson Rockefeller, Marilyn Monroe's romances with the Kennedy brothers).

Preferred star lives should evince some irony in the comparison or contrast between the individual's on-and-off screen existences (what Morin calls "the dialectic of interpenetration of actor and hero" [38]): either the two should be strangely convergent or radically opposed. Emblematic of an uncanny convergence is the figure of James Dean whose death could be construed as a realization of his screen character. Thus, he is the young movie rebel who dies off-screen at 24 years of age in a reckless car crash of his Porsche "Spyder." In the case of Louise Brooks, her biographers (and she herself) present a consonance between screen world and life story in proffering an image of a restless woman, vainly seeking desire, and constantly being thwarted. Similarly the numerous biographies of Greta Garbo thrive on highlighting a parallel between her on- and off-screen personae through presenting her as an enigma who solicits endless speculation about her life and work.

On the other hand, Marilyn Monroe is representative of the star figure that offers biographers a dramatic contrast between screen performance and life. This contrast is couched in terms of the image of a woman whose personal troubles (divorces, childlessness, and unrequited relationships with powerful men) seemed at odds with her sex goddess persona. Biographies of Monroe run the publishing gamut from routine chronicles like those of Fred Guiles and Anthony Summers to intellectual meditations like those by Norman Mailer and Gloria Steinem. At the extreme end (and perhaps characteristic of the genre's *reductio ad absurdum*) are fictional biographies like *Blonde* by Joyce Carol Oates that transpose the details of a star's life into a docu-drama. A major ingredient of most star biographies is their heavy investment in popular psychologizing. The star's narrative is structured around familial, sexual, and conjugal conflicts that are interpreted through speculation, invoking such pathologies as insecurity, neurosis, depression, anxiety, narcissism, hysteria, and self-destruction. The most egregious instances of this can be seen in biographies written by the children of stars, as in the case of those authored by the disgruntled daughters of Marlene Dietrich and Joan Crawford.

The biographical minutia of the star's life must inevitably entertain banal and quotidian material, but *scandal* can liven up the work, and this element has served as one of the guilty pleasures of fandom. The introduction of socially and sexually "deviant" material is, after all, another way of extending the spectacle of the media screen to the everyday world and legitimating the exceptional character of the star in a society that valorizes personal excess or crisis. Thus, one thinks of the gossip around Greta Garbo's, Marlene Dietrich's, or Rock Hudson's sexual preferences, around Sophia Loren's conflicts with Italian law, around John Belushi's drug addiction, around Marcello Mastroianni's sexual peccadilloes, and around Charlie Chaplin's penchant for young girls. Such titillating details have been grist for the star biography "mill" which wallows in them, obscuring more fundamental questions about how the media's engines of publicity "enable" the public in its dubious fascination with such material.

Beyond this, much writing on stardom has openly trafficked in a fascination with decadence, introducing morbid, even necrophilic details into star discourse, thereby exposing readers to the seamy side of Hollywood paradise. Here one thinks of Kenneth Anger's two-volume *Hollywood Babylon* with its map of Hollywood Memorial Park Cemetery, its photograph of Tyrone Power's crypt, its image of the deceased Valentino, its portrait of an obese and bedraggled Elizabeth Taylor, or its vision of Fatty Arbuckle hugging a bottle of booze. While such texts invite the reader to indulge in images of transgression, recent critical work has sought to rethink the dynamics of this macabre obsession. Thus, *Hollywood Headline* (edited by Adrienne McLean and David Cook) contains historically researched essays analyzing the scandals surrounding Fatty Arbuckle, Wallace Reid, Jane Fonda, Hedy Lamarr, and Ingrid Bergman. Furthermore, certain essays question the ethical and juridical premises of gossip-mongering, asking whether the critic has the "right," for instance, to inquire about an artist's sexual orientation. Such work calls attention to the problematic connections between the star and a culture immersed in and attracted to spectacles of catastrophe and death.

While the relationship between the private life of the actor and his or her screen existence has animated writing on stardom since its inception, another type of inquiry has also been evident in the voluminous literature on the subject – namely, that which examines the *star's screen presence*. In the first decades of the cinema, such writing focused primarily on Hollywood personalities, and seemed more a declaration of fascination or love than an act of analysis. For example, critics such as Kenneth Tynan "swooned" over the face of Garbo, penning essays that resembled "Odes to Beauty" more than investigations of film form. Likewise, Surrealist writer Jacques Rigaut waxed poetic about the "aura" of silent star Mae Murray, cataloging: "Her little laugh . . . her exasperating childishness . . . her tenderness . . . her incredible gaiety, and [her] . . . long, too agile body." He ends by opining: "I'm in love with Mae Murray" (128).

These critics did, however, emphasize the centrality of gestural rhetoric in star discourse, particularly that apparent in the facial close-up, a concept that has had great import for an analysis of the cinematic image. Thus, Béla Bálaázs wrote: "the film [medium] has brought us the silent soliloquy, in which a face can speak with the subtlest shades of meaning" (307). Drawing upon the expressibility of the face in cinema, Robert Benayoun focuses on the visage of Buster Keaton in accounting for the star's screen magic. As he comments: "His mask . . . is enough to knock down walls. It is a timeless icon; it belongs to a galaxy of immortal masks carved by the light of ages" (7). Similarly, Gilles Deleuze, in his philosophic analysis of the "movement-image", has commented that the face, or "faciality" as he describes it, has the power to reveal "all kinds of tiny local movements which the rest of the body usually keeps hidden" (*Cinema* I, 87–8), producing such emotions as wonder, astonishment, terror, and power.

The examination of the star's presence and more generally the phenomenon of celebrity has also been considered in terms of *myth* as exemplified by the title of Parker Tyler's book *Magic and Myth of the Movies* (1947). He wrote: "[T]hose who do not profoundly know anthropology might be astonished to learn how much of our personal life is influenced by the magical and religious beliefs . . . I assume that movies are essentially likewise" (xxi). Clearly, Tyler also applied these notions to the public's attitude toward the star. Edgar Morin tended to agree with him, noting that: "Divinized . . . stars are more than objects of admiration. They are also objects of a cult. A religion in embryo has formed around them" (71). In more recent times, Roland Barthes in *Mythologies*, characterized Garbo's visage in Platonic terms as "an archetype of the human face . . . descended from a heaven where all things are formed and perfected in the clearest light." Hence, "Garbo's singularity was of that of a concept" (57). Clearly even Richard Dyer, writing in 1987, references the "supernatural" notion of the star when he calls his book on the subject of stardom *Heavenly Bodies*. Thus, in identifying the religio-mystical dimension of stardom, critics have proposed that, in a postmodern, post-spiritual, post-aristocratic world, where deities and monarchs are dead or compromised and the universe is proclaimed as absurd, only the star is left as an icon to worship. However, there is a profound difference between identifying and reveling in these religio-mystical, cultic, and affective conceptions and finding a critical language with which to understand the basis of the star's charisma.

In a less anthropological, philosophic, or speculative vein, recent critics have sought a more rigorous analysis of stardom through *performance style*. In *Eloquent Gestures*, Roberta Pearson has examined the intricacies of silent screen acting (especially the "histrionic code" of melodrama), focusing on actors such as Henry Walthal and directors such as D. W. Griffith, both of whom perfected the melodramatic form. Similarly, Christine Gledhill's *Stardom: Industry of Desire* explores the important connections between performance and the codes of melodrama. Likewise, Charles Affron in *Cinema and Sentiment* analyzes the acting styles of particular performers. Furthermore, in his manuscript on Buster Keaton, Noel Carroll investigates the coordinated athleticism of the comic's physical being, one that he regards as opposed to the more sedentary stance of the typical American industrial worker. In focusing on sound film performance, James Naremore, in *Acting in the Cinema*, offers close readings of the behavior of performers in specific texts: be it James Cagney in *Angels with Dirty Faces* or Cary Grant in *North by Northwest*. Furthermore, he explores how "accessories" such as props, costumes, and make-up contribute to a star's expressivity. Critics have also discussed the relation of performance to film style, noting, for instance, how long-shots were used to depict Chaplin's gymnastic body, how close-ups were employed to capture Falconetti's eloquent face, how moving camera shots were engineered to render Astaire and Rogers' grace, and how static views were chosen for Busby Berkeley's mass human abstractions.

Beyond performance style, the discussion of stardom has investigated the *star persona*, exploring whether the star has been "type cast" in a limited and repetitive series of roles, and, if so, what they are and how they have evolved. Early on in the literature, Morin remarked that "Character actors are not stars: they lend themselves to the most heterogeneous interpretations, but without imposing on them a unifying personality" (39). Building on Morin's insights, in his path-breaking studies, *Stars* and *Heavenly Bodies*, Richard Dyer explored the various components and permutations of Lana Turner's roles as her persona evolved from a "sexy-ordinary image" to one of glamor and malevolence. Likewise, in the case of Marilyn Monroe, Dyer analyzed how she projected a sense of a vulnerable femininity accompanied by a healthy and liberated sense of sexuality – the *yin* and *yang* of the male erotic imagination. For Robert Sklar, James Cagney, John Garfield, and Humphrey Bogart were, quintessentially, "city boys," scrappy, edgy, mavericks who knew their way around the urban jungle. For Joan Mellen, Mae West incarnated a cynical female who willfully used her sexual powers to manipulate men, a stance that had liberatory elements despite its potentially retrograde overtones.

Since the late 1970s, with the rise to prominence of cultural studies, the examination of stardom has taken a more *social-political cast*. Most strikingly, following issues and methodologies posed by Richard Dyer, star studies have forayed beyond biographical, mythic, and formal concerns into discussions of the relation between the film industry and the broader realms of economics, politics, and social value. Thus, for example, critics like Charles Maland (working on Charlie Chaplin) have sought to locate the construction of an actor's social perspective within a historical examination of the ideology of his time.

While earlier notions of the star treated the performer as an ethereal figure who circulated in the realm of the Sublime, more engaged approaches have stressed the economic framework for the production of stardom, especially within the context of corporate Hollywood. Long ago, Hortense Powdermaker called the Hollywood cinema a "dream factory" (a phrase with clear Fordist and entrepreneurial implications); but Powdermaker was not revealing a secret – the profit-making aspect of Hollywood was always common knowledge. For example, Morin wrote that "The star is a total item of merchandise: there is not an inch of her body, not a shred of her soul, not a memory of her life that cannot be thrown on the market" (137). However, until recently, the particular character of the industry (its financial and legal structures, its modes of production, its labor practices) has been less an object of scholarship – this despite the fact that such a parameter affects the status of stardom. The actor as "commodity" involves not only the performer's salary (based directly on the box-office receipts that he or she generates), but a host of other related phenomena that film studies has begun to investigate: "tie-in" products (like fashion or clothing worn and endorsed by the star) or memorabilia (such as look-alike dolls or portrait-emblazoned lunch boxes). Among those critics who have examined the links between stardom and consumerism are: Jane Gaines, Charlotte Herzog, Charles Eckert, and Maureen Turim.

Theoretical questions concerning the social character of the cinematic apparatus have led star studies to undertake a more critical analysis of the formation of particular stars as icons of their zeitgeist, emphasizing their historical rather than their mythic dimensions. In analyses of Hollywood, this approach has resulted, for instance, in focusing on Lillian Gish as a symbol of Victorian womanhood; Joan Crawford as the quintessential 1920s flapper; James Stewart as the populist average American; Rosalind Russell as the 1940s career woman; Rita Hayworth as the postwar femme fatale; Lana Turner as the 1950s "ice maiden"; and Arnold Schwarzenegger as the contemporary Macho Man. These studies have their counterpart in the examination of international stardom (e.g. Jean-Paul Leaud as the exemplary New Wave French male, Sophia Loren as the typical Italian sexpot).

Though it is obvious that the largest body of star studies has focused on Hollywood, increasingly the field has expanded to include examinations of Asian, European, and Latin American performers. But even in their works, the specter of Hollywood looms large. While there has always been a common-sense understanding that a star expresses the cultural milieu in which he or she works (Fernandel as a prototypical French comic, Brigitte Bardot as a paradigmatic Continental sex goddess, Gracie Fields as a patriotic Englishwoman), it has been only recently that a conception of the relation between nation and stardom has emerged, another effect of the linkage of film studies to social and political analysis. With the intensified production of books on national cinemas as well as the growing critical literature interrogating the meaning and viability of conceptions of nation, star studies have expanded to incorporate critical questions concerning the manufacture of sexual, gender, racial, and class identities. Hence Aruna Vasudev has written on the star in Bombay cinema, Ana López on Latin American stars, Sabine Hake on German stars, and Ginette Vincendeau on French stars. In many cases (especially those nations boasting major cinematic institutions), it is difficult to separate the formation of national identity from the power of the screen world, suggesting (1) that national cinemas (and their major performers) have been an important factor in the formation of conceptions of citizenship; and (2) that, paradoxically, Hollywood has played a key role in shaping star images in numerous other cultures.

In connection with the attention to the material determinants of cinema, star studies have also begun to investigate the dynamic between the star and the audience through an examination of *reception*. Thus, Miriam Hansen has analyzed why the female viewer of the 1920s may have been attracted to Rudolph Valentino; Janet Staiger in *Interpreting Films* has examined the investments of gay male spectators in the films of Judy Garland; and James Damico has charted the public's reception of Ingrid Bergman's controversial and highly publicized affair with the Italian director, Roberto Rossellini. With approaches ranging from an examination of historical documents to empirical research on audience members, such scholarship has sought to assess the impact of star texts and images on the lives of spectators.

In seeking methods for understanding the bonds established between stars and their audiences, scholars have also invoked such psychoanalytically informed notions as "identification" and "affect" to account for the viewer's stake in the performer and text: Charles Affron explores these issues in *Cinema and Sentiment*, Carl Plantinga and Greg Smith in *Passionate Views*, and Janet Staiger in *Perverse Spectators*. Once the issue of viewership became a major topic, questions of gender also rose to the fore. For example, in *Star-Gazing*, Jackie Stacey focuses on British responses to Hollywood stars and discusses how notions of escapism have informed the bond between female film-goers and actresses (118, 126). By contrast, Gaylyn Studlar's study of Marlene Dietrich, based on Gilles Deleuze's study, *Masochism: An Interpretation of Coldness and Cruelty*, concentrates on the image of the star from a vantage point contrary to classical psychoanalysis. Accounting for the power of Dietrich's image and, by extension, the receptivity of audiences to her presence, Studlar challenges feminist models of spectatorship and, particularly, the reductive dimension of "male gaze theory." For Studlar, Dietrich's physical appearance and her dominating position within her film's narratives can be traced – not to the powerful, sadistic paternal figure – but to the various incarnations of the maternal Imago, often undervalued in a psychoanalytic criticism which overemphasizes the Oedipal character of language, culture, and representation. Studlar's analysis offers a fruitful examination of connections between gender and sexuality that have become increasingly central to star studies. Indicative of this, in recent years, the preponderant focus on female stars (generated by feminist criticism) has been amplified and paralleled by writings in the area of men's studies. In this type of analysis, critics have looked, for example, at the homosocial tensions between male stars and their audiences in such films as *Spartacus*, *M*A*S*H**, or *Midnight Cowboy* (Cohan and Hark).

As we have seen, Film Studies has already conceived a variety of promising and provocative approaches to the analysis of stardom. Given the plethora of such studies, what justifies yet another work on the subject? Mindful of research that has preceded, the essays gathered in *Stars: The Film Reader* address, augment, and/or modify the range, complexity, and dimension of work on stardom in the extant critical literature. Though prior work has paved the way, certain gaps remain in the field that this volume seeks to address:

1   Star studies have largely been characterized by a high degree of ethnocentrism: western cinema (and its performers) are prioritized, with American film as the favored example. This volume attempts to expand the focus of the investigation of the star phenomenon to include the *cinema of European and non-western nations*.

2   Star studies have, in general, focused on mainstream performers such as Henry Fonda, Jean Gabin, Anna Magnani, or Laurence Olivier. This volume seeks to broaden the scholarly terrain to include *performers within the avant-garde, art cinema, and independent cinema* as well as those who appeal to "*marginalized*" audiences.

3   Star studies have tended to concentrate on the cinema with the mention of television limited to certain canonical performers within the sitcom genre (e.g. Lucille Ball). This volume tries

to extend the reach and shape of the field of stardom by considering the *television talk show host*, a huge cultural force in both daytime and late night television.

4   While it is logical that star studies have centered on theatrical performers (actors paid to inhabit an illusory role), increasingly "real life" has begun to approximate a dramatic script with, for example, a soap-opera romance performed by Bill Clinton and Monica Lewinsky, a film noir intrigue lived out by Chandra Levy and Gary Condit, and a royal melodrama centered on Princess Diana and her husband and lovers. This volume seeks to explore the *emergence of the "news star,"* the individual caught in a tabloid media spotlight that conceives of the world in terms of the codes of fictionality.

5   Although star studies have focused increasingly on the material dimensions of the star as commodity (e.g. the performer's bankability, the tie-in products associated with his or her name), the *question of performance as industrial labor* has been largely ignored. This anthology attempts to fill that gap by contextualizing the star within the discourse of market value.

6   While star biographies have been given the lion's share of attention, the status and role of the biographical film in the consolidation of the star's image has not (with the exception of George Custen's work on the subject). This book will investigate the *role of the "biopic" in the creation of a broader "star text."*

7   While ethnicity has been examined within the filmic narrative – namely, whether certain films are prejudicial to "images" of Jews, Italians, or Arabs – short shrift has been given to the ethnic background of the star. This anthology seeks *to contextualize the performer within the realm of his or her cultural heritage.*

8   While the story lines of films have been subjected to ideological analysis, the roles that stars play in the actual social world has not. This volume attempts to probe the growing phenomenon of the *actor's political engagement* in the national and international context.

9   While most star studies have concentrated on Caucasian stars, this volume expands the focus to include *Asian and African-American performers.*

10   While most studies use the prototype of theater as a model for celebrity, this volume will make reference to other relevant and diverse forms of entertainment such as *the opera*.

While confronting these newer scholarly issues will augment and expand the parameters of media star studies, doing so will only scratch the surface of stardom itself – a phenomenon which is as fickle and changeable as fashion, of which it is a constituent element conceived on the human scale.

Note

1   James, Caryn. "And Now, the 16th Minute of Fame," *New York Times* (13 March 2002), p. B1, 8.

References

Note: all works cited in this section are listed in the final bibliography.

PART ONE

RE-FORMING THE STAR CANON

Introduction

The first section of this book, "Re-forming the Star Canon," will consider the mainstream Hollywood star and star system from new perspectives through the inclusion of recent critical studies that offer unique insights for an understanding of stardom beyond the familiar focus on the star's on- and off-screen biography. Among the original aspects of critical material included in this section will be a focus on the role of labor as an important determinant for considering the construction and vicissitudes of star formation, on the star "biopic" as another avenue for understanding the circulation of star texts, on issues of acting that play a key role in the personification of the star, on the rarely examined phenomenon of the star director, and on established performers who have not been accorded proper critical attention.

Danae Clark's "The Subject of Acting" concentrates on a subject that has hitherto received scant attention: the relation between stars and Hollywood labor practices. The essay offers another, more material framework from which to assess stardom. Clark describes how Hollywood studios relied on labor power differences to maintain their dominance. She outlines how, given the "fragmented state of the acting profession," studio heads were empowered to gain control over actors, reducing them to a "passive community of workers," making it difficult for them to organize collectively. Thus the issue of the value attached to the labor of performance was a perennial site of contention that has had profound implications for an understanding not only of ongoing labor struggles in Hollywood, but also for the definition of the star persona. Clark thus brings together significant strands of Hollywood history – the power of the studios, the force of labor, the material aspects of representation, the issue of unionization, questions of identity formation, and definitions of acting and their impact on the character of stardom.

The relationship between stardom, its historical construction, and its changing dimensions is evident in the genre of the biographical film. While acknowledged as an essential and conventional component of Hollywood genres, the biopic has, surprisingly, not received careful and sustained analysis for the insights that this genre form sheds on the production and circulation of the star persona. Lucy Fischer's essay, "*Marlene*: Modernity, Mortality, and the Biopic," addresses this lack of critical attention. A focus on Maximilian Schell's biopic concerning Dietrich (*Marlene*) becomes the occasion for Fischer to explore and integrate questions of the star's relations to cultural and cinematic history and particularly the impact of modernity and postmodernity in the changing perceptions of the canonical star. Crucial to a discussion of Schell's film is the fact that Dietrich refuses to appear in the film as her present-day self, although her current voice is included. Rather, the only images that we see are archival footage from her films. Thus, the biopic references the issue of aging and the female star and the manner in which visibility has always been more problematic for the female than the male actor.

While Clint Eastwood is acknowledged to be an international star, very few critical studies analytically probe the multiple social and political determinants of his celebrity persona both nationally and internationally. In "Action Movie Hysteria, or Eastwood Bound," Paul Smith offers a complex understanding of the "erotics" of masculinity that inhere in the Eastwood persona and sheds light on the psycho-cultural dynamics of male stardom. Smith connects Eastwood's image to questions concerning the changing treatment (over the span of his career) of the spectacle of his body, the narrative forms with which he is associated, and the predilections of his directors (e.g. Don Siegel). In particular, through linking Eastwood's roles to a conception of male masochism, Smith offers a method for understanding not only Eastwood's star image but, more broadly, the cultural and political character of contemporary masculinity as embodied in the star.

The Subject of Acting

1

DANAE CLARK

Labor and the commodity form

The concept of *shifting, fragmenting, and binding,* which stems from Marx's theory of commodity fetishism and which has been used in cultural studies to describe various forms of institutional oppression,[1] is particularly useful in understanding the ways that studios positioned actors as social subjects during Hollywood's Golden Era. By virtue of their labor power advantage, studio executives were able to determine the ideological boundaries of labor discourse as well as the economic boundaries of labor conditions and commodity exchange, thus limiting actors' ability to control the terms of their subjective representation. In transforming labor into commodity form, film studios first of all shifted emphasis and visibility from production to exchange. This shift masked not only the process of labor but also the antagonistic relations that existed within the sphere of production. In addition, consumer attention was shifted toward a commodity form that concealed the source of its value by "behav[ing] as though value were a property of the commodity" itself.[2] Indeed, in the case of actors, the fruits of labor produced a commodity that was particularly rich in surplus value. Even though the image or star icon was dislocated from the sphere of production, its representational form appeared to capture "the real thing," thus providing a strong source of fetishistic attachment with which to link the consumer to the actor's body in the sphere of circulation. Since this fetishization translated into money at the box office, the studios were more concerned with promoting star images than with acknowledging or improving the working conditions of actors.

Fragmentation entered this process in a variety of ways. On a structural level, the star system established a hierarchical division of actors' labor that allowed the studios to maintain economic and political control over the acting profession. The various divisions, based on cost and use value, were also necessary for efficient production. Stars represented the smallest group because they were so costly, but due to their use in regulating the industry's product and drawing audiences into the theaters, they were also extremely profitable to the studios. Character actors and bit players made up a somewhat larger group since they could be used repeatedly in films at lower wages than stars. Screen extras represented the largest group, sometimes estimated as high as 90 percent of the acting profession.[3] Extras could be paid minimal wages, and their chances of repeated use by a studio often depended upon their willingness to work below current wage standards and outside established labor guidelines.[4]

The practice of typecasting fragmented the acting profession further. Within each level or division of labor, in other words, actors were categorized according to social types based on race, age, sexual stereotype, and so on. Such typecasting not only fragmented actors' labor power (by limiting their range of performance and preventing the full potential of their skills), it fragmented actors' bodies as well. Often this fragmentation was sexualized. As Hortense Powdermaker observed in her anthropological study of the film industry,

> An actress becomes known for her comely legs, and these are accented in every picture. Another one is known for her bust; still another for her husky, sensuous voice. So obvious is the use of actors as sexual symbols that in a major studio a handsome star is colloquially referred to as "the penis."[5]

Not surprisingly, actors performed, or were coerced into performing, sexual labor. Young starlets, for example, were promised acting parts or screen tests in return for their sexual labor on the "casting couch." The labor that actors performed on their own bodies was also sexualized. Since actors were expected to maintain a certain look or body weight in order to achieve and sustain the success that accompanied stardom, anorexia and breast implants for women and rigorous body building and hair implants for men were not uncommon.

Thus, the process of fragmentation worked not only to differentiate star types in the sphere of exchange, but to create and sustain differentiated labor in the sphere of production. The overall effect of this fragmenting process, however, was to emphasize *differences* among actors. By creating and reinforcing individual differences of salary, opportunity, skill, personality, sexuality, and social type, the process of fragmentation established an "isolation effect" that placed barriers between actors and forced them into competition with each other for studio attention.[6]

The fragmented state of the acting profession gave studio heads the power to bind actors into a passive community of workers. A constant pool of unemployed and underemployed workers (mostly extras) made it possible for studios to reduce labor dissension.[7] The promise of moving up in the star system hierarchy kept hopefuls in line, while the fear of plummeting to the bottom was used to keep employed actors from challenging their employers and complaining about exploitative labor practices. Though actors were indispensable to the production of the commodity form, cooperation with studio policy was thus a precondition of achieving a livable salary and job security.

Binding was reinforced through an ideological discourse of the family that denied labor power differences, yet functioned according to a model of "paternal tyranny" whereby "love, honour and obedience were venerated and rewarded, while the neglect of them earned self-righteous retribution."[8] Actors thus found it difficult to organize their collective power. Even when they managed to form political alliances across internal divisions of labor (or with other labor groups) they had to fight against a double stronghold of management and family that threatened them with dismissal and branded them as ungrateful children. The combined effect of the shifting, fragmenting, and binding process was to limit actors' power as active social agents, constructing them as passive workers and producing them as passive images. This is not to suggest that actors subject positioning can be explained as a simple reflex of the economy. As Jane Gaines states,

Although the functioning principle of capitalism is the complete organization of social and economic life around the commodity, human needs vacillate and don't always line up with commodity use-values. In political terms, this means that the social and economic arrangements supporting capitalist production are in constant danger of coming undone.[9]

This situation is intensified by the fact that actors are caught between the forces of production and consumption, between bodily labor and commodified image. A gap exists between an actor's use value (labor) and exchange value (image). Even if a stabilized image could be established in the sphere of circulation (which was rarely possible), it would not guarantee a "stabilized" or obedient worker in the sphere of production. Likewise, although the economic and psychological effects of the star system's fragmentation may have caused actors to feel alienated from their fellow workers and from their own labor power and bodies, it could not entirely suppress or control actors' resistances.

While actors negotiated the difficult terrain between representation and self-representation, the studios attempted to appropriate the actors' labor into an economic and ideological system of profitability, mobilizing their "free consent" to establish hegemony over actors' labor and subjectivity. As Tony Bennett explains,

> It is not enough that the worker should be reproduced as someone capable of work and socially dependent on capital; he or she must also be produced as a subject of an ideological consciousness which legitimates the dominance of capital and the subordinate place which he or she occupies within its processes. . . . They must be induced to "live" their exploitation and oppression in such a way that they do not experience or represent to themselves their position as one in which they are exploited.[10]

But the lines between free consent, self-determination, and exploitation become difficult to sort out. Some actors, for example, were in a position to reap considerable rewards from the star system. The exorbitant salaries and international fame that accompanied stardom in some cases outweighed, and even diminished, exploitative labor conditions. Although wary of the consequences, actors lower in the hierarchy also stood to gain. This may explain why Alexander Walker found R. D. Laing's studies of schizophrenia apropos in describing the star as "a person [who] 'cannot make a move, or makes no move, without being beset by contradictory and paradoxical pressures and demands, pushes and pulls, both internally from himself, and externally from those around him.'"[11]

Barry King suggests, in addition, that some actors walked a tightrope in balancing the studios' demands with their own desire for control. Since performance confronted actors as a fact of employment, some attempted to utilize it in a way that met both their own needs and the needs of the institution. For example, "actors seeking to obtain stardom [would] begin to conduct themselves in public as though there [was] an unmediated existential connection between their person and their image."[12] While this strategy complied with the studio expectation that actors would develop "personalities" for purposes of public visibility, actors who initiated this process could claim some degree of control over the form their representation took. Similarly, actors attempted to control the details of their film performances in order to claim credit for their work. When successful, this strategy created the identity of a "good dramatic actor" as opposed to a "popular Warner Brothers star," thus allowing the actor (instead of the studio) to receive recognition for his or her own labor.

At the core of actor–management struggle, then, is the issue of how and how much labor is to be attached to the image. The actor, says King, is placed in a paradoxical position in relation to this issue: "While film increases the centrality of the actor in the process of signification, the formative capacity of the medium can equally confine the actor more and more to being a bearer of effects that he or she does not or cannot originate."[13] Given the displacement that occurs in cinematic practice from production to signification, the labor of performance becomes less the provenance of actors and more the property or product of the studio. This paradox, concludes King, causes the "persona" to become a site of struggle within the hegemonic discourses of the cinema: "A potential politics of the persona emerges insofar as the bargaining power of the actor, or more emphatically, the star, is materially affected by the *degree* of his or her reliance on the apparatus (the image), as opposed to self-located resources (the person) in the construction of the persona."[14]

This explanation is adequate to the extent we recognize that the persona is not a predetermined, easily defined entity, but a construction that results precisely from the struggle over the image–labor relation. But, given this, it might be better not to focus solely on the persona, but to see "the persona," as well as "the image" and "the person," as terms that arise out of the discursive struggle between labor and management. The studios, for example, worked toward separating notions of image and person as a means to construct and establish exclusive control over a coherent, salable persona. That is, by detaching the image from the person, the studio could reconstruct the relation between the two into a unified subject position called the "persona." Changing the names of actors was one way of establishing this control.[15] By erasing an actor's previous "identity" (name, personal history), the studio could create a new image and identity. An agreement of sorts was made: in return for the actor's physical body (as bearer of an image), the studio would attempt to generate for her or him the wealth and social prestige of star ranking.

The studios' power of creation and naming assured them economic and ideological, if not legal, ownership over the actor's body. Indeed, as King points out, "The established policy of building stars from inexperienced players under the studio system, can be seen to contain an element of fabricating subordination among potential stars."[16] By freely consenting to this process of fragmentation and individuation, actors lost political autonomy and forfeited some control over defining their own subject identities. It is true that one's desire for the "coherent subjectivity" of the star persona (or what King has called the single "transfilmic star person-ality image") was "in line with the star's economic interests, since the further he or she [could] enforce such an equation [between the person and the image] the greater his or her irreplaceability and bargaining power."[17] But regardless of the prestige and control that stardom might afford the individual actor, the structure of labor relations itself was not challenged, and the labor power differences between actors and management remained intact.

An actor's signature meanwhile permitted his or her "image" to become the legal property of the studio. The Screen Actors Guild reports that between 1937 and 1946, the number of players under long-term contracts to Hollywood studios varied between six hundred and eight hundred.[18] The usual contract ran for seven years, with the studio having the right to take up the option of an actor's services after six months or a year with an increase in pay. If the studio did not take up the option or wished to fire the actor (with or without stated causes), the contract was terminated. The actor, on the other hand, could not legally break the contract under any circumstances. By individualizing actors' labor power under separate contracts, producers could regulate the division of labor under the star system and enforce the use of typecasting. Since most contracts stipulated that actors must accept the roles "offered" to them, most actors found themselves playing the same type of role over and over again. The repetition of roles reinforced the illusion of a unified persona. To break from this illusion and to challenge studio regulation of the persona often resulted in suspension from the studio without pay, and, upon readmittance, the forced acceptance of even less desirable roles.[19]

The typical contract gave a studio exclusive right to "photograph and/or otherwise produce, reproduce, transmit, exhibit, distribute, and exploit in connection with [a] photoplay any and all of the artist's acts, poses, plays and appearances of any and all kinds."[20] In addition, the studio had exclusive right to determine who else might be allowed to use the actor's image for advertising or commercial purposes. With very few exceptions, actors had no right to their images and no control over how their images were exploited, divided, or transferred. It was also not unusual for actors to be unaware of how their likenesses were being used. "An actress," says Gaines, might be shocked to see her image reproduced in conjunction with products as diverse as Auto-Lite car batteries or Serta mattresses and box springs, but there was little she could do about it" – as Kay Francis discovered when she found herself advertising Compo shoe soles in a 1933 issue of *Photoplay* magazine.[21]

According to King, however, the image remained "a slippery commodity" due to the conflict that existed between the legal and physical aspects of image ownership. Although the exchange of labor granted studios the right to use or police an actor's image in ways that were profitable to them, the image was not "property" in the usual sense and could not be entirely owned:

> Whilst the contract for the employment of the star closely stipulates the limits on the utilization of the image . . . nevertheless it remains factually the case that the star is ultimately the possessor of the image, because it is indexically linked to his or her person.[22]

In effect, adds King, a legal monopoly was confronted with a physical or "natural monopoly" in a bargaining relationship. Although this gap between "the image" and "the person" cannot in itself account for the antagonisms between labor and management (which appears to be the implication of King's argument), it is true that the studios' power did not go uncontested; they were forced to bargain with actors over rights to the image.

Thus, although studios exerted considerable control over the terms of actors' contractual obligations, contracts can also be seen as a means for the two parties to work out their conflicts over the image. As Gaines notes,

> The studio used the contract to secure on-screen continuity through provisions for illness and vacations, wardrobe fittings, tardiness on the set, absences, photographic sittings and re-takes. . . . Stars retaliated with riders modifying wardrobe requirements stipulating screen billing order and typeface size on the credits, and mandating the number of closeups per picture.[23]

Yet the contract remained a paradoxical document. Although it created an imaginary relation of fair exchange between legal subjects, the contract spelled out the terms by which one party would be able to transform the labor and representation of the second party.[24] In addition, the contract exposed the constructedness of the star image at the same time it created the possibility for coherence. This is surely one reason that the studios responded so harshly when actors challenged their contracts. Such challenges ran the risk of disrupting the coherent images that studios wanted to present to the public.

Fortunately, from the studios' point of view, they did not have to rely solely on contracts to create a sense of coherency. Whereas contracts functioned within the sphere of production, realist films (and their accompanying publicity) reinforced the illusion of coherency in the sphere of exchange. As John Ellis has noted, star images function(ed) as "an invitation to the cinema."[25] Because star images were composed of character fragments, chunks of "real life," still photographs, and disembodied radio voices, the cinema's combination of voice, body, and motion promised to reveal the completeness of the star image and "the mystery of the star's essential being."[26]

Discourses of realism worked toward unifying not only actor and image, but also actor and character. While suture functioned in the case of spectators to produce identification with ego ideals, the production of actors *as* those ego ideals sutured actors into a discourse that naturalized their labor as performance and linked their performances to narrative identity. According to these conventions of naturalism, stars did not work. Though some stars were distinguished for their acting ability, it was widely thought that most stars owed their success to their personalities or photogenic qualities. In 1933, *Variety* reported:

> In hopes of finding featured talent that can be eventually developed into star material, all majors are on the widest search in picture history for new *faces*. Scouts are going into all fields which might possibly yield screen *personalities*.[27]

Viewed as "personalities" as opposed to "laborers" in a realist economy of representation, they merely displayed the qualities they possessed or the personalities that were packaged for them by others.

Character actors and supporting players fared much better in this regard. Generally considered the most talented of Hollywood actors, they were thought to carry the real burden of acting and were often relied upon to conceal a star's lack of ability. Supporting actors, in other words, were valued more for the labor they performed; they were viewed as "impersonators" (actors possessing impersonatory skills) rather than as "personalities."[28] Not surprisingly, studios spent less time and energy selling the images of character actors to the public. Hollywood dealt in personalities; the less an actor was "labor identified," the more that actor was promoted as the Hollywood ideal. In spite of this, or perhaps because of this, some actors chose the typecasting of character acting and enjoyed a professional reputation, career longevity, and financial durability not experienced by the more transitory stars.[29] In contrast, the work of Hollywood extras never established the continuity or dramatic depth of the work of other actors. Though they were sometimes used to perform unusual tasks (e.g., daredevil stunts or accordion playing),[30] extras were used in films predominantly as objects to dot a landscape (hence the term "atmosphere players"), and their filmic presence required little or no skill. Unlike stars, however, their objectified state carried no power. Extras were neither personalities nor impersonators, and were defined more by their unemployment than by their employment.

In addition to their objectified status in films and their subordinate status in the labor–management hierarchy, actors were also positioned as "other" in the Hollywood labor community. A common cliché in Hollywood, reported Powdermaker is that "there are three kinds of people – men, women, and actors."[31] Actors held the dubious distinction of being the only production workers who were visibly present in the industry's products. Technical workers who considered themselves to be the true creative artists of the industry, yet were paid (on the average) lower wages and received less recognition often resented being upstaged by actors. Stars, in particular, were perceived as a privileged class of workers that was undeservedly pampered by the front office. As a consequence, their complaints about labor practices were not taken very seriously. Stars were branded instead as "immature, irresponsible, completely self-centered, egotistical, exhibitionist nitwits" who held up production or created unnecessary problems on the set.[32] Even though the various occupational groups would have benefited from a united workers' front, actors by and large received little support, either collectively or individually, from other labor groups. Actors were resented and alienated by other workers in ways that supported the dominant discourse of labor.

Studios thus relied on a variety of labor power differences, internal and external to the actors' ranks, to maintain their own labor dominance. Through the process of shifting, fragmenting, and binding, the studios were further able to create a discourse of stardom that invited the actors' free consent and that was effective in reducing challenges to this dominance. Individual actors who did insist on contributing to their own image construction were regarded as a nuisance, but could be dealt with through contract negotiation, suspension, or dismissal. When actors struggled for collective self-representation and challenged exploitative labor practices, however, more severe measures were instituted to deny them a voice as political subjects. As actors struggled for the right to define and control their own subject identities as laborers, the studios struggled to position actors as passive objects of display fragmenting their labor power into institutionalized categories of image, performance, and profitability. Given the conflicts over systems of representation and issues of self-representation, the actors' struggle for definition was difficult.

The union question

An understanding of actors' subjectivity requires not only an investigation into labor–management relations, but an investigation into actors' shifting perceptions of themselves in relation to their work and to the cinematic institution in general. It requires, in other words, an understanding of the unifying principles around which diverse groups of actors united or formed "unions" (in the broadest sense of the term), and the way in which fragmented aspects of subject identity cohered in relation to these unions. Since the fragmented condition of subjects always tends toward unity, whether by conscious or unconscious means, whether by free consent or active resistance, the significance of subject unity lies in its political utility. For the unifying constructs of subject identity not only determined how actors perceived themselves or were perceived by others; they directly influenced relations of power in the industry and affected actors' strength as a bargaining unit.

In undertaking such an analysis, I tread upon the terrain of the "collective subject," a theoretical concept that has been all but avoided in film studies (and most Marxist criticism as well) due, I think, to its suggestion of a mass consciousness or collective will. Viewed from the perspective of labor, however, the collective subject – or a collective subject identity – takes on more useful and politically specific connotations. As Raymond Williams notes in

Marxism and Literature, collective subjectivity involves a process of "conscious cooperation" or collaboration. It is a "case of cultural creation by two or more individuals who are in active relations with each other, and whose work cannot be reduced to the mere sum of their separate individual contributions."[33] In an attempt to distance Marxist cultural theory from a bourgeois notion of the individual, Williams stresses the "trans-individual" nature of the collective subject whereby we can discover "the truly social in the individual, and the truly individual in the social."[34]

In his essay "What is Cultural Studies Anyway?" Richard Johnson argues more forcefully for the need to address the collective dimension of subjectivity. Within poststructuralist theory, he says, "there is no account of . . . *the subjective aspects of struggle*, no account of how there is a moment in subjective flux when social subjects (individual or collective) produce accounts of who they are, as conscious political agents, that is constitute themselves, politically."[35] Thus, what cultural studies must take up is an investigation of how social movements or groups "strive to produce some coherence and continuity." It must engage, he argues, in a "post-post-structuralist" account of subjectivity that returns to and reformulates questions of struggle, "unity," and the production of a (collective) political will. This involves, most importantly, a theoretical notion of the "discursive self-production of subjects, especially in the form of histories and memories"[36] – and, I would add, everyday practices.

Thus, from the theoretical perspective of labor power differences, "collective subjectivity" refers to the process that laboring subjects undergo in forming, maintaining, or protecting a collective sense of identity. Since the social relations involved in this process follow no internal logic nor create inevitable results, the project at hand must "abstract, describe and reconstitute in concrete studies the social forms through which [actors] 'live,' become conscious, sustain themselves subjectively."[37] It must locate the specific configurations of actors' collective subjectivities, which arise out of a history of struggle and labor power differences, and analyze the ways in which knowledge and experience of these collective notions are discursively produced and materially lived within the shifting context of social relations in Hollywood.

The contours and spaces of actors' subjectivity are often difficult to determine. In the earliest years of cinema, for example, a coherent or unified notion of screen acting did not appear to exist. Actors from vaudeville and the stage became part-time "picture performers" to pick up a few extra dollars during daytime hours. Or, within a motion picture company, employees who performed other duties might be asked also to "pose" for the camera.[38] By the 1910s, as the industry sought to legitimate the new entertainment form among the middle and upper classes, screen acting increasingly became defined as a specialized skill, and discourse about the acting profession began to differentiate between the theater and motion pictures. As Richard deCordova has noted, there emerged "a sort of struggle between photographic and a theatrical conception of the body, between posing and acting."[39] Distinctions were made between the live, vocal performances of stage acting and the type of acting required to create the phantom images of the silent cinema. Although film producers often played up an actor's stage experience as a way to legitimate his or her professional existence (and the film industry's existence in general),[40] actors became part of the ever-widening discursive gap between stage and screen.

Material differences also affected actors' notions of themselves and their profession. Screen acting, for example, differed not only in terms of craft, but in terms of the institutional context. From the film industry's beginning, screen actors encountered different working environments and labor power relations in the studios than stage actors encountered in the theater. In the latter, where employee–employer relations were stabilized and ownership was concentrated in the hands of a few, actors suffered a number of abuses. Alfred Harding, a historian of early stage labor, states that, in contrast, motion pictures offered lucrative and relatively stable employment conditions without the accompanying abuse by management: "There was still so much money to be made from the making, booking and exhibiting of motion pictures that the money to be gained by rigging the actors, considerable as that sum would have been, was a mere drop in a capacious bucket."[41]

As the film studios moved their operations to California, stage and screen were separated even further, and the "difference" of screen acting intensified. Once the Hollywood star system became more firmly established and divisions within the talent group were intensified, a greater distinction between high-ranking and low-ranking actors also emerged. Before World War I, screen actors formed their own labor associations, but these groups were primarily social or benevolent organizations and "had little interest in or orientation toward industrial relations."[42] Later, high-ranking actors formed the Screen Actors of America, and atmosphere and bit players belonged to the Motion Picture Players Union (MPPU). Although neither group was a radical political body, both had obtained a charter from the American Federation of Labor and established an orientation toward industrial relations.

These labor groups were challenged in 1919 when Actors' Equity Association, the political body formed by stage actors in 1913, sought jurisdiction over Hollywood.[43] Although Equity had hoped to "penetrate Hollywood peacefully," it was met with resistance, and it took several months of negotiation before the existing screen actors' unions agreed to acknowledge Equity's jurisdictional rights. By this time most screen actors were bypassing the stage and beginning their careers directly in the cinema. As Murray Ross explains, they did not know the history of labor struggles in the theater and were not interested in the stage actors' problems.[44] Equity also threatened the screen actors' professional autonomy. Because Equity had moved into Hollywood so shortly after winning a major battle with Broadway theater managers, many actors believed that the union's interest in controlling Hollywood merely stemmed from its desire to strengthen its home bargaining position.[45]

Equity members, however, argued that their actions were motivated by a spirit of collectivity and should not be interpreted as opportunistic or divisive; their goal was to protect Hollywood actors from the sort of exploitative conditions that had occurred in the theater. Although "a general survey of conditions affecting motion picture actors on the Pacific Coast revealed that at that time there were prevalent remarkably few of the abuses which had driven the dramatic actors to organize," members of Equity wanted to offset any advantage that management might gain.[46] The need for a "strong and watchful organization" was not apparent to Hollywood actors because the motion picture industry was still young and had yet to develop entrenched relations of labor–management power. But, as Equity noted, "The industry was beginning to crystallize." If protective measures were not taken soon, actors would witness "the consolidation of the field in the hands of a few strong men."[47]

During its first few years in Hollywood, Actors' Equity continued to monitor the situation without taking action. Equity felt that "the majority of motion picture actors were not yet ready to be organized" even though abuses against actors were beginning to mount.[48] In addition, unionization of the sort Equity had achieved in the theater was not yet possible, because no official employer bargaining unit existed. It was not until the Motion Picture Producers and Distributors Association (MPPDA) was formed in 1922 that Equity sought to negotiate its first standard contract.[49] Will Hays, head of the MPPDA, "noncommittally agreed to consider the request," but the matter was apparently ignored. When the Association of Motion Picture Producers (AMPP), the labor branch of the MPPDA, was formed in 1924, Equity approached Hays again. But Equity's request for a standard contract, closed shop conditions, and studio recognition of the actors' union was flatly rejected.[50]

Equity members did not push the issue further because they were unable to garner enough support in the screen community. In addition, some of the labor practices that Equity had protested against were temporarily discontinued when Joseph Schenck, president of the AMPP, intervened on the studios' behalf.[51] Thus, although interest in Equity "had been high," many screen actors thought the newly formed AMPP had responded adequately to their needs. Equity backed off, allowing their recruitment drive to come to "virtual standstill," but it refused to recede into the background.[52] In a statement issued to the press, the union declared:

> Equity wants it understood that it is not abandoning its Los Angeles office and that it is not contemplating any such action. . . . It is in Los Angeles and the motion picture field to stay, and will be there strong and vigorous long after these short-sighted actors and actresses have become dusty shadows on rolls of celluloid in somebody's storage warehouse.[53]

Equity was clearly becoming impatient with the naive and uncooperative behavior of their fellow actors in Hollywood even though the union was committed to protecting all members of the same profession.

The less than harmonious relationship between stage and screen actors, however, was not simply a matter of naïveté. Equity's attempt to protect and educate Hollywood actors also involved a control over and redefinition of screen actors' subject identity. The identity of "actor" (versus "screen actor") threatened their professional autonomy by denying the specificity of their labor and their relation to Hollywood. Screen actors were, moreover, inclined to view themselves as "picture personalities" or members of a "studio family" rather than as "industrial workers." As producer Milton Sperling observed,

> In those days in Hollywood, studio loyalty was a factor of your life. If you were a Warner employee, or a Fox employee, or a Metro employee, that was your home, your country. . . . You played baseball against the other studios. You had T-shirts with your studio's name on them. It was just like being a *subject*, and a patriotic subject at that. People who lived and worked beyond the studio walls just didn't belong, and you were prepared to fight them off, like the Philistines.[54]

But the screen actors' failure to recognize or confront the broader implications of Equity's efforts carried a high price. In their desire for an autonomy and subject identity based on film specificity, screen actors repeatedly sided with their motion picture employers and rejected the labor history and bargaining experience of their fellow workers in the theater.

The position chosen by screen actors (and fostered by the studios) left them more vulnerable to studio domination. By 1926 the Hollywood labor situation had undergone some fundamental changes. Though the major studios still maintained an open shop policy, they had signed the Studio Basic Agreement with the craft unions and were gradually becoming involved in the process of collective bargaining and collective negotiations. Studio heads realized that similar measures would be necessary if they wished to maintain their control over the creative talent groups. Thus the studios began to make certain concessions in the hopes of appeasing the demands of talent groups while forestalling their unionization. These concessions (e.g., a more equitable distribution of work for extras through the establishment of the Central Casting Corporation) were designed not only to undercut Equity's influence in Hollywood, but to discourage screen actors' identification with (unionized) actors from the stage.

As part of this new managerial approach, the producers created the Academy of Motion Picture Arts and Sciences. The Academy was made up of five branches representing the major divisions of motion picture production: producers, directors, writers, actors, and technicians. According to the original charter, the branches were to be equally represented on the Academy's board of directors, and each branch would elect an executive committee by democratic process to function as its governing voice in labor negotiations. In an effort to make the Academy a prestige organization above the status of a labor union, membership was by invitation only and based on one's distinguished accomplishments in film production. According to labor historians Louis B. Perry and Richard S. Perry, the Academy's structure was particularly attractive to major screen stars who were growing uncomfortable with Equity's attempts "to organize and control from 3,000 miles away."[55] Unlike the theater union, the Academy recognized stars as members of a white-collar profession who should be treated on the basis of individual artistry. The Academy's "method of selection, however, kept the control of the organization in the hands of a few, so that it took on many aspects of a company union."[56]

Actors' Equity was suspicious of the Academy's commitment to labor issues and believed that its formation was "calculated to give Equity a final blow."[57] Thus, when the AMPP announced a 10–25 percent reduction in salary for nonunion labor in 1927, Equity stood ready to challenge the Academy's stated commitment. The screen actors response to the situation repeated a familiar pattern. Feeling betrayed by the producers' association, they turned to Equity for assistance. But when the newly formed Academy protested successfully against the salary reduction (by convincing producers to consider the merits of each individual case), actors placed their allegiance with it. Thus Equity was once again forced into inactivity. Its presence continued to serve as a "deterrent to unlimited aggression on the part of producers,"[58] but producers still assumed the right to speak for actors through the benevolent auspices of the Academy.

The question of "a voice," of making oneself heard, took on an added significance in the battle between labor and management when the arrival of sound accentuated the voice as a material site of struggle. As Walker notes, the "economic dislocation" caused by the switchover to sound technology was also accompanied by a "human dislocation."[59] Articles in the trade press capitalized on "scare stories" and predicted an apocalyptic outcome for even the most well-established silent actors. Nervousness about learning new techniques caused some motion picture stars to enroll in voice production schools or to go to Broadway to establish themselves as stage actors. But, according to Walker, "The more insecure the talkies made these highly-priced and troublesome people feel, the better a front office liked it."[60] Producers learned quickly that while the sound crisis was stirring antagonisms between stage and screen actors, it was also increasing their control over the labor force. Producers used the crisis as an opportunity to cut the escalating salaries of stars. Since it was economically advantageous to purchase talent that was already developed, they also brought in "proven voices" from the stage at a cheaper rate. The competition and feeling of insecurity that this created among Hollywood stars subsequently persuaded them "to take cuts, or resign at a lower figure, in order to hang on to their stardom."[61]

But although the employment of stage actors provided a quick fix for the studios, producers were opening the door for the subversive potential of the voice. Of the approximately twelve hundred stage players who migrated to Hollywood to appear in the talkies, nearly all were members of Actors' Equity. These actors were accustomed to an Equity shop policy in New York theaters and had experienced firsthand the sorts of improvements that Equity had been able to obtain from theater managers. By 1929, 70 percent of all actors in talking pictures (including screen actors who joined locally) were Equity members. The membership was active, filing complaints about studio working conditions at Equity headquarters and calling for all-Equity casts.[62] With such unprecedented support from screen actors, union officials thus decided to make another stand for an Equity shop policy in Hollywood.

During their struggle to obtain the voice of effective self-representation, actors' groups underwent a series of realignments. First and foremost, stage and screen actors developed more harmonious relations. Some film actors, particularly the higher-ranked ones, continued to resent the presence of the theater in Hollywood and were suspicious of the union's attention to the newly arrived stage players. The fact that Equity had suspended several leading actors from the union (for violating Equity regulations) only added to their antagonism.[63] But the majority of actors from the lower ranks (character actors and bit players) welcomed the bargaining position that Equity could help them achieve. This vote of confidence and solidarity was forcefully expressed at a rally of Equity's members when, upon adjourning, the crowd of actors sang the song first used in the stage actors' theatrical strike of 1919, "All for One, and One for All."[64] But while these screen actors forged a unified front, of sorts, the terms of collective subjectivity remained fragmented.

It became increasingly apparent that the major split within the acting profession during this period was no longer based on medium specificity (i.e., stage versus screen), but on a hierarchical notion of actors' labor. Equity's active membership came from the lower ranks; these stage and screen actors defined themselves as workers, and the organization itself was structured along trade union lines. The major motion picture stars resisted the definition of actors as workers. They also feared that the union drive would cost them the status and power they had worked so hard to achieve. A number of them belonged to both Equity and the Academy, but as labor historians Perry and Perry point out, they were "not likely to quit the Academy in favor of a union until they found a lack of good faith in the former and were ready to consider themselves as workers in need of a labor organization rather than members of a professional group who were above organization."[65]

Gaining the loyalty and commitment of prominent actors was essential to Equity's overall success. But the stakes and issues were vastly different for stars than they were for other classes of actors. Whereas the distinguished stars could arrange contracts that guaranteed high wages and specified certain favorable working conditions, most of the industry's actors – especially screen extras – were not in a position to bargain. If they spoke out against abuses they were seldom reemployed at the same studio; and since they were never sure of continuous work, most actors kept quiet. When these actors did obtain work, they were often forced to accept contracts that were "hopelessly vague and inequitable" and essentially amounted to "tak[ing] the casting-director's word."[66] Union support from their prestigious and steadily employed colleagues would thus give them a bargaining edge that their mere numbers could not ensure.

According to a report in the *Nation*, however, producers were "resorting to every conceivable device to break the spirit of the actors."[67] They tried to undercut the union drive by offering actors tempting non-Equity contracts. Those who refused had their names passed on to other studios, where they would find it difficult to obtain work.[68] Producers also relied on the local newspapers to further their antiunion crusade. Lists of non-Equity members, for example, were published in the local press to help studios "make their hiring decisions." Both the *Los Angeles Times*, a notoriously antiunion publication, and the *Los Angeles Examiner*, owned by William Randolph Hearst (a major stockholder with MGM), printed lengthy editorials against Equity. In one, stars were warned that an affiliation with Equity would turn them into blue-collar workers, because Equity had "placed itself in line and agreement with stage-hands, ditch-diggers, janitors, iron-molders, and such."[69] Meanwhile, the local press printed interviews with several of Hollywood's top stars (Lionel Barrymore, Louise Dresser, Marie Dressler, John Gilbert, and Norma Talmadge) who praised the producers for attempting to negotiate fair – that is, non-Equity contracts.[70] These stars preferred that labor negotiations be handled by the Academy, an organization they had helped to create.

Equity once again miscalculated the unity and strength of screen actors. Although more than two thousand Equity members had turned down nonunion contracts, producers had held on to enough of the important actors to maintain continuity in production as well as a bargaining edge. The absence of prominent actors from the bargaining table, and the lack of political support, weakened Equity's position. Organized labor also retreated from the scene. Although several Hollywood craft unions had pledged their moral support and, in some cases, even their financial support to the actors' cause, they now refused to call sympathetic strikes.[71] In addition, fighting among the internal ranks of Equity resulted in the union coming up empty-handed. Although the producers, at one point, had consented to 80 percent Equity and 20 percent nonunion labor in all casts, indecision and delay among Equity officials caused producers to withdraw their offer.[72]

The breakdown in Equity leadership, the conflicting interests between high-ranking and low-ranking actors, and the lack of outside assistance resulted in an overwhelming defeat. The acting profession was now more vulnerable and fragmented than ever. And, left with no other option, actors hurried to accept contracts on producers' terms. As workers, actors once again were forced to define themselves individually – rather than collectively – in relation to producers. The political gap between high-ranking and low-ranking actors intensified, and the more harmonious relationship that had developed between stage and screen began to dissolve (or at least it became less consequential). Now that all actors in Hollywood were forced to deal directly with motion picture producers the issue of "film specificity" reemerged as the organizing principle of actors' subject identity. But this time the voice of theater was silenced on producers' terms. This would remain the case until actors were able to forge another, more collective, discourse of labor to define themselves differently.

Notes

1 See, for example, Stuart Hall, "Culture, the Media and the 'Ideological Effect,'" *Mass Communication and Society*, ed. James Curran, Michael Gurevitch, and Janet Woollacott (London: Sage, 1979): 336–42.

2 Jane Gaines, "In the Service of Ideology: How Betty Grable's Legs Won the War," *Film Reader* 5 (1982): 56. Gaines discusses at length the relation between the star image and Marx's theory of commodity fetishism.

3 Marian L. Mel, *Method of Employment of Extra Players in the Motion Picture Industry in California* (1930): 1, as quoted in Murray Ross, *Stars and Strikes* (1941; reprint, New York: AMS Press, 1967): 77.

4 Numerous instances of abuse are documented in the actors' union journal *Screen Player*. Also see Ross, *Stars and Strikes*, pp. 120–26.

5 Hortense Powdermaker, *Hollywood, the Dream Factory* (Boston: Little, Brown, 1950): 207.

6 The term "isolation effect" is from Nicos Poulantzas, *Political Power and Social Classes* (London: New Left Books, 1973).

7 "Actors' Chances Put at 10 to 1," *Variety* (9 May 1933): 7. The report states that at this time more than 10,000 persons, exclusive of extras, were hoping to gain a livelihood as actors.

8 Alexander Walker, *Stardom: The Hollywood Phenomenon* (New York: Stein & Day, 1970): 259.

9 Gaines, "In the Service of Ideology," 53.

10 Tony Bennett, "Theories of the Media, Theories of Society," in *Culture, Society and the Media*, ed. Michael Gurevitch, Tony Bennett, James Curran, and Janet Woollacott (London: Hutchinson, 1982): 52.

11 Walker, *Stardom*, 262.

12 Barry King, "Articulating Stardom," *Screen* 26.5 (1985): 46–47.

13 Ibid., 45.

14 Ibid.

15 See Walker, *Stardom*, 260.

16 King, "Articulating Stardom," 45.

17 Barry King, "Stardom as an Occupation," in *The Hollywood Film Industry*, ed. Paul Kerr (London: Routledge & Kegan Paul, 1986): 168.

18 Screen Actors Guild report as quoted in Powdermaker, *Hollywood, the Dream Factory*, 210.

19 See, for example, Thomas Schatz, "'A Triumph of Bitchery': Warner Bros., Bette Davis and *Jezebel*," *Wide Angle* 10.1 (1988): 16–29.

20 Quoted from Ginger Rogers's contract with Warner Bros., 1933. This clause was representative of many star contracts during this era.

21 Jane Gaines, *Contested Culture: The Image, the Voice, and the Law* (Chapel Hill: University of North Carolina Press, 1991): 160.

22 King, "Stardom as an Occupation," 168.

23 Gaines, *Contested Culture*, 149.

24 Ibid., 154.

25 John Ellis, "Star/Industry/Image," in *Star Signs*, ed. Christine Gledhill (London: British Film Institute, 1982): 3.

26 Ibid.; Tony Bennett and Janet Woollacott, *Bond and Beyond* (New York: Methuen, 1987): 271.

27 "Hungry Need for New Film Faces, Every Studio on Talent Hunt," *Variety* (10 October 1933): 3.

28 Powdermaker, Hollywood, the Dream Factory, 210.

29 King, "Articulating Stardom," 47.

30 See "Unsung Specialists of the Screen Who Starve Plenty Between Calls," Variety (11 April 1933): 2.

31 Powdermaker, Hollywood, the Dream Factory, 254.

32 Ibid.

33 Raymond Williams, Marxism and Literature (New York: Oxford University Press, 1977): 195.

34 Ibid., 197.

35 Richard Johnson, "What Is Cultural Studies Anyway?" Social Text 6.1 (1987). 69.

36 Ibid.

37 Ibid., 45.

38 See "How the Cinematographer Works and Some of His Difficulties," Motion Picture World (8 June 1907): 212: also see "Is the Moving Picture to Be the Play of the Future?" New York Times (20 August 1911), as quoted in Richard deCordova, "The Emergence of the Star System in America," Wide Angle 6.4 (1985): 6.

39 DeCordova, "The Emergence of the Star System," 6.

40 Ibid., 10.

41 Alfred Harding, The Revolt of the Actors (New York: William Morrow, 1929): 286.

42 Louis B. Perry and Richard S. Perry, A History of the Los Angeles Labor Movement, 1911–1941 (Berkeley: University of California Press, 1963): 337.

43 For a more complete analysis of Equity's role in Hollywood, see Danae A. Clark, "Actors' Labor and the Politics of Subjectivity: Hollywood in the 1930s" (Ph.D. diss., University of Iowa, 1989).

44 Ross, Stars and Strikes, 24.

45 Ibid., 7.

46 Harding, The Revolt, 286.

47 Ibid., 287.

48 Ross, Stars and Strikes, 24.

49 Harding, The Revolt, 356.

50 Ross, Stars and Strikes, 25.

51 Ibid., 26. Also see Harding, The Revolt, 533–34.

52 Harding, The Revolt, 535.

53 As quoted in ibid., 536.

54 As quoted in Leonard Mosley, Zanuck (New York: McGraw-Hill, 1984): 109.

55 Perry and Perry, History of the Los Angeles Labor Movement, 339.

56 Ibid., 320.

57 Harding, The Revolt, 536.

58 Ibid., 539.

59 Walker, Stardom, 212.

60 Ibid., 214.

61 Ibid., 218.

62 Harding, The Revolt, 540.

63 Ross, Stars and Strikes, 33.

64 Somerset Logan, "Revolt in Hollywood," Nation (17 July 1929): 62.

65 Perry and Perry, History of the Los Angeles Labor Movement, 339.

66 Logan, "Revolt in Hollywood," 62. "In these contracts there is no stipulation as to the

length of the working day, or the length of the entire engagement. [.] Actors are quite frequently paid nothing for rehearsals. There are instances of players being required to work from sixty to eighty hours a week. When on location, any hours, from eight to twenty, have constituted a work day – sometimes with an additional bonus, sometimes not."

67 Ibid. As quoted in Logan, "Revolt in Hollywood," 62.
68 Ibid.
69 As quoted in "Unionism in Filmland," Nation (28 August 1929): 211.
70 Ross, Stars and Strikes, 31.
71 See Perry and Perry, History of the Los Angeles Labor Movement, 341.
72 Harding, The Revolt, 542–43.

Marlene

2

Modernity, mortality, and the biopic

LUCY FISCHER

The sense of an ending

> Cinema, once heralded as the art of the 20th century, seems now, as the century
> closes . . . to be a decadent art. Perhaps it is not cinema that has ended but only
> cinephilia – the name of the very specific kind of love that cinema inspired . . . born
> of the conviction that cinema was an art unlike any other: quintessentially modern.
> – Susan Sontag

In a *New York Times* article written on the heels of centenary celebrations for the cinema, Susan
Sontag sounded the death knell for the medium, and for the fanatic love that it once inspired.
Drawing upon human/corporeal metaphors, she entitled her piece "The Decay of Cinema," and
in an anthropomorphic gesture, she likened the history of the art form to an individual
biography. "Cinema's 100 years seem to have the shape of a life cycle," she mused, "an
inevitable birth, the steady accumulation of glories and the onset in the last decade of
an ignominious, irreversible decline." But if one reads her article carefully, it is clear that
Sontag is not so much bemoaning the death of all cinema as the end of a particular filmic
mode beloved to her: namely, modernism. She speaks glowingly of the serials of Louis
Feuillade (championed by the Surrealists), the work of Dziga Vertov (influenced by Futurism
and Constructivism), and the dramas of F. W. Murnau (tied to Expressionism). Furthermore,
her essay is illustrated with stills from such modernist "masterpieces" as *Napoleon* (1927),
The 400 Blows (1959), and *Persona* (1967). Sontag is more disparaging of the "ignominious"
contemporary cinema – which she sees not only as relentlessly commercial but as "bloated,"
"manipulative," and "derivative" – a "brazen combinatory or recombinatory art."

It is not difficult to read here, in her choice of language, allusions to *post*modernism – with
its highly touted strategies of excess, contrivance, and pastiche. But Sontag regrets not only
the passing of modernist cinema, but the loss of respect for the passion it once generated.
As she notes, "Cinephilia itself has come under attack, as something quaint, outmoded,
snobbish." Again, the implied voices with which she argues are those of the postmodern
critics, who challenge art cinema's alleged elitism, and instead valorize culture's connections
to the popular. Clearly, Sontag's move here is a regressive one – as she sees the love of cinema
inherently tied to its origins and history. Hence, Sontag speaks of the cinephile's "vast appetite

for seeing and reseeing as much as possible of cinema's glorious past." For her, tradition is, by definition, superior: a remake of Godard's *Breathless* cannot possibly be as good as its source. Extending the trope of cinema as individual life, Sontag decries the recent shift to video by remarking how "No amount of *mourning* will revive the vanished rituals . . . of the darkened theater." "If cinema can be resurrected," she concludes, "it will only be through the birth of a new kind of cine-love."

These themes of individual and film history, of birth and death, of love and hate, of mourning and melancholia, circulate in a text that references issues of cinema and modernism – *Marlene* (1983), Maximilian Schell's experimental "biopic" about the famous movie star Marlene Dietrich. If Sontag sees a trajectory of success and decline in the lineage of the medium, that chronicle is doubled in the record of Dietrich's life, which begins at the turn of the century, precisely when the movies and the modernist aesthetic are in ascendancy, and ends in the 1990s, the heyday of Sontag's maligned postmodernism.

Documentary desire

> Truth value is a distinctive feature of the biopic.
>
> – George Custen (60)

In the same *New York Times* elegy, Sontag mentions the thrill audiences experienced in 1895 "when the train pulled into the station." She is, of course, paying homage to the Lumière Brothers' *The Arrival of a Train at La Ciotat Station* – an early work which she chooses to illustrate in her text, thus granting it particular importance. In so doing, Sontag references the *documentary* form – the mode that *Marlene* simultaneously invokes and deconstructs. In truth, it is a genre not always linked to cinematic modernism. Though Sontag cites Dziga Vertov, an artist associated with the nonfiction form, the majority of her references are to dramatic filmmakers: Renoir, Truffaut, Bertolucci. Significantly, along with recording the arrival of trains (or exotic locales and everyday scenes), in a biographical impulse, the early documentary captured the lives of "stars": politicians like William McKinley "at home"; actors like Mary Irwin, John Rice, and Sarah Bernhardt in performance; or industrialists like M. Lumière at breakfast with his family. In this respect, the documentary forged an early link between cinema and celebrity, one that the biopic later translated into fiction/dramatic form, and one which later still Schell would translate to Dietrich.

Clearly, what documentary film promised the spectator was a sense of a luminary's presence – a chance not only to see the dignitary, but to experience him or her at a closer range than quotidian circumstances would ever allow. It is precisely this aspiration that Schell's film perversely frustrates, for it is a star biography without a star. Though Dietrich contracted Schell to make the movie, ultimately she refused to appear on-camera in it.

What does Dietrich's defiance signify? What might it tell us about the cinema, the "biopic," film modernism, and the female star?

Body doubles

> Soon, very soon maybe, Marlene Dietrich will slink across the screen again. . . . No, this isn't Buddhist reincarnation come to the entertainment world. . . It's new computer technology that soon should be good enough to resurrect the dead.
> – David Bloom

Pursuing Sontag's call for a return to cinema's roots, I will reexamine the work of a classical film theorist in order to investigate these questions. In "The Ontology of the Photographic Image," André Bazin (1918–1958) seeks to comprehend the "essence" of cinema. Assuming a highly modern stance (and again, treating the medium like a human life), he concludes that if cinema were "put under psychoanalysis, the practice of embalming the dead might turn out to be a fundamental factor in [its] creation" (9). While on some level, all biography might be thought to "embalm the dead," or to be "aimed against death," as Bazin imagines, for him the cinematic image has a special capacity to capture an individual's existence, since it seems to assure the "continued existence of the corporeal body" (9). In her essay "Film and Theater," Sontag herself makes a similar point: "Movies resurrect the beautiful dead" (370).

Among the cinema's infamous death "productions" have been such films of the 1890s as *Electrocuting an Elephant* and *The Execution of Mary Queen of Scots* – one a documentary and one a hoax. Even before that, one of Eadweard Muybridge's photographic motion studies depicted a man shooting a chicken that seems to explode before our very eyes. Later on, there would be such experimental texts as Georges Franju's *The Blood of the Beasts* (1949) about a slaughterhouse, Stan Brakhage's *The Act of Seeing with One's Own Eyes* (1971) set in a morgue, and Hollis Frampton's *Apparatus Sum* (1972) concerning an anatomy class, as well as such commercial obscenities as snuff pornography.

Within the spectator's attraction to the cinema would seem to be two competing biographical impulses: one that is morbid and fascinated with death, and another that is vital and enchanted with immortality. Both conjoin in Bazin's image of the Mummy, simultaneously a repulsive artifact of petrified flesh and a magical icon of self-preservation. For Bazin, like mummification, cinematic representation has a special relation to reality, because unlike painting, sculpture, or the literary record, it is "indexical." As he notes, "The photograph as such and the object in itself share a common being, after the fashion of a fingerprint" (15). Hence, in its Ideal form (minus special effects or computer manipulation), the cinematic image serves an almost scientific function – as "evidence" that what it depicts once existed.

Clearly, cinema is capable of suspending the body in a flash of time – a fact that links the medium to what Leo Charney calls the modernist "cult of the momentary" (281). But Bazin saw cinema's techniques as far more sophisticated. "The film is no longer content to preserve the object, enshrouded as it were in an instant," he remarks, "Now, for the first time, the image of things is likewise the image of their duration, *change mummified as it were*" (14–15, my emphasis). Along with time, cinema also captured movement – an element traditionally associated with life, as stasis is with death (Cavell 11).

Obviously, the cinema has slyly scripted into its narratives a catalog of figures and symbols for its powers of revivification – from the corpse coming to life at its own wake, to the mummy escaping from its tomb. Perhaps, had Bazin lived longer he would have seized upon a more contemporary practice for an analogy to the cinematic process: *cryogenics*, the act of freezing live (but dying) individuals in order to thaw them out later, when a cure for their disease is found. Like cryogenics, the cinema stores a static or "frozen" image of a subject that is later "defrosted" through the heat of projection. Perhaps this is why the cinema has lately taken on the subject of cryogenics in such works as *Sleeper* (1973), *Late for Dinner* (1991), and *Forever Young* (1992). Rumor has it that Walt Disney – a man especially identified with the cinema – now lies in a state of cryogenized suspended animation (Baudrillard 154).

While Bazin's theory of cinema invoked its magical powers, he realized that no modern viewer consciously accepted its illusion of immortality. Rather, Bazin understood that the body which cinema preserved was in large part the corpus of memory. "No one believes any longer in the ontological identity of model and image," he notes, "but all are agreed that the image helps us to remember the subject and to preserve him from a second spiritual death" – the self same impulse of "conservation" that motivates the literary biography (10).

It is in fact her "second death" (in anticipation of her first) that Marlene Dietrich hires Maximilian Schell to prevent. But having hired him to create a documentary version of the biopic, why does she so stubbornly subvert his wishes? Why does she refuse to be photographed, and what is interesting about her recalcitrance?

Fading stars

> I'm ready for my close-up . . .
>
> – Norma Desmond in *Sunset Boulevard*

On one level we can surmise that Dietrich refused to appear in *Marlene* because she comprehended and endorsed cinema's "cryogenic" role. (Like Joseph Cornell's Rose Hobart, she wished to remain enshrined in "antique" celluloid.) Contrast this to the news media's proclamation in 1996 that Marilyn Monroe would have turned 70 that year, had she survived. Clearly, such reports were meant to exploit the shock value this revelation would have – fueling our grim fantasies of Monroe's feeble appearance.

As a film star from the late 1920s through the 1960s, Dietrich had been photographed in her prime, and made to look exquisite – with the aid of Hollywood lighting, makeup, and costume. This is the image of her that the public knows and adores, and one that can be restored at will. Why should she exchange it for one of an elderly diva? Clearly, like that of the legendary Greta Garbo, her impulse to hide speaks of both narcissism and savvy.

It is also a fact that Western culture supports the veiling of aged bodies, especially those of women. Patricia Mellencamp writes of her shock in perusing the Rodin Museum in Paris and finding a particular exhibit:

> Unexpectedly, amidst all this lusty creation, I came upon *Celle qui fut la belle Heaulmière*, the famous striking, small statue of an old woman, her shrunken breasts sagging away from her skeletal chest bones, her protruding stomach only folds of wrinkled skin. Her shoulders and neck were deeply bowed, her head and eyes downcast, her mouth and chin collapsed with time into a posture of calm acceptance. . . . She was beautifully old. I was startled by her familiar aging body. (248)

Dietrich also understands the inherent morbidity of the situation – the public's prurient interest in seeing her deterioration. She must have been keenly aware of the audience's potential for both devotion and deviance – for its tendency to worship stars, yet wish them a tragic denouement. Hence she hoists the cinema on its own petard, demanding to remain frozen in time. What she also counters, however, is cinema's notorious voyeurism – especially as attached to the body of the female star. It is for this reason that for the duration of *Marlene* we see only archival images of her, whether from such classic fiction films as *Destry Rides Again* (1939), or from newsreels, documentary interviews, or footage of her stage shows.

Dietrich is of course aware of the particular violence that cinema has done to the mature actress – a phenomenon that has been observed by Edgar Morin. As he notes: "In the American cinema before 1940 the average age of female stars was 20–25; their career was shorter than that of male stars, who may ripen . . . in order to attain an ideal seductive status" (46–47). The lives of many women performers were dramatically reconfigured in Hollywood's biopics, a third of which concerned female entertainers – for instance, Jean Eagels, Gertrude Lawrence, Helen Morgan, Susan Hayward, and Fannie Brice (Custen 76). But the fate of aging actresses has also been narrativized in fiction form – and quite brutally in the canonical *Sunset Boulevard* (1950). In that film, Joe Gillis (William Holden), a down-and-out screenwriter, happens upon the Gothic mansion of Norma Desmond, an old silent movie queen. In desperate need of work, he agrees to collaborate with her on a trite and dated screenplay, and finds himself the object of her delusions, rage, and sexual advances. Throughout the film, Desmond is portrayed as repulsive, predatory, and ghoulish. (In fact, when Gillis first arrives she mistakes him for a mortician she has summoned to bury her pet monkey). When Gillis eventually jilts her, she kills him, and is arrested as she hallucinates a "comeback." The film has a strangely "documentary" and "biographical" air to it, as the role of Desmond is played by a fifty-three-year-old Gloria Swanson – a major film star in the silent era (and ironically, it did produce a comeback for her). Furthermore, two venerable Hollywood directors appear as actors in the film. Cecil B. DeMille, with whom Swanson had worked, plays himself, while Erich von Stroheim plays her butler and former mentor (see Fischer, "*Sunset Boulevard*").[1]

In a strange fashion, the situation of Schell and Dietrich in *Marlene* parallels that of Gillis and Desmond in *Sunset Boulevard* – since Schell, a much younger man who was born in 1930, the year *The Blue Angel* was released, has come to the actress's Paris apartment to assist with her dubious movie project. And like Joe Gillis, he has concocted a plot of his own. But rather than allowing herself to be portrayed like Norma Desmond, fantasizing a screen revival and preparing for her "closeup," Dietrich refuses to be photographed, triumphing over Schell without resorting to murder – just as her screen persona had conquered so many men. There is also a vaguely seductive aspect to Dietrich's engagement of Schell – with whom she had worked in *Judgment at Nuremburg* in 1961. Over the course of the film the two have little "lovers' quarrels" over the shape of the narrative and Dietrich's status within it.

If one were looking for a complete contrast to Dietrich's refusal of the gaze, it might be found on numerous fronts. One thinks of the American celebrity documentary *Truth or Dare* (1991) in which Madonna (at her erotic and professional peak) parades before the camera both on-stage and off.[2] Nothing is too personal or undignified for her to share with us in this biopic, including a visit from her throat doctor, as lover Warren Beatty looks on. But the contrast between Madonna and Marlene is not just a matter of youth versus age. In the cinema verité documentary *Grey Gardens* (1976), an elderly mother and middle-aged daughter – of "interest" largely because they are relatives of Jacqueline Bouvier Kennedy Onassis – agree to be photographed in their decrepit home, and shamelessly preen for the camera. But it is also apparent that the women are mentally unbalanced – and that is, perhaps, the point. Old women, in our culture, would have to be deranged, to agree to become a visual spectacle (see Fischer, *Cinematernity* 179–213).

Yet in another text, *The Wonderful, Horrible World of Leni Riefenstahl* (1993), an eighty-nine-year-old actress/director, in complete command of her senses, happily displays herself to the camera in both scuba diving wet suits and street clothes. In addition to an elderly body, one might imagine that she has a certain "politics" to conceal, but she does nothing of the kind. The key distinction is clearly between those who respond to cinema's call for exhibitionism and those who do not.

Yet, despite Dietrich's refusal to be photographed, and her attempts (as Bazin would say) to "preserve" her life through "a representation of life" in the form of her past cinematic treasures, the specter of death re-enters the frame – like the return of the repressed (10). First of all, one has the distinct impression that both Dietrich and Schell know that the film is being made because she will soon die (which she did in 1992). In her dubbed narration, which perversely reveals, in her raspy, sluggish voice, the very age she has sought to banish from the image, Dietrich jokes about how certain Oscars are "death bed" awards – guiltily granted to their recipients on the eve of their ruin. In this sense, one might imagine *Marlene* as a "death bed" film. Though this is especially true of the biography of an octogenarian, on a theoretical level it is the case for all cinema. As Garrett Stewart has noted: "Not only . . . are all photographs . . . posthumous but they are ostensibly mortifying; telling of a death that was, they warn of a death coming" (25). Thus, it is all the more ironic that the opening credits announce *Marlene* as an "Alive" film release. For in fact it seems a "posthumous" document – and here, we might recall that in the film *Dinner at Eight* (1933), a producer refers to a has-been actor (played by John Barrymore) as a "corpse."

Several excerpts in *Marlene* highlight the theme of mortality. As early as 1931, in an extract from *Dishonored*, we see her killed before a firing squad. In a clip from *Touch of Evil* (1958), Dietrich's character tells Orson Welles (as Hank Quinlan) that his future is "all used up." In *Destry Rides Again*, the refrain of one of her songs is "And when I die. . . ." And a clip from *Just a Gigolo* (1979), her final film, talks of life going on without her.

Beyond such quotations from fiction films, the shadow of death is caught in the documentary segments of the work. At one point, for example, as part of her biographical confessions she speaks of her mother's death, and we see images of a gravestone. When Dietrich describes her own film career, she complains that she has been "photographed to death." Footage of her farewell stage performance in the 1960s reveals a Dietrich who looks already "mummified" – ostensibly through excessive make-up and plastic surgery. And significantly, although in her conversations with Schell, Dietrich refuses to admit a concern with death, and sardonically dismisses conventional notions of an afterlife, it is clear that she knows she has one, albeit in the celluloid versus celestial spheres.

As though to invoke self-reflexively the topic of Dietrich's cinematic life and death, Schell interrupts the pulsing "flow" of the film to present a series of still photographs, mostly from Dietrich's childhood – reminders of the inevitable passage of time. Likewise, he uses many freeze frames, a technique that some have seen as especially resonant with mortality. One especially powerful sequence of this kind occurs in a segment of the film that deals literally with death – Dietrich's attendance at the funeral of Gary Cooper.

Figure 2.1 Marlene Dietrich in *Just a Gigolo* (1979)
Courtesy of the Musuem of Modern Art, New York/Film Stills Archive

Imitation of life

> Whoever turns biographer commits himself to lies, to concealment, to hypocrisy, to embellishments, and even to dissembling.
>
> – Sigmund Freud (qtd. in Custen 148)

If *Marlene* merely presented a conventional star biography, it would not be a noteworthy film; neither would it contribute to discussions of modernism. It does so only because, through its self-conscious strategies, it becomes a virtual treatise on the nature of cinema, the status of documentary, the dynamics of the star system, the position of the biopic, and the role of cinematic innovation.

Schell's willingness to make a film biography of a living woman without a current appearance of her is interesting both in relation to feminist issues and in regard to the ontology of the medium. For Bazin, the cinema was defined in some sense by a cosmic Lack. On one level this pertained to its photographic production, which through its automatic quality largely dispensed with the human hand. "All the arts are based on the presence of man," Bazin notes; "only photography derives an advantage from his absence" (13). But it is mostly through comparisons between cinema and theater that Bazin surfaces issues of absence. As he writes, "the cinema accommodates every form of reality save one – the physical presence of the actor" (95). In making a biopic without the contemporary image of Dietrich, both the actress and director make a statement about the essence of the medium, which unlike the stage, always denies the spectator complete access to the performer. Despite the compensatory frenzy of movie fan culture, here Walter Benjamin's thoughts on the loss of aura in the age of mechanical reproduction are highly relevant. But Dietrich's refusal of voyeurism also draws attention to notions of woman's *genital* Lack – only here, Schell's failure of the gaze associates impotence with Man, and not with his female subject.

Yet there are other more intriguing and complex ways in which Schell, through a series of deconstructive techniques, underscores the nature of cinema. Since he has no star to photograph, he makes the production process a significant aspect of the text. As in *The Man with the Movie Camera* (1928), we repeatedly see the crew working at a film editing table, as images flicker on the Movieola screen. Frequently, they are shots we have already seen projected as part of the film, which lends the text an intricate temporal and narrative scheme. Among the crew, there is an older woman whose identity is not clear. She seems in some respects a stand-in for the elusive Dietrich.

Since Schell is not even allowed to film the space of Marlene's apartment, a request we hear her stridently refuse, he recreates her dwelling, and several moments of *Marlene* are staged in this ersatz mise-en-scène. But even the authenticity of that reconstruction is called into question when Schell admits that his memory has faded, and that he requires a photograph to refresh it. Obviously, the illusionistic nature of the medium is foregrounded here – the realization that most of what we see in dramatic, and even documentary, films is some order of set.

Behind this modernist trope is, of course, a postmodernist one – a nod to Jean Baudrillard's universe of endless "simulacra" (156–60). Extending this sense of hyperreality is Schell's dizzying use of mirrors in Marlene's fake apartment. Aside from referencing the supposed vanity of Dietrich, they invoke notions of cinema as what Bazin would call "a mirror with a delayed reflection, the tin foil of which retains the image" (97). Also circulating here is Jean

Cocteau's notion of the mirror as tied to the life cycle: if you want to see death at work, he once said, look in the mirror. Significantly, in the clip from *Dishonored*, Dietrich examines herself in a saber blade before she goes to meet her Maker. Finally, in this equation of death and self-regard, we are reminded of an anecdote told by Sigmund Freud of the uncanny horror he once felt late in life at unexpectedly catching a glimpse of his own aged face in a mirror – a visage he initially failed to recognize (156).[3] Clearly, this is an experience that Dietrich, plagued by cinematic mirrors, feels she can do without.

Further underscoring the sense of cinema as representation are the various reproductions of Dietrich that furnish her counterfeit apartment: a huge framed photograph, a bust. Finally, Schell dissolves boundaries between fact and fiction by interspersing whimsical, staged sequences into his documentary – one a tableau of three Marlene "doubles" in coat and tails; another, a simulation of Marlene being filmed in the silent era.

Violating conventional notions of the primacy of the image in cinematic discourse, Schell accomplishes a "substitution trick," and places all his faith in sound and voice – the repository of all biographical utterance in the film. "What's real?" he asks. "The tape recorder," he answers: "We can take that as our reality." As though to signal this, *Marlene* begins with a black screen and Dietrich speaking. But of course, as Stephen Heath has noted, although voice is often suppressed in the cinema, Dietrich's has been given considerable weight: "the voice is . . . a certain deposit of the body, a certain 'grain,' something else again, in excess, which the standards of Hollywood learned to pacify . . . and in specific instances to exploit (. . . the voice of a Marlene Dietrich or a Lauren Bacall)" (6).

Dietrich talks

> I then put her into the crucible of my conception, blended her image to correspond to mine, and, pour[ed] lights on her until the alchemy was complete. . . .
> — Josef von Sternberg (237)

Marlene also constitutes a meta-commentary on the relation between the film director and his star – a dynamic that traditionally has had a particular gender configuration. It is clear from the film's inception that the work inscribes a battle of wills – and sexes – between the male filmmaker and his female subject. Schell wishes Dietrich to appear in the film, and she will not; he urges her to recount anecdotes from her life, and she withholds any incident already published in her autobiography; he wants her to intellectualize about performance technique, and she mocks his pretensions; he wants to imagine her a "dreamer," and she insists on her crude practicality. In other words, while he wants her to be Galatea to his Pygmalion, rather than allow herself to be configured as the male's exotic "Other" (like the Surrealists' obscure object of desire), Dietrich insists on defining herself – even though we suspect it requires her to lie. One of the more ironic moments of this struggle occurs when Dietrich is impatient with the direction the film is taking, and lectures Schell on how it should proceed – that is, starting with her shipboard arrival in America, and moving on to her appearances in such Hollywood films as *Morocco* (1930). As though to ridicule her trite notions of linear/chronological documentary form, Schell dutifully, but condescendingly, presents to the viewer the very images that she orders, and we all chuckle at their banality.

If Bazin attempted to psychoanalyze the film medium, we sense that Schell brings his own "medical gaze" to his female subject, acting on what Mary Ann Doane has demonstrated is a male prerogative. He seems to imagine that, as part of the interview process, he will induce in Dietrich a kind of "talking cure." If for Bazin people's love of the cinema is based on the "need for illusion," Schell intends to divest his cinematic subject of this basic human requirement (11). Unlike Freud's Dora, with whom she shares a certain rebellion, Dietrich unfortunately does not depart, and is indignant when Schell walks out on her.

While Schell eventually accepts Dietrich's decision not to be filmed, he resists her refusal to watch her old movies. He sneaks a print of The Scarlet Empress (1934) into her apartment and all but forces her to view it with him. (Earlier, he had confessed that he would try to "trick" her.) Though Dietrich claims she has not seen any of her old films recently – "Me, look at myself? No really!" – it is clear that she knows every frame of them, and instructs Schell to notice particular moments. It is obviously Schell's triumph. He has bent her will, and perhaps revealed her duplicity. What he has not considered, however, is the ostensible suffering it might bring her to confront her former splendor. Or if he has, he has callously decided that it is well worth the injury. It is Marlene's compassionate assistant who slips Schell a note, quoting the words of Dante, reminding him, "There is no greater pain than the recollection of past happiness in times of misery."

But beyond thrusting upon Dietrich imposed career reminiscences, Schell attempts to prod her thoughts about her family – acting not only like a biographer and a psychiatrist, but like a detective – searching for the clues to the Marlene-enigma.[4] Schell asks Dietrich if she ever missed her father, who died when she was young. She coolly replies, "you can't miss what you never had," but we sense Schell's impatience with her guarded response. Clearly, he wants melodrama and tears, and he gets both when he raises the topic of her mother – which he sees as the key to her consciousness and to the crime of her dissembling. Though Dietrich has refused all sentimentality throughout the film, he finally causes her to break down at its end, when he asks her to recite with him a simple poem that her mother esteemed, concerning a person begging for forgiveness at a loved one's grave. Finally, Dietrich's arch superiority collapses as she succumbs to a cliché; her harsh, imperial voice cracks and we recognize the sound of muffled sobs. As Benedict Anderson has written, "nothing connects us affectively to the dead more than language" (145), and here too we recall that Michel Chion once described the cinema as "a machine made in order to deliver a cry from the female voice" (68, qtd. in Silverman 77). It is precisely this that Schell has served up. Dietrich's disintegration also confirms Custen's view that the "lesson one learns from biopic vicissitudes . . . is quite simple: with an unusual gift comes unusual suffering" (75).

In Dietrich's momentary and pathetic contemplation of the maternal, the "mummy complex" finally meets the "mommy complex" at the hands of a man young enough to be Dietrich's son. Schell has forced Dietrich to publicly grieve – for her lost youth, fame, beauty, childhood, and family – much as Welles does to his protagonist in Citizen Kane (1941), whose imagery is fleetingly quoted in Marlene. Though the moment of Dietrich's recollection is compelling, we find it vaguely pornographic – and perceive Schell as having moved from a posture of Reverence to Rape. In his biographical zeal, he has stripped Dietrich of both personal and cinematic illusions, leaving her – and us – to confront the aesthetic and psychic void. She of course retaliates later on, when she savagely orders her director to "go back to Mama Schell and learn some manners."

The painter of modern life

For Death must be somewhere in a society . . . perhaps in this image which produces Death while trying to preserve life.

– Roland Barthes (92)

The question, of course, arises as to where *Marlene* stands in relation to modernist/postmodernist debates. Clearly, *Marlene* bears traces of the postmodern (as is evident from my mention of its ubiquitous simulacra). Beyond this, Dietrich herself often assumes a rather postmodern perspective. She derides her status as a sublime screen goddess, and admits that she never especially liked sex. As the viewer watches excerpts of her museum-quality films, Schell waxes poetic about them, and urges Dietrich to do the same. Instead, she relentlessly hurls charges against them – of "kitsch" and "kvwatch" – deeming them rubbish, outdated, Camp. Again, we are not entirely sure that she means this, but at least her words pull the rug out from under the precious modernist posture. In a similar vein, when Schell informs Dietrich of the politically-correct readings of her screen persona, she announces that she hates feminists and accuses them of penis envy. Finally, she repeatedly declares herself "bored" with Schell's inquiries, and with the films that he finds so divine.

But other aspects of *Marlene* seem tied to modernist concerns. P. Adams Sitney has discussed the "resistance to vision" that subtends many such texts – a stance that questions the "status and values of seeing." As he notes, "Dramatic moments of vision occur in these works, in which nothing, or nothing dramatic is seen" (2–3). One could hardly find a better description of the central tension of *Marlene*, a film which denies the spectator visual substance and pleasure, and subverts the power of cinema as panopticon.

Furthermore, the somber and earnest tone of the film seems ultimately to belie Dietrich's parodic cynicism, and links the text to a modernist aesthetic. For the film's deconstructive techniques are never merely playful, but seek such profundities as the Truth of Dietrich's psyche, the Essence of the film medium, and the Key to human existence. If the film's concerns are "post-" anything they are more post-mortem than post-modern – invested in such sober issues as Life and Death. In this regard, it seems interesting that the site of the taping for *Marlene* is Paris – where Dietrich retired and lived until her passing. For if any locale is identified with the birth of modernism, it is this French city during the late nineteenth century – a metropolis associated with such artists as Charles Baudelaire, Arthur Rimbaud, and Stephane Mallarmé (Nicholls 1). As Peter Nicholls makes clear, the movement was tied to the theme of mortality: two of the chapters of his book on the subject are entitled "Decadence and the Art of Death" and "Death and Desire."

Similarly, in writing of the modern entertainments that preceded and presaged film spectatorship, Vanessa Schwartz focuses on the Paris morgue and the Musée Grevin – the latter, a wax works specializing in celebrity likenesses (298–311). It is the same solemn modernist contemplation of mortality that informs *Marlene*, and that links it and its actress-corpse-effigy-*femme fatale* to those historic sites of Parisian popular spectacle. If in her essay Susan Sontag calls for a new kind of cine-love to replace cinephilia, Maximilian Schell proposes an old one – necrophilia.

But, clearly, despite her alleged archival immortality, it is not only Dietrich who will age and fade, but the very film medium in which she is supposedly preserved. Hence, though long thought to have an advantage over literature, the cinema as a biographical format may bear a certain vulnerability. This issue is raised in the eccentric film *Lyrical Nitrate* (1991) – a "modernist montage" of silent film fragments that speaks to the biographical fate of the medium. One sequence of this text, a virtual treatise on cinematic impermanence and fragility, begins with a shot of a film projectionist, then moves on to some anonymous, turn-of-the-century biblical epic depicting Adam and Eve in the Garden. In the film's return to Genesis and Eden, we also recover cinema's origins and innocence – all to the strains of a female, operatic/maternal voice that would please Kaja Silverman. But in short order the scene becomes troubled, as marks on the emulsion (made from decomposition) obscure the action and view – forcing us to look "through a glass darkly." Resembling the abstract images of Stan Brakhage's *Mothlight* (1963) – created from pressed dead insect wings – the celluloid deterioration raises questions of mortality, as the intertitles speak of death and an image of the Grim Reaper appears. Fittingly, in "Falling in Love Again," Dietrich's famous torch song from *The Blue Angel*, she compares her doomed suitors to moths attracted to a flame.

But there is a moment in *Marlene* in which the filmic material also degenerates. Failing to capture a new image of the reluctant Dietrich, Schell projects an old one on the wall, and in an act of directorial passive-aggression, allows the film to combust and melt before our eyes. Here, the disintegrating celluloid is vaguely reminiscent of the portrait photographs that burn on a hot plate in Hollis Frampton's *Nostalgia* (1971) – a work whose title could not more aptly echo the bittersweet biographical themes of *Marlene*. But while *Marlene* may invoke the modernism of the primitive cinema, and of the American avant-garde, it also relates to the post-World War II European "New Wave" – a movement that Catherine Russell sees as characterized by "narrative mortality." As though to pay respect to this cinema, Schell produces an experimental sequence that blatantly alludes to such auteurs as Ingmar Bergman and Federico Fellini.

In fact, *Marlene* as a whole might be regarded as a loose remake of *Persona*, a film much prized by Susan Sontag. For like the actress Elizabeth Vogler, who will not speak, Dietrich, a performer, refuses to appear. And like the nurse who tries to uncover Vogler's biographical secrets in her summer home, Schell attempts to pierce Dietrich's defenses in her Paris apartment. Significantly, in *Persona* the psychoanalytic process is linked to cinema and death. As part of a montage that signifies a psychic break within the narrative, Bergman displays the camera, burns the celluloid, and splices in silent movie footage of a dancing skeleton.

As we have seen, Schell synchronizes his own modernist vignette with Dietrich's angry voice calling him the worst name she can think of – a "film buff" – banishing him to a "film institute," where she sentences him to communing with "old people" and savoring his relics. Here, perhaps the most fetishized actress in the history of cinema charges Schell with film fetishism. She also implicitly derides his love of the kind of "retrospectives" that play at what Sontag deems the art form's "temples" – film clubs and *cinémathèques*. It is a less celebratory sense of "retrospective" that informs *Marlene* – where filmography and biography, direction and introspection, image and Imaginary, drama and trauma, hopelessly superimpose.

In Dietrich's tone of mockery, however, we are ultimately reminded of the words of Andy Warhol, who expressed his own misgivings about fame, media, and immortality:

> At the end of my time, when I die, I don't want to leave any leftovers. And I don't want to be a leftover. I was watching TV this week and I saw a lady go into a ray machine and disappear. That was wonderful, because matter is energy and she just dispersed. That could be a really American invention, the best American invention, to be able to

disappear. . . . The worst thing that could happen to you after the end of your time would be to be embalmed and laid up in a pyramid. I'm repulsed when I think about the Egyptians. . . . I want my machinery to disappear. (112–13)

With his characteristic wit and brilliance, Warhol brings together the themes of death, celebrity, antiquity, and modernity. Though he desires an American invention that could make us disappear, he *and* we are stuck with one that makes us appear forever – the cinema.

Warhol's wish to make his own "machinery" evaporate is perhaps a secret wish to vaporize the quintessential "machine of the visible." It is against this complex notion of constituting a "leftover" – bodily, biographically, and artistically – that Dietrich so forcefully rails in *Marlene*.

Notes

1   Just how strong the legacy is of Norma Desmond is apparent from an article about a journalist's encounter with another aging actress – this time, a real one – Mary Tyler Moore. As Jonathan Van Meter noted when he visited the star's home, inscribed over the intercom are the words: "Open the Gates for Miss Desmond" (40).
2   The comparison between *Marlene* and *Truth or Dare* was raised to me by Katrin Micklitz, a graduate student in my class at the University of Pittsburgh.
3   Patricia Mellencamp recounts this anecdote in *High Anxiety*.
4   Marlene's reluctance to discuss her family background is, according to George Custen, typical of the standard "biopic," which minimizes the role of the subject's family (149).

References

Anderson, Benedict. *Imagined Communities: Reflections of the Origin and Spread of Nationalism*. London: Verso, 1995.

Barthes, Roland. *Camera Lucida*. Trans. Richard Howard. New York: Hill and Wang, 1981.

Baudrillard, Jean. "From 'Simulacra and Simulations.'" Brooker. 151–62.

Bazin, André. "The Ontology of the Photographic Image." *What is Cinema?* Selected and trans. Hugh Gray. Berkeley: U of California P, 1967.

Benjamin, Walter. "The Work of Art in the Age of Mechanical Reproduction." *Illuminations*. Ed. Hannah Arendt. Trans. Harry Zohn. New York: Schocken, 1968. 217–51.

Bloom, David. "Computers Usher in the Era of the Virtual Movie Star." *Pittsburgh Post-Gazette*, July 1, 1988: E3.

Brooker, Peter, ed. *Modernism/Postmodernism*. London: Longman, 1992.

Cavell, Stanley. "What Photography Calls Thinking." *Raritan: A Quarterly Review* 4.4 (Spring 1985): 1–21.

Charney, Leo. "In a Moment: Film and the Philosophy of Modernity." Charney and Schwartz. 279–94.

Charney, Leo, and Vanessa Schwartz, eds. *Cinema and the Invention of Modern Life*. Berkeley: U of California P, 1995.

Chion, Michel. *La Voix du Cinema*. Paris: Éditions de L'Etoile, 1982.

Custen, George. *Bio/Pics: How Hollywood Constructed Public History*. New Brunswick: Rutgers UP, 1992.

Doane, Mary Ann. *The Desire to Desire: The Woman's Film of the* 1940s. Bloomington: Indiana UP, 1987. 38–69.

Fischer, Lucy. *Cinematernity: Film, Motherhood, Genre*. Princeton: Princeton UP, 1996.

———. "Sunset Boulevard: Fading Stars." *Women and Film*. Ed. Janet Todd. New York: Holmes and Meier, 1988. 97–113.

Freud, Sigmund. *Creativity and the Unconscious*. New York: Harper and Row, 1958.

Heath, Stephen. "Language, Sight and Sound." *Cinema and Language*. Ed. Stephen Heath and Patricia Mellencamp. New York: American Film Institute, 1983. 1–20.

Mellencamp, Patricia. *High Anxiety: Catastrophe, Scandal, Age, and Comedy*. Bloomington: Indiana UP, 1992.

Morin, Edgar. *The Stars*. Trans. Richard Howard. New York: Grove, 1960.

Nicholls, Peter. *Modernisms: A Literary Guide*. Berkeley: U of California P, 1995.

Russell, Catherine. *Narrative Mortality: Death, Closure, and New Wave Cinemas*. Minneapolis: U of Minnesota P, 1995.

Schwartz, Vanessa. "Cinematic Spectatorship before the Apparatus: The Public Taste for Reality in *Fin-de-Siècle* Paris." Charney and Schwartz. 297–319.

Silverman, Kaja. *The Acoustic Mirror: The Female Voice in Psychoanalysis and Cinema*. Bloomington: Indiana UP, 1988.

Sitney, P. Adams. *Modernist Montage: The Obscurity of Vision in Cinema and Literature*. New York: Columbia UP, 1990.

Sontag, Susan. "The Decay of Cinema." *New York Times Magazine*, Feb. 25, 1996: 60–61.

———. "Film and Theater." *Film Theory and Criticism: Introductory Readings*. Ed. Gerald Mast, Marshall Cohen, and Leo Braudy. 4th ed. New York: oxford UP, 1992. 362–74.

Stewart, Garrett. "Photo-gravure: Death, Photography, and Film Narrative." *Wide Angle* 9.1 (Jan. 1987): 12–31.

Van Meter, Jonathan. "Mary, Mary Quite Contrary." *New York Times Magazine*, Nov. 26, 1995: 38–41.

Von Steinberg, Josef. *Fun in a Chinese Laundry*. New York: Collier, 1965.

Warhol, Andy. *The Philosophy of Andy Warhol (From A to B and Back Again)*. New York: Harcourt Brace Jovanovich, 1975.

Action Movie Hysteria, or Eastwood Bound

3

PAUL SMITH

There is a quite well-known photo-portrait of Clint Eastwood, made by Fran Liebowitz, which figures the star in what have become his trademark street clothes – green t-shirt, brown corded trousers, and running shoes. He is standing erect against the backdrop of what looks like the film set of a western. The rebellious, western, sometimes Promethean, hero that Eastwood so fully represents is here heavily tied by ropes around his body and legs. His hands, also heavily bound, are held out in front of the body at about waist height. His expression is perhaps not his most familiar one, but it certainly can be glimpsed occasionally in his movies: it is a look of vague bewilderment, with a slight crooking of the mouth into a mixture of amusement and annoyance as he looks back at the camera. His eyes are narrowed at the same time as his brows are arched slightly upwards. His straightened body seems to emerge from a billow of dust behind him.

This image was recently used as the cover to a Pluto Press collection of essays called *The Sexuality of Men*. I don't know how it came to be selected for that cover, but it does seem an interesting and apt choice in certain ways. The several male British authors in the book are concerned with how, as they put it, "popular versions of what it is to be a 'real man' have become so outlandish as to prompt the idea that all is not as it should be for the male sex," and consequently they are concerned with the task of breaking the silence that seems to surround this "hidden subject, resistant to . . . first investigations," male sexuality (Metcalf and Humphries 1). Eastwood's public and cinematic personae, among the most visible icons of masculinity in North American culture, can be readily taken not only as the metonym of the silence and the barriers to investigation that the authors are trying to break, but also as an obvious and symptomatic marker of the notion that "all is not as it should be" in regard to masculinity. The silence that many of his film performances appropriate as the sign par excellence of empowered masculinity – the erectness of his body and the ubiquity of what the book's editors call his "oversized gun," the careless ordinariness of his J. C. Penney clothing, the limited but stark range of his facial and bodily gestures – all contribute to Eastwood's presence within this culture as one of the more legitimated bearers of its masculinity, "real" or otherwise. At the same time, many of the movies in which he stars and/or which he directs could be understood as somewhat troubled presentations of the kind of (image of) masculinity that they popularly stand for.

The trouble is perhaps hinted at in Liebowitz's picture, where this iconic male body emerges from the waves of dust around it to stand tall as the very type of a unique masculine beauty, but where it is simultaneously marked and immobilized by these ropes, signs of a certain helplessness or, at least, of difficulty. And yet the ropes in the photo – especially the five layers that encircle Eastwood's biceps, chest, and back, and which are the focal point of the image – might also be indicative of a certain pleasure. That is, a pleasure in powerlessness – a pleasure which could certainly be grasped as an indication that "all is not as it should be" with this man, and which we might expect to be normally hidden from view in this culture and called "perverse" – that pleasure is adumbrated across the ambivalent gestures of his face, and is, I would also claim, sketched across his films. Further on I want to regard this pleasure in relation to the idea of masochism; for now it can certainly be taken to provide an emblematic starting point for discussing male sexuality in that it presents an ambivalent moment whereby this male body, objectified and aestheticized by Liebowitz's photo-portrait, comes to represent something a little "outlandish."

It has been possible for a long time now for discourses addressing North American notions of masculinity and its heroism to rhapsodize on exactly the outlandish character of a special kind of man – the westerner. There is little point in trying to demonstrate once again the long history of that man, from Fenimore Cooper's pioneering heroes, through "classic" western protagonists such as *Shane*, to a plethora in the 1980s of action heroes like Eastwood in *Heartbreak Ridge* or Mel Gibson in *Lethal Weapon*. But it is interesting to see how the male protagonist in such cultural productions always takes pleasure (and is made enjoyable, or at any rate consumable) by way of his ultimate inability to act as the solution to the narrative and social contradictions in which he is involved. Natty Bumppo's self-righteousness as he goes around killing and destroying as much or more of "the natural" as he claims to be conserving,[1] the desperate but ecstatic hypostasis of the cowboy faced with an ineluctable tide of westward expansion and modernization at the end of *Shane*, the Mel Gibson character's ineptitude in *Lethal Weapon* in dealing with the family life which renders his own heroism possible, each of these in some way fails to transcend fully the contradictions of his narratives. Now, an orthodox critique of the male heroes in these kinds of popular cultural narratives would say that they actually present too easy and transcendent a solution to contradictions; my claim is that, to the contrary, the resolutions and solutions never really come. Still less are they embodied in this long line of male heroes of which Eastwood is, of course, an especially important member. Eastwood's interest, it seems to me, resides largely in the tendency of his work to remain much longer than usual in the rather special gratification that comes of being unable to offer ultimate solutions, and, in doing so, to exhibit the symptoms of what lies behind that pleasure.

This at first sight might seem a peculiar opinion to be holding, and admittedly it is one which flies in the face of the overt narrative frames of popular movies such as those Eastwood makes and stars in. However, I want to propose that action and western movies like Eastwood's might actually exceed the familiar processes of narrative contradiction and closure and leave what I will call an hysterical residue. My point will be that these movies thus quite routinely open out onto difficult and multivalent questions about the popular cultural representation of masculinity, beyond their always rather formulaic narrative frames: indeed, that the narrative disposition of particular tropes of masculinity does not ultimately control or delimit them, and leaves unmanaged and resistant representations of a male hysteria. Of course, I am far from discounting here the significance of narrative closure as a kind of punctual return to tolerably non-contradictory positions, but I want to take the stress away from formulaic endings and ask to what extent they are but a lure beneath which particular kinds of representational and sexual-political questions are left open.

In Liebowitz's photo, Eastwood appears to emerge, almost risibly classical, from his own peculiar waves to become an objectified spectacle. At the same time, this spectacle is bound and bounded. It is with the tension between (or rather the pairing of) these two elements — the objectification and eroticization of the male body and the registration on this body of a masochistic mark — that I want to begin. I am interested in looking at the ways in which contemporary popular movies might effectively stand against some of the notions that writers in film studies deploy when talking about the interfaces of gender considerations with representation; but also I want to sketch out an argument for seeing what happens when the purportedly "outlandish" nature of representations of masculinity in popular culture are apprehended not as immediately and irredeemably contemptible but as something by and through which some of the realities of male experience are registered.

Paul Willemen, in a very short article about Anthony Mann's westerns, talks about the way in which the male heroes there are diegetically cast in two distinct ways, the one consequent on the other. First, the hero is offered simply as spectacle: "The viewer's experience is predicated," Willemen says, "on the pleasure of seeing the male 'exist' (that is walk, move, ride, fight) in or through cityscapes, landscapes, or more abstractly history." This pleasure can readily be turned to an eroticization of the male presence and the masculine body, and it is always followed up in Mann's movies by the destruction of that body. That is, the man is always physically beaten, injured, brought to breaking point. One needs to add to Willemen's formulation the obvious third stage in which the hero is permitted to emerge triumphant within the movie's narrative line, and which conventionally cannot occur before the first two. This third stage obviously provides the security and comfort of closure and is a crucial element in the production of spectatorial pleasure. Willemen proposes that both of the first stages of representation are also in their way pleasurable for the spectator. The first "pleasure" — that of voyeuristic admiration of the hero's body and presence — is followed diegetically and graphically by the "unquiet pleasure of seeing the male mutilated . . . and restored through violent brutality" (16).

This intertwining in most action scenarios of what we might call on the one hand the solidity of masculine presence, and on the other the demonstration of masculine destructibility and recuperability, is readily apparent in most Eastwood movies, whether they be the westerns or the cop movies, or even the comedies in which his co-star is an ape (*Every Which Way But Loose* [1978] and *Any Which Way You Can* [1981]). A first impulse would be to consider this as little more than an exigency of Hollywood habits and formulae, but of course it has its ideological ramifications too. I would claim that this passage — from eroticization, through destruction, to reemergence — is such a staple, not just of Mann's movies, but of action movies and westerns in general, that it can readily be called the orthodox structuring code for those movies. There are, I think, several interesting characteristics to that code that will bear commentary insofar as what is at stake is a certain erotics of the male body which demands or entails peculiar diegetic and graphic representational strategies and processes of viewer identification.

Willemen implicitly proposes that the pleasure of the first two stages is to be cast in terms of sadistic and masochistic frameworks where objectification is to be understood as the pleasure yielded by the sadistic gaze, and where the destructibility of the male body is to be grasped as a masochistic trope. Since much film theory regularly deploys the frameworks of sadism and masochism as essential heuristic notions (the notion of sadism – especially in its relation to the gaze – almost chronically, and that of masochism more recently), it might be as well to consider them here briefly.

The cinematic erotics of the male body depends first of all upon that body's objectification. It is common, of course, to regard such objectification as the standard treatment for female bodies in the cinema; equally familiar are the many critiques, deriving so often from Laura Mulvey's seminal article, "Visual Pleasure and Narrative Cinema," which tie this objectification to the sadistic male gaze, to the structure of filmic diegesis itself, and to the irredeemably homocentric nature of the cinematic apparatus. Male bodies too are subjected to cinematic objectification, but an objectification that is effected by specific cinematic means geared to the male body. The specific nature of male objectification has been dealt with most fully by Steve Neale in the article, "Masculinity as Spectacle." Taking his cue from Mulvey's analysis of the way women's bodies are objectified and made the object of the gaze. Neale also tends to take for granted the sadistic/masochistic doublet. His thesis is that, because of the power of the ritualized structures and relays of the (a priori) sadistic gaze in cinema, a male body must effectively be "feminized" by the apparatus and spectator if it is to become objectified. Dealing with the masochistic stage, he suggests that what occurs there is a "testing" of the male hero, analogous to the investigation of female protagonists in standard dominant Hollywood cinema: "Where women are investigated, men are tested" (16).

Neale's contention, that in order for the male body to be thus objectified it has to be "feminized," is open to question, not least because it relies upon a sweeping generalization (increasingly doubted in film studies) about the conventions and the apparatus of cinema – namely, upon the argument that they are oriented primarily and perhaps exclusively to the male spectator. Neale's argument is in a sense self-fulfilling, or at least circular. If it is assumed that the apparatus is male, geared to a male gaze, then any instance of objectification will have to involve the "feminization" of the object, so that the notion becomes so broad as to be useless.

Equally, instances of the erotic display of the male body are rife in contemporary film and media production, and can be shown to be geared to either (or both) male and female spectators in different contexts. There exists a whole cultural production around the exhibition of the male body in the media – not just in film, but in TV, sports, advertising, and so on – and this objectification has been evident throughout the history of Hollywood in particular, even if it has been intensified in recent years. Scarcely any of the plethora of images depends upon the feminization of the male: rather, the media and film deploy specific representational strategies to eroticize the male body.

In film, Eastwood's primary directorial mentor, Don Siegel, is perhaps one of the first Hollywood directors to foreground systematically how cinema can and does eroticize the display of the male body and turn that display into part of the meaning of his films, without deploying the particular formal strategies by which female bodies are offered to the male gaze in most Hollywood productions. That is, his work is often concerned with the activity and dynamics of all-male groups, and this concern has allowed the development of something like a cinematic obsession with the male body. Siegel has developed a repertoire of shots and conventions, often duplicated in films which Eastwood directs, which constitute a little "semiotics" of the heroized male body. Among the most frequently used devices are what I call under-the-chin shots (where the heroized male figure, shot most often from the waist up, seems to loom above the spectator's eyeline), heavily backlit shots (in which either the details of hero's whole body or his face are more or less obscured while the general shape is given in silhouette), facial close-ups (preponderantly with the actor's gaze going right to left at a roughly 45-degree angle and especially often used to deliver Eastwood's characteristic snarls and slight facial movements), and travelling shots and pans following the male body's movement (but often relatively unsmoothly, and usually avoiding centering the body in the frame).

This is a quite rough and schematic cataloguing of the kinds of objectifying shots favored by Siegel, Eastwood, and other action movie directors. But the point is that these kinds of representational strategies (developed, I think, into something like an industry standard in the last two or three decades) differ from those chronically used to objectify the female body. There is, in other words, a specific and even ritualized form of male objectification and eroticization in Hollywood cinema.

One of Neale's assumptions – that looking at the male body is something of a taboo in our culture – is contradicted by the kinds of strategies which action/western movies typically make available to themselves. It might still be true, however, that eroticizing the male body ultimately produces a mixed pleasure. According to Willemen, "the look at the male produces [in the male spectator] just as much anxiety as the look at the female" (16). Certainly it is the case that such movies defend against the possibility of such anxiety in particular ways. First and most important the two-stage, exhibitionist/masochistic process *must* always be followed by a revindication of the phallic law and by the hero's accession to the father's power in the third stage of the orthodox action movie codes. Second (that is, less obligatory than the diegetic resolution), many of these movies accompany the pleasure/"unquiet pleasure" that they establish with a quite marked anti-homosexual sentiment – which is to suggest that the masochistic moment is often crucially anti-homosexual in its significance. An example of this can be found in the second "Dirty Harry" movie, *Magnum Force* (1973), where the antagonists are a band of young extreme right-wing policemen, part of whose evil in the movie's terms is their implied homosexuality, their rather butch and leathery appearances, and their close homo-bonding. In movies where the antagonists (those who are to inflict physical damage on the hero's eroticized body) are not implied to be actually homosexual, their sexuality is usually offered as perverse in some other fashion: this is the case, for example, with the main antagonist in the original *Dirty Harry* (1971) who is marked as effeminate and perverse in many different ways. In *Sudden Impact* (1983) there is an interesting melding of the two strategies: the leaders of Callahan's adversaries (a gang of rapists) are, first, a man who is shown to be unable to conduct "normal" sexual relations with even the most voluptuous and willing female, and second, a lesbian woman ("dyke" in the movie's discourse) who procures the Sondra Locke character for her gang to rape and who seems herself to have some heterosexual desires, something the movie clearly presents as perverse.

Thus, even while these kinds of specifically masculinized representational strategies at the corporeal level are not a feminization of the male body, they do always carry with them a defense against possible disturbance in the field of sexuality. If it is actually allowed to show itself, this disturbance will always ultimately be covered over, erased, sometimes literally blown away. In what is perhaps the least well-made of the "Dirty Harry" movies, *The Enforcer* (1976), the first mention of any perversity or homosexuality comes in the final scene as Callahan blows away his antagonist with a rocket launcher and the muttered words, "You fuckin' fruit."

* * *

The several elements of popular culture's treatment of the male body are particularly evident in the Siegel–Eastwood collaboration, *Escape from Alcatraz* (1979). The first sequence of the movie, where Eastwood is a prisoner brought into Alcatraz, is especially indicative of Siegel's concerns with the male body and of his ways of working with it. In preparation for incarceration at Alcatraz, Eastwood is stripped and the camera follows his body through a kind of gauntlet of objectifying looks from the prison guards. Those looks are intercut by Siegel's typical low-angle, under-the-chin shots which do not, however, correspond directly to the direction of the guards' looks. Similarly, the guards' looks do not construct the geography of the prison's space; this is done instead by means of a series of medium-length shots with Eastwood's body moving across the screen but never centered in it. This sequence is for the most part classic Siegel, but it finishes with a slightly more unusual shot as Eastwood is then depicted as a kind of threatening gothic monster as he is deposited in a dark, barred cell to the background of thunder and lightning which irregularly lights up the body's shining chest and arm muscles. The camera lingers over this final shot in a clear prefiguration of the inevitable "testing" of that body in the rest of the film.

This objectifying passage is quickly followed by the standard routine of destruction. Eastwood is variously assaulted by both inmates and authorities in the closed space of the prison: the moment of his worst torment at the hands of isolation block guards is the prelude to the acceleration of the movie's narrative line and Eastwood's subsequent escape (escape from the masochistic moment as much as from the prison itself). The movie's final sequence has the prison governor wondering whether the escapees could have survived the icy waters of the San Francisco Bay while one of his officers muses that the men had vanished into air.

As well as following the orthodox codes of the action narrative – objectification and eroti-cization, followed by near-destruction and final apotheosis of the male body – *Escape From Alcatraz* defends against the apparent perversity and unquiet pleasure of the early stages by accompanying them with the standard anti-homosexual component. After the opening sequence has suggestively turned the guards' policing looks into the carriers of homoerotic objectification, the movie soon introduces a rather unpleasant homosexual inmate whose advances Eastwood rebuffs, the latter setting himself up for a series of attacks and fights with this man who, predictably, ends up with a knife in his body before Eastwood escapes.

Further confirmation of the strength of these rather simple conventions is perhaps best given by way of the counter-example of Siegel's *The Beguiled* (1971), in which Eastwood stars as a Yankee soldier recuperating from some serious battle wounds in a southern girls' school. The Eastwood character's lechery leads to a reaction by the women and girls in the school who punish him by rather hastily and perhaps unnecessarily cutting off his wounded leg – an amputation that is explicitly referred to as a castration. This corporeal removal is the culmination of Siegel's transgression of the standard rules for this kind of movie: the objectification/destruction/transcendence path is not followed here – at least, things are not in their proper order, since the body's damage has already been sustained before the start of the movie without any opportunity for the camera to run the usual objectification routines. Furthermore, there is no triumphant transcendence in the end: after the rushed amputation, Eastwood's anger and accusations provoke the women and girls to murder him with poison.

Audiences for *The Beguiled* have never been large, and it remains one of the least successful movies that Eastwood has been associated with, despite the fact that both he and Siegel have expressed their satisfaction with the movie. Siegel explains the failure by suggesting that "[m]aybe a lot of people just don't want to see Clint Eastwood's leg cut off" (qtd. in Kaminsky 251). Whether that is the case or not, the lack of success of *The Beguiled* underlines in a negative way the fact that dramatic Hollywood movies have induced certain expectations about the masculine corporeal, and cannot readily break them: the exhibition/masochistic stages *must* serve the end of the hero's triumph; they are inextricably part of the diegetic necessity. Another way of saying this might be to suggest that the masochistic stage of such narratives cannot be presented as a complete castration and that the possibility of transcendence must always be kept available. The masochistic trope in this sense must be no more than a temporary test of the male body.

One familiar effect, of course, of the hero's more usual triumph over the deliquescence of his once objectified body is the promotion of various metonymically associated notions of regeneration, growth, rebirth, sacrifice and reward, and so on. In that sense, one could talk of these diegetic tropes as mythical – we have a tradition of such narrative ideologies to which to appeal, including the traditional story of Christ's ascent after the crucifixion. Indeed, in much occidental cultural production the Christ figure could be said to have operated chronically as a privileged figure of the pleasurable tension between the objectification and what I will call the masochizing of the male body, and it is certainly no accident that so many of the films of the western or action hero take advantage of reference to that figure. Eastwood's movies – and especially his collaborations with Siegel – are rife with such references. Eastwood has starred in or directed several movies which make the Christ figure an easily identifiable point of reference: *Pale Rider* (1985), in which Eastwood plays a priest; *Thunderbolt and Lightfoot* (1974), where he is a pretended priest and which includes several shots alluding to the crucifixion; or even *The Beguiled*, where his role is explicitly linked to that of a long-suffering Christ, but in which there is no triumphant transcendence, only the death of his character.

Recent film scholarship has begun to investigate how the notion of masochism and its concomitant "unquiet pleasure" can be deployed in looking at the question of subjectivity (and especially male subjectivity) in filmic relations. One thinks immediately of Kaja Silverman's work (notably "Masochism and Male Subjectivity") and that of Gaylyn Studlar (*In the Realm of Pleasure*), or of Leo Bersani's *The Freudian Body* (which is not concerned specifically with film but with cultural production – "art" – in general). Part of the point in each case is to attempt to complicate and even undo to some degree the rather monolithic view of male subjectivity which film scholarship tends to propose.

In their different ways, and with disagreements, each of these three writers proposes the masochistic trope, the masochistic moment, as in some sense subversive of conventional or "normal" formations of subjectivity. Bersani, for instance, sees masochism as a formation which disturbs the fixities of literary and visual language to produce a designifying or a denarrativizing moment; more specifically, he reckons that it produces what he calls an "interstitial sensuality," responding to a reader's pleasurable "interpretive suspension between narrative and nonnarrative readings" (78). In a similar fashion, Silverman proposes masochism as a formation of suspension, though her preferred notion is that of "deferral" – masochism as a deferral of male submission beneath the Law of the Father and of the normative pressure of male sexuality. For her this is indeed a large part of the definition of perverse sexuality, that it be set against the aim-directed "normality" of the male subject.

The fully consummated pleasure of the normal subject is associated with guilt, but the suspended, showy pleasure of the masochistic fantasy is a disavowal of the paternal function, a sort of escape from it and a way of punishing its imposition: "What is beaten in masochism is consequently not so much the male subject as the father, or the father in the male subject" (56). Thus, in Silverman's account, the masochist "remakes the symbolic order, 'ruins' his own paternal heritage" (57).[2]

In these treatments of masochism as what I am calling a trope, there are considerable difficulties to be negotiated concerning the relation of theoretical schemas to textual matter, and equally to relations of reception. The assumption of my argument is that the filmic representations of masculinity act as a kind of demonstration of how masculinity is supposed to work (or, to put it another way, they proffer particular meanings around the subject of masculinity, and to the male subject). I want particularly to stress here the process of narrativization in which a masochistic moment is but a part, a single element caught up in the machinery of the proffering of significance. I want to avoid the temptation of implying that this demonstration forms male subjectivity itself or that it produces any unavoidable male spectatorial position. Film does have its interpellative effect, of course, but that does not mean to say that it inevitably or indefeasibly determines forms of subjectivity. I do not wish to suggest that cinema is simply the symptom of the spectator elaborated as it were elsewhere. In other words, I still see some kind of *décalage* between representation and subject positions which many film theorists do not. While allowing for direct spectatorial identification and thus for the cinema's proffering of subject positions, I dare say that investigation of the representational strategies of film finally is capable of discovering more about the availability of cultural ideologies than about forms of subjectivity.[3]

With such provisions in mind, it becomes difficult to accept entirely the claims of Bersani and Silverman. Each of them exploits the notion of masochism as a perversion in order to suggest that it subverts, undermines, defers, or invalidates phallic law and the fixities in both subjectivities and meanings that depend upon phallic law. Silverman perhaps summarizes this position best in her claim that the male masochist

> acts out in an insistent and exaggerated way the basic conditions of cultural subjectivity. . . . He loudly proclaims that his meaning comes from the Other, prostrates himself before the gaze even as he solicits it, exhibits his castration for all to see, and revels in the sacrificial basis of the social contract. The male masochist magnifies the losses and divisions upon which cultural identity is based, refusing to be sutured or recompensed. In short, he radiates a negativity inimical to the social order. (51)

Silverman theorizes, then, that male masochism is in itself an oppositional formation. But if, to paraphrase Judith Mayne, we submit the theory to the test of narrative,[4] or investigate the function of the masochistic moment in representational practice, it might be seen that the "inimical" nature of masochism and the pleasurableness of its self-proclamation can be sustained only provisionally: that, in other words, popular cultural narratives in effect enclose and contain male masochism.

This proposition is not contradicted by Freud's discussion of masochism. In "The Economic Problem of Masochism," while ostensibly dealing with the economic system of masochism, Freud is led to narrativize the phenomenon quite firmly. Its etiology is in what he calls erotogenic masochism, which is "found at bottom in the other forms": *feminine* masochism and *moral* masochism. Erotogenic masochism, the lust for pain, is for Freud the homeostatic result of a negotiation between the libido and the death drive (which he describes at length in "The Ego and the Id"). The relative stability of the outcome of this negotiation provokes exactly the narrative dramas of the feminine and moral forms. Strict distinctions between these two latter forms are not especially important for my purposes here. But what is common to Freud's explanation of both is that they are exhibitionist and in a sense histrionic, the exhibitionism and the drama being designed to provoke punishment. The punishment most readily comes (particularly in moral masochism) in the shape of "sadistic conscience" or in an intensification of super-ego activity. Masochism for Freud, then, is characterized by the need of the subject to "do something inexpedient" in order to bring down upon himself the gratifying punishment of the super-ego. The point I mean to stress here is that masochism's "negativity" is largely a functional catalyst in a formulaic narrative of erotic gratification.

This narrativized context for masochism might need to be considered alongside Silverman's claim for the negativity of male masochism and for the subversive potential of "bringing the male subject face to face with his desire for the father" (59) through the masochistic moment. One would certainly not want to reject Silverman's particular project as a viable way of articulating radical moments of male subjectivity; but alongside it, one might also have to take account of how, in popular cultural texts, the place of the exhibitionist/masochistic is already accounted for and already pulled by narrativization into a plot, precisely designed to eventually explode the negativity of masochism.

Indeed, it might be worthwhile making the rather more broad claim that in fact (i.e., in a narrativized frame) the male masochist in important ways obeys and serves the phallic law. Masochism (to paraphrase Lacan) is primarily a neurosis of self-punishment, partly because of the way it has of provoking the super-ego's revenge, the return of "sadistic conscience." The masochistic moment certainly promotes deferral and suspense, but a suspense that can work only if it is in the end undone. Male masochism is *at first* a way of not having to submit to the law, but equally importantly it turns out to be a way of not breaking (with) the law. Masochism might well bespeak a desire to be both sexes at once, but it depends upon the definitional parameters of masculinity and femininity which undergird our current cultural contexts. Male masochism might, finally, be seen as another way for the male subject to *temporarily* challenge his desire for the father and to subvert the phallic law, as ultimately another step in the way (might one even say the puerile way?) of guaranteeing the male subject as origin of the production of meanings. Indeed, it might be said that male masochism is a kind of laboratory for experimenting with those meanings to which ultimately we accede. The rules of masochism are, then, primarily metaphorical, and the game is a game played out unquestioningly in the thrall of the symbolic; crucially, the lessons of masochism do not last, they come and are gone, forgotten as part of the subject's history of struggle in learning how to reach symbolic empowerment triumphantly. Masochism, grasped in this way, would be a closed space where masculinity sets the terms and expounds the conditions of a kind of struggle with itself – not a struggle necessarily for closure, but a struggle to maintain in a pleasurable tension the stages of a symbolic relation to the father – a struggle in which, ironically, the body becomes forgotten.

The pleasure proffered in action movies can be regarded not so much as the perverse pleasure of transgressing given norms, but, at bottom, the pleasure of reinforcing them. This is where such movies' narratives are conservative: they marshall a certain identificatory pleasure in the service of a triumphant masculinity by employing a process girded and endlessly reproduced by the narrative conventions of Hollywood and its country's cultural heritage. But even in the most conservative and rigid kind of cultural production there is an underside, a double edge – in this instance, something that is continually being fended off. What is common to many of the action movies and westerns of the sort mentioned is the way in which the exhibition/masochism trope and its pleasure/unquiet pleasure, along with their resolution into a triumphal view of male activity, reside alongside a residual, barely avowed male hysteria.

That hysteria is often expressed narratively as the sensation of the dangers inherent in identification with women or with homosexuals (of either gender). Or else it is an hysterical formation that can be glimpsed in moments of incoherence or powerlessness in the male body and in the male presence. Sometimes it is only barely visible in the joins of the apparatus as it produces its apparently seamless cloth. The hysterical moment that I am stressing marks the return of the male body out from under the narrative process that has produced what appears to be its transcendence, but which in fact is its elision and its forgetting. In other words, although there is in these movies a conservatively pleasurable diegetic path which ends up suppressing the masculine somatic, the body nonetheless returns from beneath the weight of the symbolic. What I mean by this hysterical residue, then, is an unresolved or uncontained representation of the body of the male as it exceeds the narrative processes. The meanings proffered by these movies concern the male body as that which has to be repressed. A simple instance can be glimpsed at the climactic moments of any of these action movies where the male protagonist's control of the narrative situation is never matched by control of his own body. The body here is always represented as de-eroticized, turned into a mass of mere reflexes. The male accession to control is clearly marked as a symbolic or metaphorical matter, a process of forgetting the body, forgetting the previous stages of eroticizing and masochizing the body. And yet the body is still there, still in the field of representation, but no longer subject to the somatic meditation that the narrative has thus far constituted.

In warding off this hysterical residue, suffocating its somatic presence with the safe and deferrable pleasure of the symbolic, the male heroic text itself becomes hysterical. In the cases of *Sudden Impact* and the 1984 *Tightrope* (both movies of the "Dirty Harry" mold), as well as in *The Gauntlet* (1977, an early sketch of such movies), there is an explicit alliance on the part of the male protagonist with what is presented as the hysteria of femininity. Such alliances are always finally negated diegetically in the sense that the women involved have finally to be pulled beneath the law, their independence replaced by a traditional, disempowered status in relation to the male protagonist. And yet they leave their marks on the experience of the movie.

Some of these marks can readily be seen in the recent Eastwood directed movie, *Pink Cadillac* (1988). The female protagonist (played by Bernadette Peters) is the quarry not only of Eastwood, who plays a bail-bond officer, but also of mobsters whose money she has inadvertently stolen. As the Eastwood character attempts to help her, he is pulled into an alliance with her which involves him in increasingly serious loss of control of his body. This loss of control is signaled in many ways, but perhaps most deliberately in terms of his clothing and his facial and vocal expressions. For instance, for a good portion of the movie he is trapped in a spectacularly tacky zoot suit and suffers various kinds of physical indignities and inconveniences because of it. There is a kind of rising tide of loss of control over his body which the camera and editing produce as comic, but which is nonetheless significant for being treated so much at length. Eastwood's concomitant symptoms are constituted by an

Figure 3.1 Clint Eastwood directing *Sudden Impact* (1983)
Courtesy of Photofest, New York

exaggerated and grotesque intensification of his more familiar vocal and facial expressions; this is clearly intended as a caricature of Eastwood's usual acting style, but it also establishes the serious consequences for the male body of being allied – even temporarily – with that of the hysterical woman protagonist.

If the masochistic trope colludes with and finally reverts to narrative closure, such hysterical registrations remain as part of the history of the male body and are left floating, uncontained, untranscended by the narrative. What the hysterical bespeaks or figures is something that in an essay called "Vas" I have called, paradoxically enough, the unsymbolizable of male sexed experience. That essay is an attempt to point out and to begin to explore the male imaginary and its registration of both the body and the lived experience of male sexuality. It is generally understood in psychoanalytical theory that repression in the male subject seems to prohibit the speaking of the male body, to block its symbolization. The hypothesis entertained in "Vas" is that, in reality, repression is never complete and that some part of male somatic experience remains to be registered: this is the strictly unsymbolizable body, a body reduced to figuration outside the schemas of the phallic organization of the symbolic. This body is figured in ways that I call hysterical.

My most general conclusion is, then, that in the cultural productions of this homocentric society masculinity is represented first and foremost as a particular nexus of pleasure. That pleasure is predicated upon a specific mode of objectifying and eroticizing the male body, and is fortified by a series of operations on that male body which, while they have the trappings of a resistance to the phallic law, are in fact designed to lead the male subject through a proving ground toward the empowered position that is represented in the Name of the Father. Masochism is in a sense a metonym for another frequently deployed masculinist trope – the fun of the chase, where the hunter momentarily puts aside his innate advantages in order to intensify and prolong the pleasure of the exercise.

Within such a representational framework, something escapes or is left unmanaged. The hysterical is what always exceeds the phallic stakes, what jumps off. The hysterical is marked by its lack of containment, by its bespeaking the travails of the body, and by its task of carrying the unrepresentable of male experience. What escapes the terrible simplicity of male sexual experience and the crude simplicity of homocentric narratives is always that which cannot be represented or spoken. In that sense it is rather apt that Eastwood has become known primarily for the *silence* of his acting performances and for the sheer presence of his *body*. Furthermore, his most recent movies (*Pink Cadillac*, or *Heartbreak Ridge* [1986]), diegetically construct alliances with women which are painful and difficult for the male protagonist to sustain and which are pointed to by new kinds of pain, alteration, and decay in the Eastwood body. The generous reading of these recent movies is to say that, while they are on the face of it predictably unsubtle popular responses (albeit rather belated ones) to the impact of feminism in this culture, they do confront the difficult task of representing masculinity at the hysterical moment of its potential deprivileging and at the moment of the coming of age. These movies certainly do not represent an escape from the kind of masculinity that infuses the older ones, but they might at least be said to attempt a playing out of that masculinity in relation to femininity. These are not movies that will forge any radically new male subjectivities, but written across them in the shape of Eastwood's hysterical body are the silent signs of what might best be described as a comeuppance.

Those signs have the function too of pointing up the lure of the orthodox codes where the pleasure of masculine representations is given as essentially and intrinsically bound up with the three-stage shift from objectification to masochism to empowerment. The central masochistic moment is thus a kind of necessity in the conservation of norms of male sexuality within the discourses of popular culture; it represents a way of structuring into the full subjectivity of the egoistic hero a resistance, a way of beating the father to within an inch of his life before replacing him or allowing him to be resurrected, and finally doing it just as well as he can. In this sense, the masochistic moment, girded by its moments of pleasurably perverse display and exhibition, serves a quite orthodox version of the masculine confrontation with the father. But this also means that the masochistic moment is temporary, a kind of trial that we men know we have to go through, but which will not take all our energy. What is crucial about it, to me, is the way it so often seems here to be less a question of how we might negotiate our sexuality in lived experience, and more a question of how our symbolic dramas are channeled and recuperated. Much more on the edge, more outlandish than this nexus is the hysteria of being unable to be in control, the sheer excess of the body itself, and the hysterical symptoms we have written on our bodies which an ironically masochistic regard for ourselves cannot erase.

Notes

1   Cf. Ann Douglas's remarks on Natty Bumppo (346).
2   Studlar, too, investigates "the masochist's disavowal of phallic power" (16) in her readings of some of the Von Sternberg/Dietrich collaborations such as *Blonde Venus*; unlike Silverman, however, she is concerned to use masochism as a way of intellectually displacing the phallic schemas which so much film theory assumes. Although one has considerable sympathy with such an effort, Studlar's is insufficient insofar as she is led to posit masochism as a kind of ur-sexuality in which sexual difference is ultimately elided. The masochistic turn, in her version, does more than push toward denarrativization, as in Bersani, but actually *desexualizes* insofar as the privileged figuration of masochism becomes the androgyne. This leaves Studlar with the unfulfilled task of explaining how and why sexual difference emerges. Indeed, her way of taking masochism back to the pre-Oedipal does seem to assume the Oedipal; thus masochism serves the function of countering something which by rights it should make impossible, that is, the phallic schemas of sexual difference. Kaja Silverman's brief argument against Studlar seems right: Studlar's "is a determinedly apolitical reading of masochism, which comes close to grounding that perversion in biology" ("Masochism" 66).
3   This is obviously a schematic rendering of a longer and probably contentious set of arguments about the relation between text and subject position. Some more formal version of these positions can be found in my *Discerning the Subject*. My *Clint Eastwood* (from which the present article derives) deals more extensively with these issues (especially as they might relate to what is obviously the underplayed third term in this discussion – identification).
4   To be precise, Judith Mayne ends her article, "Walking the 'Tightrope' of Feminism and Male Desire," with the following claim from which I've extrapolated here: "But there is a fit between theory and narrative, and the intersection of feminism and male desire needs to be thought, and rethought, by submitting theory to the test of narrative" (70).

References

Bersani, Leo. *The Freudian Body*. New York: Columbia UP, 1986.
Douglas, Ann. *The Feminization of American Culture*. New York: Anchor, 1988.

Freud, Sigmund. *The Ego and the Id*. 1923. *The Standard Edition of the Complete Psychological Works of Sigmund Freud*. Trans. and ed. James Strachey. Vol. 19. London: Hogarth, 1954. 3–66. 24 vols. 1953–74.

——. "The Economic Problem of Masochism." 1924. *Standard Edition*. Vol. 19. 157–72.

Kaminsky, Stuart. *Don Siegel*. New York: Curtis, 1974.

Mayne, Judith. "Walking the 'Tightrope' of Feminism and Male Desire." *Men in Feminism*. Ed. Alice Jardine and Paul Smith. New York: Methuen, 1988. 62–70.

Metcalf, Andy and Martin Humphries, eds. *The Sexuality of Men*. London: Pluto, 1985.

Mulvey, Laura. "Visual Pleasure and Narrative Cinema." *Visual and Other Pleasures*. Bloomington: Indiana UP, 1989. 14–26.

Neale, Steve. "Masculinity as Spectacle." *Screen* 24.6 (1983): 2–16.

Silverman, Kaja. "Masochism and Male Subjectivity." *Camera Obscura* 17 (1988): 31–66.

Smith, Paul. "Vas." *Camera Obscura* 17 (1988): 89–111.

——. *Discerning the Subject*. Minneapolis: Minnesota UP, 1988.

——. *Clint Eastwood: A Cultural Production*. Minneapolis: Minnesota UP, 1993.

Studlar, Gaylyn. *In the Realm of Pleasure*. Urbana: Illinois UP, 1988.

Willemen, Paul. "Looking at the Male." *Framework* 15/17 (1981): 16.

PART TWO

THE EUROPEAN AND ASIAN POPULAR CINEMA STAR

Introduction

This section of the book goes beyond the ethnocentric focus in star studies on American cinema to include the European and Asian performer. These essays indicate how the star is not merely the product of a national culture. He or she also circulates within an international context. Despite this, as the following critics reveal, any discussion of the phenomenon of stardom in a transnational context must take into account the actual and spectral role of Hollywood.

Tim Bergfelder's study of Anna May Wong, "Negotiating Exoticism: Hollywood, Film Europe and the Cultural Reception of Anna May Wong," examines stardom not from the usual aspect of national cinema but from the perspective of international film. Focusing on the Film Europe Project of the 1920s and 1930s and on the career of Wong, Bergfelder traces the transnational character of that time. In particular, he examines how Wong's "trajectory paralleled that of her black contemporary Josephine Baker." Wong made films in Britain, Germany, and with less acclaim, in Hollywood, and her star persona "expressed an identity capable of appealing successfully across cultural and national boundaries." Beyond its careful analysis of the various expressions of Wong's persona, this essay offers a methodology that highlights the importance of analyzing the historical, economic, transnational, and cultural specificities of star analysis.

By contrast, Stephen Gundle's essay, "Sophia Loren, Italian Icon," focuses on the national dimensions of the actress's stardom and her role as "a figure of unusual importance in Italian popular culture." Tracing her career, Gundle situates her rise to prominence in the post-World War II years. In particular, Gundle links her success to several subcultural networks – Catholicism, working class aspirations, "Americanicity," and the popular culture of subaltern groups particularly in Rome and Naples. Loren's star image is a confluence of these various strands. From a winner of beauty contests and an actress in the commercial cinema of the early 1950s, Loren went on to become a star in the films of Vittorio De Sica where she was now identified specifically with "unabashed female sexuality." However, Loren also underwent Americanization, appearing in Hollywood cinema where she was divested of some of the subcultural qualities that inhered in her Italian films and publicity. Gundle's essay provides another means for assessing the relation between the local and worldwide dimensions of stardom.

M. Madhava Prasad's "Reigning Stars: The Political Career of South Indian Cinema" is an original essay commissioned for this book. It focuses on the extraordinary rise of film stars to the status of supreme political leaders in south India. While Indian democracy's electoral system has been transformed by the advent of these celebrity politicians, and new trends like "regionalism" have arisen in their wake, political theory has not been able to account for this development within its terms. This essay explores how, at a particular historical conjuncture, a lack in the political structure occasioned by the contradictory pulls of federalism and nationalism, the existence of a climate of acceptance for cinema technology, the evolution of the genre of the "social," and the linguistic reorganization of Indian states, all contributed to the production of a unique situation in which the film star became available as a supplementary site of nationalist expression.

While Tim Bergfelder's essay on Anna May Wong deals with the fate of the Asian female performer within the Hollywood industry, Kwai-Cheung Lo's article on Asian action film stars examines the place of the male body in Hong Kong martial arts cinema. In the instance of Bruce Lee, Lo finds an American-born performer who achieves international success in Chinese films and, therefore, constitutes a kind of "alien body" – devoid of local color but invested with superhuman power. Especially interesting is the non-visual aspect of Lee's performance which creates a "hole" in his screen image – his signature use of auditory "shrieks and wails." In the case of Jackie Chan, on the other hand, Lo sees a comic kung fu star who occupies both a "local and transnational space" and is, curiously, more in the tradition of Buster Keaton than Bruce Lee. On some level, despite the popularity of the Hong Kong martial arts film in the contemporary era, Lo sees a trend toward a loss of its "physical dimension" in part attributed to special effects as well as to the relentless and selective focus on the male (vs. female) screen body.

Negotiating Exoticism

4

Hollywood, Film Europe and the cultural reception of Anna May Wong

TIM BERGFELDER

As a historical case study for the problems facing integrated European film initiatives, the developments of the "Film Europe" project of the 1920s and 1930s provide a number of poignant lessons. Torn between intense competition with Hollywood, rapid changes in international production methods and technology, and self-defensive national interests, the initial enthusiasm for creating a pan-European cinema turned ultimately to inertia. To focus exclusively on the overall economic failure of this endeavour is, however, to deny the Film Europe project both its internal coherence and its cultural legacy. Many recent critical evaluations of the period have been written from the vantage point of a vested interest in a particular national cinema. The conclusions such accounts reach are not neccessarily wrong, but they tend to adopt a rather selective perspective. Thus, a scholar commenting on Hollywood's global aspirations would obviously emphasise America's overall market and cultural dominance in Europe.[1] Such an approach, however, ignores the fact that, despite an American stronghold in European distribution, not all Hollywood films achieved the same degree of popularity in different countries.[2] This approach tends to underestimate the sometimes considerable level of resistance to the cultural impact of "Americanism" and the perceived "invasion" by Hollywood, not to mention the more specific and localised objections against particular kinds of representations, genres and stars.

Some historians of French, German or British cinema, on the other hand, view the internationalism of this period as a culturally insignificant or at best transient phase after which a "self-contained" national cinema would reconstitute itself.[3] These arguments reinforce rather homogenising and narrow concepts of national cinema and national identity. They also replicate the same cultural defence mechanisms and protective strategies which hampered the objectives of Film Europe in the first place. It is perhaps not surprising that the main issues surrounding Film Europe (cultural hybridity versus national authenticity; transnational film production versus national film cultures) are being revisited in the late 1990s with renewed urgency. In a period witnessing the contradictory drives of media globalisation, multiculturalism and the violent re-emergence of nationalism, the developments of Film Europe assume a particular significance.

My intention here is not to dispute either the influence of Hollywood on the developments of Film Europe (though it was not a monolithic one), or the vital importance of nationally specific discourses. If we want to understand the Film Europe project in its own right, however, and to make productive use of its history for today's concerns, we require a critical perspective which acknowledges the dialogic and transnational nature of this endeavour. My chapter will concentrate primarily on the relationship between the German and British film industries and their respective cultural contexts. I will look at the ways in which the Film Europe project attempted to negotiate these national contexts and the impact of Hollywood with its objective of fostering "international" stars and films. I will focus in particular on the brief European career of the Chinese-American actress Anna May Wong between 1928 and 1934.

In a recent article on the industrial developments between Europe and Hollywood in the 1920s and 1930s, Thomas Elsaesser invoked the emblematic images of the "traveller" and the "voyage."[4] These two tropes are highly appropriate for many narrative trajectories and protagonists of Film Europe's international productions. Instead of circumscribing geo-political entities and centred national identities, these narratives frequently focus on the margins, boundaries and junction points of Europe. Locations may include train stations (*Rome Express*, 1932), ports (*Song*, 1928), aeroplanes (FP1, 1932), nightclubs (*Piccadilly*, 1928), or exotic islands (*Rapa-Nui*, 1927). These places are more or less self-contained, and clearly separated from a homeland or national community that might be implied but which is always absent. These spaces are inhabited by outsiders, people of indeterminate national identities, who have either just arrived at these extra-territorial locations or are about to depart from them. Many of these narratives include lengthy transnational journeys.

The films' spatial fluidity is also frequently accompanied by temporal indeterminacy. A good example of this is the genre of the "film operetta" which, in its associations with the Austro-Hungarian empire, invokes multicultural connotations as well as a nostalgic vision of the European past (see, for example, *Congress Dances*, 1931). What appears to be a lack of historical and geographical specificity in this context could, however, be interpreted as a distinctive marketing strategy. The nostalgia for a continental European cultural heritage provided a potential selling angle both within Europe and for the American market. The box-office success of Ernst Lubitsch's *Old Heidelberg* (1927) and similar productions had proven that there was a viable market for this kind of refashioned Old-European folklore in the United States.[5] The motif of transnational mobility and the idea of the multicultural melting pot also attempted to emulate the international appeal of the Hollywood product. After all, quite similar narrative and stylistic strategies of blurring geographical and cultural specificities had helped to make Hollywood films adaptable in global markets.

The theme of "uprootedness" evident in these international films finds its corollary in the circumstances of their production. During the 1920s and 1930s, a wide spectrum of film-makers were involved in transnational and transatlantic traffic, ranging from technical personnel to directors, producers and stars. The American industry, in particular, benefited from the widespread mobility of this period and actively encouraged it with its "trophy hunts," as Fritz Lang famously called the practice of Hollywood agents and producers travelling to Europe to sign up promising talent.[6] These transfers were not always as successful or as permanent as the celebrated cases of Greta Garbo or Marlene Dietrich, and there are a number of actors who resumed their European careers after a brief interlude in Hollywood (for example, Lilian Harvey and Emil Jannings).

To focus on the irresistible lure of the American industry for Europeans is in any case to ignore the considerable transnational traffic that went on within Europe during this period. For actors and actresses, such movements were arguably more risky than for those production artists for whom cultural specificities and language barriers were less crucial.[7] In fact, very few truly "European" stars emerged even during the brief heyday of Film Europe. Lilian Harvey may be considered such an exception. British by birth, she became one of the most successful stars of early German sound cinema.[8] Ideally suited for German and British language versions, her Anglo-German accent also appealed to French audiences, who found her flawed French diction a particularly charming asset.[9] However, most of the other German or French stars who attempted to conquer other national audiences had to compete not only with the indigenous stars of these countries, but also with the star appeal of the imported Hollywood product. A few stars managed to cross over into other cultural contexts, sometimes accompanied by a significant change in their star persona and status, as can be seen in the case of the British careers of Conrad Veidt, Elisabeth Bergner, or Anton Walbrook.[10]

In the same way that Hollywood tried to sign up Europeans, European film industries attempted to attract Americans to the other side of the Atlantic. From the 1910s onwards, the German film industry had tried with varying success to build imported American actors such as Fern Andra, Betty Ammann and Louise Brooks into stars. In the late 1920s and early 1930s, the British film industry similarly attempted to capitalise on the importation of Dorothy Gish, Gilda Gray and Esther Ralston.[11]

The Chinese-American actress Anna May Wong is one of the most intriguing examples in this category of transatlantic stars. Wong's brief stardom in European films (mainly Anglo-German co-productions) between 1928 and 1934 illustrates some of the most pertinent issues in the relationship between Film Europe and Hollywood during this period. It bears witness to the struggle for economic and cultural hegemony over European markets, which was fought not only in studios and executive boardrooms, but also in the contemporary film press. It exemplifies the translations and transfers of cultural products and discourses between European countries, and the conflicting urges within various national film cultures both to counter and to imitate the industrial practices and conventions set up by Hollywood. In the following pages I shall look at the ways in which Wong's European career fitted into the overall production strategies and cultural parameters of the Film Europe project. I shall also analyse how her star persona was adapted and reconstructed for European audiences, negotiating the concepts of Hollywood stardom and Americanness with notions of the "exotic other" and the Oriental woman. One of the most intriguing aspects of this analysis is the difference in the ways in which German and British commentators appropriated that star persona, articulating it differently according to the prevailing discourses of each specific culture.

Before discussing Wong's European films in more detail, I will outline briefly her earlier career in Hollywood and some of the discourses that differentiated this period from what was to follow. Born in 1905 (according to other sources, 1907) in the Chinatown district of Los Angeles, where her family had been living for three generations, Wong entered films as an extra in 1919.[12] Her first starring role came in 1922 in the first ever Technicolor feature production *Toll of the Sea*, an adaptation of the Madame Butterfly story relocated from Japan to China. Despite the film's success, she was once more assigned by a succession of different studios to minor supporting roles in a variety of genres. Of these films, the only one that can be seen as having had a significant impact on her career was the Douglas Fairbanks production *The Thief of Baghdad* (1924), in which she played a Mongolian slave girl. Though definitely marked as an exotic other in her various roles, Wong nevertheless appeared in a variety of different ethnic guises, for example as an Eskimo in *The Alaskan* (1924) and as the native American princess "Tiger Lily" in *Peter Pan* (1924).

The ethnic eclecticism evident in Wong's early roles fitted perfectly with Hollywood's appropriation of exoticism in the 1920s and 1930s. Mark Winokur has argued persuasively that Hollywood's representation of ethnicity in this period was heavily influenced by the Art Deco movement through the mediation of contemporary fashion styles and advertising aesthetics:

> By stylizing the accoutrements of ethnicity, Deco allowed its audience to maintain a safe distance from it. While using the patina of exoticism to sell everything, Deco aestheticized colonialism. Ethnic motifs became floating signifiers because they were streamlined in such a way that their original frames of reference disappeared . . . Stylization replaced the social realities of the present with the past.[13]

According to Winokur, this process of stylisation reached its perverse if logical climax by the end of the 1920s, when Hollywood's representation of the ethnic other displaced "real" ethnicity altogether, replacing ethnic actors with white performers portraying exotic characters. In the context of Hollywood exoticism and the consumption value associated with it, Wong had to remain a repressed presence for, as Winokur suggests,

> Anna May Wong's version of Art Deco does not work because she is authentically Asian; history begins to creep back into her character with an unacceptable realism, a history that would, by the 1920s, include the Chinese Immigration Exclusion Act, the ill treatment of Chinese in the United States, the special exclusion of Chinese women, and the subsequent picture bride and prostitute phenomena.[14]

It is clear from this quotation and from the social contexts it invokes that Hollywood negotiated its version of exoticism within the historically specific cultural climate of American nativism. In other words, cinematic exoticism cannot be seen as a universal and immutable ideological practice. Neither can it be exclusively determined by textual factors such as *mise-en-scène* or narrative trajectories, or even by industrial strategies. Rather, it is a constantly renegotiated and shifting discourse, dependent to a large degree on the specific frameworks of reference available at the level of reception. Hollywood's aesthetic of stylising the exotic into a global consumer product was taken up in Film Europe's narratives, which sold decentred identities to different national audiences. The appeal of Wong's star image within the context of Film Europe was that it had the potential to combine the attractions of pure exoticism with American modernity, thereby circumventing the problems of national specificity which faced many indigenous European stars. In this respect, Wong's trajectory paralleled that of her black contemporary Josephine Baker, who became a niche star in French cinema after her cabaret successes in Paris and Berlin.[15] As in the American context, however, nationally specific social discourses and repercussions, which were extraneous to the films themselves, complicated the perception of Wong's star image.

Anna May Wong arrived in Berlin in the spring of 1928, under contract to the producer-director Richard Eichberg. The reasons and circumstances of her move are open to speculation, although her Hollywood career was stagnant enough for her to consider other options. It is possible, though again not verifiable, that Wong's contact with the German film industry was initiated through her connection with the German expatriate director Paul Leni, for whom she worked in Hollywood on the Universal detective thriller *The Chinese Parrot* (1927).

Eichberg's signing of Wong can be seen as part of a wider strategy in his designs for pan-European productions. Frequently described as one of the "most American of German directors," Eichberg had made his name since the 1910s as the producer and director of action-orientated, fast-paced, spectacular and often exoticist genre films.[16] Working on the periphery of the major companies (producing independently, but with the financial support of larger firms such as Emelka and Südfilm), he was also renowned in the industry for establishing new stars (his discoveries included Ellen Richter, Lee Parry, Lilian Harvey and the operetta singer Martha Eggerth). By the time Wong arrived in Berlin, Eichberg had found production partners in London and agreed on a deal with British International Pictures (BIP) to film a series of sound productions in Elstree. In return, BIP would co-produce silent films made by Eichberg in German studios. Apart from her potentially transnational appeal as a Hollywood star and as an exotic, the signing of Wong had another practical advantage, in that her linguistic ability enabled her to be cast not only in English, but also in German language versions.

The first film to be made under these arrangements was the silent feature *Song* (a.k.a. *Schmutziges Geld*), shot at the UFA studios in Neubabelsberg, starring Wong and the German actor Heinrich George, and released in the summer of 1928. The film set the narrative pattern for most of Wong's subsequent appearances in European productions, making her the personification of female as well as racial suffering in narratives that almost always end in her death. The prototype and model for these narratives, intertwining colonialism and sexual conquest, is the Madame Butterfly story, widely circulated at the time in various literary, stage and film versions.[17] In *Song*, Anna May Wong plays the eponymous heroine, "a human piece of driftwood" (according to an intertitle) who falls in love with a rough cabaret artist and professional knife-thrower who abuses and exploits her devotion. When he is temporarily blinded, Song cares for him in disguise, wearing the perfume and fur coat the man associates with the woman he once loved. By the time he finds out the truth and finally repents, Song has been fatally wounded in a sword dance performance in a night-club.

The film was clearly intended to be a showcase for Wong's star qualities; the cinematography emphasises her face in expressive closeups, and the show numbers both display her dancing talent and provide opportunities to present her androgynous physique in a number of revealing costumes. Her great acting moments in conveying joy and tearful resignation are always played out in complete isolation. In relation to the narrative trajectory of her character, this kind of *mise-en-scène* could be seen to construct a separate space for her performance, establishing her as an outsider not only in the story, but also in visual terms. Consequently Wong's otherness remains contained, her exoticism rendered "safe." The extraterritorial location in which the narrative is set, and which conforms to the archetypal spaces of the international film I referred to earlier, adds a further distancing device.

Song not only established a stylistic and narrative formula for Wong's European films. It also set a pattern for their critical reception in the German and British press which was symptomatic of different national attitudes towards the Film Europe project in general. On the whole, German reviews conveyed a sense of much greater support and enthusiasm for the international ambitions of the European film, provided that the German industry played a central role in these endeavours. This support for internationalism, however, remained decidedly Eurocentric and drew its line at the Hollywood product. Particularly in more specialised publications such as *Film-Kurier*, the threat of American dominance translated frequently into pejorative comments on the formulaic nature of American films, and occasionally even on the Anglo-Saxon "character" (which would, significantly, include the British). Thus, attempts by European film-makers to imitate Hollywood conventions were viewed at least with reservation, if not suspicion. Eichberg's style of direction and production was often scrutinised in this respect.

If we look at the press reception of *Song* and similar films in Britain, on the other hand, we find that the the project of integrating European film industries and styles hardly featured at all. Particularly in publications aimed at exhibitors and at a mass (rather than cinephile) audience, a continental European influence on British cinema was seen as far more alien and even menacing than any Hollywood production could be. A too manifest continental style carried with it connotations of being too high-brow or too theatrical for general audience appeal. Thus, while Richard Eichberg was admonished by his German critics for following American models too closely, the British press had exactly the opposite complaint. In contrast with the position of the German press, the threat that the American film industry posed was perceived by British critics to be predominantly economic rather than cultural. Consequently, the adoption of Hollywood conventions (in other words, competing with Hollywood on its own terms), alongside a pragmatic use of continental technology and know-how, was seen as a valid production strategy.[18] The long-term prospect envisaged with this strategy was less an integrated European film culture than an economically fortified national British cinema.

Despite these fundamental differences in principle, the British and German press reception of Wong's films did converge in one respect. In both countries, reviewers could agree on the appeal of Wong herself. It was her star image which helped to alleviate the problems of narrative and style the films might cause in different national contexts. At least in this respect, the signing of Wong was a success for the international European film, although it proved a shortlived one.

For German reviewers, *Song*'s melodramatic narrative was seen as having a universal appeal, and its production and Wong's performance were perceived as great contributions to Germany's international film aspirations. The film publication *Lichtbildbühne* proclaimed: "This German film will, in its success, announce the glory of Anna May Wong throughout the world as one of the greatest film artists."[19] The evening newspaper *8-Uhr-Abendblatt* was more possessive: "Anna May Wong is ours now, and we won't let her go again." All of the reviews saw Wong's performance as the centrepiece of the film. Noting the international influences on this co-production, Ernst Jäger wrote in the *Film-Kurier*: "All the collaborators agreed on the proceedings, all differences disappeared, since the film's only intention is to serve the woman in front of the camera."[20]

The British press reception of *Song* (released in September 1928 as *Show Life*, and in the US as *Wasted Love*) equally centred on Wong's performance, praising it as a "masterpiece of subtlety."[21] For *Kinematograph Weekly*, it was a major point of appeal that this was "Anna May Wong's first starring vehicle," though with regard to the narrative it predicted that "it is a picture to attract high-class rather than popular audiences."[22]

By the time *Song/Show Life* was released in Britain, Wong was working in Elstree on the BIP production *Piccadilly*. Like *Song*, this film betrays its international aspirations. Directed by the German E.A. Dupont, who had scored an international success in 1925 with *Variété/Variety*, it starred two American actresses (Wong and Gilda Gray), and drew on the technical expertise of the German production artists Werner Brandes (cinematography) and Alfred Junge (art direction).[23] The script, by the bestselling British author Arnold Bennett, centred on the love intrigues behind the scenes of a fashionable London night-club. Wong plays the scullery-maid Shosho who eventually becomes the new dancing star at the club, replacing the former headline act (Gray) in the affections of the audience as well as the night-club owner. In the end, Shosho is shot dead by a jealous Chinese friend.

The Bioscope saw the fact that the film was a British production as an important selling angle.[24] Not all reviews were so enthusiastic about such a cosmopolitan endeavour being labelled "British." The journal *Close-Up* set the tone for a critical attitude in Britain towards co-productions and multinational film teams, a tone which would grow considerably in the coming years:

> This is the perfect British film. That means to say it was made by a German, with a German cameraman; its leading lady is an American of Polish extraction and its second lady an American of Chinese extraction; the leading man is English and the second man Chinese; the art direction is by a foreigner and the story is by Arnold Bennett, who must have had the toothache or an Income Tax paper at the time . . . There must be something wrong somewhere.[25]

After *Piccadilly*, Wong returned to Berlin and Eichberg to appear in her last silent film, *Großstadtschmetterling* (a.k.a. *Asphaltschmetterling*, a.k.a. *Die Fremde*, 1929). Like their previous collaboration, *Großstadtschmetterling* was a tailor-made star vehicle for Wong and a full-blown melodrama, this time set among the demi-monde of artists and gamblers in Nice. Wong, dressed in the latest Parisian fashions, starred as a show-girl who falls in love with a struggling artist, becomes his model and steals money for him, only to renounce her love in the end when she realises that he has found another woman. The film was again co-produced by BIP, and featured the French actor Gaston Jacquet as the principal villain.

Overall, *Großstadtschmetterling* was well-received in Germany and Britain (where it was released as *Pavement Butterfly*), and the highest praise was given to Wong's performance. The *Film-Kurier*, however, noticed an unhealthy foreign influence on the film's narrative and style, which it identified as "the Anglo-American icing on this cinematic cake, which covers the story of the poorly treated Chinese girl in saccharine." The same review also registered some exasperation with the way in which all recent Wong films seemed to dispense with her character in the course of the narrative: "The Eichberg team did not dare to let a happy white man share the same bed as the undressed body of a Mongolian woman. The erotic hypocrisy of this German Anna May Wong film could have originated in an English boarding school for girls."[26]

It is very likely that the film's perceived chasteness had more to do with the producers' desire not to get into trouble with the British Board of Film Censors (BBFC) or to jeopardise the movie's British release. Narratives of miscegenation were seen by the BBFC as highly problematic if not taboo, particularly in view of possible distribution in the colonies of the British Empire. As Ruth Vasey has pointed out, British censorship provisions regarding mixed-race relationships were largely concerned to maintain prestige in their colonial possessions.[27] All of Wong's European films, irrespective of whether they were shot in Berlin or London, adhere to a large extent to these British sensibilities. In those cases where miscegenation occurs, the repercussions for Wong's screen characters are drastic and seemingly inevitable – all of these films end in her death. In *Großstadtschmetterling*, where her relationship with a white man is not consummated, she survives.

When *Großstadtschmetterling* was released in Britain later the same year as *Pavement Butterfly*, the transition to sound in the British film industry was almost complete. Trade papers such as *The Bioscope* had by this time already established separate categories and columns for silent features, thereby signalling their phasing out. Eichberg's relationship with BIP thus entered a new stage, the production of big-budget international sound features, to be shot at Elstree simultaneously in three different language versions (English, German, French). The French co-production partner in this plan was Etablissements Jacques Haik. The first film to be made under these agreements was the Anna May Wong star vehicle *The Flame of Love* (1930, released in France as *Hai-Tang/L'Amour maitre des choses*, and in Germany as *Hai-Tang/Der Weg zur Schande*). The plot resembled those of Eichberg's previous films with Wong: as the member of a dance troupe touring Tsarist Russia, she suffers from her unrequited love for a dashing officer. To save her brother from execution, she sleeps with a villainous arch-duke; unable to live with this shame, she commits suicide shortly afterwards.

The production of the film was a difficult and costly experience. The tight planning necessary for multiple-language film-making proved to be especially problematic for Eichberg, a director who was renowned for his practice of improvising on the set.[28] Though completely in charge of the German version, he was given co-directors for the English and French versions (Walter Summers and Jean Kemm). There were also variations in the casting of the male lead (John Longden and Franz Lederer) and other supporting roles. Wong, however, played the lead and spoke her lines in all three versions.

Despite all efforts, the film was a resounding flop, and the French partner Etablissements Jacques Haik cancelled future involvements with Eichberg.[29] The British press reception of *The Flame of Love* was decidedly lukewarm. Wong was still seen as a major asset, and her "drawing power" and "very effective performance" were highlighted among some positive comments regarding the use of sound technology; but the film as a whole left no great impression: "This story . . . can hardly be said to rouse the emotions, as all the characters belong to the stage rather than to real life."[30]

The German press was equally disappointed with the film, though for different reasons. Despite positive comments on the German diction Wong had acquired for the role, her unique performance style was seen as incompatible with the new medium of sound. *Lichtbildbühne* noted: "Anna May Wong's incredibly subtle and expressive art, enhanced by her exotic appeal, was one of the greatest treasures of the silent film. With deepest regret one cannot help noticing that a lot of this appeal has been lost with the introduction of dialogue."[31] The critic Ernst Jäger came to a similar conclusion: "Anna May Wong was a silent miracle. Her intellectual diction merely adds curious novelty." The same review also included some bitingly ironic remarks about what the critic perceived as the film's British cultural influence:

It is interesting to see how well the producer Eichberg has understood the English mentality: eroticism without sex-appeal, exoticism without miscegenation; instead, tender melodies are played on the piano in a homely setting. Hai-Tang's lover is her brotherly friend, he watches her dancing, alluringly undressed, but apart from that – nothing happens between them. This is truly English.[32]

What becomes apparent in these different national reactions is that the British press was clearly more eager to embrace the new possibilities of the sound film. This required a move towards new narratives and a greater degree of screen realism – in short, a greater synchronisation with Hollywood's current sound productions. *Flame of Love*, however, was seen to resemble too much the melodramatic histrionics of silent and continental European cinema. The German press had precisely the opposite concern, and was far more reluctant to accept a technology which was seen to debase an essentially visual medium, a cherished narrative style, and the "true" qualities of silent screen acting. Since this had a detrimental effect on the perception of Wong's star image in Germany, one of the few common denominators between the German and the British reception of her international films disappeared. In its place, national differences resurfaced more strongly than ever.

The critical and box-office failure of *Hai-Tang/The Flame of Love* effectively ended Wong's career in pan-European and multiple-language productions. Eichberg announced in 1930 his future plans for collaborations with BIP, which included another star vehicle for her.[33] This project never materialised, though Eichberg continued his European co-production ventures well into the 1930s, before emigrating to the United States in 1938.[34] Wong remained in the public eye with various stage performances in Britain as well as on the Continent, but with no immediate film offers from either Germany or Britain, she returned to America in 1931.[35]

Hollywood did not perceive her as star material, and she was immediately assigned to minor roles, mostly in B-pictures. A notable exception was her supporting part as Marlene Dietrich's Asian confidante in Josef von Sternberg's *Shanghai Express* (1932), a prime example of Hollywood's own version of the "international" film. The international casts of Film Europe were replicated in *Shanghai Express*, with European actors who had become Hollywood studio properties (the German Marlene Dietrich and the British Clive Brook). But instead of Wong, the "real" ethnic other, it was Dietrich who became the locus of exoticism. As Mark Winokur has argued, "Hollywood was particularly interested in the use of white women as exotics. Their particular ethnic designation is almost irrelevant in their films, or at least very subordinate to the quality of 'exotica.'"[36]

Wong returned to Britain in 1933, but the three films she made here in the next two years can only be seen as a postscript to her earlier European career. The first of these, *Tiger Bay* (1934), was a low-budget production directed by J. Elder Willis for Wyndham Films. Neither the story nor Wong's performance had a great impact on critics or box-office results. Wong's next British feature, *Java Head* (1934), directed by J. Walter Ruben for First Division, was notable insofar as its narrative reversed the thematic priorities of Wong's earlier "international" efforts. In its focus on a colonial merchant dynasty in nineteenth-century Bristol, and in its realistic period detail, the film was more a heritage melodrama than an exploration in cultural hybridity. Recentred from the borderlines to the issues of home, family, tradition and Britain, it reduced Wong's character (the Manchu wife of one of the sons) to a colonial trophy. *Java Head* represented a quite different production and narrative strategy from the one adopted in the earlier pan-European films. Instead of blurring national distinctions, it consciously projected and propagated an image of (British) nationhood. As Ruth Vasey has pointed out, British producers became "more interested in the ready-made English-speaking market of the British Empire than in the problematic European arena."[37] Selling national narratives abroad thus became a strategy that was to be followed throughout the 1930s, most prominently in Alexander Korda's imperial epics.

Wong's final appearance in British films was in the Gainsborough production *Chu Chin Chow* (1934), an adaptation of Oscar Asche's long-running stage musical version of the Arabian Nights story "Ali Baba and the 40 Thieves." In its truly bizarre kaleidoscope of ethnic signifiers,

Figure 4.1 Anna May Wong in *Shanghai Express* (1932)
Courtesy of The Kobal Collection, London

blurred national identities and cultural registers, *Chu Chin Chow* was something of an epilogue to the internationalist style of Film Europe. It featured the Hollywood actress Wong as a treacherous slave girl next to beturbaned English music-hall comedians, operetta stars, and a German theatre and film actor (Fritz Kortner) in black face-paint. The fake-Oriental sets were built by the German-Hungarian art director Ernö Metzner and the dance sequences were staged by the choreographer of the London Festival Ballet, Anton Dolin.

The circumstances for such a production had, however, changed dramatically from the days of Eichberg's and BIP's collaborations. Kortner and Metzner, both Jewish, were effectively exiles from Hitler's Germany rather than professional travellers by choice. European film industries were in the process of reorganising themselves around notions of "national identity" rather than Film Europe, while Hollywood continued to assert its influence. The take-over of the German film industry by the Nazi state provides the most drastic and extreme example of this reorientation. By this time British cinema had rediscovered the appeal of Britain's imperial glory. It had also found a solidly national icon in the dowdy, working-class Northerner Gracie Fields.[38] Remnants of exotic glamour, on the other hand, were incorporated into the "homegrown" star image of Jessie Matthews which did not require ethnic otherness.[39] Moreover, this use of exoticism conformed broadly to the ethnic exclusiveness adopted by Hollywood. With such a shift towards addressing a defined national community and selectively targeted cultural markets, the hybrid extravaganza of *Chu Chin Chow* had passed its sell-by date. Wong subsequently returned again to the United States, her career by now in sharp decline. By the early 1940s she worked for "poverty row" studios such as Republic and PRC, and except for three minor film appearances and a shortlived TV series in the 1950s, she had effectively retired from film-making by the late 1940s. Still only in her fifties, Wong died in 1961.

In concentrating on the economic contexts and critical reception of Anna May Wong's films, I have tried to show how her involvement in European cinema originated and functioned within the overall framework of inter-European industrial co-operation and competition with Hollywood. A more exclusively textually-focused analysis of her films might, perhaps, centre much more on the sado-masochistic gender dynamic underpinning all these narratives of abuse, victimisation and self-sacrifice. It might identify the visual and narrative strategies the films employ to isolate and ultimately to exorcise the disturbing racial and sexual "other." The problem with this approach is that it tends to homogenise the cultural diversity of reading strategies and preferences which are surely crucial in understanding the trajectory of Film Europe. Any study which prioritises a film's supposedly immanent meaning ultimately displaces historical spectators and their cultural context in favour of the relationship between an "ideal" spectator and a relatively stable filmic text. While such a critical strategy may have genuinely progressive aims, it inevitably assumes the problematic notion of fixed identities and a fairly schematic interaction between films and audiences.

Equally problematic would be a critical discourse which transfers all agency solely to specific production strategies and industrial contexts. To argue that the developments of Film Europe are reducible to purely economic considerations implies that one can separate an industry from the complex social structures and cultural discourses in which it operates. Such an interpretation, however, would have to deal with the considerable paradox that Wong's films, however textually organised towards the exclusion of the "other," were simultaneously made with the intention of promoting the same "other" as a star. As I have shown, the critical response to this objective was contradictory. If we want to determine the cultural impact of the Film Europe project in general and Anna May Wong in particular, and if we want to know how concepts such as "hybridity" or "pan-nationalism" were perceived at the time, we need to consider more than production contexts and the films themselves. In shifting attention from production to reception, a multitude of different "texts" and meanings emerge, mediating historically determined positions, aesthetic conventions and expectations, social and other public discourses, and marketing strategies.

In the following pages, I shall look at some of the different meanings that emerge when British and German commentators take hold of and interpret Anna May Wong's star persona. These differences can be accounted for in terms of the culturally specific frameworks of reference which inform these receptions. What will become clear is that the international film, designed to cross national boundaries within the Film Europe network, is not a static text, loaded with determinate, immanent meanings, but a complex and hybrid text, capable of being taken up in different ways within each specific cultural context. Anna May Wong's star persona becomes a key signifier within this context of cross-cultural reception.

Perhaps not surprisingly, the contemporary European reviews of Wong's films rarely touch upon the narratives' ideology of racial representation. The comments by Ernst Jäger in the *Film-Kurier* quoted above are notable exceptions, though they are primarily directed at highlighting perceived sexual attitudes in Britain and Germany. Instead, the most common framework of reference is provided by the conventions and expectations of the silent melodrama, as ubiquitous descriptions such as "touching," "moving" and "emotional" attest. Most of the appraisals of Wong's performance focus on her acting technique, highlighting her body language, her movements and gestures, and how these elements convey particular emotions. In other words, Wong is constructed in the reviews of her films as the archetypal "tragedienne" of silent cinema, seen in the tradition of (and frequently compared with) stars such as Lillian Gish or Asta Nielsen.

The emphasis on a seemingly universal "art" of acting can be seen as a critical strategy for disavowing cultural difference. Within the economic framework of the Film Europe project, this strategy was crucial in making any star image exportable to a wide range of different countries. That German and British reviewers associated Wong predominantly with her acting seems to imply that this strategy worked, at least up to the point of the introduction of sound when different expectations of screen acting emerged in both countries. However, such a discourse had to be reconciled with Wong's quite visible ethnic otherness. Articles and publicity material on Wong approached this issue quite differently in Germany and Britain, but what emerged in both countries was a projection of contemporary, culturally specific conceptions of identity and exoticism onto Wong's perceived star persona.

Since the late nineteenth century, exoticised concepts of China were explicitly used in public discourses in Britain to justify Anglo-American colonial and imperial interests, and later to strengthen the ideology of the "yellow peril" in the face of Chinese immigration. The way in which Wong's ethnicity was perceived in Britain was largely dependent on these extra-textual discourses, and how they were negotiated with the image Wong projected on screen. In Germany, the link with China and the Far East was far less tangible: Germany had lost all of its colonies at the end of the First World War, and Asia had never been a significant factor in its imperialist endeavours. For Wolfgang Reif, the exoticist discourses on Asia in Germany in the 1910s and 1920s had highly conflicting and divergent ideological agendas.[40] On one hand, exoticist projections could be used as a critique of Western industrialisation and modernisation. On the other hand, exotic motifs formed an integral part of modern leisure and consumption – in the marketing of tourism, fashion and design.[41]

It is worth noting that none of Wong's European films rooted her in a distinctly Chinese or even Asian setting, or gave her roles a past or family background. In most cases they carefully avoided assigning her screen characters a definite "Chinese" identity. Even in those films where she is identified as Chinese, this identity is frequently offset by adding "Western" characteristics to her image, such as her eclectic fashion style, or her "shimmy" dance in *Piccadilly*. In contrast, Wong's off-screen persona and her ethnicity were discussed in Germany in more or less essentialist terms. Though there are occasional comments on her career in Hollywood, she is not generally referred to as an American citizen, or even as a Chinese-American, but as resolutely Chinese. However, the way in which this perceived ethnicity is portrayed through constant references to and comparisons with Chinese art, crafts and literature, effectively turns Wong into an artefact herself, a figurine in the style of Western chinoiseries. An interesting as well as representative example of this can be found in the art director Ali Hubert's portrait of her, published in 1930:

> She personifies the spirit of the great Li-Tai-Pe, and brings to life for us the tales of 1001 nights . . . On her tender and youthful body, expressing every movement with the indescribable grace of the Oriental woman, towers her head which, although com-pletely Mongolian, is beautiful by European standards. Her eyes, for a Chinese unusually large, deep and dark like a Tibetan mountain lake, gaze with enormous expressiveness. Her well-shaped, slightly voluptuous lips form a striking contrast to the melancholy darkness of her eyes. Her hands are of outstanding beauty, slim and perfectly formed. Only a Van Eyck or a Holbein could capture her on canvas . . . Externally, she appears American: smart, confident, and chicly dressed. But inside, she is purely Chinese, wearing long hair, and believing in reincarnation, convinced that in her next life she will swing as a humming-bird on the branches of a pepper-tree.[42]

One could say a great deal about the fetishising tendency of this portrayal, and its almost literal "mapping" of Anna May Wong's body. What is equally interesting, however, is the eclecticism of its ethnic and national descriptions (Oriental, Mongolian, Tibetan, etc.) and its cultural references (Arabian Nights, Chinese poetry and nature drawings, classical Western painting) Though ostensibly intended to authenticate Wong's Chinese identity and to render her Americanness as merely superficial, the portrait actually refers back to a much more diffuse concept of projective exoticism.[43]

The persona that comes across in the British press portraits and articles on Wong during her years in Europe is quite different, and allows for a more complex, though no less ambivalent, consideration of ethnic issues. Most importantly, Wong's Americanness becomes a much more central aspect of her identity. Almost all British portraits make lengthy references to Wong's roots, upbringing and early career in Los Angeles. In a *Picturegoer* portrait, programmatically titled "East meets West in Anna May Wong," the author, Marjory Collier, goes to great lengths to define the actress as a contemporary Western female film type, the "flapper," and stresses her "American timbre." The article reverses the "external–internal" distinction set up by Hubert, claiming that, "exteriorly, Anna May Wong is Chinese. But her mental outlook is almost entirely Western."[44] Written ostensibly for a female readership (the article was published in a column entitled "Screen Types – As A Woman Sees Them"), Collier correlates contemporary ethnic and gender discourses. She argues that the sexual freedom Wong projects both in her films and in her off-screen persona is incompatible with the repressed social status of women in Chinese society.

Having established the otherness of the perceived "pure" Oriental woman, the article then sets up Wong as an intermediary: "Hybridism is inherent in all her screen performances, and for all her distinctive face and features one hesitates to pronounce her as representative of a type." Collier juxtaposes a number of quite different sets of reference: the acceptable Asia of the chinoiserie ("gardens, mountain scenery, Sung vases and K'ang Hsi plum blossom jars"), the unemancipated state of Chinese women, and Wong's hybrid identity. It is, however, precisely the link between Wong's "hybridism" and her American identity which allows Collier to celebrate the actress as a modern and progressive female icon which defies stereo-typing. Wong's Americanness distances her from the more "threatening" manifestations of hybridity and miscegenation, resulting from breakdowns in colonial segregation or from Chinese immigration (in the contemporary British crime novels of Edgar Wallace and Sax Rohmer, for example, mixed-race Chinese were marked as particularly villainous). In its clear separation of value-different conditions and contexts for hybridity, this reading strategy might explain why progressive attitudes towards Wong herself could be accommodated to the discourses of the "yellow peril."

There are several other British star portraits of Wong during this period which adopt a seemingly "progressive" attitude, as long as issues of repression and prejudice can be located elsewhere. In an interview article in *Film Weekly* Wong complains about the stereotypical representation of Chinese characters in Hollywood: "I was so tired of the parts I had to play . . . Why is it that the screen Chinese is nearly always the villain of the piece? And so crude a villain – murderous, treacherous, a snake in the grass."[45] She then continues to express her gratitude to British producers, who have offered her roles that were "real, not film, Chinese." The article as a whole leaves an ambivalent impression. Its title, "I Protest," strengthens Wong's plea for more complex representations, although it is debatable whether her European film roles actually achieved this. In any case, the piece is accompanied by a photo-graph of Wong that can be seen to undermine the text's apparent intentions: she is portrayed as staring menacingly sideways, and clutching a dagger in her hands, thus visually conforming to the Hollywood stereotype of the "Dragon Lady" the article sets out to critique.

For the historian of the 1920s and 1930s, the transnational trajectory of Wong's career provides an exemplary case study of the economic and cultural limitations and possibilities of the Film Europe project. As exotic other and as an American, Wong provided a solution to the problem of finding a star image which would be acceptable to a wide range of different national markets. It is evident from these examples that the marketing and mediation of Anna May Wong's star persona in Europe did not add up to a coherent or unified image. The fact that her image was bound up in contradictions and conflicting cultural perceptions was not an obstacle, however, but part of the success of the image. In other words, Wong's public persona (blending her on- and off-screen image) functioned to some extent as a free signifier which could be imbued with various meanings. The casting of Wong was thus one of the strategies which enabled her films to be relatively successful in different European markets, which was one of the central aims of the Film Europe initiative.

From the beginning Wong's European producers and directors aimed at rendering her exotic identity indeterminate and therefore widely consumable. At the same time, Wong's image was taken up within and adapted to specific Orientalist and social discourses in different countries. Wong's German reception showed a particular resistance to accepting the American dimension of her persona, and interpreted her instead within an essentialist framework of Asian ethnicity. The British press, on the other hand, was more perceptive of her status as a "cultural hybrid," but dissociated this notion from any social significance within a British context. Indeed, wider socio-political considerations, and especially those of

British colonial prestige and immigration, imposed a constraint on the kinds of narratives that were permissible for Wong. A way out of this minefield of ethnic discourses was to concentrate on Wong's performance style as an example of a universal art of acting. Yet again, an Anglo-German consensus of what constituted screen presence and acting quality was only in evidence up to the advent of sound, after which national expectations began to differ sharply. To a large extent, it was this development in audience preferences, coinciding with the economic implications of the conversion to sound, that ended Wong's transnational appeal.

For a time, however, Anna May Wong's roles in various pan-European co-productions demonstrated one of the ways in which the international film could succeed. Contrary to those who see the international film as a bland or standardised product with no national-cultural roots, the focus on reception indicates the extent to which such texts could be taken up meaningfully within different national-cultural contexts. Anna May Wong's star persona articulated the complex hybridity which rendered those texts more or less acceptable in the different markets that made up the pan-national distribution networks central to the Film Europe project. Wong thus expressed an identity capable of appealing successfully across cultural and national boundaries.

To consider Anna May Wong's European career a success for Film Europe, if only a temporary one, still requires some qualification. German and British critics frequently referred to enthusiastic audience feedback and to a firm base of Wong admirers. Yet, compared to the top Hollywood and national stars of the time, and despite the hyperbole in the contemporary press, Wong never became a major box-office attraction. Her role as a cultural rather than a purely economic emblem for Film Europe is, however, significant. If we want to assign any cultural importance or legacy to the Film Europe project, and if we want to avoid national parochialism, we need to reassess the multiple interactions between films, secondary discourses, and audiences. In such a process, the perception or negotiation of identity and "otherness" becomes crucial. As my case study suggests, particular film cultures are constructed through culturally diverse interpretive strategies at the level of reception. Some of these strategies may conform to what we perceive as dominant representations or social discourses (the expression of an imagined national consensus, ideology, or unity) but they may also reveal interesting sidelines, diversions and productive contradictions. This approach might help to widen the scope of what any national cinema could encompass – in terms of transnational narratives and stars, or cross-cultural influences. One of the most important lessons of the Film Europe project might be that such "interferences" form an integral part of any film culture. In concentrating on this aspect, we might arrive at a more inclusive view of film history, and become less dependent on static hegemonic oppositions.

Notes

Thanks to Peer Moritz, Hans-Michael Bock, and Deniz Göktürk for their help and inspiration.

1 The standard text for this approach is Kristin Thompson, *Exporting Entertainment: America in the World Film Market, 1907–1934* (London: British Film Institute, 1985).
2 See, for example, Joseph Garncarz, "Hollywood in Germany. The Role of the American Film in Germany," in David W. Ellwood and Rob Kroes, eds, *Hollywood in Europe: Experiences of a Cultural Hegemony* (Amsterdam: VU University Press, 1994), pp. 94–135.

3 See, for example, Ginette Vincendeau, "Hollywood Babel," in Screen, vol. 29, no. 2, pp. 24–39; for a German perspective see Uta Berg-Ganschow, "Deutsch, Englisch, Französisch," in Wolfgang Jacobsen, ed., Babelsberg. Ein Filmstudio (Berlin: Argon, 1992), pp. 169–174. See also Andrew Higson, Waving The Flag: Constructing a National Cinema in Britain (Oxford: Clarendon Press, 1995).

4 Thomas Elsaesser, "Heavy Traffic: Perspektive Hollywood: Emigranten oder Vagabunden," in Jörg Schöning, ed., London Calling: Deutsche im britischen Film der dreißiger Jahre (Munich: Edition Text + Kritik, 1993), pp. 21–41.

5 See my "Surface and Distraction. Style and Genre at Gainsborough in the late 1920s and 1930s," in Pam Cook, ed., Gainsborough Pictures (London: Cassell, 1997), pp. 31–46.

6 Elsaesser, "Heavy Traffic," p. 23.

7 See my "The Production Designer and the Gesamtkunstwerk," in Andrew Higson, ed., Dissolving Views: Key Writings on British Cinema (London: Cassell, 1996), pp. 20–37.

8 See Christiane Habich, Lilian Harvey (Berlin: Haude und Spener, 1990). See also Katja Uhlenbrok, "Verdoppelte Stars. Pendants in deutschen und französischen Versionen," in Sibylle M. Sturm and Arthur Wohlgemuth, eds, Hallo? Berlin? Ici Paris!: Deutsch–französische Filmbeziehungen 1918–1939 (Munich: Edition Text + Kritik, 1996), pp. 155–68.

9 Uhlenbrok, "Verdoppelte Stars," p. 157.

10 On Veidt, see Sue Harper, "Thinking Forward and Up. The British Films of Conrad Veidt," in Jeffrey Richards, ed., The Forgotten Thirties (London: Tauris, 1998).

11 See Andrew Higson, "Way West. Deutsche Emigranten und die britische Filmindustrie," in Schöning, ed., London Calling, p. 47.

12 For more biographical information on Wong, see Philip Leibfred, "Anna May Wong," in Films in Review, vol. 38, no. 3, March 1987, pp. 146–53; and his "Anna May Wong's Silent Film Career," in Silent Film Monthly, vol. 3, no. 2, February 1995, pp. 1–2.

13 Mark Winokur, American Laughter: Immigrants, Ethnicity and 1930s Hollywood Film Comedy (Basingstoke: Macmillan, 1996), p. 202.

14 Ibid., p. 212.

15 Nancy Nenno, "Femininity, The Primitive, and Modern Urban Space: Josephine Baker in Berlin," in Katharina von Ankum, ed., Women in the Metropolis. Gender and Modernity in Weimar Culture (Berkeley: University of California Press, 1997), pp. 145–62.

16 See Corinna Müller, "Richard Eichberg," in Hans-Michael Bock, ed., Cinegraph. Lexikon zum deutschsprachigen Film (Munich: Edition Text + Kritik, 1985), pp. D1–6.

17 See Gina Marchetti, Romance and the "Yellow Peril." Race, Sex, and Discursive Strategies in Hollywood Fiction (Berkeley: University of California Press, 1993), pp. 78–89.

18 See my "The Production Designer and the Gesamtkunstwerk."

19 Lichtbildbühne, 25 August 1928.

20 Film-Kurier, 21 August 1928.

21 The Bioscope, 19 September 1928.

22 Kinematograph Weekly, 20 September 1928.

23 Andrew Higson, "Film Europa: Dupont und die britische Filmindustrie," in Jürgen Bretschneider, ed., Ewald André Dupont. Autor und Regisseur (Munich: Edition Text + Kritik, 1992), p. 46.

24 The Bioscope, 6 February 1929.

25 Close-Up, vol. 5, no. 1, July 1929.

26 Film-Kurier, 11 April 1929.

27 Ruth Vasey, *The World According To Hollywood*, 1918–1939 (Exeter: University of Exeter Press, 1997), p. 148.

28 *Filmjournal*, February 1980, p. 22.

29 *Filmjournal*, February 1980, p. 22.

30 *The Bioscope*, 12 March 1930.

31 *Lichtbildbühne*, 28 February 1930.

32 *Film-Kurier*, 27 February 1930.

33 *Film-Kurier*, 1 February 1930.

34 Müller, "Richard Eichberg."

35 See Leibfred, "Anna May Wong," p. 2.

36 Winokur, *American Laughter*, p. 209.

37 Vasey, *The World According To Hollywood*, p. 91.

38 See Higson, *Waving The Flag*, pp. 142–62.

39 See my "Surface and Distraction."

40 Wolfgang Reif, *Zivilisationsflucht und literarische Wunschträume. Der exotistische Roman im ersten Viertel des 20. Jahrhunderts* (Stuttgart: Metzler, 1975); see also his "Exotismus und Okkultismus," in H.A. Glaser, ed., *Deutsche Literatur: Eine Sozialgeschichte, Band 9: Weimarer Republik–Drittes Reich: Avantgardismus, Parteilichkeit, Exil* (Reinbek: Rowohlt, 1983), pp. 155–68.

41 Eckhart Schütz, "Autobiografien und Reiseliteratur," in Bernd Weyergraf, ed., *Hansers Sozialgeschichte der deutschen Literatur, Band 8: Literatur der Weimarer Republik 1918–1933* (Munich/Vienna: Carl Hanser, 1995), pp. 549–601.

42 Ali Hubert, *Hollywood Legende und Wirklichkeit* (Leipzig: E.A. Seemann, 1930; reprinted Heidelberg: Das Wunderhorn, 1988), pp. 106–7.

43 For a similar view, see Walter Benjamin, "Gespräch mit Anna May Wong. Eine Chinoiserie aus dem alten Westen," in Tilman Rexrodt, ed., *Walter Benjamin. Gesammelte Schriften. Vol. 4, Part I* (Frankfurt: Suhrkamp, 1972), pp. 523–7.

44 *The Picturegoer*, May 1930, p. 26.

45 *Film Weekly*, 18 August 1933, p. 11.

Sophia Loren, Italian Icon

5

STEPHEN GUNDLE

Early in 1989 Italian newspapers reported on a curious series of events that began with a proposal to erect a statue of Sophia Loren. The suggestion itself was bizarre enough but, for a few weeks, new twists were added to the story almost every day. The size of the statue was discussed, the materials to be used, the identity of the preferred sculptor and also its eventual site, on the waterfront of her native town of Pozzuoli, on the northern edge of the Bay of Naples. Here it was thought that Sophia could greet visitors in the same way that the Statue of Liberty hails those entering the port of New York. A referendum was even held, in which the idea was endorsed by some seventy-eight per cent of the town's population. Eventually the whole scheme came to nothing, Loren herself intervening to quash it. But the episode revealed that Sophia Loren is no mere showbusiness personality; rather she is something much more enduring and significant, a figure of unusual importance in Italian popular culture. As well as being the best-known and most celebrated Italian actress, she is seen as a timeless symbol of her country's spirit, someone who stands above fashion and shifts in popular taste. This is confirmed by the event which gave rise to the proposal for the statue. In a poll jointly sponsored by the national lottery and the Saturday evening television variety show *Fantastico*, several million people elected her Italy's national idol (*mito nazionale*) in January 1989.

From one point of view none of this should be surprising. After all, Sophia Loren has been a star for forty years and has made some very popular films. A woman of striking looks whose dark features and opulent figure have long been associated with a certain idea of Mediterranean beauty, she also proved herself to be an actress of rare spontaneity whose talents could be turned to dramatic roles as well as to comedy or farce. In addition she is perhaps the only Italian actress to have established herself as an international star, a figure who is widely seen as conveying something of the character of Italy to people the world over.

Yet in fact Sophia Loren's consecration as the most universally admired of Italian stars was not as predictable or obvious as might be thought. At the start of her career her looks were held to be too vulgar and exaggerated and she was cast mainly in non-Italian parts. For a considerable period she also had the handicap of being viewed with scepticism and distaste by many Catholics. Finally a large section of the public was deeply offended when she was arrested at Rome's Fiumicino airport in 1979 and charged with illegally exporting capital, non-payment of taxes and other financial irregularities. When she returned to Italy in 1982 to serve a one-month prison sentence arising from her conviction on these offences it seemed that her popularity had reached a nadir.

To investigate how and why Sophia Loren became a cultural icon and even a national symbol is therefore a worthy and potentially useful enterprise. From an exploration of her resilience and success something may be learned not only of her and of relations between stars and their publics, but also of Italy and the nature of Italian identity. First, however, it is necessary to say something of the problems involved in tackling these themes.

Italian identity after 1945

Since 1945 there has been an absence of any conventional national discourse in Italy. With the collapse of Fascism and the impossibility of restoring the values and political forms of the pre-Fascist era, a series of old ideas about the nation and its destiny fell into abeyance. Instead four subcultural networks or areas of differing consistencies and characters provided a structure to civil and political life. Two of these, the Catholic and the socialist areas, have been studied by political scientists. The Catholic subculture was in many ways the most widespread and deeply rooted in society. It was also the only one that represented a degree of continuity with the official framework of the past. At its core there was a strong attachment to the Church, the Pope and to the religious hierarchy. At the centre of the left-wing culture there lay a strong identification with the working class and a belief in its role in remaking society. The Soviet Union offered an international reference point while the Resistance was taken as having provided the impulse to a new framework of domestic political values and alliances.

The third subculture was less formalised and drew strength from the massive input of American films, music, fashions and consumer products in the post-war years. First associated with the American troops who arrived with the liberation, these consolidated their appeal in subsequent years as Italy was integrated into the Western camp. Exciting, dynamic and modern, American culture and its derivations offered young people a form of liberty and a promise of individual social mobility that nothing else could match. So powerful was the idea of prosperity it offered that its appeal extended across all subcultures to some extent.

In addition to the above networks there was a strain of autonomous popular culture that contained a mixture of values and norms typical of all subaltern worlds, but which also possessed a strongly independent identity. Primarily associated with the urban poor of Rome and Naples it extended in various forms across vast areas of rural Italy. Pre-industrial and pre-modern in nature, it was a culture of rebellion, pride, honour, self-assertion and invention. To one degree or another these subcultures included most of the population. They therefore need to be borne in mind in any discussion of the symbols through which a shared identity was constructed in the post-war years.

A starlet is born

Central to the mythology of Sophia Loren are her humble origins. Born Sofia Scicolone in a Roman charity ward on 20 September 1934, she was the illegitimate daughter of a good-for-nothing father, Riccardo Scicolone, and an aspirant actress, Romilda Villani. Her upbringing in the earthquake-prone port of Pozzuoli, eight miles from Naples, was marked by the privations of the war years, to which she has continued to refer in interviews. In the final eighteen months of the war the double occupation, first by the Nazis and then by the Allies, provided a further crucial character-forming experience. Although Sofia was aged only ten in 1944, the Liberation from Fascism and Nazi occupation made a vivid impression on her. In the English language autobiography she wrote in 1979 in collaboration with the American journalist A. E. Hotchner, she describes it as a strange experience involving fear, delight, novelty and discovery.[1] The presence of troops and the machinery of war was certainly intimidating, but the Americans also brought with them DDT, chocolate, tinned foods and the unfamiliar sound of big band jazz. Moreover, like many others, Sofia began going to the cinema at this time. The films she saw, however, were not the masterpieces of neorealism for which the Italian cinema of the period is remembered. Rossellini and Visconti seem never to have reached Pozzuoli and even Anna Magnani, the popular Roman actress who was the most representative screen heroine of their films, passed unnoticed. Rather it was the Hollywood films that poured into Italy in vast numbers which captured Sofia's imagination, as she later recalled:

When Pozzuoli's only movie theater reopened, it offered Hollywood movies for the first time. Before the war only drab Italian films had been shown. The Hollywood films took me into a world far removed from the desolate years of my childhood. But it was not the opulence I saw on the screen that overwhelmed me; it was the stars themselves and the roles they played. Fred Astaire dancing with Ginger Rogers was a fairy-tale dream. Gable, Cary Grant, Linda Darnell, Rita Hayworth, Sinatra, Betty Grable, Gene Kelly, June Allison, and, above all, Tyrone Power. He was the god of my adolescence; when he appeared in the melodramatic epic *Blood and Sand*, I went to see him twelve times. And each time I sat through as many shows as I could. I had to convince someone in my family, usually my aunt Dora, to sit with me because my grandmother would not allow me to be in the movie house by myself . . . I felt a real physical pain each time I had to leave the theater, no matter how many times I saw the film. After I saw Rita Hayworth in *Gilda*, I started to comb my hair the way she wore hers; later I switched to Veronica Lake's hairstyle when one of her pictures captivated me.[2]

It has been suggested that although Hollywood films were immensely popular in Italy, they did not have a profound impact on consciousness because they were too far removed from the experience of everyday life.[3] Yet while it is true that the rich, bright lights world of Hollywood was distant from reality in a country that was poor and prevalently rural, it nonetheless provided images and ideas whereby diffuse aspirations for social improvement and individual mobility could be articulated. This was particularly true for young women, who found in stars such as Rita Hayworth a model of beauty, glamour, sophistication and elegance that broke radically with the ideas of womanhood which the Catholic Church sustained and which Fascism had broadly adopted.

Under the twin influences of American troops and cinema, beauty contests assumed a key function in permitting these hitherto secret aspirations to rise to view. Such competitions were not completely unknown, a precursor of the post-war Miss Italia contest having been held in 1939, but they became commonplace only after the Liberation. For most participants the ultimate goal was a chance at screen stardom. Thousands of teenage girls, mostly of humble, lower class backgrounds paraded before juries in the hope that they might be noticed by a journalist or film director. The prospects of this occurring were of course remote, but in a number of instances it did happen. Gina Lollobrigida, Lucia Bosè, Gianna Maria Canale and Eleonora Rossi Drago all began to work in films after taking part in the 1947 final of Miss Italia. Naturally these rare cases further fuelled the aspirations of those who saw in cinema one of the few means of escape from poverty and drudgery.

Unlike many girls with screen ambitions, Sofia did not encounter any objection from her mother. Before she became pregnant, Romilda Villani had cultivated similar ambitions after winning an MGM-sponsored Greta Garbo look-alike contest in the early 1930s. No sooner had the blossoming Sofia turned fourteen than she was entered for a competition organised by the Neapolitan daily newspaper Il *Mattino* to find a "queen of the sea" and twelve princesses.[4] The result was very promising. Even though she was dressed in an evening gown hastily made from her grandmother's best curtains, she was chosen as one of the princesses and awarded a prize consisting of a train ticket to Rome, several rolls of wallpaper, a table cloth with matching napkins, and 23,000 lire.

Fired by this success and driven on by her mother, Sofia responded like thousands of others to a call for extras launched early in 1950 by the production of Quo Vadis, an American historical epic about to begin shooting in Rome. Both women were given two days' work on the film but no other opportunities followed. One reason for this was the limited quantity of films being made in Italy. Hollywood still dominated the nation's screens and Italian cinema had not yet recovered from the devastation of the war. Rather than return home or abandon her showbusiness aspirations, Sofia turned to the photoromance magazines for employment. A typical byproduct of the Americanised subculture of the post-war years, these publications constituted pocket cinemas that were passed from hand to hand by working-class women who looked to them for romance and fantasy. Although Sogno, Cine Illustrato and other photoromances catered amply to the local taste for melodrama, they also borrowed much from Hollywood and fuelled the mass myths of beauty, glamour, love and wealth. With her dark looks and slightly exotic air, Sofia quickly became a favourite with readers. Under the pseudonym of Sofia Lazzaro (translated in English as Lazarus – so chosen because her beauty was said to be violent enough to awaken the dead) she was cast most frequently in the part of the foreign temptress or slave girl, usually of Arab or gypsy origin.

This point is important because it demonstrates that Sofia was not viewed as a typical Italian beauty at the start of her career. Whatever was thought later, she simply did not match the standards of appearance which won approval in the 1940s and early 1950s, which mixed the innocence and poise of the American pin-up girl with the more familiar features of Mediterranean womanhood.[5] This was proved by her lack of success in the beauty competitions she continued to enter in the hope of attracting the attention of a director or a producer. Even though she was still a teenager, her appearance was considered to be too dark and earthy, her mouth was too large and she was too tall. Moreover her blossoming figure suggested more torbid passions than was deemed appropriate for the average beauty queen.

The credit for discovering Sofia and launching her on the road to screen stardom is normally attributed to Carlo Ponti, the Milanese producer who became first her lover and eventually her husband. But there is in fact little evidence to suggest that the meeting between the two at a Cervia night club in 1951 heralded any immediate turning point in her career. For some considerable time Sofia was only one of many aspirant actresses Ponti followed and although he obtained a number of screen tests for her, these netted no more than a few bit parts in productions of dubious quality. In a succession of films now mostly forgotten she played a foreign princess, a slave girl, a waif of uncertain origins and an Oriental night-club hostess. Even when she was selected for a few more prominent parts Sofia seemed unable to break out of the sort of low budget production that constituted all too significant a part of Italian cinema as it put itself on a surer industrial footing in the 1950s. Tinsel subproducts produced rapidly to cash in on the domestic and foreign markets opened by Hollywood, they were the underside of an expansion that saw the local industry match a rapidly increasing demand for cinema throughout the peninsula.

In what is widely recognised as one of the better productions she was involved in, Sofia was blackened from head to foot as the Ethiopian slave girl Aida to whom Renata Tebaldi lent her soprano voice in the film version of Verdi's opera. Another film was *Africa sotto i Mari* [*Africa beneath the Seas*], an underwater documentary drama in which she starred with a former boxer, the American Steve Barclay.[6] In order to enhance this film's box-office appeal by disguising its origins, it was even decided to change Sofia's surname from Lazzaro to Loren, in the hope that people might mistake her for a minor Swedish actress recently arrived in Italy, Marta Toren. At the same time the Italian "f" in her forename was substituted with a more cosmopolitan "ph" to make Sophia. The only person to notice this change or voice opposition to it was Carlo Mazzoni, the editor of *Sogno*, who took it as a sign of the contempt with which the film world viewed the photoromances. By turning Sofia into a beauty in a bathing costume and giving her a name to match, he argued, film producers ensured that her future would be as an Italian Esther Williams.[7]

To save her from such a fate was the matinée idol and neorealist director Vittorio De Sica, who was the first to sense Sophia's true screen potential and who was the real architect of many of her subsequent successes. In contrast to the cheap glamour image others had sought to impose on her, he wanted to uncover what he saw as the hidden dimension of her personality, that of a loud, passionate Neapolitan woman with a strong character and spontaneous charisma that escaped the confines of any show business packaging. While some might have found Sophia's appearance exaggerated or too plebeian, De Sica raised no such objection, for he aimed to turn the clock back, to capture a dimension of Italy and particularly of Naples before the Americanising phenomena of the late Forties had begun to influence popular identity. In the episode film of 1954, *L'Oro di Napoli* [*The Gold of Naples*] all the leading representatives of Neapolitan popular culture were present including the actor-playwright Eduardo De Filippo and the comic Totò. The result was a celebration of a world and a culture that seemed proud, joyous and self-sufficient. In her episode Sophia designed her first memorable role as a sexy and unfaithful pizza girl. Although she was by nature far more introverted than De Sica imagined, in his hands she appeared so natural on screen in the part that for many she became totally identified with *la pizzaiola*. In an Italy in which the traditional values of Catholic morality provided the only officially recognised norm of behaviour, Sophia became the embodiment of a highly subversive idea of unabashed female sensuality that was both attractive and seen as typical of the spontaneous popular world. In one celebrated scene in the film she walks quickly through the sidestreets of Naples under the rain followed at a distance by her dullard husband who is forced to witness the stares and wolf whistles his wife provokes in her trail. This in a sense symbolised both the way in which she became a target of the male imagination and yet remained totally free of objectification. Defiant and flirtatious, she was a woman who retained control of her sexuality and administered herself as she best thought fit.

The enormous success which this film achieved helped make Sophia a nationally known personality. The aura of glamour with which Ponti and others had tried to surround her was by no means eroded by this sudden fame. Indeed it provided an impulse to a number of film projects in which it was actually consolidated. Moreover, as a rising young star of Italian cinema, Sophia was automatically a model of interest and emulation to the readers of film magazines and to young people in general. But the praise and admiration she drew from the ranks of normally severe intellectuals and critics was entirely due to the connection De Sica had made with a recognisable strand of popular culture. Giuseppe Marotta, author of the tales on which the episodes of L'Oro di Napoli were based, was one of many who saw in Sophia an authentic Italian personality. Moreover, her most popular films were those in which she returned to roles similar to her celebrated portrayal of the pizza girl. In Pane, Amore e . . . [Scandal in Sorrento], for example, the third film in a successful series of provincial comedies in which De Sica had starred with Gina Lollobrigida, she took the latter's place, offering a much less coy interpretation of bountiful womanhood. As a widowed fish vendor determined not to be evicted from her home by De Sica, the proprietor who wishes to take possession of it himself following his retirement from the Carabinieri, she employed a wide variety of seductive stratagems. In one scene she danced a mambo at an open air party, unwittingly tormenting her antagonist with suggestive physical gyrations. The only sign of her status as a widow that she displayed was a small black strip attached to the edge of the plunging neckline of a flaming red dress that showed off her well-rounded figure to maximum advantage. In this way Sophia's reputation as a "bad" woman, a siren so attractive that she could not help but drive men crazy, was enhanced while her strength of character and dignity were also maintained.

Thanks to such films, Sophia became one of the most popular new stars in Italy. As a poor girl who had made the most of the opportunities open to her to reach success, she attracted particular interest and enthusiasm. Moreover, her films were a hit not only in Italy but also abroad. In Europe and America she began to emerge as an actress of great potential who might add sparkle and lustre to any story. For the successful launch of the next phase of her career this was a vital premise.

The Americanisation of Sophia

With the help of Ponti, who went out of his way to make the necessary connections with the Hollywood director Stanley Kramer, Sophia made her first American film in 1957. It was The Pride and the Passion, an historical epic of the Napoleonic wars set in Spain. The film was no great artistic achievement; indeed it has been described as an indigestible pot-boiler notable mainly for the extraordinary miscasting of its stars, Cary Grant and Frank Sinatra. But, despite her uncertain English, Sophia made a favourable impression in the role of a Spanish camp follower. As a result she made two further American films in quick succession on location in or near Europe. The first was Boy on a Dolphin, the story of a Greek peasant girl who finds a precious statue on the sea bed whilst diving for sponges, in which the male lead was played by Alan Ladd. The second film was The Legend of the Lost, a tale of the rivalries and jealousies of two Americans hunting for treasure in the North African desert. On this occasion the star was John Wayne. In all cases Sophia added youth, a love interest and the necessary indigenous flavour. She was supposed to incarnate the primitive settings against which the plots unfolded and to this end it was always the wild, almost animal-like intensity of her looks that was accentuated.

The reaction of Italian critics to these films was not at all favourable. Profoundly hostile to the large-scale, cosmopolitan styles typical of American movie-making, they argued that the natural verve and vitality of Italy's favourite starlet was gradually being crushed or refined to the point where it ceased to be recognisable. After seeing her dominate the screen in home-grown films, it was a shock to have to adjust to her new role as a supporting actress who added local colour and spice to foreign productions dominated by often ageing Hollywood stars shipped across the Atlantic for the occasion. Giuseppe Marotta was one of the first to object to what he saw as a brusque process of Americanisation which had deprived Sophia (or Sofia as he and others preferred to write her name) of her roots.[8] But he was by no means alone. Hollywood make-up and photography made her seem artificial even to Arturo Lanocita, critic of Il Corriere della Sera, who judged that she had been turned into a "grotesque mannequin".[9] Perhaps the sharpest criticism of all however came from the film magazine Cinema Nuovo. "For the Americans the vital energy of our star must represent a rather difficult problem to resolve," its reviewer wrote. "Unable to place her in a contemporary setting, or fearful of doing so, they have for the time being confined her and rendered her ugly by hunting her to a vaguely gypsy-like Mediterranean cliché – olive skin and rags – that is monotonously familiar even when the chronological frame changes."[10]

Advanced at the very beginning of what was destined to become a long and highly successful international film career, criticisms of this type would recur frequently in Italian reactions to Sophia Loren's American films. Yet in fact there was nothing either strange or shocking in her seeking to pursue her involvement in cinema beyond the confines of her native country. Hollywood was no less a part of her own film culture than it was of most of the Italian population. To appear on screen with some of its most celebrated stars there-fore was a highly attractive prospect. Indeed, as she recounts in her autobiography, she could scarcely believe it when she heard that Ponti had managed to win her the role in The Pride and the Passion: "When I heard the names of my co-stars I almost passed out – Cary Grant and Frank Sinatra. I, little Sofia Scicolone, was to play opposite two of those romantic figures of my Pozzuoli dreams, in an English-speaking multi-million-dollar spectacle film!"[11]

Other factors were important too. Hollywood had a long history of attracting talent from abroad. Indeed one of the secrets of the universal appeal of its productions lay pre-cisely in the ability to embrace and to assimilate people of a wide variety of gifts and backgrounds. Alida Valli and Rossano Brazzi had been early examples of Italians who had made the trip across the Atlantic; in the 1950s and 1960s numerous actresses followed, including even Anna Magnani, who won an Oscar in 1955 for her performance in the screen version of Tennessee Williams' The Rose Tattoo.

Sophia's immediate predecessor was Gina Lollobrigida, the first starlet of the post-war era to attract American attention.[12] Although she was physically smaller than Loren and more of a girl-next-door type, Gina nonetheless appealed because she was perceived to be incredibly sexy with respect to the prudish American standards of the early 1950s. Humphrey Bogart, her partner in the 1953 film Beat the Devil, declared that she made "Marilyn Monroe look like Shirley Temple" while similar comments were attributed to Burt Lancaster and Tony Curtis, her co-stars in an improbable circus drama, Trapeze. In pre-Bardot days this view was echoed in Europe. For René Clair, her director in Fanfan La Tulipe, she was "the hottest thing in Europe today."[13] Yet Gina's period of international popularity was in fact quite brief, not least because she managed very quickly to create an unfavourable impression of herself. "Gina has a star's compulsive vanity," *Time* confided to its readers in August 1954. "She has 300 dresses and 70 pairs of shoes, keeps 15 handsome, leather-bound scrapbooks filled with newspaper clippings about Gina; one scrapbook is devoted entirely to observations about her bosom."[14]

Sophia was viewed from the start as a carefree, unspoilt beauty who was more natural and easy-going than Lollobrigida. Perhaps the first time many Americans heard of her was as a result of a remarkable presentation which appeared towards the end of the 1954 *Time* article on Gina, in which the new names of Italian cinema were mentioned. "Sophia Loren (38, 24, 37), 19, is the youngest of Italy's screen queens," the short paragraph read. "She has a thick Neapolitan accent and in the sultry Roman evenings loves to turn on the record player, throw off her clothes and dance." *New York Times* critic Bosley Crowther drew frequent attention to her fiery spirit and well-proportioned figure, helping confirm her image as an untamed native beauty. Yet another touch was added in August 1955 when *Newsweek* ran a four-page spread on her entitled "Italy's Sophia Loren, a New Star – A Mount Vesuvius." Thus well before she made a Hollywood film Sophia had acquired a reputation and a loyal following in the expanding art house circuit where foreign films were shown. In Michael Bruno's view numerous European stars acquired fans among the *habitués* of these cinemas, but "everyone went to see Sophia Loren, just for the sheer pleasure of looking at a beautiful woman, a pleasure denied movie-goers since the hey-day of Hedy Lamarr."[15]

Although Americans liked to think of Italian actresses as the main natural resource of a hopelessly backward country, by the mid-1950s Italian cinema was no longer the Cinderella industry it had been only a few years before. Under the impulse of an expanding domestic demand it grew rapidly and even began to challenge Hollywood in international movie markets. The older actors who still insisted on afternoon shooting only ("it is impossible to make art before midday" the comic Totò loved to repeat) began to feel out of place in an enterprise that was conforming ever more to the rigid schedules and professional standards of a modern system of entertainment production.

Not by chance, the emergence of Italian cinema as a powerful international force coincided with the decline of Hollywood. By 1950 the golden age of cinema had come to an end in the USA and film-going was no longer the major pastime it had once been. Yet for Italians Hollywood remained the unrivalled dream factory. Home-produced films might often be more popular, but America continued to be viewed as the centre of true cinema for which all else was but a substitute. Thus it was seen as an extraordinary honour, a fairy tale almost, if an Italian actress were fortunate enough to be invited there. When Sophia Loren prepared to make her first visit across the Atlantic in 1957 there was enormous public interest. The weekly magazines were filled with news of the elegant dresses and ball gowns that comprised her wardrobe as well as speculations about the celebrities she could expect to meet. Curiosity was particularly intense because of the firm footing on which the trip was set. Whereas other actors and actresses had gone to Hollywood to appear in this or that film, unaware of what the future might hold, Sophia had a two million dollar contract with Paramount to make five films. Because of the success which her three location movies had brought, everyone knew she would be guaranteed royal treatment in Hollywood.

The first Italian star to be absorbed successfully into the American star system, Sophia quickly became a favourite with the public and a household name the world over. Yet it is probably true to say that her popularity was achieved despite rather than because of her films. To this extent the Italian critics who had reacted so negatively to her first contact with

Hollywood had a point. The light comedy *Houseboat*, in which she played once more alongside Cary Grant, was one of very few films to show her to good effect. As an Italian governess who gradually wins the favour and then the heart of a widowed diplomat and his three small children, she gave a relaxed and spontaneous performance that won much acclaim. In none of the other films she made in Hollywood did Sophia appear so much at ease. American movie-makers seemed not to appreciate the fact that European stars could not simply be inserted in mainstream productions which took no account of their specific histories and personalities. As Sophia put it in her autobiography, Hollywood moguls "had never been able to accept a foreign actress for what she was. They felt they had to change her. That's what happened to me."[16] As an actress who had achieved fame playing lower class women, she found herself called upon to play aristocrats and noblewomen in historical dramas and glamour productions which offered American middle-class audiences a taste of the elegance and sophistication they allegedly yearned for. In such films exotic colouring and foreign-sounding accents possessed a special allure. As Gargano and Renzetti explain in their discussion of female stars, Loren's "physically exciting attributes" and her function as an "unconscious object" of male desire made mobility easy,[17] but films of this type inevitably seemed tired and old-fashioned in the 1950s and 1960s. In crisis at home and abroad Hollywood appeared unable to maintain the originality and charm that had contributed to its wide appeal in earlier times. Part of the difficulty derived from the witch hunt of the McCarthy era, which not only saw a purge of several leading scriptwriters and directors but also served to render the overall output more bland and less controversial. Foreign actresses often found themselves cast in films which could just as well have been made in the 1930s. Furthermore, they were frequently given parts in which their ethnic origins were either confused or eradicated completely. In Loren's case this was especially apparent in her final contract film with Paramount, George Cukor's *Heller in Pink Tights*. Paired unsatisfactorily for the third time with Anthony Quinn, she found herself in a blonde wig playing the actress manager of a theatrical company touring the Wild West. According to Stefano Masi this film signalled that Sophia's image, now proximate to the standards of the Hollywood star system, had profoundly evolved. "Her popularity had benefitted from the potent channels of diffusion of the American industry, capable of reaching every angle of the globe," he wrote. "Sophia was no longer Italian or Neapolitan: she was by now one of those actresses without a homeland, citizens of the world who in every film play above all themselves."[18]

Sophia did of course play Italians from time to time and even Neapolitans. But when she did they were inevitably portrayed in an utterly conventional light. No better example exists in this respect than *It Started in Naples*, a 1960 film in which she was partnered by Clark Gable in his penultimate screen performance. The plot was simple. Gable played a mature American lawyer who arrives in Naples with the intention of rescuing his recently orphaned nephew and taking him back to civilization. However he runs up against the opposition of the child's current guardian, his wayward maternal aunt, played by Loren. Despite his efforts to convince the boy with talk of hamburgers and baseball, Gable himself is gradually seduced by the more casual, easy-going life style he finds in Italy and in the end, having succumbed to Loren's charms, he opts to stay. What is striking about the film is its wholly stereotypical depiction of Italy. The spectator is presented with a picture postcard image of the country that would be "instantly recognisable" to anyone. Italians moreover are seen as a people more suited to singing and dancing than to work. In the midst of this, Sophia, giving an attractive performance as an undisciplined and unpredictable night club artiste, functioned to guarantee the timeless, unchanging character of the Italians. As Patrizia Carrano has observed, she offered "the image of Italy as the eternal country of bell-towers – all pizza, generosity and love."[19] It seemed irrelevant that by 1960 the country in reality was emerging as a dynamic industrial power on a par with most of its European partners.

In general however Masi was right, as even a cursory glance at the range of films Loren was involved in during the 1960s and 1970s will show. With the decentralisation of film-making advancing further and faster than before, Loren became one of the first stars of the jet age, a stable fixture in international productions of virtually every type. She appeared in grandiose historical epics such as El Cid and The Fall of the Roman Empire and a varied selection of cosmopolitan extravaganzas including Arabesque, Judith, Five Miles to Midnight and Operation Crossbow in which her nationality could be British, Israeli, Arab or German. In addition she even made a number of relatively high brow screen adaptations of contemporary literary works, including Sartre's The Prisoner of Altona.

In the course of her international career Loren co-starred with a long list of leading men including some of the most celebrated names in the history of cinema: Cary Grant, John Wayne, Gregory Peck, William Holden, Charlton Heston, Jean Gabin, Anthony Quinn, Clark Gable, Peter Sellers. She also starred with Marlon Brando in Chaplin's last film A Countess from Hong Kong. But in very few cases did the partnership work. One problem was that producers and directors tended to see her purely as a woman of beauty without recognising the strength of character that her background gave her. Even Time magazine, which in 1962 described Sophia's body as "a mobile of miscellaneous fruits and melons," recognised this. If she often dwarfed her partners on screen, it noted, it was because "she was matched with leading men whom she could have swallowed with a glass of water".[20] This was particularly true of Tab Hunter and Alan Ladd (once unflatteringly described by Raymond Chandler as "a small boy's idea of a tough guy")[21] but many others lost something of their aura in her proximity. Of all her American co-stars perhaps only Cary Grant was an ideal partner.

Despite the questionable nature of many of the films she made, Sophia's international achievements won her a special status at home. After the reconstruction and recovery of the early 1950s, Italy stood on the brink of the most rapid and extensive transformation of its history. From a predominantly rural economy it was rapidly becoming a modern industrial state. With her success abroad and particularly in the heart of the most developed society in the world, Sophia symbolised Italy's re-emergence on the international plane. But at the same time, as a glamorous, much admired film star, she was also associated with the vast changes that were occurring on the plane of social mores and morality as a consequence of urbanisation and development. The rearguard battle the Church fought against innovation in these areas thus found in her a target.

The Vatican's extreme hostility towards Sophia was not triggered so much by the immorality of her films as by her personal conduct. As long as the relationship between Ponti and Loren had been essentially a private one, no one had voiced disapproval, even though the producer was a married man and there was no possibility of divorce in Italy. But in the Autumn of 1957 things took a different turn. Goaded into action by the rivalry of Cary Grant, the producer arranged a hasty divorce and a proxy marriage which took place in Ciudad Juarez in Mexico on 17 September 1957, during the shooting of Houseboat. As Sophia reports in her autobiography, it was hardly the wedding she had dreamed of – two Mexican lawyers in a courtroom a thousand miles away pretending to be her and Ponti – but at least it appeared to be legal.[22] What no one seemed to have bargained for was the reaction of the Church hierarchy in Italy, which denied all validity to proceedings of divorce and civil marriage. Those who engaged in such practices, the official newspaper of the Holy See announced in a scarcely veiled reference to the celebrated actress, were public sinners subject to ex-communication. Sophia was not a practising Catholic but, as she later said, "emotionally Catholicism was my heritage and ex-communication was a chilling threat."[23]

In a country that was witnessing the first startling signs of a long process of secularisation, Loren and Ponti found themselves held up as examples of everything the Church condemned. Catholic organisations urged a boycott of Sophia's films, while newspapers willingly took up the campaign against her. For strict Catholics, Sophia the sexy starlet had always been a questionable figure, but now a campaign was launched that was designed to mobilise a much larger segment of the population against her. For women she became the concubine and the home-breaker, the siren who had stolen a man from the breast of his family without regard for morality or the sentiments of others. Ponti, for his part, risked incrimination on charges of bigamy should he have set foot in Italy.

This campaign had no tangible impact on the economic fortunes of Sophia's films. But at another level it profoundly compromised her public image. At the very moment when she might have broadened her support and won the affection of all Italians, she not only failed to do so but actually provoked considerable enmity in an important sector of the population. She was portrayed as having become remote from true Italian values and as conforming more to the standards of behaviour of international show business than to those of respectable people.

In the 1960s a major effort was made to overcome these negative perceptions and restore Loren in a position of favour in the affections of the Italians. But it is doubtful if this would have succeeded had she not made a significant number of highly popular Italian films in the course of the decade, which enabled her to restore and considerably enrich the familiar, down to earth dimension of her personality and attenuate the scorn with which some viewed her.

The chameleon rearguard of neorealism

Although he played a supporting role in It Started in Naples, Vittorio De Sica strongly disapproved of the Americanisation of Sophia. Her master and guide in L'Oro di Napoli, he much preferred her spontaneous exuberance to the stylised grooming to which she had been subjected in Hollywood. It was appropriate therefore that he should be the director of the film which more than any other contributed to her recognition as an actress capable of touching the deepest chords of a common Italian sentiment. Released in 1960, La Ciociara [Two Women] secured for Sophia an Oscar for best actress as well as various other awards in Cannes, London, Tokyo, Madrid, Santiago and Berlin. More importantly it revealed Loren in a dramatic role for the first time and in a part that was recognisable to Italians as being a component of their heritage. This was essential to her winning the respect and approval of a left-wing public which, while not previously hostile, had never regarded her with special affection.[24] Given the significance of this film, it is worth examining its genesis in a little detail before going on to discuss its relationship with subsequent films in which Loren was also directed by De Sica.

A best-selling novel by Italy's most popular writer, Alberto Moravia, La Ciociara described the period leading up to the liberation of Rome from the point of view of a woman evacuated with her daughter to the hills of the surrounding countryside. By any standard the story was a bleak one. Although the women escape the vengeance of the retreating Nazis, they are trapped and raped by a band of Moroccan soldiers enrolled in the French army of liberation. It is therefore a tragic aspect of liberation that is highlighted at the expense of the more conventional triumphant dimensions.

For the part of Cesira, the mother, it was thought that Anna Magnani would be ideal while Sophia Loren might play her daughter. However, Magnani, a temperamental actress who made no secret of her distaste for the new generation of screen beauties, rejected out of hand any suggestion that they might appear together. If it was so vital that Loren be in the film, she suggested sarcastically, then perhaps she should take the role of Cesira herself. This in effect is what happened and the parts were rewritten to lower the mother's age from fifty to thirty plus (Loren in fact was twenty-five) and that of the daughter from eighteen to thirteen.

In her autobiography Loren recalls how the shooting of La Ciociara was a testing experience. On the night before the filming of the rape scene, she stirred up her emotions by bringing to mind memories of the fear she had felt herself during the closing stages of the war when some Moroccan soldiers were stationed near her own home in Pozzuoli. But, once again, the director's contribution was essential. "Without De Sica," she reports, "I could not possibly have performed the part as I did. He gave me the confidence to go far beyond where I had ever gone before, into an area where I could not have dreamed to venture . . . Before I made Two Women I had been a performer. Afterwards, I was an actress."[25] That this was widely acknowledged is evident from the almost unanimously positive reaction to the film. By so successfully taking on a dramatic role, Sophia opened a new range of professional possibilities which before would have been precluded to her. In effect she took on the mantle of Magnani. Only later did the Roman actress realise the mistake she had made in renouncing the role of Cesira. "Since Ponti discovered that his wife can do the films that were offered to me in the past, I no longer have a place in Italian cinema," she remarked bitterly.[26]

Sophia's new-found credibility amongst even the more difficult and demanding sections of public opinion derived largely from the fact that La Ciociara seemed just like a neorealist film. Scripted by Cesare Zavattini, directed by De Sica, and made in black and white, it recalled the grainy masterpieces of the late 1940s that won Italian cinema a worldwide reputation and the undying hostility of the authorities in its country of origin. Even the theme of ordinary people caught in the vortex of war was familiar. It was, Time wrote, "a brutal but honest film."[27] In this sense it was not out of step with the new mood which swept through Italian cinema between 1959 and 1962. After a ten-year period in which controversial topics had been mostly banished from the country's screens, Monicelli's La Grande Guerra [The Great War] tackled the theme of war and Rossellini's Il Generale Della Rovere [General Della Rovere] the issues of Fascism and the Resistance. But to address these questions in the early 1960s was not at all the same as dealing with them in the urgent climate of the 1940s. They were no longer actuality but history. Moreover, De Sica's film did not actually raise any issue that was controversial and the tragedy at its centre was strictly personal rather than political or social. A huge box-office success in Europe and America, La Ciociara was in reality an international star vehicle made in accordance with the practice of the industrial cinema of the period. This was perfectly clear from the cast. In addition to the international celebrity Sophia Loren, an American girl (Eleanor Brown) played the daughter while a rising star of French cinema, Jean-Paul Belmondo, took the part of Michele, the doomed left-wing intellectual loved by both women.

Figure 5.1 Sophia Loren in *Two Women* (1960)
Courtesy of the Museum of Modern Art, New York/Film Stills Archive

For proof that De Sica was moving in a direction quite different to neorealism, it is sufficient to look at the films he made subsequently with Sophia Loren, in which her most frequent co-star was Marcello Mastroianni. These include the episode "La Riffa" [*The Raffle*] in *Boccaccio '70*, about a fairground girl who concedes her body every Saturday night to the winner of a raffle, the three-part film *Ieri, Oggi, Domani*, in which Loren played a happy-go-lucky slum dweller, a prostitute and a society woman, and *Matrimonio all'italiana* [*Marriage Italian Style*], a remake of Eduardo De Filippo's play *Filumena Marturano*. Despite variations of social class – although the preferred environment remained that of the Neapolitan sub-proletariat – all these characters were distinguished by their independence of official morality and, at the same time, by their conformity to a normative system that matched the easy-going impulses of a recognised popular sentiment. In short, even in their transgressions they aroused popular sympathy and approval. Yet despite their veneer of daring non-conformism, none of these films engaged with the pressing issues that were dividing the dynamic, changing Italy of the boom years. While directors such as Marco Ferreri and Pietro Germi sought to give cinema a sharp focus, and make it a force for social and cultural change, De Sica took refuge in a celebration of an Italian spirit that belonged to the past and which was symbolised by Loren and Mastroianni. Although they were made between 1962 and 1964, a period in which the processes of urbanisation, modernisation and motorisation were all well advanced, these films, like *La Ciociara*, were for the most part set in an Italy that was mainly southern and in any event rural or pre-industrial. There were no signs of the recent, rapid transformations that had altered the face of the country; consumerism and modernity in general were notable by their absence. To this extent it may be argued that, far from representing an element of renewal, they constituted a regressive current in a cinema that in other respects was beginning to recover its critical edge after a long phase in which passive entertainment had been the norm. The image of the country offered in these films was not problematic, but cheery, sunny and timeless.

Abroad, De Sica's films of the 1960s did especially well. *Ieri, Oggi, Domani* unexpectedly took the Oscar for best foreign film in 1964 while Loren won an Oscar nomination in 1965 for best actress for the role in *Matrimonio all'italiana*, as well as a Golden Globe from the Hollywood foreign press corps, a David of Donatello and the best actress award at the Moscow Film Festival. One of the reasons, Vittorio Spinazzola has acutely observed, was the close connection between these works and Hollywood convention.[28] In both, Italy was presented in exactly the same way, as a country that was defined in terms of a set of unchanging stereotypes recognisable to all. The Italians appeared as a roguish but essentially lovable people whose principal defect was that they were irredeemably ill-suited to the ways of modern, industrial society. To many this seemed like an authentic portrait. As *Time* wrote, the country fair that formed the backdrop of "La Riffa" "is alive with superb detail, from the smallest of the watermelon seeds to the largest of the paunchy farmers with hot breath and sausage fingers. In this milieu, Sophia is not a star showing off but a figure that belongs."[29]

In Italy not everyone took the same view. In the south, the region that featured most frequently in this type of cinema, reactions were mixed. Vittorio Ricciuti, critic of the Neapolitan daily *Il Mattino*, was particularly vociferous in his attack on what he saw as its false authenticity. In his view the films lacked human vitality and in any case a celluloid creation like Sophia Loren was not a worthy successor to Anna Magnani or the star of the first screen version of *Filumena Marturano*, Titina De Filippo.[30] In the north the story was a different one. As Spinazzola's analysis of the distribution of box-office takings reveals, De Sica's films of the early 1960s were highly successful in the more industrial regions and in particular in the provincial centres of the north and centre of the country.[31]

Motherhood and reconciliation

If for Sophia Loren the 1960s were a period of great popularity, it was not only because she played recognisable and sympathetic parts in films that were themselves box-office triumphs.

Crucial to her success was the campaign to overcome the negative publicity deriving from her Mexican marriage, which continued to be an object of controversy until Ponti took action to have it annulled. Nothing was known of this campaign until 1984, when the two leading press agents who directed it, Enrico Lucherini and Matteo Spinola, published a volume of memoirs in which they discussed their role in reconstructing Loren's image. "The aim," it was explained, "was to reconcile Sophia with the Italian mammas and detach her from that terrible term: 'family-breaker'." Already during the shootings of La Ciociara action was taken to this end. As Spinola reports:

> It began with the capillary distribution of a series of photographs in which, during a pause in shooting, she played with the little boys of the quarter or held in her arms a new born baby. Once she fainted and we hinted to the journalists that maybe she was pregnant: in this way there was a lot of fuss when the sensational news was released and equal attention when we were compelled to issue a denial. We kept up this story for eight years until Sofia resolved the problems that really stopped her having a child. By that time she had definitely recaptured the heart of the whole of the public.[32]

In April 1966 Loren and Ponti were married legally in France, soon after they were granted French citizenship in recognition of their respective contributions to international cinema. But this was not the only problem standing in the way of Sophia's motherhood. Before she could achieve this state she had to fight a long battle marked by miscarriages, medical examinations and finally by six months of seclusion in a Geneva hotel where she could be guaranteed maximum tranquility prior to giving birth. The press coverage of these developments was massive. Perhaps never before had the intimate details of a celebrity's private medical record been so openly publicised and debated. Yet by spectacularising her struggle to become a mother, Sophia rendered herself more human and acceptable even to those who had long viewed her with distaste. As the large circulation Catholic weekly Famiglia Cristiana acknowledged in 1967, "The misfortunes of Loren render her more human and bring her nearer to us. They make her poorer than she appears, more simple and therefore more worthy of compassion."[33] When her first son, Carlo junior, was born in December 1968, it was almost a moment of national celebration. Among the many telegrams she received, was one from the President of the Republic, Giuseppe Saragat, congratulating her "in the name of the Italian people."

This was perhaps the highest point of Sophia's popularity. For the first time she had succeeded in reconciling the four component elements of Italian popular culture, all of which could recognise themselves in one facet or another of her public and "private" image. The left could identify with her personal struggle against adversity and her portrayal of combative ordinary women. This also sat well with the spontaneous current of popular culture in which her sexy image had initially been grounded. For the upwardly mobile, for migrants from the rural south and for people coming to terms with consumerist prosperity, the glamorous, cosmopolitan dimension to her success and to her screen personality offered an example of achievement which in a way matched their own aspirations. Finally, the Catholics, the section of the population most resistant to her charms before the late 1960s, joined with everyone else in hailing Sophia's motherhood. The symbol of an Italy that had overcome at least some of its contradictions and seen its basic human and material needs satisfied, she enjoyed unrivalled status as a national icon, a cultural reference point for the country as a whole.

Loren's centrality was not disturbed even by the great wave of social and industrial agitation which profoundly shook the texture of Italian society between 1968 and 1973. Her films of this period were a little more controversial and thus matched the changing mood. In particular *La Moglie del Prete* [*The Priest's Wife*] and *Bianco, Rosso e . . .* [*White, Red and . . .*] could broadly be seen as contributing to the secularisation of society. The former was the tormented story of a love affair between a failed Neapolitan singer (Loren) and a priest (Mastroianni), the latter a rather old-fashioned melodrama in which the pop singer turned actor Adriano Celentano played a Communist militant who falls in love with a nun working in a Milanese hospital. As Sister Germana, a woman torn between her heart and her vows, Loren gave a sensitive performance in what was fundamentally an anti-clerical film. Given her own personal difficulties, Loren was also able to take a credible public stand in favour of divorce in the controversy which followed its introduction in 1970. She also expressed genuine, if not blanket support for the aims of the women's liberation movement in the early 1970s.

Italian icon

Although Sophia Loren seemed definitely to have conquered a pre-eminent place in the gallery of Italian stars in the 1960s, the successive decade witnessed a remarkable decline in the public favour she enjoyed. Sophia's position remained unaltered up until the mid-1970s, when her films suddenly seemed to lose their appeal for mass audiences. Part of the blame must be attributed to poor choices on her own part, for a number of very mediocre productions in which she was involved, such as the low budget comedy set in the customs hall of J.F. Kennedy airport, *La Mortadella*, could not but disappoint. Similarly, the general standard of the international films she made, which in any case had never been high, sank further, reaching a historic low point in the adventure films *Cassandra Crossing* and *Brass Target*. But even De Sica was not exempt, after a long string of successes starring Loren and Mastroianni: his last film *Il Viaggio* [*The Journey*] was a flop.

The principal cause of this development was not the exhaustion of the populist ideology De Sica championed and with which Loren was strongly, if not totally identified. This was amply proven by the triumph of *Una Giornata Particolare* [*A Special Day*] in 1977. Directed by Ettore Scola, the film told the story of two lonely people left alone in a big Roman apartment block the day Hitler visited Rome. Mastroianni played a radio announcer dismissed from his post on account of his homosexuality while Loren took the part of a prematurely aged lower class housewife, whose life spark is reawakened in a day long affair with her unlikely counterpart. Cast rigorously against type, the pair struck a chord with their memorable performances. For Loren, however, this was her last big screen success. Although she made a number of Italian films and a handful of international spectaculars in the late 1970s, it appeared that her days as a major box-office draw were over. The main cause of this was the serious decline in cinema attendance which took place everywhere in the 1970s. From a high starting point, Italian audiences began to drop markedly from 1975, thereby initiating a trend which would accelerate throughout the 1980s.[34] The first casualty of this downturn was the sort of middle-of-road film in which De Sica, Monicelli, Risi and others specialised and of which Sophia was the uncrowned queen.

The late 1970s and early 1980s also saw a dramatic erosion of Loren's personal popularity. Just at the time when it seemed that *Una Giornata Particolare* had restored her to public favour after a period of professional uncertainty, an unpleasant sequence of events damned her to ignominy. In March 1979 she was arrested at the Fiumicino airport in Rome and interrogated for several hours about a variety of financial offences including the illegal export of capital and massive tax evasion. In the investigation that followed, fifteen properties and various works of art of undeclared origin – with a collective value of twenty million dollars – were confiscated. The public reaction was one of outrage. At a time when the country was in an economic crisis and the Lockheed bribery scandal had recently broken, people were appalled that a popular symbol, the emblem of a healthy Italy uncompromised by scandal or dishonesty, should become so tarnished. Outside the Cinecittà studios, several hundred extras organised a noisy protest and raised placards hostile to Sophia. Even when she returned to Italy in 1982 to serve the one-month prison sentence to which she was condemned in her absence, the public mood was unfavourable. Combined with the box-office flops in which she was involved in immediately successive years, this led Patrizia Carrano to conclude in 1985 that "the amorous enchantment between Sophia and Italy, now definitively compromised, is beyond renovation . . . The time of veneration for the poor girl whose progress reached even to the firmament of existence is far off."[35]

This judgement proved to be premature. Loren may not command the universal admiration and affection that she did in the late 1960s, but her role as a cultural icon is undiminished. After an eclipse lasting some ten years she returned in the late 1980s to incarnate once more women of strength and courage with whom the population could identify, as her election as a national idol in 1989 testified. The vehicle for this revival was offered by three television mini-series produced by Ponti for the American network NBC and Silvio Berlusconi's Reteltalia: *Mother Courage*, the story of a mother determined to stop at nothing to save her son from drug addiction; *Mamma Lucia*, an adaptation of Mario Puzo's novel of Italian immigrants to America *The Fortunate Pilgrim*; and, finally, a small screen remake of *La Ciociara*, broadcast in Italy in April 1989. In each case Loren played highly traditional, ferociously protective mother figures, of the type she had frequently played since the original version of *La Ciociara*. This was not only an image by now fixed in the minds of older spectators, but one which was also familiar to the younger generation thanks to constant television showings of Sophia's old films on the private networks which mushroomed in the 1980s. For the whole of the public it was entirely natural that television should be the means whereby Sophia added a postscript to her screen career.

Yet while it is not difficult to understand why the conventional and even historical portrait of Italian values contained in these mini-series should appeal to foreign audiences, an explanation is needed for the striking audience figures they obtained in Italy. On the face of it, it would appear to be even more inexplicable in the late 1980s than in the 1960s that such outdated characterisations should achieve a wide resonance. After all, in the context of dynamism and recent growth, surely such images were static and irrelevant. Why should a country which had struggled to free itself of underdevelopment and immobilism rejoice in such a retrograde representation of itself?

These questions clearly raise broad issues, but it is important to address them because such a significant part of the Loren myth is founded on a backward-looking picture of Italy which, in its more positive connotations, highlighted continuity, courtesy, charm, cheerfulness and generosity and, in its less rosy moments, the everyday struggle to overcome disadvantage, misfortune and adversity. In the case of the former, exemplified by several of the films Loren made with De Sica, nostalgia was probably an important element. It is significant that *La Ciociara, Ieri, Oggi, Domani* and *Matrimonio all'italiana* were all released as Christmas films. In addition to being a great time for film-going in Italy, Christmas is also of course the season of goodwill, when sentimentalism reigns and reunited families find comfort in tradition and continuity with the past. But this is not the only reason. The existence of the second dimension suggests that the issue is more complex.

To find an answer it is necessary to consider broader issues. As Joseph La Palombara has observed, there has been strong cultural resistance to change in Italy. Although in recent decades it might have become a thriving industrial country, beneath the surface patterns of change have been slow. In terms of eating habits, recreational activities, saving and spending, and the family, innovations occurred within a broad framework of continuity.[36] The new, in short, was grafted onto the old and, by means of these conservative mechanisms, the impact of any disruption was cushioned and mediated. However, this is not a new process and nor is it specific to Italy. To greater or lesser extents all countries look to a pre-industrial, rural past as a resource for the construction or maintenance of national identity. But in Italy it may be argued that the preservation of a conservative image of society was more marked. Only there did it fix the sole possible coordinates of a collective identity. Giulio Bollati has explained why this should be so. Ever since the early 1800s intellectuals and politicians expressed ideas relative to social and economic development in such a way as to minimise the impact on existing structures. The idealisation of rural life was "not only the mythical disguise of the economic form prevalent in Italy, but also a vaccination or ideological antidote to the risks of industrialism."[37] Furnished by a ruling class keen not to have to seek legitimation by modern means, the ideology of backwardness was also accepted, albeit in a variant of its own, by the left. There was thus a broad vision of the rural world as the primary repository of Italian values which survived the transformations of the 1950s and 1960s to be challenged for the first time, but not actually displaced, in the 1980s. Needless to say, the picture of an unchanging country, content with its own self-image, was not one that could ever be popular in the poorer rural areas or in the teeming metropolises of the south. It was a fiction that was adopted principally in the more advanced areas of the country. But with the extension of prosperity in the post-war period it on the one hand ceased to be necessary as an element of social integration and on the other acquired universal acceptance as a representation of the past. Thus it may be said that by conforming to the rural vision, Italian cinema at once eased social transition and acted as a channel for the maintenance of collective identity. Sophia Loren is the star who most successfully embodied the desire for a break with the past, for economic progress and social mobility. Even today, by her cultivation of a glamorous public image fed by magazine stories of society galas and friendships with Elizabeth Taylor and Michael Jackson, she maintains faith with the reality of a mature capitalist society and its need for models of consumption. Despite her nearly sixty years, she became increasingly identified from the late 1980s with Italian fashion, lending her support first to Valentino and subsequently to Armani, in whose company she was frequently photographed. In 1994 she consolidated this new aspect of her enduring image by her role in Robert Altman's satire on the fashion world *Prêt à Porter*. However, the real key to her success as a cultural icon lies in the construction of a screen image in which a perfect identification was achieved with the different variants of the dominant Italian ideology. In so far as this was matched by a stress on motherhood and on a secularised vision of family values acceptable to all, Loren guaranteed for herself a permanent place in the symbolic universe of the Italian people.

Notes

1 A. E. Hotchner, *Sophia Living and Loving: Her Own Story* (London, 1980), pp. 38–42.

2 Ibid., pp. 49–50.

3 Goffredo Fofi, introduction to Lorenzo Pellizzari, ed., *Cineromanzo: il cinema italiano* 1945–1953 (Milan, 1978), p. 3.

4 Hotchner, *Sophia Living and Loving*, pp. 54–56.

5 On the type of beauty current in Italy in the 1940s and early 1950s, see Renzo Renzi, *Gina Lollobrigida* (Milan, 1955), pp. 24–31.

6 These early films are examined in some detail, together with the rest of Loren's screen career, in Stefano Masi and Enrico Lancia, *Sophia Loren* (Rome, 1985).

7 Cited in ibid., pp. 33–34.

8 See the two pieces entitled "Nessuno s'inginocchia davanti a Ischia o a Taormina dicendo grazie" and "Sofia Loren rinnova con ogni suo film il miracolo giudiziario di Frine" in Giuseppe Marotta, *Marotta Ciak* (Milan, 1958).

9 *Il Corriere della Sera*, 20 December 1957.

10 *Cinema Nuovo*, 8:128, 1 April 1958, p. 218.

11 Hotchner, *Sophia Living and Loving*, p. 94.

12 On the impact in Italy and abroad of Gina Lollobrigida, see Maurizio Ponzi, *Gina Lollobrigida* (Secaucus, NJ, 1982).

13 Hollywood on the Tiber, *Time*, 16 August 1954, p. 34.

14 Ibid., p. 34.

15 Michael Bruno, *Venus in Hollywood: the Continental Enchantress from Garbo to Loren* (New York, 1970), p. 185.

16 Hotchner, *Sophia Living and Loving*, p. 110.

17 Patrizia Gargano & Emmanuela Renzetti, *La Mercificazione dell'immagine femminile nel cinema italiano* (1960–71) (Trento, 1978), pp. 56 and 77.

18 Masi & Lancia, *Sophia Loren*, p. 82.

19 Patrizia Carrano, "Sophia Loren" in Aldo Bernardini *et al.*, *Le Dive* (Bari, 1985), p. 182.

20 Much Woman, *Time*, 6 April 1962, p. 44.

21 Cited in Dorothy Parker & Katherine Sorley Walker, eds., *Raymond Chandler Speaking* (London, 1962), p. 217.

22 Hotchner, *Sophia Living and Loving*, p. 115.

23 Ibid., p. 118.

24 However it should be noted that in 1954 Sophia acted as the "Godmother" of the annual beauty contest organised by the Communist illustrated weekly *Vie Nuove*.

25 Hotchner, *Sophia Living and Loving*, p. 135.

26 Giancarlo Governi, *Nannarella* (Milan, 1981), pp. 183–184.

27 Much Woman, *Time*, 6 April 1962, p. 44.

28 Vittorio Spinazzola, *Cinema e Pubblico: lo spettacolo filmico in Italia* 1945–1965 (Milan, 1974), p. 289.

29 Much Woman, *Time*, 6 April 1962, p. 48.

30 *Il Mattino*, 20 December 1964.

31 Spinazzola, *Cinema e Pubblico*, pp. 288–289.

32 Enrico Lucherini & Matteo Spinola, *C'era questo, c'era quello* (Milan, 1984), p. 43.

33 Che cosa pensare di Sofia Loren, *Famiglia Cristiana*, 12 February 1967, p. 3.

34 See Stephen Gundle, From Neorealism to *Luci rosse*: cinema, politics, society 1945–1985, in Zygmunt Baranski & Robert Lumley, eds, *Culture and Conflict in Postwar Italy* (London, 1990), pp. 220–221.

35 Carrano, "Sophia Loren", p. 195.

36 Joseph La Palombara, *Democracy Italian Style* (London, 1987), p. 14.

37 Giulio Bollati, L'italiano, *Storia d'Italia*, Vol. 1, I *Caratteri Originali* (Turin, 1972), p. 1004.

Reigning Stars

6

The political career of south Indian cinema

M. MADHAVA PRASAD

The problem

The film culture of southern India has attracted the attention of a number of social scientists (Hardgrave Jr. 1979; Sivathamby 1981; Pandian 1991, 1992; Dickey 1993) intrigued by a phenomenon for which there seems to be no parallel. For in this corner of the world, since the proclamation of the Republic in 1950, a strong and durable link has been established between the institutions of cinema on the one hand and political life on the other.[1] Let us briefly outline the diversity of forms assumed by the relation between cinema and politics, in particular the widespread participation of film and television actors in political life, before isolating and defining the specificity of the phenomenon that we are concerned with.

The earliest instance of the use of cinema for political action is that of the Indian People's Theatre Association (IPTA), a cultural movement launched under the aegis of the Communist Party in 1943, which during the 1940s, turned to filmmaking, resulting in the film *Dharti ke Lal* (1943), a socialist-realist melodrama on agrarian exploitation. While IPTA's foray into films was brief, many IPTA workers and others influenced by the broad left cultural agenda, made careers for themselves in the film industry. The films associated with IPTA, however, did not include any direct form of party propaganda.

Meanwhile in the southern state of Tamil Nadu, a party called the Dravida Munnetra Kazhagam or DMK (Dravidian Progressive Front) was launched by a group of intellectuals from the rationalist, anti-caste Dravidian social movement led by E. V. Ramasami Naicker. As writers and orators of great skill, they used the cinema in the 1950s to spread the party's message, which combined rationalism and criticism of Brahmanical ideology with Tamil nationalism. Through the efforts of other Tamil nationalists meanwhile, the Tamil language had come to acquire a classical image akin to that of Sanskrit, and high rhetoric employing this language was a prized element in the new culture (Ramaswamy 1998). What are known in film history as the DMK films are a product of the combined efforts of the intellectuals of the party and the already well-established film industry in Madras ("Tamil Cinema" 1997). Party propaganda as well as more general lessons in rationalism, atheism and egalitarianism were the main distinguishing features of these films which were otherwise indistinguishable from the then prevalent genres of folklore and social melodrama. Thus in *Parasakthi*, considered emblematic of the genre, the scene of the attempted rape by a priest inside a temple which leads to the famous oration by the victim's brother, Gunasekaran, about the goddess: "It will not speak, it is a stone." The impact of these scenes is rendered all the more powerful by the dialogue, which constantly rises to a high level of persuasive rhetoric, penned by some of the masters of Tamil prose (in this instance M. Karunanidhi, who later served as chief minister of the state several times). As Pandian (1991) has shown in his fine analysis, *Parasakthi*, released in 1952, already shows the signs of ideological compromises that a social movement reconstructing itself as a political party is forced into. The lesson in atheism, for example, is not as sharp as it first appears. And on the question of women's chastity, an issue tied up with that of Tamil national identity, the film takes a retrogressive stand (Pandian 1991: 769). Nevertheless, these DMK films are markedly different from the films that were later to be assigned the function of political campaigning by the same party, in the emphasis they laid on the communication of messages. Sivaji Ganesan, who played Gunasekaran in *Parasakthi* was identified with the traditions of good acting that were familiar to audiences from the stage. His task was to lend his power of dialogue delivery to the task of communication of radical messages, a task he performed admirably in the film. Of the combination of elements that constitutes a film, it is the dialogue – or rather the intermittent monologues – that dominate as they critique, satirize, accuse, condemn and exhort.

Sivaji Ganesan did not stay with the DMK. It was M. G. Ramachandran (known popularly as MGR) who became the principal "star vehicle" (to modify the meaning of that term) of DMK propaganda. His rise also coincides with the party's decision to enter electoral politics. As Sivathamby suggests, the rise of MGR as an autonomous charismatic entity transcending the party programme coincides with the politics of compromise that led DMK into parliamentary politics. Sivathamby divides the history of the DMK film into two phases. In the first phase, "which depended on social criticism from the writer's point of view, the emphasis was more on the arguments adduced than on the character of one personality, though, even in those films, the character was identified with the cause propounded" (Sivathamby 1981: 41). However,

> In the second phase of the DMK oriented films when MGR was the chief personality, the entire argument was woven round the protagonist himself. The whole concept was personalized in that it was shown as emanating from the personality of the actor. Here the emphasis was equally placed on the actor as it was on the story. Here too it is the dramatic narrative that is important, but the world of conflict exists only as a world centred round the hero and his personal emancipation symbolizes the emancipation from the social evil depicted. If we accept this position, and see it in the background that the particular actor chooses to act only in particular roles then it becomes easy for identification of the actor with the character. Such was the case with MGR.
>
> (Sivathamby 1981: 41–42)

Sivathamby thus highlights a dramatic shift that took place within the genre of DMK film, at the height of MGR's career as the DMK's star campaigner both off- and on-screen, a shift we might characterize as a reversal of relations between the propaganda message and the charismatic bearer of the message. It is as if charisma had reverted to its role as message in itself, subsuming all other messages of a concrete nature, related to party ideology. *Nadodi Mannan* (*Vagabond King*, 1958) is often cited as the film that marks the turning point in this history. (Many years later, when he was asked what he would do if he were chief minister, MGR told the interviewer – who was incidentally the actress Jayalalitha, who now heads the party he founded – that he had already answered the question in *Nadodi Mannan*.) The party, reaping the benefits of MGR's popularity, and oblivious to the developments that lay in store, organized a massive public reception at which he was taken out in a procession on a chariot with the rising sun (party symbol) as painted backdrop, and garlanded by elephants (Pandian 1992). Rivalry between M. Karunanidhi and MGR after the death of Annadurai, led to a split. MGR formed his own party in 1972 – the All India Anna Dravida Munnetra Kazhagam, named after Annadurai – which came to power in 1977, from which time until his death in 1987 MGR remained the chief minister of the state. Since then these two parties have dominated the political scene in Tamil Nadu, with the national parties reduced to minor partners in alliances with them. If Tamil Nadu remains the pre-eminent instance of the cinema–politics nexus even today, it is because of this unprecedented role that the cinema has played in the political life of the state.

But let us look at other manifestations of this nexus. In the state of Andhra Pradesh, N. T. Rama Rao (popularly known as NTR) was the most popular star with a following to match that of MGR. He was particularly associated, at least in the minds of commentators in the press, with the so-called mythologicals – films based on stories drawn from the epics and *puranas* of ancient India – where he played roles of epic heroes and gods like Krishna, Rama, Arjuna, Bhima, etc. Apart from taking active part in social causes like raising money through public appearances for victims of cyclones, NTR had not shown, until the late 1970s, any noticeable inclination towards a political career. Nor was there a party in Andhra Pradesh ideologically similar to the DMK. Politics in the state was largely dominated by the Congress and the communists, both with a national outlook. Beginning in the late 1970s, however, a series of developments, including the release in quick succession of several propagandistic films, culminated in NTR launching a new party, the Telugu Desam (Telugu nation), which scored a spectacular victory in the state elections in 1983, on a platform of Telugu pride and identity. This was a most unexpected development and has since transformed politics in the state drastically. In spite of many ups and downs, the Telugu Desam Party remains a powerful force in the state and is now, in the hands of NTR's son-in-law Chandrababu Naidu, the party in government there, attracting international attention for its initiatives on the information technology front. Between them, Tamil Nadu and Andhra Pradesh have contributed much by means of this link to cinema, to the elaboration since the 1970s of a regionalist politics which has transformed the political life of the nation.

In yet another southern state, Karnataka, the film star Rajkumar enjoys a popularity that matches that of his above-mentioned counterparts. Although Rajkumar did not follow his colleagues in launching a party and bidding for political power, his public career took a distinctly political turn when, in the early 1980s, he came out in support of the so-called Gokak agitation, a movement demanding primacy of place to the state language Kannada in education and administration. His entry catalysed the movement and drew vast numbers of people into the agitations, marking a turning point in the state's history. Despite widespread speculations about his political ambitions, and appeals from parties and fans, Rajkumar desisted from entering electoral politics. Today he occupies a symbolic position of power in the state, while fan clubs swearing allegiance to him are active in various agitations around issues of language, river water-sharing between states, etc. When the current Congress chief minister assumed office, the very first thing he did was to visit Rajkumar to "seek his blessings".[2]

Some other events can be briefly mentioned to complete the story of the cinema–politics nexus. Amitabh Bachchan, the most successful star of Indian cinema, entered politics on the advice of his friend Rajiv Gandhi, and won a spectacular victory over the seasoned socialist leader H. N. Bahuguna, putting an end to the latter's career. Although he subsequently withdrew from the political arena, he has lately been campaigning for the Samajwadi (Socialist) Party. Apart from stars who get nominated to the Upper House of Parliament regularly, a number of them have lately been attracted to the Hindu nationalist BJP, including Shatrughan Sinha, Vinod Khanna, the "Lady Bachchan" action star of Telugu films Vijayashanti, and Hema Malini. Rajesh Khanna, long after his film career had started to decline, launched himself into full-time politics, although few would claim that the stupendous fan following of his early days in filmdom had anything to do with this. Television actors were also inducted into politics to exploit their role identifications, especially after the success of the television *Ramayana*. In Tamil Nadu, Sivaji Ganesan, MGR's rival for the top slot in the film industry, extended the rivalry to politics as well by joining the Congress for some time. There are numerous other instances of this phenomenon all of which fall into the same category of periodic mobilization of stars by political parties.

Considered in such exhaustive detail, this picture of widespread political mobilization of star charisma points to a general problem of interest to political scientists, concerning the nature of democratic political life in India. However, it is my contention that this large picture actually conceals two distinct phenomena, which should not be confused with each other. In brief I would describe the developments in the three southern states as constituting one distinct historical phenomenon, and club all the rest together under the general category of extra-political infusions into the political process. Of all the numerous instances that fall under the second category, only the case of Amitabh Bachchan may have some relevance to the issues brought to the fore by the first category. Otherwise, it is safe to say that film stars, like football and cricket players, generals and other public personalities, try to cash in on a valuable asset called "name (and face) recognition". In this essay, therefore, we will leave these aside and concentrate on the southern developments that I have included in the first category as constituting a unique historical event. The question may then be formulated as follows: Why did three southern states produce film stars, one in each state, who became or had the power to become powerful political leaders?

The explanations

Social scientists and film critics have sought answers to the mystery of the south Indian film miracle. The most popular explanations combine certain Indological/cultural psychological truisms about the Indian psyche with a behaviourist reading. Thus the critic Chidananda Das Gupta, an inveterate champion of the alternative cinema, surprised himself by writing an entire book on popular cinema, "the urge for [which] came with N.T. Rama Rao's meteoric rise to power in 1983 in Andhra Pradesh" (Das Gupta 1991: ix). Das Gupta regards the gullibility of the masses, their inability to distinguish reality from the illusions of the screen, as the primary reason behind the success of film stars in politics. The adulation stars enjoy is seen as a variant of devotional activity of the religious kind, which is said to figure in the cinema–audience relation in two ways: first, the masses relate to stars with the attitude of *devotion* specific to the sphere of religion, thus establishing a relationship that, both in its internal substance and external manifestation, bears the marks of a popular religious cult. Second, the industry produces mythologicals (films based on themes from the epics and *puranas*), in which the audience see their favourite stars appearing as gods and goddesses and consequently, the argument goes, stars who play gods on screen can hope to be mistaken for a Krishna or Rama by voters who naturally prefer to vote for immortals over humans. In this way star charisma joins superstition and other pre-rational phenomena which are used to rig the electoral process. When NTR launched his political career in the early 1980s, explanations for his popularity began to converge on the idea that the Telugu public saw him as a god. "The picture that his name conjures up in the minds of ordinary voters," a newspaper reported, "is that of a god, killing demons and evil doers" (*National Herald*, 21 December 1982). Another critic explained that his image combined the charisma of Krishna (a role he played several times) as well as that of Rama, in support of which she cites a number of his films with the word Rama in the title, although these were not mythologicals. Here it is assumed that there is a sort of transfer of qualities from a frequently essayed role to the actor himself, as if in the course of performing these roles, he had acquired the power of the god himself.

The second, behaviourist part of the explanation, of which Sivathamby is an early proponent, supplements the Indological tale: of course, there is star popularity verging on devotion, but it is the political propaganda messages that these stars convey which go deep into the spectators' psyche and affect their voting patterns. The difference between the two positions hinges on whether charisma is a message in itself or a medium for the effective communication of political messages. This "political communication" thesis finds its evidence in the example of the DMK film.

It is not our purpose here to rescue the masses from accusations of gullibility and restore them to an exalted position of instinctual and unerring wisdom. It would be ridiculous to deny that the majority of people of India are constantly being taken for a ride by a variety of forces, including the film industry. Nevertheless, the point is that the case for such an explanation seems to rely on the obviousness of its own presuppositions than on anything else. Not that there is no evidence to support this view. The south Indian fan is known in common parlance as a *bhakta* (devotee), although the more ambiguous and formal designation *abhimani*[3] has tended to replace it in recent times. The press occasionally prints stories about temples being built to stars (MGR, NTR, but also actresses like Khushboo). Mythologicals were once immensely popular among audiences and while their appeal has waned as television took over with its historic productions of *Ramayana*, *Mahabharata*, and other *pouranic* serials, the other related genre of *devotionals* (where the emphasis is on the intervention of gods in the secular modern sphere), continues to draw audiences. (When silicon technology and other new special effects became available to local producers, south India erupted in a series of new-look devotionals about fierce goddesses (*Devi*, *Ammoru*).) The actors who played the lead roles in the television Ramayana entered politics or campaigned for political parties. All this seems to confirm the suspicion that stars' fan following, being of a quasi-religious nature, entails absolute loyalty which is reflected in election results.

But the difficulty arises around the question how and why all this devotion and superstition gets channelled into so unlikely an area of everyday life, electoral politics. And further, why it does so in only some regions of this more or less uniformly benighted country. Third, why are south Indian film stars, who have far less glamorous off-screen personae than their Bombay counterparts, more successful in convincing their audiences about their superhuman ability and status? The contrast between screen roles and real life personae among southern film stars is particularly striking. At the height of their careers, some of these stars, especially of the first generation, would appear in public in extremely unfashionable dhoti and shirt, their bald pates exposed, and would even celebrate their children's weddings lavishly in full view of the public, while their films showing them as glamorous college students were playing in the halls. On the gullibility question it must be added that it is not something particular to cinema, but a logic of religiosity which is indifferent to the form of manifestation of divinity. Thus even in popular state mythologicals, where often audiences are watching their own friends or neighbours playing the roles of gods, the moment of performance produces a relation of devotion at specific moments which are designated for the purpose, irrespective of who the performer is. If the cinema too produces similar devotional fervour, it is not because the people cannot distinguish between illusion and reality like the fabled early spectators of the cinema who rushed to the screen to rescue the heroine, but because such a distinction is not pertinent to the experience of the moment. The spectator's assumption about the presence of the divinity is not, in other words, based on a *realist* premise, which is the mistake positivist commentators make. Rather, it relies on the idea that divinity can manifest itself by using even a fool as its vehicle.

As far as NTR is concerned, he did play Krishna and Rama, but he also played Arjuna and Bhima and other roles with no religious connotations. Audience appreciation in mythologicals, derivative of appreciation in the theatrical tradition, is focused on the quality of the performance, not on the role – the performer's versatility, in being able to play the ferocious Bhima or the villainous Ravana as effortlessly and impressively as Krishna or Rama, being a crucial factor. Besides, a simple statistical analysis shows that the output of mythologicals in NTR's career was relatively low, while the social[4] dominates throughout his career.[5] On the other hand, MGR in the neighbouring state of Tamil Nadu, never acted in a mythological film in his entire career, and while Rajkumar did act in some, the Telugu mythologicals had such a successful run all over the south that NTR's association with *pouranic* heroes remained strong even outside Andhra Pradesh. Besides, it is through the socials that all the three stars elaborated the persona that alone generates identificatory possibilities.

Thus any explanation that falls back upon the psychic dispositions of the spectators of the cinema and the manipulative designs of film-makers and politicians cannot explain:

1   Why only some stars succeeded and not others who did everything they did;
2   Why they succeeded in only some parts of the country and not in others;
3   Why other political parties did not try or did not succeed in similarly propagating their political message through the cinema.

Work in star studies (Dyer 1979; Gledhill 1991) has proved very useful in the few studies that have been attempted of the Indian star systems (Srinivas 1997). But they are of little help in approaching the situation we are dealing with. This is because star studies have largely been preoccupied with issues of individual subjectivity, with the question of *imaginary* identifications through which individual fans supplement their lives with meaning or seek avenues for pleasures (such as a sense of community, or forbidden sexual fantasies) that real life deprives them of. It is thus in the intra-psychic or *pathological* dimension of social existence that star studies seeks and finds its explanations for why people identify with stars.

In the *cine-politics* (as I will henceforth refer to it) of south India, however, we are confronted with the *objectification of identifications in political institutions*. It is as if the fantasies that spectators could indulge in as long as they were aware that these were only fantasies (which is the case with individual fans' relations to their favourite stars), had suddenly turned into reality, so that the fantasy itself occupies the position of the formerly repressive agency, whose presence had necessitated this detour through fantasy identifications. It is thus no longer in the realm of individual, intra-psychic fantasy, but in concrete programmes of political utopia, realized in the social and affecting even those who never participated in the fantasy. Fantasy here reaches out and occupies the place of the universal, the law itself. There is thus a need to reconstitute the object "cinema and politics" to take into account factors ignored by the political communication model, the Indological model or the imaginary identification model of star studies. Neither the specificity of the cinematic institution nor the complexity of the political processes in a peripheral modern nation-state is given its due by such models of explanation.

Elements for an alternative approach to the problem

In this essay I propose no more than the beginnings of an alternative approach, supported by some speculations arising out of the combination of elements I invoke as essential to any analysis. My main proposition is that the sociological and cultural-psychological approaches (which explain any star identification whatsoever) have to be replaced by a historical approach which treats the phenomenon in question as a unique historical event occurring at a crucial conjuncture. Not because the sociological and star studies methods are not useful but because they ask and answer a very different question: why do people identify with stars. Our question is, however, different: we are concerned with why and how this proclivity of film spectators, observable in all parts of the world, contributed in this corner to a set of political projects which clashed with the projects of the national parties and reconstituted the political field itself in accordance with a new logic of regionalism.

In speaking of a historical conjuncture as the birth place of the event in question, we must also acknowledge another reality. One reason why star studies is preoccupied with individual spectator identifications and their psychic origins and consequences is that in the First World situations that it usually studies, the separation of political, economic, cultural/ideological *instances* is assumed to be complete. It is only in the indirect form of ideological inscription that we recognize, in cultural analysis, the *politics* of this or that text or discourse. In this instance, however, we must be alert to the non-separation of these spheres, to the prevalence of a relatively undifferentiated field of socio-political activity.

We must discard the serial, infusionist model whereby something from cinema comes into something called politics and affects its character. Most commentaries on south Indian cinema discuss the politics question only in relation to electoral battles: in other words, it is only when film stars become politicians that the link is seen and taken seriously. Instead we must acknowledge that neither politics nor cinema as we know it (distinct from each other and with their respective roles marked out) remains the same. This is not to say that such a distinction is unheard of in south Indian society, simply that that distinction was blurred, jettisoned in a specific fashion in order for cinema to function as a supplementary political apparatus. In other words it is not only when stars entered politics but throughout the nearly five decades of south Indian film history since the constitution of the Republic in 1950, that we must expect to find a cine-politics in operation. The still unsettled question of *political representation*, which supersedes all other issues in the career of Indian democracy and extends to the question of the *state form* itself, is at the heart of the issue.[6]

The elements of the conjuncture which are essential to our attempt to reformulate the question about south Indian cinema are as follows:

1   The birth of the sound film, which at the level of narrative posed the problem of language and the authority of speech, and gave rise to linguistically homogeneous markets for cinema in India;
2   The end of colonial rule, which made visible the void in the place of patriarchal authority;
3   The constitution of the Republic, the advent of electoral politics and the reorganization of the states according to dominant languages;
4   The decline of the film studios and the increasing dependence on star value as a factor in film production;
5   The ideology of passive revolution which made developmental/pedagogic relations between rulers and ruled, literate and illiterate, cultural producers and consumers, an essential feature of social and cultural life.

Without proceeding in any determinate order, what follows will draw on all these elements in an attempt at a historical construction that reveals the conditions of possibility for the elaboration in film culture of what I will refer to as a *supplementary structure of political representation* that introduces an excess or surplus of representation over and above that inscribed in the political apparatus while at the same time filling a gap in the symbolic chain that threatened the legitimacy of that apparatus.

Thus one distinctive feature of the south Indian case is the fact that adulation is based upon the ascription to the star[7] of the status of a representative. The star is taken to represent the *linguistic community* for whom his films are made. If it were only a question of the political messages, if the "rebel" image, for instance, were the source of the popularity, there would be no difference between the Hindi star Amitabh Bachchan and say, NTR, many of whose films were remakes of Bachchan's hits. Or, given the much wider fan following of Bachchan, it would seem reasonable to expect him to be politically more successful than NTR, which we know was not the case. The difference hinges on an extra dimension: NTR is taken to represent the Telugu "nation" in a way that Bachchan cannot be – within modern India a separate nation of Hindi-speakers is difficult to conceive, since the identity of the Hindi-speaking regions is far more comprehensively merged into the Indian national identity. Indeed our stars rarely appeared as rebels against the system in their formative years. They played characters who worked to restore a better, improved version of the existing order. There is thus little evidence here of a dynamic of counter-identification, of the sort we find in the case of Amitabh Bachchan[8] where the marginal figures that he played seemed to hold particular appeal to a subaltern, lumpenized population. In those films, it was as a leader of the oppressed in a hostile environment that Bachchan gathered a mass following. The star persona was explicitly inscribed with the oppressive burden of the world, and words often failed the hero, who would withdraw into a brooding silence. In the southern films in question, however, it is rare to find such failure of subjectification, these stars are always firmly entrenched in the symbolic order that they represent, and they speak effortlessly about the predicament of the characters they portray.

Another unusual feature that we have already mentioned is that this generation of stars never tried to reproduce in real life the image they had on the screen. All of them appeared in public in traditional clothes and in real life roles that were a far cry from their screen images as youthful, virile heroes. Their public image, in other words, was that of elderly, respected members of traditional society. The main reason for this has to do with the history of the emergence of the sound film in India. These stars, as well as others like Sivaji Ganesan, Nageswara Rao, etc., began to enter the industry in the years after the Second World War, when film production in these languages was still relatively undeveloped. This was the early era of the sound film, when the advances in silent cinema were temporarily annulled by the necessity of having characters that spoke. In such a situation, a filmmaker does not make the same films with dialogue and sound added, rather he looks for plays. The early talkies in the south were predominantly derived from the stage. The actors too came from there. At that time, all over south India (as in other parts of the country), there were many successful touring theatre companies (sometimes called boys' companies because they recruited their performers young, and especially hired boys (like Nageswara Rao) to play the female roles) inspired by the success of the Parsi theatre companies,[9] which would put up mythologicals and social dramas. These companies usually had a very paternalistic social structure with elders and youth given roles of command, obedience and deference, relations which would also figure in the assignment of acting roles. When the cinema began to talk, the old order collapsed, you could no longer choose your actors for their looks alone. Nor did the cinema evolve its own dramatic devices, partly because the theatre companies themselves saw in this an opportunity to expand their activities. Thus the actors who came into the cinema in those early years were from the stage, the *bhagavatars* as they were known – Honnappa, Thiagaraja, etc. These actors often enjoyed immense popularity for their versatility, and some would be identified by the kind of roles they played. The Tamil film *Rajapart Rangadurai* (Rangadurai of the Raja roles or parts 1973) pays homage to that tradition. While the first actors to thus come into the film industry maintained a great degree of continuity with the company theatre tradition, both in terms of the roles they played and the skills they brought to their parts, as well as the kind of appreciation they enjoyed, it is the second generation of stars, the ones we are concerned with, whose careers see an irreversible transition to the cinema. All the three stars, and many others of their generation, came from theatre companies. They had very brief stage careers compared to their predecessors before they succumbed to the lure of Madras, which was by then the primary location of the film industry in the south. They still sported their "bhagavatar crop", which was a generic hairstyle recommended for the male stage actor, where the hair reached down to about the middle of the neck and curled inwards. Rajkumar recalls in his autobiography how he had to get rid of his bhagavatar crop after entering films.[10] In the course of the careers of these stars, we may observe the transition from the bhagavatar era (when stage and screen were parallel and interlinked institutions) to the era of the more autonomous narratives of the social genre in cinema, which hence-forth became the primary defining element of their star status. We can capture this transition in miniscule in the fact that the modern hairstyle became the norm for the stars and whatever other roles they might play, their identity was fixed by this look. They thus bridged the bhagavatar era, when there was as yet no star persona for actors, to the present era, when star persona reigns supreme.

While their careers were almost entirely in the cinema, these middle generation of stars remained bhagavatars at heart. In other words, while in many ways their careers witness a decisive and irreversible rupture between stage and screen, there also remained many continuities at the level of production cultures as well as performance. One important factor of continuity lies in the tradition of performance and the culture of appreciation that went with it. In their real lives, these actors, even after they became big stars, retained the image of the bhagavatars, the best among whom were regarded as eminent members of society who commanded respect (or not) for their skills of *abhinaya* (acting). It is this tradition that explains the oft-lamented fact that 50-year-old stars play college students: the aesthetic in question privileges the display of *abhinaya* over the compulsions of realism.

The rise of the male star

The careers of these stars, who are, historically, the first generation of male stars in the industry, acquires added significance when seen against the background of a cinema that was, prior to and for some time after their arrival, organized around the female star as the primary attraction. This tradition went back a long way. In 1931, in an article in *Filmland* entitled "Choice of 'Heroes' from a Lady's Standpoint" the writer observes: "Producers think that if the female artistes are not good, people will curse them and so they do not care so much about male actors. They are in the wrong. Heroes should be as befitting as heroines" (Bandyopadhyay 1993: 63). A four-year survey of the industry published in *Moving Picture Monthly*, 1935, confirms this observation. The section on "players" starts thus: "Among the players Gohar and Sulochana still hold the supreme places, with Madhuri coming for a close second." This is followed by a second paragraph that deals with male actors: "India seems to be lacking in heroes" (Bandyopadhyay 1993: 26). In the 1930s, at the beginning of the sound era, the industry was still organized around female stars, but some people were beginning to express dissatisfaction with this state of affairs.

While the above remarks were not made in reference to south Indian films, the same situation prevailed here as well. Indeed, it is enough to look at some of the early films of our trinity to see how, both in terms of narrative and visual primacy, it is the female characters who win out. *Sodari* (*Sister*, 1955), Rajkumar's second film, is a good example. The title refers to the heroine, sister of the king of Jayanagara, who marries the king of a neighbouring kingdom (Rajkumar). Her brother promises to adopt her son and make him king after him. The queen of Jayanagara, instigated by a maid, tries to scuttle this plan in her own son's interests. The brother goes to war and in the neighbouring kingdom drought ravages the land and the king (Rajkumar) gives away all his wealth to save the people. He leaves the palace, so that his wife can return to her brother's. After this Rajkumar more or less disappears from the narrative and returns in brief scenes as he wanders aimlessly, until the climax. After many trials, his wife reaches her brother's palace where in his absence his queen inflicts a series of cruelties on her until the king's return. He inquires after his sister and the rest of the action is taken up with his trying to set things right. Rajkumar returns at the end, but by then his wife has died, along with their son.

As the husband of the heroine, Rajkumar plays a role that is, within the logic of the narrative, central in a purely symbolic fashion and his name tops the cast credits. After Pandari Bai, the heroine, he is the most important character, more so than the heroine's brother. He is the more handsome, aristocratic figure. From the point of view of narrative *movement*, however, he is a marginal figure. He makes nothing happen. The entire gamut of plots and counter-plots, actions and reactions, through which the narrative moves forward is initiated by the king of Jayanagara, his wife, her maid and others, including the heroine herself, who is the pathetic centre of the narrative. In a revealing farewell scene that follows the wedding, Rajkumar stands at the edge of the frame with a look that suggests that he has no connection with the goings on. This indicates the somewhat secondary status of the male "lead" in that kind of cinema as well as the unimportance of the hero to the plot. A similar bias towards the heroine can be seen in other films as well, such as *Rayara Sose* (K. Ramamurthy/ K. S. Murthy, 1957); *Mohini* (Lanka Sathyam, 1948); *Manthirikumari* (Ellis Dungan, 1950); *Shavukaru* (L. V. Prasad, 1950) to mention only those starring our heroes (note that all the titles except one refer to the main female character). These are from the late 1940s and 1950s, when the trend towards male star-centred narratives had already begun. The entries for the period 1920–40 in the *Encyclopedia of the Indian Cinema* (Rajadhyaksha and Willemen 1999) indicate the extent to which female stars, and therefore female characters, dominated the scene before the transformation brought about by the entry of our southern trinity.

Why and how does this dominant tendency get reversed in the course of about fifteen years? Given the non-availability of an adequate number of early silent and sound films, it is difficult to come to any reliable conclusions about this phenomenon. It is not even certain that a transformation such as this can be really understood through an examination of the films alone. In any case, this is undoubtedly one of the most momentous transformations in the history of Indian cinema and it is strange that it finds no mention in film historians' accounts. It is one of those phenomena that would appear to have been rendered invisible by virtue of having been too familiar. At this distance and with the limited resources available to us, we can only approach the problem in an indirect fashion, hoping at best to eke out some speculative propositions that might guide future research.

If the advent of the talkies is one of the historical transitions that seems to have a bearing on this question, the other is the birth of the new nation itself. In matters of cultural change such as this, where each instance of the social has its own temporality, it would be disastrous to assume direct cause–effect relations between texts and historical developments. For the same reason, neither the date of advent of the talkies nor the exact moment of Independence is here implied but the period in which these events take place, including the years leading up to Independence, which is already a time of preparation for a new day. Periodization is further complicated by the fact that in the case of the sound film, different language cinemas in India have their own temporalities, so that it takes some of them much longer to make certain transitions in terms of genres, than it does others.

What then are we to make of the fact that as narrative films evolve, the dominant genre that has come to be known as the "social" acquires an andro-centric structure? Does it indicate the lifting of a constraint that prevented such a structure from prevailing earlier? Or does it signify the imposition of a fresh constraint, a new order, made possible or necessary by the withdrawal of the colonial power? In the mythologicals, which were the first, spontaneous choice for talkie producers, speech was not a problem. What was to be spoken, who was to speak, what mannerisms of speech were to be employed – all these problems were solved by the existence of a ready resource, the stage mythologicals, with their established modes of stentorian dialogue delivery, bursts of singing, etc. But in the "social", speech brings with it the problem of authority, the necessity of a narrative centre from which moral authority flows. In a film like *Schoolmaster* (Panthulu, 1958), an elderly patriarch serves as this centre and makes possible the imagining of a world, whose coherence and integrity are troubled by an invading modernity. The important thing here is how a new world which can *represent* the society of modern India is imagined, using the joint family as model and, as D. R. Nagaraj has argued, an ambivalent attitude towards romantic love as both an important element of this construct and a threat to its integrity (Nagaraj 1996). If romantic love is a "formal requirement" of the popular cinema, as well as, increasingly, its energetic centre, it appears to have become so only in a process of re-formation that allows the centrality of patriarchal authority to be maintained without foregoing the visual pleasures of glamour, sensuality, etc.

The relatively weak position of male leads in pre- and immediately post-Independence films is also related to the problem of the peculiar predicament that Indian society faced under colonial authority, where the overarching power of the colonizer rendered difficult the ideological conception of a coherent patriarchal authority *internal* to the society. A reading of some of the pre-Independence films would show how this impasse is disavowed at the same time that it is reflected by the strategy of emphasizing female roles. As the new nation consolidates itself, however, filling the void becomes a necessity as well as a possibility, but this cannot be done at the national level in the absence of a cultural/linguistic homogeneity where patriarchal authority can be unproblematically identified and elaborated.

The long-drawn process of a restructuring of the dominant narrative form which installs a new patriarchal order as the moral–legal framework within which narratives unfold is the background against which we must plot the rise to importance of male stars, whose image henceforth includes not only glamour and beauty but also the authority of a patriarchal figure. Nothing illustrates this more vividly than the *paternal* relation that these heroes often have with the heroines. At the height of their career as star-representatives of the linguistic community, these stars cannot indulge in romance without maintaining, as a supplementary feature of their subjectivity, a paternal function which extends to all characters in the film, including the heroine. The mandatory sub-plots of sister-love in the south Indian cinema, with their emotional excesses, are also part of the narrative technology that assists in the elevation of the male star to a paternal status. The sister in these films is a *cause*, a figure in need of protection, that the hero takes up and through which he elevates himself from a state of immanence in the diegesis, rising above it as a position of transcendence. Sister-love is an ingenious solution for the problem of narrative authority that the popular cinema faces. It enables the hero to take the place of the elderly patriarchal authority, like the schoolmaster of Panthulu's film, while he pursues his own romance and other goals. In the presence of a "schoolmaster", the characters indulging in romantic love look innocent, carefree, and in need of protection. In his absence, the male member of the romantic couple becomes a protector, acquiring the attributes of the schoolmaster/parent. Thus it is not surprising to see Rajkumar, in *Bidugade* (Y. R. Swamy, 1973), admonishing the heroine in song for neglecting her studies. The father/schoolmaster, a figure of traditional authority, is thus replaced by the brother, who, while respectful of traditional authority, has the skills to get on in the modern world.

We have established the preconditions which enable the star system to reconstitute itself around male stars and male-centred narratives, and make a decisive entry into a distinct cinematic genre of narratives in contemporary settings. In the 1950s, a new situation arises where these stars have to assume a further burden, that of representing the audience figured as a linguistic community, a nation. Here we approach the question of how, among the many stars who acquired popularity through a combination of the above strategies and circumstances, one in each of the three states rose to represent the nation or linguistic community.

In approaching the problem, I turn to the distinction, now taken for granted, between political and aesthetic representation. Marx, in the *Eighteenth Brumaire*, employs this distinction in a stunning analysis of the rise of Louis Bonaparte to power. In a brief discussion of Marx's analysis, Gayatri Spivak (1988) introduces a problematic that, albeit indirectly, has relevance to the question we are considering. The discussion concerns the two senses of the term that we have noted above: "representation as 'speaking for,' as in politics, and representation as 're-presentation,' as in art or philosophy." In Marx's German, these two terms translate as *vertreten* and *darstellen* respectively, a fact obscured by the English translation. The distinctions between *vertreten* and *darstellen* come into play in a complex argument about a political situation where a "model of social indirection" prevails in the absence of transparent modes of representation based on a calculation of interests alone. Thus representation takes the form of *substitution*, a process through which Louis Bonaparte comes to be recognized by the French peasants as their leader. Here, political representation "behaves like" aesthetic representation or *Darstellung*. The *name* of Napoleon substitutes for a capacity to "make their class interest valid in their proper [own] name" (Spivak 1998: 278). To summarize, the argument here is that sometimes political representation is not effected through acts of election or delegation, but through substitution, i.e. through the unexpected arrival of a figure who seems to be already endowed with the legitimacy to represent us. In such instances, the figure of representation as substitution has the added dimension of *darstellen* or aesthetic representation. The two orders of representation, in other words, collapse into one.

In the political order of post-Independence India, we have a situation that gave rise to a similar deadlock of representation, although the entities involved are not classes, but linguistic communities emerging into a shadowy nationhood within a federal polity. The linguistic reorganization of states which came to a culmination in 1956, led to the dissolution of the Madras Presidency[11] and the constitution of new states, incorporating territories from the erstwhile Madras Presidency, Bombay Presidency, and the princely states. The territorial map of south India was thus redrawn according to the spread of the dominant languages. For long a demand expressed by Congress leaders, linguistic reorganization was nevertheless resisted by the Nehru government. The demand from the regions, especially from Andhra, however, could not be ignored. The main reason for resisting linguistic reorganization was, of course, because from the centre's point of view, the states were purely administrative units. National identity had to be one and indivisible – Indian. Linguistic reorganization automatically implied that there were different nationalities within the federation of states. While in the north, to a large extent, a measure of linguistic homogeneity worked against the state = nationality equation, in the south and the east, language communities, if not already defined as nationalities, had the potential to move in that direction. Thus for a central government preoccupied with the deepening and expansion of national unity and identity, regional demands for the territorial affirmation of linguistic identities naturally appeared as divisive. Separatist voices occasionally arising from the south would only have confirmed the central machinery in this fear.[12]

The anxiety was not unfounded.[13] Linguistic reorganization created the conditions for the development of national identities in these states. A movement that, prior to Independence, was largely confined to the educated classes, and elaborated in literary texts, now found itself appealing for the affiliation of the poor and the unlettered as well. There is no logical reason why cinema should become entangled in such a situation. But if there is already a strong film industry in existence, and the redrawing of boundaries creates new boundaries within the market, the cinema, a talking cinema what is more, would necessarily reflect this change in some fashion. *Ranadhira Kanteerava* (N. C. Rajan, 1959), one of the most popular films of the post-reorganization era in Karnataka, begins with a call to a constituency that cinema had never directly addressed before: *"Geleya kannadigare swagathavu nimage"* (Welcome, fellow Kannadigas"). Based on the story of a legendary king of the Mysore dynasty, who is reputed to have restored the kingdom to its former glory, the film features Rajkumar in the lead role. Scenes of confrontation with challengers from other kingdoms in the region emphasize the Kannadiga versus Tamil/Malayali dimension. Here the direct address to the spectators as Kannadigas and the thematic reinforcement of the appeal serve to define a new market.

The entire process of the dissolution of the presidency and the gradual re-centring of cultural production in the state capitals or within the new state boundaries is of great relevance to the story we are trying to tell. This process has many dimensions, of which only those which concern cinema will engage us here. While initially films in south Indian lan-guages were made in many production centres all over India, Madras soon became the primary site of production. In the socials produced here, the narrative authority rested in a particular zamindar type based on local models, and elaborate plots full of familial intrigues often required a sutradhara[14] type of figure to intermittently announce the next step in the story. In such complicated plots, the hero had the sort of symbolic centrality noted above, with the attendant romantic scenes, songs, etc., but there would also be many scenes that were unconnected, with the main plot. L. V. Prasad's Telugu films (e.g. *Appu Chesi Pappu Kudu* (1958)) are typical of this genre, which we can call, for convenience, the studio genre. The comedy track, for instance, was often totally unconnected to the main plot and sometimes for long periods, the comic and the hero never met. These films, in other words, showed a world in which the romance of the lead pair was the central, but not the only preoccupation. On the whole, we could identify here a self-image of the elite of the presidency, concentrated in Madras but with landholdings in the outlying regions, adding up to a sort of presidency aesthetic which looked pretty much the same across language barriers. Since it is through these "socials" that the heroes acquire their final star-identity, it is useful to look at how this narrative structure changes with the dissolution of the presidencies.

We have already noted how the sub-plot of sister-love contributes to the transformation. Another such important change is the process by which the comedian's existence within the film becomes more and more strongly linked to the hero's. From a parallel "hero" of an inde-pendent comedy track, we see the comedian becoming a sidekick, a friend who is nevertheless marked as subordinate, and in the moment of the star's apotheosis, as in a film like *Namnaadu* (1969) the comedian has become indistinguishable from a fan. In Kannada, this identity of the comedian as fan is prefigured very early, in *Nandadeepa* (M. R. Vittal, 1963), where Vadiraj plays Rajkumar's "follower". Indeed, as these stars become more and more powerful, comedians are reduced to an essentially subordinate function, and constitute a crucial link to the audience, serving as a sort of go-between, seeming to give expression to the spectators' admiration for the star.

This process of narrative streamlining, whereby the hero's position (though not yet the hero himself) soon determines all the action, coincides with the rise of these stars to repre-sentative status. This status also acts as a constraint: while female stars and lesser male stars take up roles in more than one language, representative status imposes on the top male star a language restriction. He cannot or will not act in a language other than the one he is identified with. Further, the re-centring process leads to a situation where the fact that the stars from Karnataka and Andhra reside in Madras becomes a contradiction that they are forced to resolve or find explanations for. They build studios, acquire an interest in distribution and/or exhibition and in other ways entrench themselves as key players in the developing regional industry. The entire industry's fortunes begin to depend upon the star value of the top hero and one or two of his rivals. New stars pay their obeisance to the "elders" (partly in continuation of the culture of theatre companies) or are forced by fans to do so (as in the case of Vishnuvardhan – once Rajkumar fans are reported to have made him get out of his car and march in a procession in honour of their star). Fan clubs regulate the size of the cutouts and "stars"[15] that are erected outside the cinema halls, so that a rival cannot have bigger cutouts without incurring their wrath. Thus a whole series of major and minor phenomena go to construct for the top star the supreme position within the local pantheon.

In all the three industries, there also emerges a division of labour among stars that hints at the different forms of representativeness that are involved in the public's relation to cinema. Thus each of these top stars has a counterpart or set of counterparts who by contrast, have a more middle-class image: Nageswara Rao in Telugu, Sivaji Ganesan and Gemini Ganesan in Tamil, Kalyan Kumar in Kannada. These stars' images tend to be invested with a sense of *cultural authenticity*, whereas, as the case of MGR makes clear, cultural authenticity is not the primary factor in the representative status achieved by the top star. With MGR, NTR and Rajkumar, what we have is a point of symbolic identification, based more on monarchic or Bonapartist logics, rather than on cultural familiarity. Here we may also note the role of film genres in producing this division of labour. When we examine the careers of these stars closely, we notice that the leader stars are those who achieved big success in the genre called the "folklore" films, which include the Douglas Fairbanks-style film, as well as other stunt and adventure genres, which attracted the masses as opposed to the "classes". However while this is crucial for identifying the stars' "mass base" as it were, it is through the "social" that the leadership position is elaborated. In terms of iconography, the choice of top star was clearly decided in favour of a face that was associated with adventure and stunt films, where the body acquires primacy over acting ability. Physical attributes that, thanks to various conventions prevailing in the visual culture at large, are associated with princes or other exceptional beings, parts which these stars often played, are prized over ethnic familiarity. In the films that the subalterns favoured, identification had a symbolic dimension, where one identifies with the Other precisely for the qualities that make him different from us, superior to us.

Thus, considered in the light of recent history, against a backdrop of the rise of disavowed nationalisms for which no legitimate grounds of political expression were available within a federal polity that was in competition with the regions in its attempt to establish a non-linguistic pan-Indian national identity, cinema in the southern region confronts us with a unique case of a cultural form serving as a shadow structure of political representation, a political "supplement" in the Derridean sense. The entry of these stars into everyday electoral politics may then be read as marking the end of cinepolitics, rather than its beginning, the conclusion of a phase in which among certain nationalities political representation had to have this double structure, a supplementary, virtual one subsisting underneath the parliamentary system.

Cine-politics is not about the infusion of star charisma into electoral politics, nor about the use of cinema to disseminate party slogans. It is a distinct form of political engagement that emerged in some of the linguistically defined states of southern India at a certain historical juncture where Indian nationalism's ideological suturing could not take care of certain gaps in the symbolic chain. A set of contingent factors led to a situation where cinema, a form of entertainment that was then learning to speak, came to be chosen as the site of a strong political investment, where audiences responded with enthusiasm to an offer of leadership emanating from the screen and, through the fan associations that emerged later, established a concrete set of everyday practices that reaffirmed the position of the star as leader.

Cinema offered certain distinctly novel possibilities, which Indian filmmakers exploited to bring about such a social scenario. To get at this, we must pose the question of the cultural significance of the *screen* as a site of discovery of images. The pioneering Indian filmmaker Dadasaheb Phalke's story about how he was inspired to take up film production when he was watching a film on the *Life of Christ* and felt a strong desire to see Hindu gods and heroes on the screen, is indicative of the primacy that the screen, as the site of projection of images, has had in the Indian imagining of a cinematic culture (Prasad 1998b). The possibility of seeing Indian images on the screen was what Phalke cited as the motivating factor behind the launch of his *swadeshi*[16] film production enterprise. The screen here has the status of one of those neutral spaces that modernity produces, whose very existence compels all nations to relocate themselves in them. Like History itself, within whose gaze every nation seeks to install itself, the screen too is, beyond the fact of its western provenance, a space that can be rendered neutral, and hospitable to diverse imagery. The underlying metaphor here is that of parliament, an assemblage of the world's diversity, providing an opportunity for all to represent themselves in its spaces.

Whether they later entered electoral politics or not, the first generation of south Indian male film stars in three states participated, through their films and the cultural *organizations* that grew up around them, in the construction of a sort of *virtual state* which gave to linguistic communities embedded within a larger nationalism a concrete sense (albeit ideological) of their own nation-statehood. Thus the film industry of the period became a part of the political machine, filling a lack in the actual parliamentary democratic structure and demonstrating the ineffectuality of the Indian-nationalist programme, a deficiency which the Hindutwa movement is now trying to overcome.

Notes

An earlier version of this paper was published in the *Journal of the Moving Image*, no. 1 (2000).

1 The four states of Karnataka, Tamil Nadu, Andhra Pradesh and Kerala are generally clubbed together as "south India", and each of these has its own dominant language, respectively, Kannada, Tamil, Telugu and Malayalam. These belong to the family of "Dravidian" languages which linguists treat as a distinct group in comparison with the languages of northern India which, being more Sanskritic in character, are considered to be offshoots of the Indo-European family. A broad north–south cultural divide is often assumed to be operative, for which this linguistic difference is cited as a chief factor. Of the four states, Kerala alone is not part of the history of cine-politics that we are discussing, although there too, the actor Prem Nazir did once toy with the idea of a political career.

2 Rajkumar was recently abducted by a bandit, a sandalwood smuggler, who held him captive in the forest for months, leading to a minor political crisis in the state – but that's another story. See Prasad (2000).

3 A word, all of whose various meanings would be pertinent to our concerns. It means one who not just admires, but takes pride in, the star and asserts an emotional claim over him or her.

4 "The social" is how the genre of social melodrama with narratives set in the modern world is known. This is a very loosely defined genre, capable of incorporating a wide variety of elements, which has dominated film production in India as a whole. The term "social" is used throughout this essay to refer to this genre. For a discussion of the genre question in Indian cinema, see Prasad 1998a.

5 The figures are (out of 250 of the 274 films that can be clearly identified): 170 socials, 40 mythologicals, 40 folklore films.

6 On this question and its relevance to a study of Indian film, see Prasad 1998a.

7 Unless otherwise specified, the word star will henceforth refer to one or all of the three stars – M. G. Ramachandran or MGR, N. T. Rama Rao or NTR, and Rajkumar. Each of them averaged more than 250 films in careers that lasted about four decades.

8 See Prasad 1998a, especially chapters 5 and 6.

9 See entry in Rajadhyaksha and Willemen 1999.

10 *Kathanoyakana Kathe* (Hero's story) *Vijayachitra*, June 1978, p. 40. The Kannada writer Purnachandra Tejaswi recalls in his memoirs about his father, how as a child he (Tejaswi) used to get his hair cut short in the modern style. This was so novel in the Mysore of those days that his friends used to call him "taki bola" (talkie baldie). The modern hairstyle was still associated with the movies. This does not mean that everybody sported a bhagavatar crop in those days, only that the very short haircut was still rare.

11 Apart from the central authority in Delhi, British India was governed from three metropolitan centres, Madras, Bombay and Calcutta, which were the headquarters of the *presidencies* named after them. The presidencies were multilingual territories which, after Independence, had to be dismantled in order to form states as administrative units.

12 For this and other details concerning the language question in India, see King (1997). King argues that Nehru's foot-dragging on the language question was, in the context, a sign of greater wisdom than is acknowledged.

13 Although it also demonstrates the failure of the Indian state to proactively realize a federal, multinational society, opting instead for a nationalism that, when challenged, can only claim a Hindu religious basis for itself, a fact which has come home to roost in the current Hindutwa crisis.

14 A sort of master of ceremonies from Sanskrit dramaturgy who presided over the proceedings on the stage and addressed the audience between scenes with various messages.

15 Made of coloured paper and cane and hung up outside the theatres on the day of the release. See Srinivas (1997) for a detailed discussion of the culture of fandom in south India.

16 Literally, "of one's own country" the name of a movement during colonial rule to promote Indian industry.

References

Bandyopadhyay, Samik, ed. 1993. *Indian Cinema: Contemporary Perceptions from the Thirties*. Jamshedpur: Celluloid Chapter.

Das Gupta, Chidananda. 1991. *The Painted Face: Studies in India's Popular Cinema*. Delhi: Roli.

Dickey, Sara. 1993. *Cinema and the Urban Poor in South India*. Cambridge: Cambridge University Press.

Dyer, Richard. 1979. *Stars* London: BFI.

Gledhill, Christine, ed. 1991. *Stardom: Industry of Desire*. London: Routledge.

Hardgrave Jr., Robert L. 1979. "When Stars Displace the Gods: The Folk Culture of Cinema in Tamil Nadu," in *Essays in the Political Sociology of South India*. Delhi: Usha.

King, Robert D. 1997. *Nehru and the Language Politics of India*. New Delhi: Oxford University Press.

Nagaraj, D. R. 1996. "Adhikara vighataneya athankamaya maththu hasyamaya rupagalu," *Sahitya Kathana*. Heggodu: Akshara Prakashana.

Pandian, M. S. S. 1991. "*Parasakthi*: Life and Time of a DMK Film," *Economic and Political Weekly*, March 1991, 759–770.

—— 1992. *The Image Trap. MGR in Film and Politics*. Delhi: Sage.

Prasad, Madhava. 1998a. *Ideology of the Hindi Film: A Historical Construction*. Delhi: Oxford University Press.

—— 1998b. "The State in/of Cinema," in Partha Chatterjee, ed. *Wages of Freedom*. Delhi: Oxford University Press.

—— 2000. "Where Does the Forest Begin?" *Economic and Political Weekly*, November 18.

Rajadhyaksha, Ashish and Willemen, Paul. 1999. *Encyclopedia of the Indian Cinema*, 2nd edition. Delhi: Oxford University Press.

Ramaswamy, Sumathi. 1998. *Passions of the Tongue: Language Devotion in Tamil India, 1891–1970*. New Delhi: Munshiram Manoharlal.

Sivathamby, Karthigesu. 1981. *The Tamil Film as a Medium of Political Communication*. Madras: New Century Book House.

Spivak, Gayatri Chakraborty. 1988. "Can the Subaltern Speak?" in Cary Nelson and Lawrence Grossberg, eds. *Marxism and the Interpretation of Culture*. Chicago: University of Illinois Press, 271–316.

Srinivas, S.V. 1997. "Fans and Stars: Production, Reception and Circulation of the Moving Image". Unpublished Ph.D. dissertation, University of Hyderabad.

"Tamil Cinema: History, Culture, Theory." 1997. Dossier of the Workshop held at the Madras Institute of Development Studies, Chennai, 15–19 August, 1997.

Tejaswi, Purnachandra. 1996. *Annana Nenapu*. Mysore: Pustaka Prakashana.

Muscles and Subjectivity

A short history of the masculine body in Hong Kong popular culture

KWAI-CHEUNG LO

About a year ago, watching David Letterman's *Late Show* on CBS, I was surprised to find that Jackie Chan was the show's second guest, there to push his new release *Rumble in the* Bronx (1996). Asian faces, especially those directly from Asia, are rarely shown on US television. At the time, I happened to be teaching a course on Hong Kong popular culture in an American university, and my students were excited about Jackie Chan's action movies. I can't remember exactly how I felt when I saw Chan on Letterman's show, but I may have been a little bit nervous. I did not really want to admit that I was concerned about Jackie Chan, or about his popularity in the US, or about what he said on the show, partly because we come from the same place, but also because, besides the news footage of Hong Kong's 1997 handover to China, Chan is the only popular Hong Kong subject consistently covered by the American media.[1] But I was eager to have my image "correctly" represented by a Hong Kong action hero, especially as I was living in the States at the time. I would prefer to believe that I was concerned because I wanted to see my teaching materials transcend the restricted boundaries of area studies and become a part of everyday life. Perhaps I fantasized that Chan's celebrity would elevate Hong Kong from its location in a particular field to a universal realm, moving from the ghetto of Chinatown to the blockbuster chart of the first-run theater.

What fascinated the audience of the *Late Show* that night were the clips of acrobatic action scenes and the incredible physical stunts from Chan's movies. Chan showed off his athleticism live by somersaulting to his chair and kicking bottles from a table. He teasingly told Letterman that his American fans had asked him to come to kick the host's butt. Letterman responded by exchanging his jacket with Chan's and trying it on to demonstrate that he was bigger than the Asian star. For a while, the show was full of jokes about bodies. I felt embarrassed afterwards. In front of the American audience, Chan played the role of silent film comedian or cartoon character. I worried about his representativeness for Hong Kong. Would the American audience see the Hong Kong subject as a muscular, though slight, man who only knows how to use his body to amaze them and make them laugh?

It is commonplace to associate action movie stars and superhero figures with the (dis)play of their body. Hong Kong popular culture has become famous for its production of muscular bodies – from Bruce Lee, through the kung fu comics, to Jackie Chan. John Woo's tightly choreographed gunfight sequences are a sheer deployment of virile bodies. In the movies of Tsui Hark and Wong Kar-wai, the action bodies go beyond their physical dimensions and constitute a new kind of signification. These bodies are identified as the unique contribution that Hong Kong has made to cultural production in the world. They play a role in the self-invention of Hong Kong. But while they appear solidly material on screen or page, Hong Kong bodies are of a peculiar make and significance. While global circulation of films and comics makes these bodies conspicuous as Hong Kong cultural products, they remain at some levels inscrutable. Despite their importance as components of the self-invention of Hong Kong, they allude to no positive, descriptive cultural features from which Hong Kong identity can easily be drawn. As such, their import evades its own articulation and, by the same move, escapes representation in familiar critical discourse. Instead, the Hong Kong male body serves as a "sublime body" which paradoxically presents what is unpresentable of Hong Kong subjectivity.

That is to say, what the sublime body can provide is precisely a failed and negative representation of this subject position. What "sublime" generally refers to is something measureless, incommensurable, unimaginable and formless.[2] It is often described as a feeling one has in the face of raw nature – though, I will elaborate, there is no "raw nature" when it comes to bodies, and specifically in this case, "the Hong Kong body." Nonetheless, the word usually designates the inadequacy of form to content. I would like to use this concept of "sublime" to understand the complex cultural formation of Hong Kong identity through the muscular body. As a sublime entity, this body is paradoxically a material signifier of that which is unsignifiable. This itself is a product of material conditions. Because of its historical specificity, Hong Kong culture is situated in between Chinese tradition and Western influence, but problematically, a commitment to Hong Kong cannot mean reclaiming native culture or identifying with British colonial traits, either of which will only eliminate the possibility of cultural agency. Hong Kong's cultural selfawareness is precisely an awareness of its "in-betweenness," its impurity, its difference at the origin, or its changing indeterminacy. This impossible representation of Hong Kong identity has been discussed perspicaciously and rigorously by a number of critics.[3] Here I concentrate, through a reading of how the muscular body is portrayed in popular cultural forms, on how the failed representation is inscribed as an essential part of the Hong Kong subject formation.

The pumped-up bodies of the kung fu movie stars and the heroic figures of the comic-books have a fantastic quality that cannot be fully articulated by historical interpretation. Although these bodies are the products of the history of Hong Kong, they cannot be approached directly as so many positive ontological entities that endorse a definite historical meaning of cultural identity. However, their peculiar quality does not refer to a timeless world or a place beyond history. On the contrary, these sublime bodies occupy an empty space without any positive content or intrinsic meaning, and their void can only subsequently be filled through the specificity of their particular historical milieu. What they indicate is only the impossibility of fixed definition. The sublimity of the muscular body thus creates an initially empty place for the emergence of the Hong Kong subject, which is correlatively embedded in this "hole" of identification. The body may fail to offer a completely coherent representation corresponding to Hong Kong subject formation, but its inadequate presentation constitutes the real dimension of this subjectivity. This is the reason why *either* a total denial of any symbolic meaning *or* a conventional historical explanation of the bodies represented in Hong Kong kung fu culture can never grasp the complicated mechanism of subject construction.

In a historical study on the construction of Hong Kong identity from the sixties onward, Matthew Turner argues that, after the political separation from China, the image of the Hong

Kong body was designed to fit the modern Western mode of health, posture and physique. He points out two particular types of Hong Kong male bodies popular at that time: those associated with Fei Jai and Mr. Hong Kong. Fei Jai was a rebellious teddy boy who gelled his long hair, wore sunglasses and led a "corrupted" Western lifestyle, whereas Mr. Hong Kong was a muscle-building competitor associated with the image of Western wrestling shows on television. Both types converge into the seventies' image of the popular movie star Bruce Lee and the comic-book figures of Wong Yuk Long's *Siu Lau Man* (Little Rascals), later renamed *Lung Fu Moon* (Dragon and Tiger Kids). Turner explains: "Icons of the Hong Kong male were transformed from the weaklings of earlier Cantonese comedies and given new identities as stylish playboys or muscular heroes. A unique combination of Western body building and Chinese Kung Fu (with an admixture of James Bond karate and Mainland flying action) were brought together in the figure of Bruce Lee and the characters of Wong Yuk Long's early comics."[4]

For Turner, the representation of the Hong Kong body functions almost like an ideological state apparatus (although Althusser's name is never mentioned in the text). As a chronicler of the social control of Hong Kong identity construction, Turner focuses on the ways in which the formation of identity is monitored to meet the political, economic and cultural demands of the times, how the individual in Hong Kong is interpellated as a Hong Kong subject. In this sense, Hong Kong identity is a mere reproduction of the existing power structure: the bodies are basically created and trained by the rules of the dominant system. However admirable his empirical studies of Hong Kong history, Turner's perception of the relationship between history, identity, and the body is thus based on a simple model of causality. It is always the result of a political cause that identity is designed, dissolved and rearticulated. Determined by a political break, the subjectivization of individuals into "Hong Kong people" occurred, according to Turner, in the sixties, which demarcates a "before" and an "after":

> Before the sixties, Hong Kong exhibited an ambivalent identity, like many displaced *huaqiao* (Chinese expatriate) communities and overseas Chinese . . . A decade later it was evident that local life-style was displacing traditional cultural attachments as the basis of identity, to the point where, in the mid-eighties the great majority of the population identified themselves as "Hong Kong people," not "Chinese people."[5]

Yet the clear historical cut in this analysis trims off the radical heterogeneity of the effect by tying it up neatly with the cause. Such an approach of mechanical determinism fails to acknowledge that the surface phenomenon itself could be more than the appearance of an underlying content. The body as a representation of Hong Kong identity is precisely not a transparent medium for straightforward historical explanations. The body should be thought in its specific autonomy in relation to Hong Kong subject formation.

Nevertheless, if Turner's approach is too direct, missing that dimension of Hong Kong subjectivity which resists historicization, I do not concur with some film critics who read Hong Kong kung fu culture as pure visual and aural spectacle and bliss either.[6] For those critics, the spectacle of kung fu has no historical or ideological association. Rather, it performs the function of undoing all narrative and representational fixities in its simple excitement, vitality and electricity.[7] In this view, the jouissance of bodily spectacle defies all meaning and designates the limit of historicization and ideological interpretation. The anti-historical understanding of Hong Kong muscles may succeed in substantializing the body as a new object of study, but it ignores the body's intimate connection with the political reality of the colonial city.[8]

In distinction to both of these approaches, I propose to understand the relationship between the cultural identity of Hong Kong and its body image by focusing on the unrepresentable, corporeal aspect of subject formation – that is to say, the body part that eludes a direct ideological critique and that cannot easily be symbolized in any objective historical sense. On the one hand, this bodily aspect is not a simple reflection of the meaning of history; it is always already a part of the historical transformation of Hong Kong self (re)construction. But, on the other hand, the unrepresentable corporeality can only be made sense of in its inherent connection with the historical changes of Hong Kong society. It is like a "remainder" of history which cannot be directly symbolized nor fixed by historical explanation; yet an ahistorical approach would entirely fail to grasp its existence.

The cultural identity of Hong Kong may not be readily articulated or presented in any positive terms, like distinct values, customs, or lifestyle. On the contrary, that identity is something which might be determined by a series of negativities and contradictory properties. To put it differently, Hong Kong identity may be accessible to the local inhabitants only in a way that both Chinese nationalist discourse and a Western global perspective fail to grasp or fully understand. But, at the same time, that identity is so fragile and unstable that it is constantly changed, dissolved, endangered, and threatened by the mere presence of other subjects, including new immigrants, British colonial bureaucrats, and Chinese communist officials. In the following, I examine Hong Kong's body culture (focusing primarily on kung fu cinema and comics) in relation to its subject formation and argue that the subject posited is not always a definite, substantial entity but is rather a site of indeterminacy or an ambivalent space to be filled out with different historical contents.

The hole punched out by Bruce Lee's body

Without any doubt, Bruce Lee was the most popular kung fu star in the West, and he has become a token for Hong Kong action cinema. If the image of Bruce Lee facilitates and promotes the construction of Hong Kong identity, the role of agency it plays is far more complicated than that of being an ideal ego for identification. When Lee came from the US to Hong Kong to make his first kung fu movie *The Big Boss* (1971), the Hong Kong Cantonese film industry was in a severe decline because of the competition from Mandarin films.[9] Lee's films were all originally dubbed and released in Mandarin.[10] He never spoke the common dialect (Cantonese) of the majority of Hong Kong people in any first release.[11] The characters Lee played were also more generically "Chinese" than distinguishably "Hong Kongese." He was broadly held as a "Chinese hero" who used the power and philosophy of kung fu to defeat the Westerner and the Japanese, arousing a Chinese nationalistic fantasy in the Hong Kong audience more strongly than any particular local identification.[12] If Lee's onscreen figure primarily advocated an encompassing Chinese national spirit, then how can we account for his contribution to the invention of a Hong Kong subjectivity?

It is only possible to clarify Lee's unlikely role in the formation of Hong Kong subjectivity by deviating from the traditional inquiry into the meanings of his filmic image.[13] What is at stake in understanding the connection between Bruce Lee and Hong Kong is neither a stable signifying link nor any positive causality, but rather the inherent inconsistency of Lee's signification. What prevents Lee's image from falling entirely into the category of a "Chinese hero" is paradoxically the kind of Chineseness invoked in his films. The China portrayed in Lee's films is a remote space emptied of social and political reality, an imaginary and void China with which Hong Kong inhabitants can associate. The nationalistic feeling stimulated by Lee's kung fu exercised its influence through this alienation and distance. As such, Hong Kong identity could be said to have derived from an ambivalent emotional attachment to a fictional China. The ambiguity cloaking a phantasy object of identification – the fictive China is further complicated by Lee's own background. His mother is Eurasian, and he was born in San Francisco; he married an American and was himself an American citizen. Before making the Mandarin films, he was already known to the people in Hong Kong through his appearance on the US television series *The Green Hornet*.[14]

Herein lies the impossibility of the linear determinism of Hong Kong identity through Lee's body. Consistency of identification derives from an inconsistency of the signification. If being the first Hong Kong movie star to become widely famous across the world qualifies Bruce Lee for a role in the constitution of Hong Kong subjectivity, there is nonetheless little trace of local culture in his movies. His fame is as a foreign body, an inconsistency in the field of symbolic signification. But it is precisely because of this lack of localism that a Hong Kong identification with Lee is possible. His alien body ("alien" both as a deficiently localized figure and as a superhuman screen image) gives new symbolic meaning to the community, even though – or because – he is not an integral part of it. The icon that his body image provides for identification is not immanent, but comes from afar; it does not belong to that symbolic

Figure 7.1 Bruce Lee
Courtesy of Photofest, New York

order which it is made to uphold, and, it even pierces a "hole" in the conventional signification of that identity. Suffice it to say that Lee's body is unable to offer a solid ground for locating a specific entity, "Hong Kong." However, this "hole" becomes the new symbolic center for identity construction. The invention of Hong Kong subjectivity is structured around this hollow space punched out by Lee's muscular body.

To illustrate this problem of causality further, I want to focus on the famous gimmick used in Lee's movies: the shrieks and wails he emits to disturb his opponents in combat. The tactics of shrieking or sneering at the opponent have been interpreted as bespeaking a profound bliss in the self, a reinforcement of Lee's own subject position.[15] But in my perception of Lee's films, though Lee's mouth is moving, the shrieks do not come from a particular source or a subject.[16] The animal-like voice is all pervasive and free-floating, unfixed to any definite visual object on the screen: it is not a noise caused nor uttered by any individual subject. Disembodied, this animal voice, this sound from nowhere, seems to have a life of its own, even as it is, conversely, looking for a body to fill out. The chain of cause and effect is thus somewhat reversed here. The ecstatic and intoxicating sound associated with Lee as star suggests more of a loss of control than mastery by any speaking subject. This mythic voice is an object that cannot be mastered by the subject, but is rather constitutive of that subject, acting precisely like an empty placeholder in the causal chain.

[. . .]

The outtakes of Jackie Chan

Bruce Lee's body reveals the hollowness of Hong Kong identity. What does the image of Jackie Chan, this well known muscle man, tell us about the mechanism of identity construction in Hong Kong? Over the last two decades, Hong Kong has changed from a local community to an international metropolis. Although Hong Kong culture may not accurately be described as a national culture, its colonial history and its need for a specific identity in face of the 1997 handover to China do not allow Hong Kong to let go its particular local elements. The muscular image of Jackie Chan developed over the years by Golden Harvest, a Hong-Kong-based multinational film production company, also reveals this ambiguity of being both local and international at once. As a result of this position, Chan is never like a conventional kung fu movie star since he occupies both a local and transnational space simultaneously. As well, he is more like a comic book hero become real, occupying the roles of hero and comedian simultaneously. Generally seen as the successor of Bruce Lee, Chan tells an American reporter in an interview: "'How can I get rid of the Bruce Lee shadow and be Jackie Chan? Then I look at Bruce Lee all the film. O. K. When Bruce Lee kick high, I kick low. When Bruce Lee punch, he is the superhero; when I punch, ahh!' – he shakes his hand. 'It *hurts*.'"[17] This is how the reporter tries to capture Chan's funny tone as well as the flaws in his English. Chan does not mind exposing his weakness to the public, which he does with good humor.[18]

The movies Chan makes are therefore more like action-packed comedies than traditional kung fu films. It is Buster Keaton, not Bruce Lee, who is Chan's role model. In every new movie, his ambition is to outdo the most daring stunts of the previous one. Yet in the movies he is never a kung fu master. In Bruce Lee's films, especially in *The Way of the Dragon* (1972), combat is a serious, intense duel between two equally powerful kung fu masters who have to perform a series of rituals before and during the fight: taking off their outer clothes, flashing their muscles to warm up, pausing when an opponent falls down, etc. By comparison, Chan's combat is a street fight. There are no rules, and it can happen in any place at any time. He does not even have the time to take off his street clothes and warm up. And though he is the star, the action sequences of Chan's films are not just solo performances; they heavily depend on collective work and coordination. Chan's movies are thus multiple loops of actions and stunts. The narratives are weak and the messages ambivalent: spectacular performance, not heroism, occupies the center stage. Indeed, a signature feature of Chan's films is the homage they pay, tongue in cheek, to stunt-driven action.

Chan's movies began a tradition of showing the outtakes of stunt mishaps behind the closing credits. No Jackie Chan fan will leave during the closing credits of his films. Significantly, it is precisely the outtakes of the flubbed stunts that create the myth of Jackie Chan. Portrayed as a comedian, a common man in the films, Chan becomes a superhero in his outtakes. The clips do not really debunk the illusionism of the movies. Instead, they reveal to the audience how hard Chan works. He may be only an ordinary human being – he makes mistakes and gets injured – but, precisely because he does not have an invincible body – real flesh-and-bone is imperiled before your eyes: these are not the workings of blue screens and computerized technologies – the stunts produce a phantasy effect. As with other films, viewer identification is with superhuman accomplishment. Yet, revealing the failed stunts explicitly acknowledges the existence of a subject willing to believe. The credibility of the film is solidified by this imaginary subject. Because of the presence of this believing subject, the outlandish stunts are given a reality status, even though they are just made for a movie. Through this combination of "real" and "imaginary" elements, the films confirm the "truth" of the spectacular stunts, and the audience is posited to identify with the "subject supposed to believe" even as its limits are exposed.

At first, there may seem to be no point in watching Chan fall fifty feet from a clock tower and hit the ground with his head (*Project* A), or jump off a railing in a department store and crash through several glass ceilings (*Police Story*), or hang dangling from a flying helicopter over the city of Kuala Lumpur and bump into a billboard on a skyscraper (*Super Cop*), or skip across a snowy mountain with only a sweatshirt to keep himself warm (*First Strike*). Clearly, his stunts are imbued with masochistic intensity for comic effects. However, these spectacular abuses of the human body perform another function as well. In the revelation of the outtakes, they become part of the structure of the entire "reality." In other words, it is the fantasy element (the subject supposed to believe) that gives consistency to the "reality" of Chan's body image. The international stardom of Chan emanates from the support of this phantasy identification with "unreal realism": the outtake's revelation of the enactment of the impossible.

In *Armour of God* (1986) directed by Chan himself, he plays an Indiana Jones character named Asian Hawk. He is a world famous adventurer who is good at stealing archaic treasures. Some satanic monks abduct his ex-girlfriend in order to force Asian Hawk to give them the "Armour of God" (an antique five-piece set). The Armour of God is like a "MacGuffin object"[19] in the movie. The MacGuffin is an essential but irrelevant object, around which all action turns. The object triggers off the story and the chase, but it has no significance in itself at all. Unlike the treasures of the Indiana Jones movies, the Armour of God has no magical power or special contents. It is not even mentioned at the end of the film. It is just a pure medium or empty form that instigates action and incites relationships among the characters. In many ways, the mission of Asian Hawk is itself like a MacGuffin. It has no purpose but to affirm the unconditional want for action. The hero is portrayed simply to satisfy Asian audiences' fantasies about the ideal image of the Asian hero before the Western gaze of highly developed societies: he is well respected by the Westerners and is driving a hi-tech sports car manufactured by Mitsubishi (which is also the film's sponsor), chasing other cars off-road in a European city. Between the African tribal group from whom he steals the God's Armour and the evil European monks with whom he battles, Asian Hawk denounces and sneers at all beliefs and rituals. He presents himself as a pure action hero supported by unlimited resources, but not motivated by any inner conviction. This is typical of Chan's films: in general, the image of Jackie Chan offers no ideological cause with which an audience might identify. As an icon and sublime figure, he is neither global nor particularly local. However, the pure action itself is the very thing that calls for identification: it does not signify but only indicates a space that gives a sense of reality to the impossible, non-existent subjectivity of Hong Kong.

The disappearance of bodies

From the eighties into the nineties, the representation of Hong Kong kung fu culture is losing its physical dimension. For instance as Ackbar Abbas argues, in Tsui Hark's martial arts movies, the real heroes are not the kung fu stars, but the special effects.[20] The bodies stand as an alibi for the "culture of disappearance."[21] He further elaborates that the problem new Hong Kong cinema faces is how to represent a subject which is always on the verge of disappearing. My notion of disappearance, however, has a different focus. As I have discussed above, the sublimation or the disappearing of the material bodies is a necessary condition to understand the history of identity constitution in Hong Kong. I would also suggest that Hong Kong identity is constructed historically at the expense of female bodies. Even though the positivity status of the masculine bodies in popular cultural forms is being weakened, it does not follow that women can play a more progressive role in representations. It is true that the muscle men (like Yuen Biao and Sammo Hung in Zu: Warriors from the Magic Mountain (1982) or Jet Li in Once Upon a Time in China (1991)) in Tsui's films are simply support props for the intensive effects work. Interest in kung fu technique and human athletic ability do not survive his obsession with creating a political allegory for Hong Kong history. Not bodies, but excessive technical prowess, over-rapid editing, breakneck-speed narration and video-game-like cinematography are what convey the impossible representation of Hong Kong culture in its chaotic transitional moment. Even while the phobia of losing one's virility and literally becoming a woman, as is evident in Swordsman II (1992) produced by Tsui, might suggest a materiality of bodies,[22] in Tsui's films, the Hong Kong body is actually no longer confined to any individual or sex. It encompasses a larger social body characterized by restlessness, high-speed movement, the force of dislocation, and instantaneous comings and goings. The only stabilizing force acting on the Hong Kong body is the constant play of flux or incessant motion.[23]

A different and subversive manipulation of the figure of the kung fu master is seen in Wong Kar-wai's two recent films, Ashes of Time (1994) and Fallen Angels (1995). Wong's ultra-stylistic productions not only redefine the kung fu and action genres (Ashes of Time is a historical martial arts genre freely adapted from the popular swordsman fiction by Louis Cha, and Fallen Angels is a hit man story with John Woo inspired violence), but they also reshape the heroes' bodies by filling them with desire for love. The heroes and the heroines in both movies fall in love with the ones they cannot have; like their opponents, all their love objects are elusive and unattainable. In *Ashes of Time*, the hero, Ouyang Feng, is deeply in love with a woman, but because of his pride, he does not express his love to her. The woman, who has the same affection for Ouyang, is angered by his pride and marries his brother. Ouyang exiles himself to the desert to hurt the woman who still cares for him, and each year, she sends someone to spy on him there. In *Fallen Angels*, the female assistant of the hit man falls desperately for the hero, even though circumstances forbid their rapprochement. As these descriptions suggest, the sexual drive in these two movies corresponds with the drive for combat, but love does not lead to body intimacy or physical consummation. Precisely because of the elusiveness and impossibility of the objects of love, desire can never be extinguished and action is futile. While the traditional action genre stresses the hero's masculinity and physical invulnerability, Wong's movies empty the bodies out and fill them with excessive emotional drives.

The bodies are haunted and persecuted by the pure desire for the impossible; the desire that dominates them presents itself as an unconditional imperative. Desire in its pure form has no object, yet it is only via this empty form that desire constructs and effects the subject. The spectacular imagery of the wild desert and the wide-angle shots of the Wan Chai streets supply somber ambience for their futile maneuvers of these subjects and objects. But since pure desire has no goal other than itself, movement will bring about nothing but the failure of action. Kung fu, violence, or love, as Wong's films show, cannot achieve anything; they only affirm action's invalidity and impotency. In both films, the action heroes have lost whatever it was that might have defined their beings. Their angst bespeaks the social atmosphere of Hong Kong at the near end of time.

A history of the body in Hong Kong popular culture is a history of its gradual disappearance. Indeed, no matter how show-offish the muscles from Hong Kong are, they are only a fetish that marks a sublime absence. Furthermore, it is a history almost monopolized by men, the female body absented to the margins of this scene. However, less than a year before the colony's return to China, a female windsurfer, Lee Lai-shan, won the only Olympic gold medal Hong Kong will ever have. Her muscular body intervenes in the politics of Hong Kong cultural identity and becomes a rich symbol of the city. Suddenly, the "real" female body poses a challenge to the "unreal" male body, giving rise to a new possibility of identity construction in Hong Kong. Her strong, independent image of womanhood is further confirmed by the relationship with her boyfriend who is also a windsurfer and is happy to play a supportive role in her career. Different from the physically powerful women portrayed in Hong Kong cinema, Lee no longer has to sacrifice her career in order to save her man's face.[24] But Lee's popular image has been quickly capitalized upon by sponsors. In a soap commercial, her body is ogled as she becomes a typical feminized object: a woman in the shower, her muscles are veiled by the bubbles. Not unlike Jackie Chan's body in his American media appearances, Lee's is an iconic representation not defined by her individuality but by some recognizable social types that characterize the dominant commodified culture. In Hong Kong, identity construction is not only a process of body building, but also a process of body vanishing.

Notes

I would like to thank Ackbar Abbas, Rey Chow, Lynne Joyrich, and Amelie Hastie for providing useful suggestions and comments on this paper.

1 Chan also appeared on Jay Leno's *The Tonight Show*, *Entertainment Tonight*, *The* MTV *Movie Awards*, and *The Academy Awards* around that time.

2 While grounded in an intellectual history extending from Loginus and Kant to more recent contemporary critics, my invocation of the notion of the sublime primarily stems from a colloquial understanding of the term in order to develop a specific concept that helps us understand better the cultural identity of Hong Kong.

3 The impossible representation of Hong Kong identity has been keenly discussed by a number of critics. See, for instance, Rey Chow, "Between Colonizers: Hong Kong's Postcolonial Self-Writing," *Diaspora* 2.2 (Fall 1992): 151–70 and her selection of articles *Xiezai jiaguo yiwai* |Alternative Perspectives on Hong Kong Culture| (Hong Kong: Oxford UP, 1995); Ackbar Abbas, "Building on Disappearance: Hong Kong Architecture and the City," *Public Culture* 6.3 (1994) and "The New Hong Kong Cinema and the Déjà Disparu," *Discourse* 16.3 (Spring 1994): 65–77; Ping-kwan Leung, *Xianggang wenhua* |Hong Kong Culture| (Hong Kong: Hong Kong Arts Center, 1995), *Xianggang wenhua kongjian yu wenxue* |Hong Kong Cultural Space and Literature| (Hong Kong: Youth Literary, 1996), *Yuejie shujian* |Letter Across Borders| (Hong Kong: Youth Literary, 1996) and "Liuchang de shujian: zenyang keyi tongguo bieren de kuanjia qu shuoziji" (The Fluent Letters: How to Look at Oneself through the Frame of the Other); *Evans Chan's To Liv(e): Screenplay and Essays* Wong Tak-wai, ed. (Hong Kong: Hong Kong University, 1996), 151–5.

4 Matthew Turner, "Hong Kong Sixties/Nineties: Dissolving the People" *Hong Kong Sixties: Designing Identity* Matthew Turner, ed. (Hong Kong: Hong Kong Arts Center, 1995), 38.

5 Turner, "Hong Kong Sixties/Nineties," 23–4.

6 The typical example is often found in non-academic popular writings, such as the following: "[I]n describing Hong Kong cinema . . . film-school polemics fail. There is no pointy-headed, white-wine-and-baked-brie philosophizing that adequately describes its 'scalding propulsion,' the force that blasts you out of your seat and rearranges your popcorn, because over-intellectualizing film denies the primary purpose of moviegoing: entertainment. And Hong Kong movies are, simply, some of the most entertaining films on the planet." See *Sex and Zen & A Bullet in the Head: The Essential Guide to Hong Kong's Mind-bending Films* Stefan Hammond and Mike Wilkins, eds. (New York: Fireside, 1996), 11. The popular reception of Hong Kong movies – especially of John Woo's films – in the West always celebrates their notorious scenes of violence. Many Western critics writing for popular magazines eulogize the excessive violence in Hong Kong cinema as ballet choreography or orchestration of pulverized bodies. The question of how the violence relates to the historical background, the semantic function and the narrative articulation is seldom raised. For a critique of such an ahistorical Western reception, see Julian Stringer, "'Your tender smiles give me strength': Paradigms of Masculinity in John Woo's *A Better Tomorrow* and *The Killer*," *Screen* 38.1 (Spring 1997): 25–41.

7 See, for instance, Claudine Eizykman, *La jouissance-cinéma*, (Paris: Union generale d'editions, 1976). See also Jillian Sandell, "Reinventing Masculinity: The Spectacle of Male Intimacy in the Films of John Woo," *Film Quarterly* 49.4 (Summer 1996): 23–34; Dana Polan, "Brief Encounters: Mass Culture and the Evacuation of Sense," *Studies in Entertainment: Critical Approaches to Mass Culture* Tania Modleski, ed. (Bloomington: Indiana UP, 1986), 167–9; Stuart M. Kaminsky, "Comparative Forms: The Kung Fu Film and the Dance Musical," in his *American Film Genre* (Chicago: Nelson-Hall, 1984), second edition, 73–80.

8 The recent scholarship on Hong Kong cinema, and John Woo's movies in particular, often sees the cinematic body of work as responsive to the political crisis of 1997. Hence, the cinema is a way to express the Hong Kong people's anxiety, uncertainty and vulnerability to the takeover of Chinese government. See Tony Williams, "Space, Place, and Spectacle: The Crisis Cinema of John Woo," *Cinema Journal* 36.2 (Winter 1997): 67–84; Stringer, "'Your tender smiles give me strength.'" Like Matthew Turner, these critics, though offering interesting readings of Woo's films, tend to over-emphasize the direct historical reflexivity of Hong Kong cinema.

9 Although Hong Kong people are Cantonese speaking, a lot of Mandarin films were produced in Hong Kong following the 1950s, nearly extinguishing Cantonese cinema in the early 1970s (only one Cantonese film was made in 1971–2). At the time, Mandarin films were more cosmopolitan, technically sophisticated, and related to the modern urban world. Cantonese films, with their lower budgets, were considered to be too parochial and of poor quality.

10 Lee was only able to complete four features in the three years before his untimely death in 1973. They are *The Big Boss, Fist of Fury* (also named as *The Chinese Connection*), *The Way of the Dragon*, and *Enter the Dragon*.

11 When Cantonese cinema revived and swept away the entire Mandarin film industry, Golden Harvest redubbed Bruce Lee's movies in Cantonese. As a child Bruce Lee had starred in several Cantonese films, such as *My Son Ah Cheung* (1950), *Thunder Storm* (1957), and *The Orphan* (1961). For biographical studies of Bruce Lee, consult Bruce Thomas, *Bruce Lee: Fighting Spirit* (Berkeley: Frog Ltd., 1994); Wen Juan, ed. *Li Xiaolong yanjiu* [The Studies of Bruce Lee] (Hong Kong: Just For Fun Book, 1992); Linda Lee, *The Bruce Lee Story* (Santa Clarita: Ohara Publications, 1989); Robert Clouse, *Bruce Lee: The Biography* (Burbank: Unique Publications, 1988).

12 One critic even argues that the popularity of Bruce Lee is intimately associated with the Chinese "Boxer Rebellion idea" and anti-Western and anti-imperialist attitudes of that time. See Cheng Yu, "Anatomy of a Legend" *A Study of Hong Kong Cinema in the Seventies*, ed. Li Cheuk-to (Hong Kong: Urban Council, 1984), 18–25.

13 Many studies on the meaning or the ideological content of Bruce Lee's films decode him as either a nationalist or a narcissist. See, for instance, Tony Rayns, "Bruce Lee: Narcissism and Nationalism," *A Study of Hong Kong Martial Arts Film*, ed. Lan Shing-hon (Hong Kong: Urban Council, 1980), 110–12; Stephen Teo, "The True Way of the Dragon: The Films of Bruce Lee," *Overseas Chinese Figures in Cinema*, ed. Law Kar (Hong Kong: Urban Council, 1991), 70–80.

14 This American connection of Lee is played up in the Hollywood film, *Dragon: Bruce Lee Story* starring Jason Scott Lee, which obviously attempts to reclaim Bruce Lee's body as an incarnation of the myth of the American dream. In the film, Lee is portrayed as a struggling immigrant who is able to overcome racial discrimination, smoothly developing a harmonious relationship with other minorities, fighting against the conservative Chinese and making his dream of success come true at the end. He is also described as a faithful husband and a responsible father.

15 See Rayns, "Bruce Lee: Narcissism and Nationalism," 112.

16 While this phenomenon is probably produced through the technical problem of the post-synched soundtrack, I believe its significance extends well beyond the technical dimension.

17 Fredrie Dannen, "Hong Kong Babylon," New Yorker 23 (7 August 1995): 33. Emphasis in the original.

18 Jackie Chan came from a poor family. His parents once offered to sell him for twenty-six dollars to a British doctor, and they later left him in a Beijing Opera training school for ten years when they migrated to Australia. He never received any formal education and only learned English in Los Angeles when he was sent by Golden Harvest to crack the American market in 1979. For the early history of Jackie Chan, see Cheng Long (Taipei: Linba chubanshe, 1981).

19 A MacGuffin object originates from a joke told by Alfred Hitchcock in an interview with Francois Truffaut. His joke goes as follows: MacGuffin is a Scottish name which relates to a story about two men on a train. One man says, "What's that package up there in the baggage rack?" The other man answers, "Oh, there is a MacGuffin." The first one asks, "What's a MacGuffin?" "Well," the other man says, "it's an apparatus for trapping lions in the Scottish Highlands." The first man says, "But there are no lions in the Scottish Highland." The other one answers, "Well, then that is no MacGuffin!" See Francois Truffaut, Hitchcock (New York: Simon & Schuster, 1985), 138.

20 See Ackbar Abbas, "Cultural Studies in a Postculture," Disciplinarity and Dissent in Cultural Studies, ed. Cary Nelson and Dilip Parameshwar Gaonkar (New York & London: Routledge, 1996), 298.

21 When he refers to Hong Kong culture as "a culture of disappearance," Abbas does not merely mean that its cultural specificity is going to be extinct after the handover to China in 1997. "Disappearance" is understood as a kind of pathology of cultural presence which no familiar modes of representation can contain. Abbas believes that filmmakers like Stanley Kwan and Wong Kar-wai are able to work with disappearance and invent a form of visuality that problematizes the visual itself. See Abbas, Hong Kong: Culture and the Politics of Disappearance (Hong Kong: Hong Kong UP, 1997).

22 This costume martial arts movie is about a man who, in order to learn a powerful fighting skill, pays the price of emasculating himself and transforming into a woman. Although the film implies that the foundation of phallic power is paradoxically based on the loss of penis, and the fluid sexual identity the film displays also reveals the gender confusion of today's situation; I still think a feminist critique of the film is valid. For a direct criticism of the film, see Tammy Cheung, "Who Are the Women in Hongkong Cinema?" Cinemas 3.2–3 (Spring 1993): 182–8. Cheung fails to offer a sophisticated reading of the film, but she has surveyed more than one hundred Hong Kong films made between 1989 and early 1993; she comes to the conclusion that, despite the increasing physical strength of the female roles on screen, they continue to be subordinate to men and are portrayed as those who are better at using their fists than their brains.

23 For a further discussion of Tsui Hark's movies, see my "Once Upon a Time: Technology Comes to Presence in China," Modern Chinese Literature 7.2 (Fall 1993): 79–96.

24 There were a number of blockbusters in the early nineties in which an invincible and skillful female character is depicted, such as Saviour of the Soul (1991), Justice, My Foot! (1992), Fong Sai Yuk (1993), and The Heroic Trio (1993). But these female characters are either unintelligent or contented to be housewives when they are not saving the world. See Tammy Cheung, "Who Are the Women in Hong Kong Cinema?"

PART THREE

THE AVANT-GARDE AND UNDERGROUND STAR

Introduction

This section moves beyond stardom in the popular narrative film to consider celebrity in other types of cinema: the avant-garde and the underground film. Clearly, these works circulate in a different context than commercial cinema, often involving ties to gay and political subcultures as well as to the world of galleries and museums. This section also explores the instance of the star/director: the individual who is not only the author of a filmic work but its primary screen presence.

Maria Pramaggiore's essay, "Performance and Persona in the U.S. Avant-Garde: The Case of Maya Deren," focuses on a rarely examined phenomenon in cinema study, namely the connections between experimental cinema and stardom. Pramaggiore acknowledges that Maya Deren was never a mass cultural figure. However, the tendency in academic criticism has been to seal off an analysis of her work and persona, relegating them to a separate sphere of cultural analysis that belongs "to the modernist claims to the autonomy of art." Certainly, there are differences between Deren's work and that of mainstream cinema, but this essay probes important ideological connections. Pramaggiore offers an analytic perspective from which to regard the points of contact between dominant and marginal cultures, particularly as both are determined by the ideology of individualism. For several generations of film students and for the growing cinematic culture conveyed through museum exhibition, Deren, the "mother of the American avant-garde," has become a canonical figure, fascinating for both her work, her life and her alluring, photogenic image. As director and actor in her own films, her work evokes the characteristics of stardom: exoticism, primitivism, youthfulness, and eroticism. Her persona also emphasized her bohemian lifestyle and her films (such as *Meshes of the Afternoon*) focused on her body and on different psychic states. In effect, what Pramaggiore's essay seeks to do is identify the common elements of celebrity status without violating Deren's innovative contributions to experimental cinema.

In his essay, on John Waters's famous gender-bending diva, "Camping with Lady Divine: Star Persona and Parody," Dan M. Harries explores the complex relations between mainstream stardom and questions of camp – revealing the various venues in which star value travels throughout the culture. Beginning with a discussion of the carnivalesque as derived from Bakhtin, Harries challenges negative assessments of the performer, Divine, as akin to a sideshow "freak" and focuses rather on the "subversive" aspects she exemplifies. He undertakes an analysis of the "multi-leveled operation of parody which occurs in the star persona of Divine." Among the levels that Harries identifies are the roles of androgyny, cross-dressing, and transvestitism, all of which are components of camp sensibility. Arguing against those critics who regard the exaggerated performances of femininity as misogynistic and as reinforcing patriarchal constructions, Harries asserts that Divine's image is not that of a transvestite in the films but of a man playing a woman, and, further, a gay man playing a woman. Thus, he argues that the parody is directed against all gender roles and, more particularly, Hollywood stardom and its versions of glamour. This essay thus raises a number of critical questions and controversies about the social and political effects of parody in the star system of underground film.

Performance and persona in the U.S. Avant-Garde

8

The case of Maya Deren

MARIA PRAMAGGIORE

Maya Deren's persona illustrates the similarities between practices of stardom in mainstream and alternative film, and Deren's use of film as a performative art highlights the relationship between film images and persona.

In his examination of the formative years of the Hollywood star system, Richard de Cordova calls for a "reassessment of the manufacturer's place" to balance a number of historical accounts which argue that public demand single-handedly fueled the creation of the star system.[1] Richard Dyer concurs with this approach, characterizing stars as commodities produced and circulated by a profit-making economic apparatus. Furthermore, in Dyer's view, stars embody and disseminate prevailing notions of what it means to be an individual.[2] De Cordova and Dyer consider the Hollywood manifestation of stardom but do not address the way star production functions in other contexts, such as that of avant-garde film.[3] Although the concept of stardom may seem antithetical to the avant-garde, the practice of star making is not: Patricia Mellencamp writes that avant-garde film in the United States has always had a star system of its own, where "success was not measured by money, cars, houses and designer fashion, it was embodied in famous names and landmark films, and fueled by gossip."[4] In keeping with Dyer and de Cordova's focus on the manufacture of stardom and following Mellencamp's characterization of stardom in the avant-garde, this essay examines one case of persona construction: that of Maya Deren, one of the most celebrated figures within alternative film culture.

Clearly Deren was not, and probably never will be, a mass culture figure in terms of name or image recognition. Nor was she a star product owned and marketed by a Hollywood studio. Nevertheless, Deren participated in a process of persona construction during the 1940s which looks surprisingly similar to the construction of mainstream film stars in that era. After her death in 1961, film scholars and filmmakers have carried on the work Deren began, celebrating her "legendary status" as the now-absent "Mother of the avant-garde"[5] who gave "birth" to U.S. avant-garde film.[6]

By examining Deren's extratextually constructed persona in relation to her film performances, I hope to provide insight into the ways that commodity capitalism informs avant-garde culture, despite modernist claims to the autonomy of art. My analysis also suggests that specific meanings and practices of stardom may not differ greatly between dominant and marginal film cultures, primarily because ideologies of individualism that infuse mass culture also influence alternative practices.

In the U.S. avant-garde, for example, a filmmaker's personal relation to his or her films is the object of a great deal of interest much the same way that mainstream film actors are connected in some personal way to their films. In fact, directorial auteurism has always been the dominant paradigm of stardom in alternative cinema.[7] Mellencamp comments, in somewhat ambivalent terms, that the growth of experimental film culture in the 1960s and 1970s depended upon the accessibility of the director through live appearances: "As the great film would reveal the hand of the artist, so could we meet him, in person. The 'personal' was both the glory and the pitfall of the movement, without a national structure of permanent exhibition . . . dependent on stalwart individuals."[8] This reification of the artist obeys the modernist logic of authorship Roland Barthes lays to rest, arguing that the author is a convenient fiction which imposes "a limit on that text . . . [and] furnish[es] it with a final signified."[9] Because avant-garde exhibition has been "clearly framed by presence and anecdote," Patricia Mellencamp cautions, the "personal appearance system . . . risk[s] placing 'meaning' totally within the author."[10] Along similar lines, but placing less emphasis on the cult of the individual, Jim Peterson argues that avant-garde film viewers depend upon filmmakers' appearances at screenings because they provide explanations to an audience engaging in "problem solving" at cognitive and thematic levels.[11]

Avant-garde film spectators, then, may expect that film viewing in itself will constitute an event, framed as it often is by the live appearance of the filmmaker.[12] Thus, the distinction between filmgoing as event and on-screen events may not be as definitive for avant-garde film culture as it has been for Hollywood cinema. Whereas de Cordova posits a shift in attention from exhibition as performance "toward . . . the performance of those who appeared in films"[13] as one precondition for the emergence of the Hollywood star system, this shift may not accurately describe avant-garde cinema spectatorship. I am not suggesting that avant-garde spectators are necessarily resistant or critical, only that active viewing and expectations differ across mainstream and alternative contexts.[14] Furthermore, on-screen performances and the live exhibition event converge through the figure of the filmmaker, the director/actor/star who often appears on screen and in person. Because the filmmaker serves as both director and actor, director-as-auteur and actor-as-auteur models are not mutually exclusive.

In this manner, avant-garde film culture, like mainstream cinema's star system, links stardom to historically specific notions of individualism. Unlike mainstream cinema, however, U.S. avant-garde cinema couches individualism in the specifically modernist vocabulary of the artist's role in – and alienation from – society.[15] A filmmaker's live appearances confirm the status of the film object as art and the filmmaker's status as artist. In the process, historical and cultural ideas about the artist come to inform star discourses.

An examination of the ongoing construction of Maya Deren offers insight into the way stardom has operated in an avowedly oppositional subcultural context, that of experimental film culture in the United States in the mid-twentieth century. I analyze the manufacture of Deren's persona through live appearances at film screenings, film reviews and interviews, and the circulation of her photographic image and conclude that Deren's marketing strategy does not differentiate avant-garde film culture from mainstream film as much as might be expected, given the anti-Hollywood rhetoric of the U.S. avant-garde. I discuss the 1940s "trance" films *Meshes of the Afternoon* (1943), *At Land* (1944), and *Ritual in Transfigured Time* (1946) in terms of the relationship between Deren's performances and persona. I argue that Deren's promotional efforts helped create an image of the modernist artist-auteur (inflected by contemporary discourses of gender), whereas her multiplied and fragmented film protagonists refuse to "guarantee" textual meaning through persona. In fact, Deren's films, which draw heavily from her study of dance and ritual possession, explicitly deconstruct notions of individualism and engage an aesthetic of depersonalization. My concluding remarks point out that Deren's film performances and her marketing activities reflect an ethic of participation, an aesthetic and political practice which in some ways does link Deren's promotional work to her formal contributions to experimental cinema.

Marketing persona

Maya Deren was an expert at manipulating images: although committed to exploring their aesthetic potential, she was no innocent when it came to exploiting their commercial appeal. In a 1945 letter to Sawyer Falk, her former mentor at Syracuse University, Deren suggested a media event to publicize a screening of Meshes: "if, by chance, you have made any stills, we could use them in the advertising and in whatever program we print. Add to this a picture of yourself which would, most likely, get into the downtown papers."[16] Personalizing the event, marketing the film by publishing portraits of locals such as Falk and the film director herself, was characteristic of Deren's promotional strategy. She may have learned about such tactics as a writer for the Syracuse Post-Standard or as a publicity director at Syracuse University (two items listed on her 1941 résumé).[17] Deren also had the opportunity to gain marketing experience as secretary, publicist, and sometime chauffeur to anthropologist and choreographer Katharine Dunham, with whom she toured just prior to making her first film in 1943. Millicent Hodson, coeditor of the first volume of The Legend of Maya Deren: A Documentary Biography and Collected Works, notes that "[Deren] used [a] photo on posters and flyers to publicize her screenings and film business. It heralded her arrival at colleges and museums as she traveled around the country, urging visual freedom from Hollywood and promoting independent production and distribution."[18] The photograph Hodson refers to is the well-known frame enlargement from Meshes of the Afternoon, a shot which has become an icon and visual mantra for aficionados of avant-garde film.

The shot captures Deren in an apparent act of contemplation: standing at a window, she is literally caught in the act of looking through the glass. The camera's soft focus is enhanced by the screening or veiling effect of the glass window, rendering an abstract, unblemished vision of Deren's face. Anaïs Nin, an acquaintance of Deren's, wrote of the shot: "When Sasha [Deren's second husband, Alexander Hammid] filmed her, as he loved her and found her beautiful, he caught a moment when Maya appeared behind a glass window, and, softened by the glass, she created a truly Botticelli effect."[19]

Nin's reference to Botticelli's Primavera brings the rhetoric of classical painting to bear on this portrait of Deren. The portrait's cultural work, however, was more akin to that of the photographs Hollywood studios circulated in the popular press to mythologize their star products. The film industry had perfected the use of photographs as promotional weapons as early as 1910,[20] and by the 1940s glamour photography was an industry of its own, with its own representational conventions.

Images of female glamour during the 1940s, for example, differed from the "cosmetic, refined" glamour embodied by Marlene Dietrich and Carole Lombard because they emphasized "naturalness."[21] Naturalness was the term applied to photographs taken at locations, such as at the star's home, on the set, or on tour with the USO, rather than in a studio. Natural shots appeared to be candid rather than posed compositions, although they too were posed.[22] Deren's enigmatic image from *Meshes* is poised between the pale Madonna of the *Primavera* and the dominant standards of 1940s glamour: although not candid, the shot appears to be a moment captured by, rather than posed for, the camera. Deren's loose, informal hairstyle and simple clothing emphasize her "naturalness," and her gesture at the window, despite her gracefully curved hands, appears to be an everyday gesture, not an actorly or exaggerated stance.

The visual rhetoric of "naturalness" encompasses Deren's physical characteristics as well. Both classical painting and glamour photography associate female beauty with a regularity of female features, either prohibiting or masking racial and ethnic variability.[23] Deren's prominent facial features are perhaps more suited to the code of 1940s naturalness than to the slinky artifice of the previous decade's beauty queens – not least because, according to the press and Deren's personal friends, her appearance and behavior were considered "ethnic," "exotic," and bohemian.

Deren's friends' and acquaintances' comments regarding her appearance and personality emphasize "exotic" qualities underscored by her "ethnic" physical features, including her stocky physique, and her flair for the dramatic in clothing and behavior. Anaïs Nin called her "Maya, the Gypsy, the Ukrainian gypsy, with wild frizzy hair, like a halo around her face."[24] Alexander Hammid told the coeditors of *The Legend*, "[Maya] had a great flair for Russian-like clothing. She sewed very well and she made her own fantasy clothes, kind of folksy, embroidery type."[25] Third husband, Teiji Ito, remembered: "Maya was always a Russian. In Haiti she was a Russian. She was always dressed up, talking, speaking many languages and being a Russian."[26] In her diary, Anaïs Nin emphasized a "primitive" quality about Deren's face by first naming and then displacing Deren's ethnicity entirely: "She was a Russian Jewess. Under the wealth of curly, wild hair, which she allowed to frame her face in a halo, she had pale-blue eyes and a primitive face. The mouth was wide and fleshy, the nose with a touch of South Sea-islander fullness."[27] It is not surprising that these facial emblems of Deren's "exoticism" and "primitivism" are not the features that invite comparison to the face of the woman in Botticelli's painting. Instead, the glass has the effect of regularizing, perhaps "softening" Deren's features. This abstraction, this flattening of Deren's facial features may explain why the shot is likened to classical European art, why it worked so well as a promotional photograph in the United States from the mid-1940s onward, and why Deren used the shot to publicize her work.[28]

Patricia Mellencamp and the coeditors of *The Legend of Maya Deren* question Deren's choice of this particular photograph to represent herself. The coeditors conclude that Deren sought to preserve not her youth or beauty but "the transparency of the glass" because she saw "in many dimensions at once."[29] Mellencamp, however, argues otherwise: "Deren knew about the gap between the real and the appearance, the performer and the filmmaker, women and woman, the contradictions to which women are held."[30] Her comment suggests that Deren's promotional strategy was just that: unavoidably implicated in ideology and economics, specifically in terms of the marketing of women's bodies in the Hollywood film industry and in U.S. culture generally. Although Deren was not owned by a Hollywood studio, she constructed herself, in part, in the vocabulary of the dominant cinema. Named for the actress Eleanora Duse, Eleanora (Maya) Deren created a persona by exploiting the public's desire for particular kinds of images of women. A case in point is the photograph of Deren which appeared in *Glamour* in 1946. Here Deren does adopt a pose: hair swept back, arms behind her, smiling winsomely as she gazes off to her right, she assumes the posture of a glamour girl, even as the curves of her back and neck reveal a self-conscious stiffness. Deren's "exotic" difference is hinted at through her beaded necklace, and her body is both framed and shielded from view by the chair back in a "peek-a-boo" rather than overtly exhibitionist fashion. This photograph, like the Botticelli, adheres to the visual codes of commodified female beauty, albeit in the historically specific vernacular of glamour photography rather than the supposedly timeless vocabulary of high art.

As this shot and the numerous other photographs which accompanied interviews and reviews of her films suggest, Deren's persona capitalized upon her physical appearance and bohemian lifestyle as much as, if not more than, her technical explorations and rigorous film theory. An interview published in the *New York World-Telegram* on April 17, 1946, opens with the following statement: "A good deal of what Maya Deren says about her creative work in motion pictures sounds like long-hair double talk. But it is as agreeable to listen to as she is to look at."[31] The hook for a Louise Levitas review is Deren's appearance: "Miss Deren, who you can see is as photogenic as this month's Miss Subways, is a movie producer on a skinny shoestring."[32] A caption accompanying a photograph in *Esquire* in December 1946 reads: "Maya Deren experiments with motion pictures of the subconscious, but here is finite evidence that the lady herself is infinitely photogenic.

Deren's attractiveness was often linked to what critics described as her bohemian, Greenwich Village lifestyle. Manny Farber's *New Republic* review (October 1946) refers to Deren as a "Greenwich Village purist who has the ambition, belief in her own genius, love for esthetic verbalizing, ginger and push of a whole colony of artists."[34] Mary Braggiotti's "Classicism on a Shoestring" (1946) leads with a description of Deren that conflates an aggressively coifed and passionate bohemian artist with woman as image: "A lot of people casually mention motion picture-making as an art. Down in Morton St., in Greenwich Village, lives a small-sized young woman with large gray eyes and an aggressive cloud of curly brown hair, whose belief in films as an art form amounts to a passion."[35] Reviews that emphasize Deren as "agreeable to look at" may not directly undermine her status as an artist, yet they do shift the focus to her appearance. Clearly, the discourses of glamour girl, ambitious filmmaker/promoter, and bohemian artist clash with and inform each other in these extratextual discourses.

A number of reviewers relate Deren's film work to her poetry and dance, promoting her as a multifaceted modern artist. Deren herself actively sought to be identified as an artist and to define film as an art form: she excerpted these reviews in a four-page promotional brochure entitled "Cinema as an Independent Art Form."[36] Her assistant, Miriam Ashram, recalls: "A lot of her efforts had to do with how one separates oneself from the rest of the world. In her case, the rest of the world meant the non-artists, that's all. . . . . Self-sufficiency was the artist's pride – the idea that one's artistry should extend itself to every aspect of daily living."[37] Deren embraced the dominant concepts defining the modern artist, including the necessity of living for one's art and the inevitable alienation from mainstream society.

Deren's portrait, her films, and her persona,[38] not for sale in any conventional way, were nevertheless products which fueled interest in and consumption of avant-garde film. Deren's picture personality enhanced her own "legendary" status, publicized experimental filmmaking as noncommercial, iconoclastic art making, and encouraged the serious contemplation of such films. Lauren Rabinovitz writes that "Deren became the best known representative of the postwar independent cinema discourse, perhaps because she herself was the object of attention as often as the films and ideas."[39] These filmmaking and film-promoting activities consumed Deren's energies through the 1940s.

The difficulties of exhibiting and distributing experimental films during this period cannot be overestimated. Deren reportedly began screening her films on the wall in her New York apartment and, when friends of friends began asking to see them, she arranged theater showings and college and university screenings and sent out a rental price list to any organizations that might have an interest in experimental film. In January 1946, Deren "averaged 7 university or museum rentals of the film program per month" and lectured twice a month at screenings.[40] Ultimately, she arranged for the Provincetown Playhouse screening in February 1946 which made history in its own right and encouraged the development of other venues such as Amos Vogel's Cinema 16.

Deren not only developed exhibition channels but did so with what David Curtis calls a "dynamic approach to the screening of films by the film-makers themselves that led to a complete restructuring of non-theatrical distribution in the United States."[41] Deren's performance-based approach to exhibiting avant-garde film, while bound up in the economics of independent film distribution, also reflects a modernist aesthetics of presence wherein the author – in this case, the attractive, bohemian artist – adds an important layer of meaning to the text.

There is no doubt that the Botticelli photograph played a particular role in creating Deren's persona and perpetuating her singular status in avant-garde film history. After her death, Deren's "legend waned, almost to the point of obscurity," write Hodson, Neiman, and Clark, yet the *Meshes* portrait "played a vital role in keeping the legend alive, appearing, so it seemed, every season."[42] That portrait also adorned the program for the 1994 Society for Cinema Studies conference, held at Deren's alma mater, Syracuse University. Another photograph of Deren (dancing and immersed in the ocean) is featured on the cover of Stan Brakhage's recent book,[43] and a shot of Deren behind her camera is one of the postcards Anthology Film Archives routinely sends out. Deren's image thus continues to circulate as a signifier of avant-garde film, although now primarily within film studies circles.

Certainly one must ask if Deren could have secured recognition for noncommercial filmmaking if she had not exploited her public's desire for a particular kind of star – one whose glamorous exoticism was matched by her bohemian lifestyle and her ambition. It is important to remember that the period in which Deren's legend arose was a period in which visual artists such as Jackson Pollock and Andy Warhol were celebrated for their public and private lives as well as for the works they produced. Furthermore, academic and popular film criticism seized upon the notion of auteurism during the 1950s, encouraging a cult of the film director in mainstream cinema that persists, although its intensity cannot rival the idolatry of the film actor.

Deren was by no means the first avant-garde filmmaker in the United States.[44] Yet, she has been designated experimental film's most prominent practitioner and, in the still-pervasive ideology of female domesticity, its "mother." Deren's status as the "mother" of avant-garde film, a comment Stan Brakhage credits to James Broughton, can be read as a trivialization of Deren's promotional work (merely motherly nurturance) and a conflation or displacement and domestication of her public efforts to the private sphere of familial relationships. The shift from bohemian artist to maternal figure suggests an anxiety of origins and, perhaps, a desire to embrace the oppositional stance Deren and others proclaimed for film artists without relinquishing traditional notions of gender.[45] Certainly her early death contributed to her unique location within the avant-garde as well. If absent mothers are figures of both resentment and reverence, then a dead mother whose much-circulated image resembles that of a classical Madonna is particularly likely to enjoy the latter.

Deren's participation in the circulation of her "Botticellied" image implicates her in the star-making apparatus of commodity capitalism, where images become commodities. The shot from *Meshes* operated and still operates as a fetishized commodity, but its cultural work differs from that of commercial cinema's artifacts in several crucial respects. Deren's marketing strategy was designed to encourage noncommercial filmmaking among artists, not to consolidate a financial empire. Deren helped to develop new perspectives on film art as she promoted her work at universities and museums. Certainly her legend is infused with notions of the importance and exoticism of the modern artist as alienated individual, notions that Deren herself shared. And certainly Deren's persona was and still is tied to her appearance and bohemian lifestyle.

It is not my purpose to indict Deren for participating in the process of persona construction; rather, I am interested in examining the contradictions that arise in the context of oppositional social practices. I am not surprised that some of Deren's promotional activities resemble those of the commercial film industry. The ideology of individualism, embodied in the ambitious and seductive star, artist, or auteur (or all three), captures the imagination of and speaks to the myriad desires of spectators and would-be practitioners and, in this manner, becomes mainstream and experimental cinema's most powerful tool of self-promotion.[46]

Performance and persona in Deren's films

The particular meanings accruing to a star persona are drawn from film roles and extratextual discourses, according to de Cordova. Deren's film performances, however, present more than merely a counterpoint to her promotional work. The film "roles" do not help to seamlessly construct a star persona; in fact, they contradict the assumptions upon which persona construction depends by undermining the self-containment and stability of the individual. Deren's film performances and experimental techniques deconstruct oppositions – interiority versus exteriority, surface versus depth, image versus reality – which help define the individual as self-sufficient, integrated, authentic, and stable.

Three of Deren's 1940s films, aptly named "trance" films by P. Adams Sitney,[47] explore the visual implications of simultaneously assuming the positions of object and subject, agent and action, observer and observed. Deren's fragmentation and multiplication of her body in these films suggests more than a reversal of the subject–object dichotomy, however. In *Meshes*, *At Land*, and *Ritual in Transfigured Time*, Deren questions the artifice of the visually represented individual. The films manipulate images in the formal sense in which all films use images, but, more importantly, they are concerned with issues of mobility in relation to Deren and her images and with the camera's ability to capture, create, and participate in movement. Deren's persistent interest in dance and ritual, expressed most overtly in her book and unfinished film on Haitian religious practices, *Divine Horsemen: The Living Gods of Haiti*,[49] manifests itself in these films as an obsession with images of bodies in motion and an exploration of the implications of movement for the individual body.

Deren's interest in dance preceded her work in cinema. She toured the country with African American anthropologist, dancer, and choreographer Katharine Dunham in the early 1940s, in part because she was interested in collaborating with Dunham, whose master's thesis concerned ritual dance in Haiti. In her letter of introduction to Dunham, Deren writes of her "very deep feeling for the dance with some uncultivated talent" and of her desire to write a children's book on dance which would be "anthropological but not academic."[50]

Catrina Neiman writes that Deren's film career "deflected" her study of Haiti.[51] Deren published an article on religious possession in dancing in 1942. Alexander Hammid remembered her interest in possession, trance, and dance: "I think she must have had some notions about Haitian rituals which always involve dancing in a kind of trance-like state, that's also how the Bali dancing interested her, and that's where possession came in. A dancer, like a whirling dervish, working up motion and then extending it – the dancer seems to be possessed by another being."[52]

Annette Michelson argues that Deren's socialist activities predisposed her toward collectivity; this, Michelson explains, is why she developed an aesthetics of anonymous ritual rather than of individualistic psychology.[53] It may be that Katharine Dunham's emphasis on "primitive" rhythms and collectivities in motion deepened Deren's interest in the relationship between movement and depersonalization.[54] Whatever the impetus, Deren's mannered acting, her use of repetitive, ritualized gestures in place of narrative continuity, and her fondness for matches on action that distribute movement across performers' bodies all promote the sense of bodies subsumed by forces different from and larger than the individual will.

Deren's films treat movement as a force which mediates subjective and objective experience as an event which is not independent of bodies but is independent of any one person's body. In *Ritual in Transfigured Time*, Deren joined "together a shot of one person beginning a movement and another person continuing it and still another completing it. These shots are held together not by the constant identity of an individual performer, but by the motional integrity of the movement itself, independent of its performer."[55] Movement and repetition – both that of the camera and of the actors – depersonalize her films and connect filmmaking to ritual:

> I have called this new film ritual, not only because of the importance of the quality of movement . . . but because a ritual is characterized by the de-personalization of the individual. . . . The intent of such a depersonalization is not the destruction of the individual; on the contrary, it enlarges him beyond the personal dimension, and frees him from the specializations and confines of "personality."[56]

This enlargement or extension beyond the individual is made possible because the camera can represent movement so that it no longer is associated with a single body. Deren's camera choreography renders movement in ways that reorganize subject and object categories.

In particular, Deren uses motion and choreography to animate: "if it can move, it lives. This most primitive, this most instinctive of all gestures: to make it move to make it live. So I had always been doing with my camera . . . nudging an ever-increasing area of the world, making it move, animating it, making it live."[57] To animate the world, Deren does not merely "add" a category of objects that move. Rather, the act of animation forces one to reconsider the entire structure of movement and the role and location of the individual object/body. In each of the three films I discuss, Deren unsettles traditional relationships between bodies and motion and questions the stability and cohesiveness of the individual, explicitly critiquing gender relations and the politics of image production in the process.

Meshes of the Afternoon

Deren's first film was a collaboration with her second husband, Czech filmmaker Alexander Hammid. As a result, Meshes bears a strong resemblance to Hammid's own first film, Aimless Walk (1930), particularly in terms of the iconography of the doubled self.[58]

Meshes appears to record a woman taking an afternoon nap in a house whose interior becomes increasingly and surprisingly gothic, given that the dream takes place, in Manny Farber's words, "on a lazy California day in a stucco bungalow."[59] By depicting the dreamer's imaginative representations of herself and meshing those dream representations with the film's initial "reality," the film questions the stability of vision, the power of (self-) images, and the integrity of the individual. Deren acts as the dreaming protagonist whose body is both divided and multiplied; her movements are repeated, and certain inconsistencies arise which are incapable of recuperation in the figure of the initial dreamer. Deren's notes suggest that the film "does not record an event which could be witnessed by *other* persons."[60] But in fact, the point-of-view structure is such that no person within the film could witness all the events, not even the dreamer who appears to be the origin of the film's events.

Repetition and symbolism displace narrative in Meshes. The use of spatial and temporal triples – in the stairway sequences and through the three dream doubles – ensures that the film conveys a mood of obsessive, ritualistic reiteration.[61] A key falls out of Deren's hand before she enters the house and reappears from a different location (e.g., her mouth) each time a dream double attempts to enter the house. Deren watches her double chase a robed, mirror-faced figure and enter the house three times; she and her dream doubles climb and fall down the stairs in pursuit of the figure. The three dream doubles confer over the dining room table, apparently determining which one will kill the dreamer. When the third double approaches Deren with a knife, the now-restless dreamer is awakened by the kiss of her male lover, played by Hammid.

We are encouraged to think the dream has ended when the lover hangs up the telephone Deren left off the hook prior to the dream. Yet, the dream is not over; for after she follows him upstairs to the bedroom, his sexual caress, which visually parallels her earlier autoerotic caress prior to her nap, incites her to slash him with a knife. Her gesture reveals that the space where his head appeared has become, or always was, a mirror – possibly the mirror face of the robed figure in which the woman has not been able to see her reflection. The mirror shatters: through a frame of broken mirror we see the ocean, and the next shot depicts shards of a mirror falling onto a sandy beach. In the final scene, the male lover enters the house to find the dreaming woman in her chair covered with seaweed and apparently dead. These final point-of-view shots are inconclusive, however: if the dreamer's imaginative world seeped into the film's "reality," then viewers must also question the male lover's "reality."[62]

P. Adams Sitney argues that the woman in Meshes "encounters objects and sights as if they were capable of revealing the erotic mystery of the self."[63] Sitney is correct in observing that objects, vision, and the erotic are important to the film's construction of a repressed and resistant female sexuality and subjectivity. Sitney's is one of several excellent readings that provide insight into the film's psycho-sexual tensions and suggest their source in the Deren–Hammid relationship.[64]

My focus, however, is on the fact that objects and sights in this film, most importantly the protagonist's sights of her fragmented and multiplied self, undermine vision as a sense which offers access to the truth of the individual. This process is not without gender implications, of course; the notion of woman as knowable through her image is one that the film takes issue with. Deren argued that photographic images always refer to other images but also constitute their own reality,[65] and her images emphasize that constructed, photographic reality at the expense of the referential reality of the subject–effect. The framing of Deren's face by its own reflection in the Botticelli shot, for example, foregrounds that vision cannot guarantee one's position – we see the face and its reflection as both objects and subjects. Later in the film, an image of Deren's moving reflection in the knife blade echoes and answers the Botticelli shot by demythologizing and, in fact, deforming Deren's face.

Lauren Rabinowitz writes that in *Meshes* "the relation of subject to object is reversed: the woman becomes passive while the objects act aggressively."[66] Yet bodies and inanimate objects are not easily distinguishable as either subjects or objects in *Meshes*, Deren's treatment of the properties of subjects and objects thwart our expectations regarding the definitions of those categories. For example, the sequence in which the dreamer enters the house contains a shot of a knife falling out of a loaf of bread. The key the woman drops early in the film bounces down the outdoor steps in slow motion. Later, the woman is forced down the stairs several times and in several different ways. In each scene, an "object" falls down, yet each time the repetition of the act of falling is complicated by the peculiar behavior of the object itself. By virtue of the slow motion filming, the key seems to dance in the air, to be suspended in its rebound from each step, and to almost intentionally avoid capture by the hands that seek it. The dream figures, however, resist falling down the stairs; one grips the edges of the stairs, and another moves down and up the stairs, coming to rest in a variety of locations on the staircase in a series of disconnected shots. Inanimate objects like the key are fluid and mobile in this film, whereas the human bodies move stubbornly and appear gravity-bound.[67] The knife easily slides from the bread onto the table, yet it initiates the fall by an apparently self-induced pulling away from the density of the bread. In these moments, the behavior of the objects does not conform to expectations regarding the volitional nature of human bodies (which move according to the will of the subject) and things (which are objects acted upon by subjects).

Furthermore, the interplay of subjective and objective camera angles prohibits any clear distinction between the dreamer and the dreamed event, a confusion emphasized by the woman's apparent death at the end of the film. The cameras positioning varies from subjective (in the tunnel zoom shot that begins the dream sequence) to objective (we see the dreaming Deren from positions that are neither her optical point of view nor that of any of the doubles). Neither position, nor the combination of them, provides a stable ground from which to assess the dreamer's identity or even her bodily integrity. This ambiguous camerawork is signaled in the opening sequence, where the establishing shot of the street and house reveals the protagonist's body in shadow; viewers see her "whole" body only as a silhouette.

By investigating the problems of the individual body in terms of subject, object, singularity, and multiplication, *Meshes* makes it apparent that conventional films construct personas through single-bodied images, conventional point-of-view structures, and realist acting conventions. The film probes the relationship between the real (presumably the dreamer) and the role (the dream doubles), ultimately confounding the distinction between the two. Annette Kuhn writes: "In effecting a distance between assumed persona and real self, the practice of performance constructs a subject which is both fixed in the distinction between role and self and at the same time, paradoxically, called into question in the very act of performance."[68] The multiplied representation of the female protagonist produces a distinction between the dreamer (self) and the three dream doubles (roles), then calls that distinction into question. The use of Deren herself as dreaming and dreamed woman/women, the agency and autonomy of the dream doubles (they apparently succeed in doing violence to the dreamer), and the complex use of camera angles and editing confound the distinction between "role" and "self." The film thus calls into question the continuity, stability, and location of the ostensible "self" or subject while at the same time confirming the power of images – and, importantly, women's images of themselves – to produce their own realities.

At Land

The title of this 1944 film is a pun that reverses "at sea," and the opening scene cites the final scene of *Meshes*: the ocean's waves roll (in reversed-motion photography) as Deren's body is washed up on the sand. In the scenario for *At Land*, Deren describes the woman's relationship with the ocean in these terms: "She watches the sea desert her with inactive longing, accepting the sand which, as she dries off, slowly collects around her."[69] Deren's language reflects the reversed relationship between the human as active subject and the sea as passive object – the sea "deserts" the woman, and she inactively longs for it. As in *Meshes*, the woman confronts a hostile and uncaring environment, although the settings are not claustrophobic domestic spaces but are oceans, fields, and other public spaces. Unlike *Meshes*, where the protagonist is multiplied, embodied four times over, here she is single and decidedly solitary until the concluding sequence, often "pass[ing] invisibly among [the] people" in the film.[70]

Repetitive motions and Deren's body structure the film. The montage editing, organized around Deren's body and her eyeline matches, juxtaposes vastly different locations but presents them as continuous. In a sense, Deren's body performs the work of continuity editing because her body and the chess piece she pursues are the figures that create graphic and narrative connections among the scenes.[71] Her body stretches across these spaces to create continuity, yet she is also fragmented because she occupies, and sutures together, impossible spaces.

After she emerges from the sea, Deren crawls from a piece of driftwood on the beach up to a table; eyeline matches suggest that her body occupies both spaces simultaneously. She crawls along the table, unnoticed by the people sitting at the table, and spots an unusual chess game. The chess pieces move themselves across the board. When a white piece moves itself off the board, she watches intently; like the key in *Meshes*, however, it escapes her, tumbling into a stream of water. Deren then encounters a man along a country road and enters a house in which a man lies in a bed and stares at her. A cat suddenly appears in her arms and leaps from them, initiating the motion which allows her to escape from the room. In the final scene Deren returns to the beach and watches two women play chess. Deren steals the white queen as it is about to be conquered and runs down the beach in a series of shots

Figure 8.1 Maya Deren in *At Land* (1944)
Courtesy of Photofest, New York°

edited so that Deren is seen looking at herself from several locations and so that she appears to make extremely rapid progress across vast sand dunes.

Body doubling and division occur not only in terms of Deren's body in the final sequence but also in the sequence where Deren encounters the man. Her first male companion, presented in two-shots with Deren and in close-ups, is Hammid. Through cuts, he metamorphoses into film critic Parker Tyler and then into composer John Cage. The man's transformation differs from Deren's self-multiplication in *Meshes*, however. In *Meshes*, Deren's subjective dream state motivates her fragmentation into dream doubles whose bodies are identical but who behave differently. In *At Land*, the multiplication of the male figure results in different male bodies but similar behavior. Like the *Meshes* dream doubles, each man appears slightly more hostile than the last, a trait emphasized near the end of the scene, when the final man walks too fast for Deren to keep up. The nature of the interaction with Deren, the physical movements, and the relative location of the seemingly generic man does not vary; what changes is the physical body which inhabits the location. Deren's body creates continuity in relation to the ever-changing man. The social relation between the men and the woman – expressed in physical proximity and facial expression – seems prearranged and scripted. From the perspective of the female protagonist in the film, the physical distinctiveness of each man is irrelevant. The "dance" that the woman performs with the series of men constitutes a ritualized relation, recalling the tension-charged relationship between the dreamer and her lover in *Meshes*.

In the film's final scene, Deren watches the women play chess on the beach, strokes their hair in a sensual gesture, and then steals the white queen as it is about to be taken. Her triumphant run down the beach seems to celebrate the capture of the queen and the escape from oppressive social, sexual, and aesthetic rules.[77] The chess game may be a metaphor for the social positionality of males and females, of pawns and their superiors, but it also asserts the importance of location and movement in determining both social and aesthetic relations. Chess pieces obey a rigid hierarchy that determines their relative mobility, power, and importance. That Deren identifies with and/or desires a chess piece and rejects human contact is interesting in itself: it indicates that the (gendered and color-coded) definitions of subjectivity and objecthood depend upon who defines those terms and upon the social hierarchy which determines such relations.

Deren's identification with and desire for the white queen signifies a recognition that both of their identities are determined by gender, color, and position in a social hierarchy. The queen, despite her gender, is a powerful figure: the only female figure on the board, she is unique and, importantly, more mobile than even the king. What Deren claims for herself at the end of At Land is thus an identification with and possession of an object which is marked by gender yet singular in status and more powerful in her ability to move than the king, whose immobilization by the opponent ends the chess game. In At Land, Deren's possession of the queen ends the game and the film.

After her successful theft of the queen,[73] a series of shots of Deren in different spaces is cut together; the effect is of different aspects of the woman watching from different locations in space and time, unified for a moment by watching her own escape. Deren's comments on the film's protagonist reveal the importance of the fragmentation and unity of that figure, who, "instead of undertaking the long voyage of search for adventure, finds instead that the universe itself has usurped the dynamic action which was once the prerogative of human will, and confronts her with a volatile and relentless metamorphosis in which her personal identity is the sole constancy."[74] Yet the woman's constancy is compromised by the techniques Deren uses to destabilize her as a coherent body which moves as a body should. In the program note for At Land, Deren calls attention to her body's enhanced physicality: "[in] the dune sequence . . . the camera stops, permitting the figure to move a considerable distance before photographing again (but the result looks continuous) . . . [this] results in a diminution in the size of the figure, which carries a strong emotional effect and is an event which could not possibly be translated out of cinematic terms into any other."[75] Here, Deren's moving body creates the illusion of continuity, the woman running down the beach, but also produces a "strong emotional effect" because it distorts spatial and temporal relations that normally govern human bodies. The film addresses the contradictions between singular body and plural subject, but it does not resolve them.

The whole, vibrant, moving Deren running down the beach at a pace faster than humanly possible does, however, offer a stark contrast to the immobile, seaweed-draped dreamer at the end of Meshes. The camera's more "objective" treatment (in contrast to the dream-motivated subjectivity of Meshes), Deren's fascination and alliance with objects, and her triumphant rejection of both heterosexual/social and homosexual/social relations all point toward the cult of the artist-individual. In other words, At Land rewrites the apparent self-destruction that concludes Meshes and valorizes the power of one woman's sexual and creative autonomy. The game of chess is about structured relations; each piece acquires its value from the rules of the game and is powerful only in relation to the movements of other pieces.

In *At Land*, Deren seems to claim the queen's position and mobility and also to leave the game behind.

This film does not neglect the fact that a woman such as the radical individualist protagonist is produced by film, is embodied within particular relations of looking. The woman running down the beach is watched by others of herself. Her ability to look at herself many times over is not threatening, however, possibly because she is aware of and defies the strictures of the chess game, or, perhaps, because she occupies both subject and object position and new definitions of those terms are produced. If *Meshes* questions male-centered definitions of women and investigates women's internal self-representations, then *At Land* affirms the woman's right of access to the symbolic order, figured by the chess game, and her choice of positions within symbolic representation.

Ritual in Transfigured Time

In this film, Deren revisits themes of self-doubling, replacing thematic repetitions such as climbing the stairs or chasing the pawn with formal repetitions: specifically, the use of slow motion and the freeze-frame. *Ritual* explores the individual persona in the context of quotidian rituals of social interaction and the mythic dimension of the masculine aesthetic tradition.

Deren uses editing to enable two distinct bodies to occupy a particular social position. Deren and dancer Rita Christiani meet as distinct beings and then mutually inhabit and move through the same spaces.[76] In the opening scenes of the film, Christiani watches Deren roll a ball of yarn with a partner who is hidden from view. After passing through an intermediate chamber to arrive in the room where Deren sits, Christiani discovers that the chair opposite Deren is empty. Christiani sits down in the chair and takes the place of the unseen former occupant. The camera moves to a medium close-up of Deren as her hands twist the yarn and as she tosses her head and smiles in conversation with Christiani. Deren is shot in slow motion, which emphasizes the fluid, dancelike quality of her gestures. The position from which Christiani first looked at Deren is shown in a reverse shot to be a doorway, guarded by a distinctly Cerberean Anaïs Nin.

Christiani passes through the threshold Nin guards and enters a room filled with party goers, who interact by flirting and dancing. Deren's camera breaks these activities down into their component gestures and renders them dancelike through slow motion and freeze-frames. Christiani's costume changes as she passes through the doorway; as she enters the party, she wears a black garment that suggests widow's weeds or a nun's garb. After several minutes of the party scene, during which Christiani stands out against the white party goers both because of her costume and her racial difference (she is the only African American woman in the scene), a cut transports Christiani, two other women, and dancer Frank Westbrook to an outdoor sculpture garden.

The three women dance together and then become involved in a game that resembles the children's game of Roman Statues. Westbrook dances with each of the women in turn and spins them off to dance on their own. As they begin their own dances, they are frozen by the camera and turn into statues in freeze-frames. Westbrook leaps onto a statue pedestal and momentarily becomes frozen himself, but he turns toward Christiani and begins a slow-motion and freeze-frame pursuit.

Christiani seems to understand the effect of the *danse macabre* with Westbrook and attempts to escape from this game of objectification into immobility. A tightly edited match on action editing sequence alternates shots of Christiani and Deren; as Christiani turns to flee, a cut inserts Deren's body finishing the gesture begun by Christiani. Their movements are continuous across two bodies. The two women are never photographed in the same frame, and they wear the same dress and shawl, encouraging the interpretation that they inhabit the same space and time. Their scene culminates with the women immersing themselves in the ocean, still in sequential match on action shots.

As they plunge into the sea, they are shot in negative, so that the dark dress becomes a white gown. Their movements in the water are detached from any ground, free of gravity's restrictions. The film ends with a shot of Christiani floating upward in the frame in the now-white gown. Once again, the use of ocean imagery invites comparison with *Meshes* and *At Land*. In the former, the freedom attained by dream doubles – that they were capable of behaving in a manner at odds with the dreaming woman who created them – is only capable of being represented as the possible death of the dreamer at the hands of her mental "objects." The active figures in *Meshes*, the doubles, are then left unaccounted for; if the dreamer is made inaccessible to representation, what is the status of her doubles? *At Land* foregrounds the rule-bound nature of social interaction, like *Ritual*. The protagonist embraces the inanimate queen and, implicitly, symbolic representation yet rejects the game by running down the beach along the ocean from which she emerged. In *Ritual*, the ocean can be read as a symbol of rebirth-in-motion as opposed to the immobilizing transformation of the Roman Statues game. This symbolism is heightened by the white bridal, initiate, or christening gown. The transformation also involves a breakdown in rules of representation – the switch to negative images – and the rules of individualism – Deren and Christiani are both same and different.

The transition to negative in this sequence calls up associations with the figuration of woman as lack in Freudian and Lacanian psychoanalysis.[77] *Ritual* can be read as refiguring this definition of woman as lack, not by reversing the image but because the negative has the potential for an alternative enactment of identity as a shared, but not identical, experience. In "Cinematography: The Creative Use of Reality," Deren discusses negative images as more than simple reversals: "the photographic negative image is still another striking case in point. This is not a direct white-on-black statement but is understood as an inversion of values. When applied to a recognizable person or scene, it conveys a sense of critically qualitative change."[78] Sameness and difference are cast as a dividedness of the body in *Meshes* and as an expansion of the individual body to partake of more impersonal, universal movements and gestures in *Ritual*. Deren does not develop an absolute equivalence between herself and Christiani through visual techniques, yet she forges an identification between the two through their bodies' actions as they flout the stasis of statuesque art objects. Women's images – both still and moving – are at stake in this film. Deren clearly makes a distinction between the art object's immobility (the statues) and the woman/women's shared motion in the water; in the process she reveals that film techniques permit objects and subjects to be differentiated through the manipulation of moving images in space and time.

Conclusion

Anaïs Nin wrote that Deren had ruined *Ritual in Transfigured Time* because she refused to develop individual characters: "The theme of interchangeable personalities is not clear, and I might even say that in destroying the characters. Maya destroyed the film. When gestures are broken at the party, heads cut off, it is not human beings who lose arms and heads but the film which loses its meaning. I feel this film is a failure."[79] It is certainly true that Deren's films do not regard the individual as immutable or sacrosanct. The three films in which Deren appears are all concerned with individual women, and yet all are unable to "guarantee" a singular position for the protagonist or a stable meaning for the text. In *Meshes*, the protagonist is multiplied by her own dreaming imagination. Her dreams produce a hall of mirrors that defies codification as internal or external, reality or role. In *At Land*, Deren's body moves through and across impossible spaces and times, ultimately fleeing ritualized social interactions. At the moment of her individuation, however, the figure watches herself run along the beach from several vantage points. In *Ritual*, women escape from stasis, from male-defined aesthetic representation, into the ocean, enlarging their personalities beyond the boundaries of the individual body. By refusing to occupy the position of either subject or object, Deren's protagonists stake out positions of "in-betweenness" and indeterminacy and thus intervene in the power hierarchy associated with looking relations as well as unsettling expectations regarding individualized characters with whom spectators might identify.

As with most star constructions, Deren also occupies an indeterminate position: she is both highly individualized and generic, inviting and refusing spectator identification. She is a highly individualized special case – partly because she has been canonized as the mother of avant-garde cinema. She is not a special case at all when we see that her legacy reproduces the myth of the exotic, uninhibited, and solitary artist at odds with her culture. One final image captures the contradictions of Deren's particular star persona: the unresolved tensions between performer and persona are signified by the juxtaposition of Deren's face, the artificial mannequin arm (which appears in the opening of *Meshes*), and the glass barrier, a metaphor for the camera lens or screen whose position between the real and the constructed determines how we see them both. The doubling of Deren's right eye suggests the doubleness of occupying subject and object positions on either and both sides of the camera, the ambiguous nature of reflected images, and the camera's potential to exploit the unreliability of vision to create its own realities.

Finally, the modernist aesthetics of presence that has characterized avant-garde cinema has direct bearing on the relationship between performance and persona in Maya Deren's life and work. Her appearances at film screenings (which she referred to as performances) and the circulation of her images were essential to the construction of her persona, yet, paradoxically, her films question the idea of the individual that underwrote the activities that promoted the development of the avant-garde.

For Deren, film performances were never limited to the screen, and film was by its nature a performative art, enacting and creating a particular form of reality. In search of a theory of performative film, Peggy Phelan asserts that "rather than asking again what makes a good film performance, [we should ask,] how do films and videos become performative?"[80] One answer to that question is Deren's ethic of participation – visible in her textual engagement with destabilizing the subject–object opposition as well as in her Haitian footage, which must be the subject of another essay, and in her work promoting the growth of experimental film.

Notes

I thank Jim Morrison, David James, Gaylyn Studlar, Martha Henn, Ann Ingram, Kim Loudermilk, Kim Whitehead, David Desser, Craig Fischer, and two anonymous readers for their helpful comments and suggestions. I also thank Lise Carlson, Bill Nichols, Akira Lippit, and all the participants at the Maya Deren symposium at San Francisco State University in April 1996; though this essay was in the final stages of revision, many of its topics were discussed there, and the enthusiasm of so many scholars for Deren's work was invigorating. I would also like to express my deep appreciation for the help provided by Jonas Mekas and for the work of VeVe Clark, Millicent Hodson, and Catrina Neiman.

1 Richard de Cordova, *Picture Personalities: The Emergence of the Star System in America* (Urbana: University of Illinois Press, 1990), 7.

2 Richard Dyer, *Heavenly Bodies: Film Stars and Society* (New York: St. Martin's Press, 1986), 5, 8.

3 Here I follow in the footsteps, or perhaps I should say footnotes, of Patricia Mellencamp, William Wees, and Scott MacDonald, who all note that "avant-garde" is a problematic term. In *Indiscretions: Avant-Garde Film, Video and Feminism* (Bloomington: Indiana University Press, 1990), Mellencamp discusses the uneasy relationship of "avant-garde" to modernism and postmodernism (xiv–xv). In *Light Moving in Time: Studies in the Visual Aesthetics of Avant-Garde Film* (Berkeley: University of California Press, 1992), Wees writes that "experimenting with the medium and opposing the dominant film industry suffice to make a filmmaker avant-garde – though I readily acknowledge that there are more rigorous ways of defining the term, just as there are other terms (for example, experimental, underground, visionary, personal, poetic, pure, free, independent, alternative) that have been applied to films I call avant-garde" (ix–x). In *Avant-garde Film: Motion Studies* (New York: Cambridge University Press, 1993), MacDonald notes the same slippage, remarking that this problem of definition "is evidence of the size and diversity of this particular area of film history, as well as of the on going debate about how to understand it. No one term seems entirely satisfactory – including *avant-garde film* . . . in general avant-garde film-making has been a derivation of the industry, a response to it in content and form" (15–16, emphasis in original). Like Mellencamp, Wees, and MacDonald, I use the term *avant-garde* to designate cinema practices that critically respond to and/or oppose dominant cinema in terms of form, content, and/or, I would add, production and exhibition.

4 Mellencamp, *Indiscretions*, xiii.

5 Quotation credited to James Broughton by Stan Brakhage in *Film at Wit's End: Eight Avant-garde Filmmakers* (New York: McPherson and Company, 1989), 13.

6 The case for Deren's role as "mother" of the avant-garde may have been made implicitly by P. Adams Sitney, whose *Visionary Film: The American Avant-garde* 1943–1975, 2nd ed. (New York: Oxford University Press, 1979), begins in 1943 with the Deren/Hammid collaboration on *Meshes*. See Lauren Rabinowitz's *Points of Resistance: Women, Power and Politics in the New York Avant-garde Cinema*, 1943–71 (Urbana: University of Illinois Press, 1991), for a discussion of the various New York artists working in experimental film.

7 In keeping with my argument that mainstream and alternative cinema practices are not always divergent, I should point out that director-stars are not uncommon in mainstream cinema, although the conflation of star and directorial persona has been much more

limited: Orson Welles, Alfred Hitchcock, Clint Eastwood, Spike Lee, Martin Scorsese, Woody Allen are the most obvious examples. It is interesting to speculate upon the increasing importance of the film director as star in the midst of the recent wave of independent studio hybrid films (e.g., Quentin Tarantino).

8 Mellencamp, Indiscretions, xiv.

9 Roland Barthes, "The Death of the Author," in Image, Music, Text, ed. and trans. Stephen Heath (London: Fontana, 1977), 147.

10 Mellencamp, Indiscretions, 9, 11.

11 See Peterson's provocative Dreams of Chaos, Visions of Order: Understanding the Avant-garde Cinema (Detroit: Wayne State University Press, 1994), esp. chaps. 1 and 2.

12 In Avant-garde Film: Motion Studies, MacDonald argues that conventions of spectatorship are usually established before one sees an avant-garde film and that these films force us to question our habits of film viewing (1–2). This questioning may become an expectation of avant-garde film viewers that enhances the sense of the immediacy of avant-garde spectatorship. In other words, one difference between mainstream and avant-garde cinema viewing practices may be the conscious awareness that avant-garde film viewing constitutes a temporally and spatially immediate event/practice.

13 De Cordova, Picture Personalities, 29–30.

14 See Judith Mayne's Cinema and Spectatorship (London: Routledge, 1993), 3–4, for a discussion of the paradigm developed by 1970s film theorists that divided film spectatorship into an active or passive activity depending upon the context (mainstream or alternative).

15 Prominent twentieth-century star-artists in the United States include abstract expressionist painter Jackson Pollock, author Norman Mailer, and Beat poet Allen Ginsberg. The countercultural stardom of these figures was dependent upon discourses about their public performances, their works, and their private lives. The conflation of star and artist is also evident in mainstream film culture in a limited way. For example, the discourse of method acting, which legitimized acting as a craft, rendered stars such as Marlon Brando both artists and actors.

16 VeVe Clark, Millicent Hodson, and Catrina Neiman, eds., The Legend of Maya Deren: A Documentary Biography and Collected Works, vol. 1, part 2 (New York: Anthology Film Archives, 1988), 254.

17 Ibid., vol. 1, part 1, 432.

18 Ibid., ix.

19 Anaïs Nin, The Diary of Anaïs Nin, 1944–47, ed. Gunther Stuhlman (New York: Harcourt Brace Jovanovich, 1971), 76. Nin appeared in several of Deren's films, including At Land and Ritual in Transfigured Time.

20 See de Cordova, Picture Personalities, 50–97.

21 Paul Trent, The Image Makers: Sixty Years of Hollywood Glamour (New York: McGraw Hill, 1972), 19.

22 Ibid., 21.

23 Emphasis on particular features varies across historical periods and cultural locations and can be associated with dominant cultural concerns, for example, the importance placed on the sensuality of the protruding female belly during the Renaissance. The regularity of features characterizing both the glamour queens of the 1930s and the natural beauties of the 1940s may, in fact, have had a great deal to do with anxieties surrounding Americanness and ethnicity. For an excellent study of glamour photography in relation

to women's spectatorship practices, see Jackie Stacey, *Star Gazing: Hollywood Cinema and Female Spectatorship* (New York: Routledge, 1994).

24 Clark, Hodson, and Neiman, eds., *The Legend*, vol. 1, part 1, ix.

25 Ibid., xx.

26 Ibid. Despite these references to her Russian origins, Deren's Jewishness, her tenure as national secretary of the Young People's Socialist League, and her membership in the Trotskyist wing of the Socialist party in the 1930s are rarely mentioned in contemporary or subsequent accounts of her life, possibly because of post-World War II anxieties concerning Communism and Jewish identity.

27 Nin, *The Diary of Anaïs Nin*, 1944–47, 76.

28 More than one acquaintance of hers has commented on Deren's ambivalence toward her Jewish heritage. Harry Roskolenko (Harry Ross) claims that Russian Jews who supported Trotskyist ideas did so in order to hide their Russian Jewish identity. Clark, Hodson, and Neiman, eds., "From an Interview with Harry Roskolenko," in *The Legend*, vol. 1, part 1, 332–39. In an interview Deren's personal assistant Miriam Ashram claims that Deren "ignored or denied any connection" to her Russian Jewish background. Ibid., vol. 1. part 2, 441.

29 Ibid., vol. 1, part 1, xiv.

30 Mellencamp, *Indiscretions*, 34.

31 Clark, Hodson, and Neiman, eds., *The Legend*, vol. 1, part 2, 230.

32 Louise Levitas, "How to Make Your Own Movies on a Shoestring," *P.M.*, 19 March 1946; reprinted in ibid., 388–89.

33 *Esquire*, December 1946; reprinted in ibid., vol. 1, part 1, 418.

34 Manny Farber, "Maya Deren's Films," *New Republic*, 28 October 1946, 555.

35 Mary Braggiotti, "Classicism on a Shoestring," *New York Post*, 28 October 1946; reprinted in Clark, Hodson, and Neiman, eds., *The Legend*, vol. 1, part 2, 408.

36 This brochure is reprinted in ibid., 345–48.

37 Ibid., 440.

38 What I am referring to as Deren's persona – the complex amalgamation of film performances, live appearances, press discussions, and the impressions those who knew her are left with – is perhaps the antiromantic version of what Hodson, Clark, and Neiman call Deren's "legend." Both terms imply Deren's control or participation. I choose persona because it is the term used by scholars who study the American star system to describe a star's deliberately packaged personality. The term "legend" implicitly romanticizes the filmmaker as modern artist.

39 Rabinowitz, *Points of Resistance*, 49.

40 Clark, Hodson, and Neiman, eds., *The Legend*, vol. 1, part 2, 367.

41 David Curtis, *Experimental Cinema* (New York: Universe Books, 1971), 50.

42 Clark, Hodson, and Neiman, eds., *The Legend*, vol. 1, part 1, xiv.

43 Brakhage, *Film at Wit's End*.

44 See Rabinowitz, *Points of Resistance*, especially chapter 3, "Avant-garde Cinemas before World War II," for an account of a number of New York artists working in experimental film.

45 This transition from young artist to mother is undoubtedly due to the way youth and aging are (de-)gendered and (de-)sexualized. Women past a certain age, for example, are considered motherly whether they have children or not. Deren died at forty-four without having had children. It is also interesting to consider Broughton's comment in light of his

characterization of his own parents as repressive, particularly in relation to sexuality, and his film *Mother's Day*. See Brakhage, *Film at Wit's End*, 67–89.

46 This phenomenon is not limited to the historical avant-garde. A discussion with experimental filmmaker Barbara Hammer in early 1994 led to the conclusion that the desire for stars is operative in contemporary gay and lesbian film culture.

47 Sitney, *Visionary Film*, 20.

48 These contradictions are made concrete in the Botticelli portrait from *Meshes*. Described by Leslie Satin as "draw[ing] attention to the fact of vision, of watching and being watched," the shot positions Deren as object of the camera's vision and as a subject who looks. Leslie Satin, "Movement and the Body in Maya Deren's *Meshes of the Afternoon*," *Women & Performance* 6, no. 2 (1993): 44.

49 Maya Deren, *Divine Horsemen: The Living Gods of Haiti* (New Paltz, N.Y.: Documentext, 1991).

50 Maya Deren letter to Katharine Dunham, in Clark, Hodson, and Neiman, eds., *The Legend*, vol. 1, part 1, 431.

51 Catrina Neiman, "An Introduction to the Notebook of Maya Deren, 1947," *October* 14 (fall 1980): 4. Neiman may be countering Stan Brakhage's claim that Deren's interests in spirituality derailed her film career (*Film at Wit's End*, 111).

52 Clark, Hodson, and Neiman, eds., "Interview with Alexander Hammid," in *The Legend*, vol. 1, part 1, 410.

53 Annette Michelson, "On Reading Deren's Notebook," *October* 14 (fall 1980): 49–50.

54 See Joyce Aschenbrenner's "Katharine Dunham: Reflections on the Social and Political Contexts of Afro-American Dance," *Dance Research Annual* XII (New York: CORD Inc., 1981) for a view of Dunham's work in historical context and a discussion of her own use of the term "primitive."

55 Deren, "Film in Progress: Thematic Statement," *Film Culture* no. 39 (winter 1965): 12.

56 Deren, "Notes on Ritual and Ordeal," *Film Culture* no. 39 (winter 1965): 10.

57 Deren, "Letter to James Card," *Film Culture* no. 39 (winter 1965): 32.

58 See Thomas Valasek, "Alexander Hammid: A Survey of His Film-Making Career," *Film Culture* nos. 67–69 (1979): 250–322.

59 Farber, "Maya Deren's Films," 555.

60 Deren, "Program Notes on Three Early Films," *Film Culture* no. 39 (winter 1965): 1, my emphasis.

61 In other words, doubling can signify repetition, but three signifies a series.

62 The "unreliability" of the dreamer's "reality" is signaled in the first sequence inside the house, where she sees a knife pull itself out of a loaf of bread on the table: this scene takes place well in advance of the apparent dream sequence.

63 Sitney, *Visionary Film*, 11.

64 Several excellent readings of *Meshes* emphasize the sexual dynamics within the domestic space, reminiscent of film noir's depiction of heterosexual union as threatening, and the woman's imprisonment. See Mellencamp, *Indiscretions*, 33–35; Rabinowitz, *Points of Resistance*, 55–65; and Sitney, *Visionary Film*, 3–19. All these readings offer useful insights, but I focus here on the multiplication and fracturing of the protagonist and the animation of her domestic space.

65 See Deren, "Cinematography: The Creative Use of Reality," *Daedalus* 89, no. 1 (winter 1960): 150–67; reprinted in Gerald Mast and Marshall Cohen, eds., *Film Theory and Criticism*, 3rd ed. (New York: Oxford University Press, 1985), 51–65.

66 Rabinowitz, *Points of Resistance*, 62.
67 There are exceptions to this, for example, the flight through the curtains in the bedroom window, but these moments are overshadowed by the dense bodies struggling up and falling back down the stairs.
68 Annette Kuhn, *The Power of the Image: Essays on Representation and Sexuality* (London: Routledge & Kegan Paul, 1985), 52.
69 Clark, Hodson, and Neiman, eds., *The Legend*, vol. 1, part 2, 174.
70 Sitney, *Visionary Film*, 22.
71 Ibid.
72 Catrina Neiman notes that Marcel Duchamp was a mentor of Deren and influenced her thinking about games, including chess, in relation to the construction of art ("An Introduction to the Notebook of Maya Deren, 1947," 7).
73 Shango initiation rites include a period of ritual theft, in which initiates are expected to steal small items (for example, food), signifying that they are not subject to the laws of society during this period. Judith Gleason, *Initiation of a Shango Priest*, screening and discussion at Emory University, Atlanta, Georgia, 9 February 1993.
74 Deren, "Cinematography: The Creative Use of Reality," 63.
75 Clark, Hodson, and Neiman, eds., *The Legend*, vol. 1, part 2, 194.
76 Rita Christiani was a dancer Deren became acquainted with when she toured the United States with Katharine Dunham's dance group in the early 1940s.
77 See Luce Irigaray, "This Sex Which Is Not One," chap. 2 in *This Sex Which Is Not One*, trans. Catherine Porter and Carolyn Burke (Ithaca: Cornell University Press, 1985).
78 Deren, "Cinematography: The Creative Use of Reality," 60.
79 Nin, *The Diary of Anaïs Nin*, 1944–47, 149.
80 Peggy Phelan, "Arresting Performances of Sexual and Racial Difference: Toward a Theory of Performative Film," *Women & Performance* 6, no. 2 (1993): 7.

Camping with Lady Divine

Star persona and parody

DAN M. HARRIES

9

A gross caricature, an underground sensation, the darling of French and English discos, the he-she that ate poodle doo, a temperamental, mean-spirited artist, a 'male actress' who aspired to take up where Sydney Greenstreet left off, Divine (born Harris Glenn Milstead) was nothing if not singular. Projecting his oh-so-mortal flesh from the streets of Baltimore into national notoriety, he became one of the few media eccentrics who was more than a 15-minute personality.

– Divine's Obituary, 1988[1]

As a critique of the organized social order, Mikhail Bakhtin's carnivalesque semiotics relishes the "anticipation of another, utopian world in which anti-hierarchism, relativity of values, questioning of authority, openness, joyous anarchy, and the ridiculing of all dogmas hold sway, a world in which syncretism and a myriad of differing perspectives are permitted."[2] Bakhtin's carnival theory can be usefully applied to film parody analysis, particularly in terms of its subversive disruption of social order and the eventual acceptance and recuperation of disruptive elements within the mainstream.[3] During carnival, social conventions are temporarily subverted – only to be restored after the carnival ends. An interesting distinction arises, then, in the comparison with film parody, for parody seems to leave a residual effect which cannot be completely ignored. Unlike carnival, parody injects social disruption at unpredictable moments. While the recuperation of order is probable and expected, there is an uncomfortable lag – an uncertainty about how well mainstream society can withstand these subversive episodes. Robert Stam argues that

> by appropriating an existing discourse and introducing into it an orientation obliquely or even diametrically opposed to that of the original, parody is especially well-suited to the needs of oppositional culture, precisely because it *assumes* the force of the dominant discourse, only to deploy that force . . . *against* domination.[4]

This interpretation stipulates that the subversiveness of parodic transformation affects more than the parodied text – it alters the social order.

In fact, a residual subversion is also evident in Bakhtin's semiotic analysis of carnival where the social disruption is not fully mended. The predominance throughout history of carnival and carnivalesque texts (which Bakhtin documents), indicates that carnival is authorized, but he suggests that this authorization is inevitable – the result of the inescapability of these subversive tendencies. Societal awkwardness allows some amount of subversion to escape, and then linger within uncomfortable folds of mainstream consciousness. In this respect, carnival theory lends itself even more readily to the analysis of film parody.

The carnival "freak," embodying a double-sided social phenomenon, is a major player in the cultivation of the carnivalesque. "It" is not only different (as a breach in social standards), it is also quite the same ("one of us"). As an instance of transmutation, the freak manifests both transformation and replication. Madonna Kolbenschlag writes that "freaks are threatening and disruptive because they challenge conventional boundaries between male and female, sexed and sexless, animal and human, plant and animal, life and death. They disrupt the proper 'scale' of the universe, they disorder the basic 'distinctions' which constitute our sense of reality."[5] What the freak in the carnival is to society, parody is to source texts. A strong indication of this relationship and a way into parody's subversive power can be found in the analysis of one of the recurring "freaks" in American independent cinema, the late actor Divine.

Divine's film career spanned over twenty years in which he[6] starred in eight feature films, six of them directed by John Waters.[7] At well over three hundred pounds and dressed in an evening gown and pumps for most of his performances, Divine was uncontestably one-of-a-kind, and always controversial. John Waters dubbed his favorite *leading lady* "The Most Beautiful Woman in the World." Vincent Canby, however, chided Divine for being "a grotesque extension of the fantasies of all little boys who grew up in the forties and fifties wanting to be Marlene Dietrich or Mae West,"[8] and Divine's parodic (and often misogynist) representation of certain aspects of traditional women's roles in patriarchal society has drawn justifiable criticism from feminists and others.

It is the purpose of this essay to analyze the multi-leveled operation of parody which occurs in the star persona of Divine. Personae are constructed both intra and inter-textually throughout an actor's career and can be studied as an amalgamation of specific forces. In other words, various factors, constructed through specific performances (both on and off-screen) as well as other ancillary activities (such as film reviews and publicity ventures), coalesce to form a star persona.

Analyzing a complex star persona, such as that established by Divine, can be especially fruitful for the enterprise of looking at how cultural forms both support and subvert the society which generates them. Parody plays a large role in Divine's persona, and I intend to address its functions in conjunction with theories of carnival and camp.[9] In line with the spirit of carnival, parody and camp's energy is invested with subversiveness – turning social norms upside down and constantly challenging the normalized boundaries of the social order.

In the following analysis, I will discuss three specific variations of parody operating in and contributing to Divine's star persona: (1) a parody of gender roles; (2) a parody of the institution of Hollywood stardom and of specific "glamour" stars; and (3) a form of self-parody in which Divine parodies his own established star persona.

A central facet of Divine's star persona is its function as a parody of normalized gender roles. Parody, the carnivalesque, and camp all utilize certain forms of incongruity – the most common being the contrast of masculine/feminine.[10] Androgyny, cross-dressing, and trans-vestism have all contributed to camp sensibility and as Susan Sontag notes, "Allied to the camp taste for the androgynous is something that seems quite different but isn't: a relish for the exaggeration of sexual characteristics and personality mannerisms."[11] Sexual incongruity and ambiguity can be seen in many of the costumes found within the carnivalesque – especially men dressed as women. An important element of camp is the exaggerated dressing and acting like women by men. Divine, a male actor playing female characters, is parodic, operating through the collapse and reformulation of gender boundaries deemed normal in Western society and thus exposing the construction of such roles.

Fully within the realm of the carnivalesque, Divine's persona embodies a double-edged representation. On the one hand, there is the problem of men dressing as women, which has long been the focus of feminist critique. Whatever the subversion of traditional roles, the uneasy suspicion persists that Divine's transvestism is wholly acceptable within a patriarchal framework, in much the same way that the subversion of carnival depends for its acceptability on the inevitable return of order. At the same time, there is a liberating aspect to Divine's image. It cannot be disputed that the subversion of gender role demarcation is a considerable challenge to the dominant patriarchal social order. The question arises, does the possibility of Divine's misogyny, which is undeniable at moments, invalidate the damage which is nonetheless done to patriarchal order?

From the perspective of feminist thinking, men's cross-dressing often fortifies men's societal position by mimicking (and thus reinforcing) the marginalized status of women. Quite often, such instances of transvestism are coupled with a strong misogynist tendency. Kolbenschlag argues that "the image of woman as 'temptress,' 'witch,' and demonic source of evil has . . . been a constant motif in the misogynist tradition."[12] Divine's persona relies on many of these elements, but they are not central to his critique. Divine's parody shatters all conventionalized notions of gender and traditional behavior. That the persona exhibits such misogyny, whether frequently or not, is clearly a problem for any critic examining Divine's work as parody, but it does not interfere in the limited scope of Divine's critique of patriarchal conventions.

Much of Divine's persona is derived from patriarchal notions about what constitutes femininity and what defines a normal woman. Such notions are usually exaggerated to such a degree that they become parodic. Gaylyn Studlar argues that this exaggeration reinforces patriarchal expectations of "normal" femininity. Discussing Divine's character in *Pink Flamingos*, Studlar writes:

> As Babs Johnson, Divine's makeup is so extreme that her hairline must be shaved back to accommodate her sweeping eyebrows, and her huge 'breasts,' gigantic extensions into free space, are important twin signs of woman's mythical hyperbolized sexuality. . . . Divine's masquerade parodies woman's performance of femininity, but fails to expose the origins of this performance in patriarchal culture's demand for its construction.[13]

In many ways, Divine's persona does exactly this. Richard Dyer argues that "crossdressing and play on sexual roles can be seen as a way of heightening the fact that sex roles are *only* roles and not innate or instinctual personal features."[14] I would argue that the mere excessiveness of Divine's characterization of femininity necessitates the reading of gender roles not as self-styled and innate qualifies, but as constructions – conventionalized norms – which usually border on the effete. The parody functions by taking constructed sex role expectations and transforming them beyond credibility, thus exposing the system which reinforces such norms.

In Mary Ann Doane's view, "male transvestism is an occasion for laughter; female transvestism only another occasion for desire."[15] In both cases, men make women the subject of a patronizing study, and woman's power to define her own parodied persona is obstructed. This is the great problem of transvestism according to many feminist critiques. Elaine Showalter numbers among feminist critics who cite films like *Tootsie* and *La Cage aux Folles* as examples where the transvestism is problematic. Laughter is generated when the male character dresses as a woman yet accidently slips back into his original male role. The shifting in and out of masculine and feminine roles, in order to exert a "masculine power disguised and veiled by the feminine costume . . . [promotes] the notion of masculine power while masking it."[16]

The intensity of this problematic can be defused by calling attention to the fact that Divine does not portray a transvestite in his films. Divine is to be accepted as a woman from the film's start to its finish, rather than as a male character who is narratively motivated to dress as a woman. Thus, Divine's persona operates less as a male "discovery" of woman's weaker position, and more as a direct, female, assault on patriarchal structure, using the medium of a (parodied) woman as a strong vehicle of attack. Divine thereby engenders a view that recognizes and attempts to dispel the myth of the weakness of women's roles.

In analyzing Divine's persona in terms of its parody of constructed feminine sex roles, one must also consider that Divine the actor is not only a man playing a woman – he also is a gay man. Studlar's argument that "the antierotic, parodic treatment of Divine guarantees that the position of the heterosexual male viewer will not be problematic,"[17] seems to be rendered questionable by this important point. Divine, like women, is a marginalized other and his "female" persona can be read as an instance of solidarity with women. As in carnival, where "all those who have been socially marginalized . . . take over the symbolic center of the city,"[18] Divine's persona combines many facets of the oppressed "other." Thus, the heterosexual male viewer's position is problematized by Divine's presence on the screen – his "gay man playing a woman" persona threatens the patriarchal social structure. Again, the threatening disruption moves beyond the contained subversion of carnival. Nowhere is this more evident than in the homosexual acts performed by Divine within his characterizations, such as in *Pink Flamingos* when she performs fellatio on her son. The parody of femininity becomes more of a critique of the system which constructs gender roles than a criticism of the oppressed who play out such roles.

Divine's cross-dressing not only undermines sex role expectations, it also initiates an outright attack on what is considered "decent" in our society. Actresses quite often become "plasticized" through Hollywood's effort to manufacture glamour and to create an aura of desirability. With Divine's persona, quite the opposite is achieved. Bakhtin defines the "grotesque body" as one which consists of many parts that are open to the outside world, with an emphasis on "the open mouth, the genital organs, the breasts, the phallus, the potbelly, the nose."[19] In many ways, this sounds like an accurate physical description of Divine's persona – traits which are mimicked as a parody of the "perfect woman." Although Divine's characters carry themselves in a glamorous fashion, particularly in terms of clothing and mannerisms, their disproportionally large breasts and protruding stomachs seem to negate any sense of normalized glamour and indeed parody such expectations.[20] Characterized as a "strong woman," Divine's persona also plays with the juxtaposition between feminine qualities and his enormous size. This, in turn, fosters his subversive parody of what a woman *should* be in terms of size and stature. The primary means of achieving this is the "animalization" of Divine's persona, equating Divine with large animals. Umberto Eco argues that the comic hero in carnival goes through a transformation into some sort of animal association. He writes that "carnival is the natural theater in which animals and animal-like beings take over the power and become the masters."[21] Some examples of Divine's animalization occur in Mondo Trasho (1969) when a wounded Divine is driven out to a pig farm and proceeds to roll around in pig dung (accompanied by a Wagnerian score and pig grunts); then again when she is called a "Fat Hog!" in Pink Flamingos, a "cow" in Female Trouble (1974), and an "ant-eater" and a "pig" in Polyester (1981). One film critic even referred to Divine as "some sort of overgrown, mutant rooster."[22] In all of these instances, Divine is reduced to an animalized form, a freak and subversive threat who parodies the social order through a grotesque transformation.

Another factor in Divine's persona which parodies the separation and immutability of distinct gender roles is the casting of Divine in dual roles within certain films. Unlike films such as Some Like It Hot, where Tony Curtis and Jack Lemmon's switch into drag is narratively motivated, Divine's characterizations revolve around his doubling up in a male *and* a female role. In Hairspray, Divine plays both the "frumpy," congenial housewife Edna Turnblad and the evil segregationist Arvin Hodgepile. Such dual roles function as parodies through the transformation of gender roles and the collapsing of the character/actor relation of Hollywood films.

As with the grotesque realism found in carnival, the two gendered roles often relate to each other in terms of the lower stratum of the body, transgressing societal norms regarding sexual behavior. In Mondo Trasho, Divine is not only a wandering woman, but also the rowdy male yahoo who "moons" her while driving his car. In one of the most unconventional scenes in cinema history, Divine plays both Dawn Davenport and Earl Peterson in the film Female Trouble. In a feat of cinematic manipulation, Dawn and Earl have sex with each other on the side of a rural road. Later in the film, Earl makes the definitive inside joke when he tells Dawn to "Go fuck yourself!"

Divine's portrayal of dual gender roles and multiple characters in his films is further complicated by his numerous references to other Hollywood stars. Stardom and the cult of the star are central elements in the composition of Divine's persona. Most of Divine's films revolve around his character trying to become a star. One example of such a parody focuses on the Hollywood institution of the sacred Academy Awards. In Female Trouble, Dawn Davenport starts out as a go-go dancer, then works her way up to a job as a night-club entertainer with her own show. The film climaxes when Dawn "shoots random members of her night-club audience. For this she gets the Electric Chair, the Oscar of her crime, her proudest moment. . . ."[23] In the last scene, Dawn gives her final acceptance speech while being strapped to the chair, thanking all of those who had helped with her career in crime. This parody of the Oscar ceremonies, complete with a long-winded acceptance speech, connects (and critiques) the absurdity of such awards with the grotesque realism of a criminal about to be electrocuted.

At another level, Divine's persona is a critique of Hollywood glamour stars. Divine's persona is both modeled after and parodies three primary stars: Jean Harlow, Mae West, and Jayne Mansfield. He also constantly mimicks and refers to Russ Meyer's "nasty pussycats" in such films as, Faster, Pussycat! Kill! Kill! and Vixen.

Jean Harlow contributes her demeanor to Divine's persona. Molly Haskell, in describing Harlow's characters, writes that "through no fault of her own, Harlow's toughness and

Figure 9.1 Divine in *Hairspray* (1988)
Courtesy of Photofest, New York

intelligence were used as a weapon to clobber other women."[24] Throughout Divine's performances, her characters are at war with other women – usually for the possession of a man. In *Pink Flamingos*, Divine prepares to kill her closest rival and proclaims: "You're Connie Marble and you're gonna pay for being Connie Marble! And you're gonna pay royally, bitch! Let this be a lesson to you just in case there *is* reincarnation: it's virtually impossible to be filthier than Divine! . . . 'Cause you're gonna be dead, Connie, YES DEAD!" Like Harlow, Divine is tough, but this is a toughness far beyond any of Harlow's exploits and thus carries out the parody to a perverse extreme.

It is not hard to see the similarity between Divine's persona and that of Mae West, a star who has long been a model for drag queens and female impersonators, especially in terms of her androgyny and insatiable sexual appetite. Molly Haskell writes that, "So complete was West's androgyny, that one hardly knows into which sex she belongs, and by any sexual-ideological standards of film criticism, she is an anomaly – too masculine to be a female impersonator, too gay in her taste to be a woman."[25]

There are two prime instances in Divine's performances which make direct references to Mae West. In *Mondo Trasho*, Divine is seen driving down the road, her hair piled high on her head. When she spots a male hitchhiker on the side of the road, she begins to mentally undress him accompanied by a voice-over of Mae West stating: "Like I say, it's not the men in your life that counts, it's the life in your men!" Divine's character of Rosie in *Lust in the Dust* (1985) is a dead-on copy of West's Diamond Lil from *She Done Him Wrong*. Much of the parody of West occurs in the exaggeration of her mannerisms as well as in the fact that Divine, like West, usually possesses the ability to attract men for her sexual pleasures. Yet unlike West, and more like a Black Widow spider, Divine usually ends up torturing and/or killing her mate. Many of the semantic qualities of West exist within Divine's characterizations and persona, yet the manner and trans-contextualization of those elements on a syntactic axis become transformed, producing critical distance – hence the parody of West's persona.

Divine's persona, especially those elements culled from his earlier films, is also heavily influenced by 1950s' glamour star, Jayne Mansfield. John Waters said that both he and Divine "idolized Jayne Mansfield, and since Divine was getting quite heavy, we agreed she could play the perfect takeoff of a blond bombshell."[26] Yet, Divine added, "when you think of a bomb-shell, you think of Monroe or Mansfield, you don't think of a three-hundred-pound man."[27] The parody here revolves around societal expectations of what constitutes a "bombshell" and Divine's actual gender and size – both excluded from the normal definition. But Divine's costumes, makeup, and mannerisms (semantic constituents), all point toward the Mansfield persona.

Studlar comments that "Divine's excess femininity is that of the blonde bombshell whose undulating walk, 'cha-cha heels,' tight skirt, and clinging sweater define woman as a walking sexual minefield."[28] In fact, Divine's persona becomes somewhat of a "parody of a parody, Marilyn Monroe's 1950s bombshell mediated through Jayne Mansfield's mindboggling too-much-ness."[29] While Mansfield's extra large breasts, overly bleached hair and sultry mode of speech mimicked (and parodied) Monroe, one quality that seemed to elude Mansfield is Monroe's sense of naturalness and purity. Divine's persona, in turn, parodied Mansfield with even larger breasts, "too-platinum-to-be-real" hair in *Mondo Trasho*, and a strained falsetto voice; moving even further away from Monroe in terms of naturalness.

Divine's persona, as a critique of glamour stars, is composite in nature, exhibiting various qualities. Yet, it is held together by a common element: as Divine so aptly describes, "They're all bitches." Another element which surfaces in Divine's persona that seems to be gleaned from past female stars is, as Haskell mentions, that many of these stars were "hedonists, unshackled sensualists who would rather go to hell than achieve salvation at the price of erasing all those moments of carnal bliss. They are all the goddesses of sex and yet are not, being earthly rather than divine."[30] In a sense, Divine both celebrates, by means of homage, these past "superwomen" (to appropriate Haskell's term), yet also parodies them through exaggerated mannerisms and behavior. The characterizations of these women become "tame" in comparison to Divine's atrocities. By dressing up like a glamour star (beyond the cocktail dress and wig, the similarities end), and by narratively placing himself in situations which connote past stars (yet often carrying these narratives to their gruesome extremes), Divine's persona oscillates between instances of difference and similarity.

Combined with the breaking of gender roles and his parody of Hollywood glamour stars, self-parody serves as a third variation within Divine's persona. Apart from the stars discussed above, Divine himself became a minor screen cult star. His status was reinforced by exposure in the various media and by films which featured him in central roles – roles built around his established persona. Even Divine's name became a sort of self-parody. Often, a character's name reveals specific attributes associated with that character. As Dyer suggests, the "character's name both particularises her/him and also suggests personality traits."[31] The parody here exists within the ironic use of the term "divine," which is grotesquely removed from any of Divine's characters. Divine's name becomes conflated, referring not only to the actor himself (he legally changed his name), but also to the characters in many of his films. Critics discussing Divine's work rarely refer to Divine's characters by their role names. This is not only the sign of a very established star persona, one which transcends single filmic roles, but also is another form of subversion, and a critique of how roles are constructed and maintained.

Mark Booth states that "camp self-parody presents the self as being willfully irresponsible and immature, the artificial nature of the self-presentation making it a sort of off-stage theatricality."[32] In one way, all of Divine's performances seem to consist of some level of self-parody, always making light of the actor-as-playing-a-role. Yet in his later films, the degree of self-parody increases dramatically After his first four feature films, Divine's characters began to stray from his earlier established persona of "the Bitch" to a parody of the "evil" Divine. Divine's characters of Francine Fishpaw in *Polyester* and Edna Turnblad in *Hairspray* are both campy attempts at creating a sympathetic character, attempts which usually falter – possibly instances of "failed seriousness," a major criterion of camp itself. It is quite hard to see these roles as anything more than spoofs of Divine herself. Francine tries her best to be the "perfect housewife." At the dinner table with her porno theater owner husband and two delinquent children, Francine is by far the most "civilized" member of the family, insisting on saying grace and reinforcing table manners. But the facade cannot last throughout the film; Francine is eventually jolted back into the "monstrous" Divine. When Francine catches her daughter sniffing glue with her trouble-making boyfriend in his car, an angry Francine rips the car door completely off of its hinges. When she senses that her husband is having an affair, she breaks down the hotel door to catch him in bed with another woman.

Edna, the responsible mother in *Hairspray*, reverts back to the old Divine as she yells at her daughter in a husky, baritone voice to turn the television set down. Divine's portrayal of both Francine and Edna is also colored by her over-acting which is combined with many direct addresses and a self-conscious bravura style. Divine's self-parody, suggested through his stage name and the parody of his own persona, demonstrates the fluid movement of this technique.

Carnival, parody, and camp have, at their core, a subversive and liberating quality. Joseph Dane suggests that parody functions on a scale which moves between "affirmative" and "subversive" poles, where both interplay in parody's double-sided critique.[33] Yet some theorists argue that this critique is limited by the very system it subverts. J. G. Riewald describes the "quality of *controlled* exaggeration of the salient characteristics of its subject in which lies the value of parody as criticism."[34] Linda Hutcheon adds to this, arguing that,

> The parodic text is granted a special license to transgress the limits of convention, but, as in the carnival, it can do so only temporarily and within the confines dictated by 'recognizability'. . . . [Thus] parody's transgressions ultimately remain authorized – authorized by the very norm it seeks to subvert.[35]

Yet it seems as though the surplus generated by Divine's persona is too great to be recuperated after the instance of transgression. In social semiotics, this is described as the *weakening* of conventionalized codes by the act of parody. Many people have described a frustration with the fact that they cannot take an old Western film seriously after watching *Blazing Saddles*. In the case of Divine's persona, after exposure to his films, it is hard to look at gender roles quite the same way, or view Mae West in a manner untainted by Divine's parodic endeavors. The effects of parody are lasting, not temporary. The fact that Divine cultivated a devoted cult following based on his parodic activity seems to further attest to parody's lasting effect.

Susan Sontag argues that the "camp sensibility is disengaged, depoliticized – or at least apolitical,"[36] yet as we have seen, Divine's persona is quite subversive and political. Because parody (or camp or the carnivalesque) has a subversive effect which does not immediately subside after the moment of critique, its relation to satire must be reevaluated. Hutcheon argues that "parody is an 'intramural' form with aesthetic norms, and satire's 'extramural' norms are social or moral."[37] She also states that parody can be used for satirical purposes (i.e. to critique the social order) while satire can equally make use of parody to perform its function, but that they are still quite separate in "intent." Because parody is constrained by the very norms it subverts does not mean it is any more apolitical than satire. As Joseph Dane adds, "when parody calls attention to the norm, it criticizes the very system on which its own plane of expression depends."[38] In fact, because the act of subversion of *any* norm is political, this would sensibly mean that *all* parody is a form of satire. (And yet, not all satire would be considered parody). We must move away from the antiquated idea that there is a great separation between aesthetics and social signs. All aesthetics are socially based and any violation of their existence is political. This is indeed a political gesture – conscious or not.

Within the analysis of Divine's persona, we have seen how all three variations of parody discussed, each centered on different targets, seem not only to capture some of the essence of that which is being parodied, but also work to dislodge and critique a social order which still prescribes sexist gender roles, while continuing to worship the cult of the manufactured movie star. Divine's presence will go on subtly ripping apart the societal fabric, providing an on-going critique of a repressed culture. Although Divine is dead, his persona, a campy combination of various parodies, remains, if not on new strips of celluloid, then in the deep recesses of our psyches.

Acknowledgments

I would like to thank Nick Browne, Rhona Berenstein and David Gardner for their advice on this essay.

Notes

1 Craig Lee, "Divine's Obituary," *Los Angeles Weekly* (March 17, 1988): 41.

2 Renate Lachman, "Bakhtin and Carnival: Culture as Counter-Culture," *Cultural Critique* 11 (Winter 1988–89): 118.

3 The three primary works by Bakhtin which focus on the carnivalesque are *Rabelais and His World* (Bloomington, Ind.: The Indiana University Press, 1984), *The Dialogic Imagination: Four Essays by M. M. Bakhtin* (Austin, Tex.: University of Texas Press, 1981), and *Problems of Dostoevsky's Poetics* (Ann Arbor, Mich.: Ardis, 1973).

4 Robert Stam, "Bakhtin, Eroticism and the Cinema: Strategies for the Critique and Transvaluation of Pornography," *CineAction!* 10 (Fall 1987): 16.

5 M. C. Kolbenschlag, "The Female Grotesque: Gargoyles in the Cathedrals of Cinema," *Journal of Popular Film* 6, no. 4 (1978): 329.

6 To avoid confusion, I will use "he" when discussing Divine the actor and the few roles in which Divine played a male character and will use "she" for Divine's typical female characterizations.

7 *Mondo Trasho* (1969), *Multiple Maniacs* (1970), *Pink Flamingos* (1972), *Female Trouble* (1974), *Polyester* (1981), *Trouble in Mind* (1985), *Lust in the Dust* (1985), *Hairspray* (1988).

8 Vincent Canby "When Movies Take Pride in Being Secondrate," *New York Times* (June 7, 1981): 19.

9 One of the most influential discussions of camp can be found in Jack Babuscio's "Camp and the Gay Sensibility" in *Gays and Film*, ed. Richard Dyer (London: British Film Institute, 1977).

10 Jack Babuscio, "Camp and the Gay Sensibility," 41.

11 Susan Sontag, "Notes on Camp," in *Against Interpretation and Other Essays* (New York: Farrar, Straus & Giroux, 1986), 279.

12 M. C. Kolbenschlag, "The Female Grotesque," 332.

13 Gaylyn Studlar, "Midnight S/excess: Cult Configurations of 'Femininity' and the Perverse," *Journal of Popular Film and Video* 17, no. 1 (1989): 6.

14 Richard Dyer, *Stars* (London: British Film Institute, 1986), 67.

15 Mary Ann Doane, "Film and the Masquerade: Theorising the Female Spectactor," *Screen* 23, no. 3/4 (1982): 81.

16 Elaine Showalter, "Critical Cross-Dressing: Male Feminists and the Woman of the Year," in *Men in Feminism*, eds. Alice Jardine and Paul Smith (New York: Methuen, 1987), 123.

17 Gaylyn Studlar, "Midnight S/excess," 8.

18 Joao Luiz Vieira and Robert Stam, "Parody & Marginality: the Case of Brazilian Cinema," *Framework* 28 (1985): 22.

19 Mikhail Bakhtin, *Rabelais and His World*, 26.

20 For a critique of Bakhtin's discussion of the grotesque body, see Mary Russo's "Female Grotesques: Carnival and Theory," in *Feminist Studies, Critical Studies*, ed. Teresa de Lauretis (Bloomington, Ind.: The Indiana University Press, 1986).

21 Umberto Eco, "The Frames of Comic 'Freedom,'" in *Carnival!*, ed. Thomas Sebeok (Berlin: Mouton Publishers, 1984), 3.

22 F. Rich, "Review of *Female Trouble*," *New York Times* (February 21, 1975).

23 D. Lyons, "Film Review – *Female Trouble*," *Andy Warhol's Interview* 5, no. 3 (1975): 37.

24 Molly Haskell, *From Reverence to Rape: the Treatment of Women in the Movies*, Second Edition (Chicago: The University of Chicago Press, 1987), 115.

25 Ibid., 115.

26 John Waters, *Shock Value* (New York: Dell Publishing, 1981), 54.

27 Ibid., 154.

28 Gaylyn Studlar, "Midnight S/excess," 6.

29 Ibid.

30 Molly Haskell, *From Reverence to Rape*, 109.

31 Richard Dyer, *Stars*, 122.

32 Mark Booth, *Camp* (London: Quartet Books Limited, 1983), 18.

33 Joseph Dane, "Parody and Satire: A Theoretical Model," *Genre* 13, no. 2 (1980): 152.

34 J. G. Riewald, "Parody as Criticism," *Neophilologus* 50, no. 1 (1966): 127.

35 Linda Hutcheon, A *Theory of Parody: the Teachings of Twentieth-Century Art Forms* (New York: Methuen, 1985), 74.

36 Susan Sontag, "Notes on Camp," 277.

37 Linda Hutcheon, A *Theory of Parody*, 25.

38 Joseph Dane, "Parody and Satire," 153.

PART FOUR

RACE AND ETHNICITY AND THE AMERICAN STAR

Introduction

This section introduces the problematic of race and ethnicity as it subtends conceptions of American stardom and capitalizes on the growing work that has been done in this area in recent years. Clearly, this is a counterbalance to the fact that, until recently, the largest share of critical attention has been devoted to Caucasian actors. With the expanding concern with identity formation, studies are now increasingly focusing on non-white performers and on aspects of ethnicity in the cinema. Critics have returned to Hollywood history and reexamined the compromised stardom of such figures as Dorothy Dandridge, Louise Beavers, or Lena Horne. Other studies now focus on the new role played by contemporary black stars like Denzel Washington, Samuel L. Jackson, or Morgan Freeman and by director/actors like Spike Lee. Similarly, studies of Carmen Miranda and Dolores Del Rio bring to the fore questions concerning the character and price of stardom for Latin American performers. The essays in this section, written from varying perspectives, critically review the issue of race and ethnicity in relation to American stardom.

Ian C. Jarvie's essay, "Stars and Ethnicity: Hollywood and the United States, 1932–51" asks, "How representative were Hollywood stars of the nation as a whole" during the cinema's "golden age?" To answer this question, he, first of all, indicates the difficulty of clearly delineating who was and who was not a star. He finds equally troublesome the absence of methods and criteria to categorize discrete ethnic groups and to know the stars' own ethnic self-descriptions. To begin to tackle this scholarly problem, Jarvie constructs a table based on available sources about the stars (reference books, birth names, and personal testimony). On the basis of his research, Jarvie concludes that "overwhelmingly, actors and actresses are white, Christian, European, native English-speakers, American-born, and highly assimilated." Where they are not, such subterfuges as a name change was often employed in order to appear more mainstream. Moreover, Jarvie asserts that there was "what the statisticians call good agreement among the ethnicity of the actors, the ethnicity of the star personae they assumed, and the ethnicity of the roles or vehicles in which their star personae were displayed on the screen." Often, of course, this was unavoidable, due to the appearance of the performer or associations with his or her accent. As for the films of this period themselves, they are most informative about the processes of cultural assimilation in the production of images of "mainstream America."

Sarah Berry's essay, "Hollywood Exoticism" further explores the treatment of ethnicity in the Hollywood cinema. Her piece analyzes the "popularization of imperialist fantasies and ethnic stereotypes," citing the "Latin lover" roles played by such actors as Ramon Novarro, the "Latin, Asian, and South Seas beauties" played by Dolores Del Rio, Lupe Velez, and Hedy Lamarr, and the "Orientalized" roles played by European stars such as Greta Garbo and Marlene Dietrich. Berry asserts that Hollywood's ethnicity arose "in the context of social anxiety about race but also represented an ongoing attraction and fascination with idealized forms of ethnicity." While the studios employed émigré performers as central to their designs on international distribution, they did this in a contradictory fashion, seeking to appeal to both audiences abroad and in the U.S. While the use of "foreignness" sought to engage the American audience's tastes for exoticism and their interest in multicultural characters, this had to be portrayed within the confines of racial stereotyping despite the desire appeal to non-domestic viewers. Clearly, there was a tension between the desire for international profit and the strictures of racism and xenophobia in the U.S. Berry explores further how "Hollywood exoticism" was realized through the important uses of costume, cosmetics, and Technicolor film stock – all aspects of the creation of exoticism on the American movie screen.

In "Paul Robeson: Crossing Over," Richard Dyer examines the stardom of an African-American who until very recently received scant attention in studies of both the American and British cinema. Dyer conceives of Robeson as fundamentally a star who traverses a number of boundaries. Robeson appealed to both black and white audiences and he shuttled between a variety of media: theater, film, and music. While Dyer admits that Robeson's image was, of course, bound up with blackness (in his association with Negro Spirituals, for example), there was considerable controversy within the black community as to the depth of this racialized image and Robeson's commitment to his own people. Dyer is interested in retrieving a multiple reading of the Robson persona and does so through examining two films. In *Body and Soul* (1924), made by black director, Oscar Michaux, Robson is cast as Isaiah, an escaped prisoner who poses as a preacher. Dyer argues that, in this film about hidden ghetto life, Robeson's sexual allure is both fascinating and dangerous. *Borderline* (1930) was directed by Kenneth Macpherson, a member of the avant-garde group associated with the film journal *Close-Up*, a progressive publication with ties to the Harlem Renaissance. It concerns sexual tensions and violence that erupts between two couples (one black and one white) both of whom reside in a small village inn, while simultaneously raising questions about the broader community's racial prejudices. As Dyer notes, "the film is organised around the basic antimony of black and white at every level, aesthetic, metaphorical, ethical, ethnic." Furthermore, the use of Robeson in the film partakes in a "general discourse that deactivates the black person even while lauding her or him."

Marcia Landy's essay, "Opera, Folklore, and Ethnicity: The Case of Mario Lanza," addresses changing conceptions of ethnicity in Hollywood cinema. Landy examines the pivotal cultural role played by Mario Lanza's stardom in the 1950s as well as the resurrection of his screen image in the 1990s. Lanza was a significant departure from prior Italian stars such as Rudolf Valentino. Lanza's biography and the roles into which he was cast provide a narrative of the changing character of stardom in Hollywood of the 1950s that is connected to new cultural imperatives concerning ethnicity, masculinity, and musical performance. Lanza's image, in contrast to the dominance of certain Irish stars in Hollywood (e.g. Cagney), demonstrates that the Italian and Italian-American was seen as an indeterminate identity, more broadly classed as Mediterranean. He was acknowledged to have broken comic stereotypes and parodies of the opera singer, providing different and more respectful images of opera and its performers. In sum, an examination of the roles he played and his popularity provides an indication of changes in notions of star profitability, of historical conceptions of star construction, and of indices of cultural value in relation to the cinema.

Stars and Ethnicity

10

Hollywood and the United States, 1932–51

IAN C. JARVIE

> We shall call "ethnic groups" those human groups that entertain a subjective belief
> in their common descent because of similarities of physical type or of customs or
> both, or because of memories of colonization and migration; this belief must be
> important for the propagation of group formation; conversely, it does not matter
> whether or not an objective blood relationship exists.[1]

How representative were Hollywood stars of the ethnicity of the nation as a whole? It is
often presumed that they were not. They certainly did not represent the 10 percent or so
of the nation who were black. As far as the other ethnic identities within the nation are
concerned, the data are difficult to interpret and easy to exaggerate.

 Before presenting data and analysis, preliminary questions of selection and reliability
must be addressed. First, there are problems concerning how to use the concepts of stars and
ethnicity.

Stars

Who should be classified as a star is far from clear. Consider some criteria of that status such
as an icon on a dressing room door. This is a contractual matter between actor and studio;
like other contractual matters, for example, a name above the title, were it to be used as a
criterion of stardom the result would be to inflate the numbers of stars greatly by the addition
of now-unrecognizable names.[2] As an alternative, if the contractual matter of salary were
used as a criterion of stardom, that would have the additional shortcoming of making the
population of stardom subject to all the unreliability of Hollywood bookkeeping and rumors,
as well as excluding big stars in their early and lower-paid years.

 If contracts do not provide satisfactory criteria of stardom, what about public acceptance?
Sampling public opinion by such means as questionnaires, or the existence and size of fan
clubs, would make stardom a simple function of public opinion. Although in the last analysis
the public decides whether or not someone is a star, that decision is made at the box office,
and its results may not agree with what is said to the researcher. Another route to public
opinion is the press. But to accept as a star everyone whom the press names as such is to give

undue weight to the views of a small group of journalists. No doubt they try to fathom whom the public has made a star, but tendencies to hyperbole and exaggeration, not to mention optimism and even payola, scarcely make the press a reliable guide. The box office, then, appears to be the best guide.

In addition to the difficulty of deciding whom to classify as a star, questions arise of which stars to study and by what criteria such a selection is to be made. Many writers on stars simply select those who happen to interest them; just as unsatisfactory is to select past stars who are presently remembered and revered. Neither approach generates a representative group, and only a representative group will sustain generalizations about the ethnicity of stars and the latent content of what the star system projected. However, box-office attractions do constitute the sort of representative group necessary.

Ethnicity

Confusion about ethnicity is greater than that over stars. The long history of our ways of categorizing fellow humans – into barbarian and civilized, into races, by cultures – is a melancholy one, for the categories were usually normative. That there has of late been a strong reaction against the judgmental use of ethnic categories is manifest in the current United States census form on which ethnicity is ascribed by self-description – no set of categories being suggested to help or direct the answer. From a social science point of view, this is a very untidy practice. Ethnic self-identity claims employ diverse criteria: general appearance (WASP), surname (Hispanic), religion (Jewish), skin color (black), nationality (ItalianAmerican), hemisphere (Oriental), and language (Creole). Because all categories can be permutated with hyphens, the possibilities are endless.

The census form makes ethnicity subjective. Another approach – which we can call "objective" – is possible. This begins from the idea that ethnicity designates concrete groups with restricted membership and mappable boundaries. Max Weber, the classical authority on the subject, warned, however, that ethnicity disappears during any attempt to define it too closely.[3] Furthermore, he thought the phenomena which were interesting were a political creation of the larger group. Ethnicity was a property of minority groups. Since his time the view has emerged that we are all ethnics. It follows that even the majority group – in this case called WASPS – is an ethnic group. In the period chosen, with few exceptions, stars belonged to the majority WASP group – in fact, in persona, and in screen roles.

In combination the two troublesome notions of stars *and* ethnicity present a number of further difficulties. The stars' ethnic self-description, that is, how they would have described themselves on their census forms, is unavailable. Their public was not surveyed systematically about how they would ethnically classify this or that star. As if these difficulties were not enough, a threefold ambiguity of reference exists. Stars and public might both respond differently depending on whether the question of ethnicity referred to the ethnicity of the *actor* who signs the contract (ethnicity 1 "real"); the ethnicity of the *star* embodied in that actor (ethnicity 2 perceived); or the ethnicity of the *roles* that star played on the screen (ethnicity 3 on screen).

For example, the Austrian-American actor Paul Muni (Muni Weisenfreund) played Italian, Oriental, Mexican, French, and many other roles.[4] Did he have any determinate ethnicity (ethnicity 1) for the public? Did he try to project an ethnicity of his own? He seldom played a

Jew, although he might have classified himself as one on the census form. Did his star persona (ethnicity 2) take on the ethnicity of his roles (ethnicity 3), his (real life?) Jewishness, both, or neither? Was he perhaps taken by the public to be ethnically WASP but capable of making himself up as exotics? The case is undecidable for lack of information. It is not crucial because I have cheated: Muni does not make the list created by the box-office criteria used herein.

Other out-of-bounds examples would be Mickey Mouse and Donald Duck, as well as Snow White and the Seven Dwarfs. The ethnic classification of the first two presents grave problems, although they seem to me to be WASP.[5] Some books claim these two cartoon characters were "stars," and that Snow White "starred" in one of the most popular films of the year. Be that as it may, their absence from the lists compiled by using my chosen indicators simplifies the matter.

With the foregoing difficulties in mind, my procedure was as follows. Without solving once and for all the problem of who is and who is not a star, assume there were stars. Within the group of those who were stars, focus on the big box-office attractions. To decide their ethnicity, I became the census respondent on their behalf, checking my attributions by running the same stars by an ethnic cross-section of my students (self-identified). In effect there were three census forms to be completed for each person: one for the actor (ethnicity 1), one for the star who is the actor's doppelganger (ethnicity 2), and one for the roles with which the star is associated (ethnicity 3). While I identified the ethnicity of the actor behind the roles (ethnicity 1), this was primarily for background information. What interested me most were the ethnic identification of the off-screen star persona (ethnicity 2) and the ethnic content of the roles themselves (ethnicity 3).

How, exactly, to choose a representative sample of box-office stars? My special interest is Hollywood in its golden age, when its products predominated on world screens.[6] That period ended early in the 1950s with the rapid shrinkage of the American film industry. Sound films are more tractable than silent because more are readily accessible. This focuses a twenty-year period, from 1930 to 1950, and it so happens that a useful reference book provides data from 1932 on.[7] These data are the exhibitors' reports on the ten top-drawing stars of each year, compiled for Quigley publications *Motion Picture Herald*, *Motion Picture Daily*, and *Motion Picture Almanac*. Subject to the same lack of precision as all Hollywood data, these were, however, used to make industry decisions. Fifty-six names appear from 1932–51 (Table 10.1). All of the films that these stars made while on the list have been researched and listed in an endeavor to identify the ethnic profile drawn by those roles.

The first glance over Table 10.1 creates a few surprises. Names virtually never mentioned by present-day experts on the stars – such as Abbott and Costello and Sonja Henie – feature prominently. Males outnumber females in all but four years.[8] Apart from the child stars, entrants are usually of quite mature age on first appearance in the list. (Because one or two birth dates are in dispute, figures are rough.) The mean age at entry for males is around thirty-six, with a standard deviation of 8+. The mean age at entry for females is 28.5, but if we eliminate the two children, Temple and Withers, and the far from anile Marie Dressler, the mean rises to thirty-three, with a standard devation of 10+. Public perception is invalid that stars of either sex "made it" very young; many worked primarily in light entertainment with no pretensions to be anything more. Were I more attentive to current critical practice I should also discuss those names not present in the list: the "presence" of significant absences.[9]

It is assumed that readers will know what the listed stars look like. That information, plus their stage name and a general feel for the star persona is all we have to start with; we cannot

Table 10.1 Top box-office stars 1932–51

Star name	Real or given name	Age of entry to list	Where born	Ethnicity 1 "real"	Ethnicity 2 perceived	Ethnicity 3 on screen	Years on list
Abbott, Bud	William Abbott	46	U.S.A.	WASP	Same	Same	7
Astaire, Fred	Austerlitz, Frederick	36	U.S.A.	WASP	Same	Same	3
Autry, Gene	Same	33	U.S.A.	WASP	Same	Same	2
Beery, Wallace	Same	46/51*	U.S.A.	Irish?	Same	WASP?	5
Bergman, Ingrid	Same	31	Sweden	WASP	Same	Same	3
Bogart, Humphrey	Same	44	U.S.A.	WASP	Same	Same	7
Brown, Joe E.	Same	43	U.S.A.	WASP	Same	Same	3
Cagney, James	Same	36	U.S.A.	Irish	Same	Same	6
Cantor, Eddie	Iskowitz, Edward Israel	41	U.S.A.	Jewish	Same	Same	1
Colbert, Claudette	Chauchoin, Lily Claudette	30	France	French	WASP	Same	3
Cooper, Gary	Cooper, Frank J.	35	U.S.A.	WASP[†]	Same	Same	12
Costello, Lou	Cristillo, Louis	35	U.S.A.	Hispanic	Italian	Same	7
Crawford, Joan	Le Seuer, Lucille	29	U.S.A.	WASP	Same	Same	5
Crosby, Bing	Crosby, Harry Lillis	33	U.S.A.	Irish	Same	Same	12
Davis, Bette	Davis, Ruth Elizabeth	31	U.S.A.	WASP	Same	Same	4
Day, Doris	Kappelhoff, Doris	27	U.S.A.	WASP	Same	Same	1
Dressler, Marie	Koerber, Lila Von	63	Canada	WASP?	Same	Same	3
Farrell, Charles	Same	31	U.S.A.	WASP	WASP	WASP	1
Faye, Alice	Leppert, Ann	26	U.S.A.	WASP	Same	Same	2
Flynn, Errol	Same	30	Australia	WASP	Same	Same	1
Gable, Clark	Same	34	U.S.A.	WASP	Same	Same	15

Table 10.1 continued

Star name	Real or given name	Age of entry to list	Where born	Ethnicity 1 "real"	Ethnicity 2 perceived	Ethnicity 3 on screen	Years on list
Garbo, Greta	Gustafson, Greta	27	Sweden	WASP	WASP	WASP	1
Garson, Greer	Same	34	U.K.	WASP	Same	Same	5
Gaynor, Janet	Gainer, Laura	26	U.S.A.	WASP	Same	Same	3
Grable, Betty	Same	26	U.S.A.	WASP	Same	Same	10
Grant, Cary	Leach, Archibald	40	U.K.	WASP	Same	Same	3
Harlow, Jean	Carpentier, Harlean	22	U.S.A.	WASP	Same	Same	1
Henie, Sonja	Same	27	Norway	WASP	Same	Same	3
Hope, Bob	Hope, Leslie Townes	38	U.K.	WASP	Same	Same	11
Johnson, Van	Johnson, Charles Van	29	U.S.A.	WASP	Same	Same	2
Ladd, Alan	Same	31	U.S.A.	WASP	Same	Same	1
Lewis, Jerry	Levitch, Joseph	25	U.S.A.	Jewish	?‡	WASP	1
Loy, Myrna	Williams, Myrna	32	U.S.A.	WASP	Same	Same	2
MacDonald, Jeanette	Same	33/34	U.S.A.	WASP	Same	Same	1
Martin, Dean	Corcetti, Dino	34	U.S.A.	Italian	Same	Same	1
O'Brien, Margaret	O'Brien, Angela Maxine	8	U.S.A.	Irish	WASP	WASP	2
Peck, Gregory	Same	31	U.S.A.	WASP	Same	Same	1
Powell, Dick	Same	31	U.S.A.	WASP	Same	Same	2
Powell, William	Same	45	U.S.A.	WASP	Same	Same	1
Power, Tyrone	Same	25	U.S.A.	WASP	Same	Same	3
Rogers, Ginger	McMath, Virginia	24	U.S.A.	WASP	Same	Same	3
Rogers, Roy	Slye, Leonard	33	U.S.A.	WASP	Same	Same	2
Rogers, Will	Same	56	U.S.A.	WASP	Same	Same	4

continued

Table 10.1 continued

Star name	Real or given name	Age of entry to list	Where born	Ethnicity 1 "real"	Ethnicity 2 perceived	Ethnicity 3 on screen	Years on list
Rooney, Mickey	Yule, Joe, Jr.	18	U.S.A.	Irish	Same	Same	4
Scott, Randolph	Crane, Randolph	47/52*	U.S.A.	WASP	Same	Same	2
Shearer, Norma	Same	32	Canada	WASP	Same	Same	3
Stewart, James	Same	42	U.S.A.	WASP	Same	Same	1
Taylor, Robert	Brugh, Spangler Arlington	25	U.S.A.	WASP	Same	Same	3
Temple, Shirley	Same	6	U.S.A.	WASP	Same	Same	6
Tracy, Spencer	Same	38	U.S.A.	Irish	WASP	WASP(?)	10
Wayne, John	Morrison, Marion Michael	47	U.S.A.	Irish	WASP	WASP(?)	3
Webb, Clifton	Hollenbeck, Webb Parmelee	57	U.S.A.	WASP	Same	Same	1
West, Mae	Same	41	U.S.A.	WASP	Same	Same	2
Williams, Esther	Same	26	U.S.A.	WASP	Same	Same	2
Withers, Jane	Same	11	U.S.A.	WASP	Same	Same	2

Sources: Cobbett Steinberg, *Reel Facts* (New York: Vintage Books, 1981); numerous reference books.

Notes

* The reference books give differing dates of birth.

† Cooper, like a number of others I have classified as WASP, was Roman Catholic. Some stars, especially Irish and Italian, emphasized their religion as part of their persona.

‡ It is unclear whether in his Martin and Lewis days Lewis was recognizably Jewish to the audience.

be familiar with every single film each of these stars made in the twenty-year period. Nevertheless, reviews, stills, and biographies can supplement film libraries, VCR tapes, and memory. On that basis we can proceed to ethnic matters by looking at the evidence of names (s 1), accents (s 2), appearance (s 3), roles and reality (s 4), and their relation to the dream of America (s 5).

Names as ethnic signifiers

First, contrary to popular opinion, the WASPishness of the stars was not a disguise. Of the fifty-five star names, forty-two (or possibly forty-three if Marie Dressler is included) were unequivocally WASP (or Roman Catholic) by stage name and real name; seven more were Irish by name; two Italian by stage name (Costello and Martin); Cantor was Jewish by stage name and Lewis, who was Jewish, had a stage name that was not manifestly Jewish. A great many of the stars used their "real" names, or a very close variant thereof, for example, "Gary" instead of Frank J. Cooper. There seems to have been an esthetics of names – "Roy Rogers" rather than Leonard Slye; "Gary Grant" rather than Archibald Leach – that was separate from ethnic disguise because the alteration does not shift the star to another ethnic group. In some cases the surname is a help to the actor's ethnic assignment; especially in black and white movies, nothing in appearance distinguishes, for example, an Irish actor from a WASP.

Lou Costello (Louis Cristillo) may be Italian-American or Hispanic (ethnicity 1), he surely is white, but not likely Anglo-Saxon Protestant. The same goes for Eddie Cantor (Edward Israel Iskowitz), who seems to have settled for a stage name more euphonious to the English-speaking audience but still undisguisedly Jewish (ethnicity 1 = ethnicity 2). Beery, Cagney, Crosby, O'Brien, Rooney, and Tracy are all, it seems to me, unmistakably Irish surnames, and those of Catholic Ireland at that. "John Wayne" is not an Irish name, yet its possessor was aggressive in affirming off-screen loyalty to that ancestral connection.

A fascinating case is that of Tyrone Power (his real name). Both Christian name and surname smack of Eire, the former more than the latter. Undoubtedly much of Power's appeal came from his very handsome face. Whether his Irish descent (ethnicity 1) was apparent to the movie fans who had not read his biography is hard to tell. Usually Power played WASP heroes with appropriate names (ethnicity 3), but he was also one of the handful of top stars who tackled roles which involved a shift of ethnicity (ethnicity 1 and 2 = ethnicity 3). He played Frenchmen twice in 1938 (*Marie Antionette* and *Suez*), a turbaned East Indian in *The Rains Came* (1939), and Hispanics in *The Mark of Zorro* (1940) and *Blood and Sand* (1941). He was not named to the top ten after 1940, and he did not play Latins or exotics at all after that. Whether there is a causal connection and which way it flowed is thus moot.

In addition to euphony, there seem to have been a number of other "esthetic" criteria at work in the choice of names: avoidance of the ordinary and avoidance of the fancy, for example. Myrna Williams became Myrna Loy, Harry Lillis Crosby became Bing Crosby, and Ruth Davis became Bette Davis – all cases of lessening the ordinary. Meanwhile, Spangler Arlington Brugh became Robert Taylor, Lucille Le Seuer became Joan Crawford, Harlean Carpentier became Jean Harlow, and Webb Parmelee Hollenbeck became Clifton Webb – all cases of lessening the fancy. However these renamings came about, they reveal an interesting tendency akin to reversion toward the mean. If the mean is WASP for ethnicity 1 and 2 and the names that go with it, there seems to be a middle ground between ordinariness and uniqueness toward which the name altering tends.

German-American ethnicity was clearly avoided in names: Frederick Austerlitz became Fred Astaire, Doris Kappelhoff became Doris Day, Lila Von Koerber became Marie Dressler, and Charles Van Johnson, presumably Dutch, became Van Johnson. Such disguise needs little explanation beyond noting the vitriolic anti-German sentiments associated with the World War I and revived by World War II.

Also to be avoided were names that are also ordinary words or their homonyms: hence Rogers not Slye, Rooney not Yule, Scott not Crane, and Gaynor not Gainer. No rule is without its exceptions, so, although Leach had to go, its replacement, Grant, is a word, and Gumm was replaced by Garland; no change occurred in Hope or in West.

Figure 10.1 Eddie Cantor
Courtesy of Photofest, New York

What can we learn from these name changes? It cannot be concluded that there was consistent concealment of ethnicity by name change among this group of top box-office stars. There was a good deal of name changing, it is true, but for different purposes. Here the limitations of the sample population are evident. No doubt a good many actors and actresses with non-WASP names changed them for that reason alone, a practice that contrasts with present custom, when such names as Mandy Patinkin and Meryl Streep are retained. The selected group showed more complexity; clearly one result of "we are all ethnics now" is that names which proclaim ethnicity are retained.

The third category is composed of names as indicators of role ethnicity. I have noted how Tyrone Power played a number of roles wherein the character's Hispanic surname immediately indicated that he was supposed to be neither WASP nor Irish-American, Power's two possible ethnic identities as actor and star. The three Scandinavians in the list – Bergman, Garbo,[10] and Henie – invariably played characters whose name designated them as foreign, obviating explanation of their retained accents. In compiling Table 10.2, I have included the films of the year before the star entered the top ten box-office attractions list, assuming that they contributed to the achievement. With the exception of "Susan Lennox," the character names are to be taken as "foreign" – but French, German, and Russian as easily as Scandinavian.

Table 10.2 Scandinavians as generically "foreign"

Film	Character's name	Character's nationality
GRETO GARBO		
Inspiration, 1931	Yvonne	French
Susan Lennox, Her Fall and Rise, 1931	Susan Lennox	U.S.
Mata Hari, 1931	Mata Hari	Dutch
Grand Hotel, 1932	Grusinskaya	Russian
As You Desire Me, 1932	Maria (Zara)	Italian
SONJA HENIE		
One in a Million, 1936	Greta Muller	Swiss
Thin Ice, 1937	Lili Heiser	Swiss
Happy Landing, 1938	Trudy Erickson	Norwegian
My Lucky Star, 1938	Kristina Nielson	Norwegian
Second Fiddle, 1939	Trudy Hovland	U.S.
Everything Happens at Night, 1939	Louise	Swiss
INGRID BERGMAN		
Notorious, 1946	Alicia Huberman	German
Arch of Triumph, 1948	Joan Madou	French
Joan of Arc, 1948	Jeanne D'Arc	French

Accents as ethnic signifiers

The three Scandinavian stars mentioned previously retained traces of their "foreign" accent even after long residence in Hollywood. It was hard to put them into sound films playing native-born Americans. Their accents were seldom used to designate Scandinavian origin specifically; Bergman and Garbo often played Germans, and sometimes Russians. The same was true of foreign-born stars who did not meet our box-office criteria, for example, Marlene Dietrich, Charles Boyer, Conrad Veidt, Paul Henried, and Louis Jourdan.

Yet there was no consistent policy. Particularly puzzling was the treatment of actors with British accents. Cary Grant and Greer Garson were British-born and so spoken, yet little or no effort was made to limit the parts they played. Some claim that Grant developed a trans-atlantic accent, but I am skeptical; his accent remained English, just as Clifton Webb's, however clipped, remained American. The differences were, however, very subtle and the attribution of transatlantic character clearly an effort to explain the combination of ready comprehensibility and hard-to-place. One reason sometimes given in this period for not distributing British films more widely in the United States was that they needed subtitling in certain regions. The evidence of the use of accents in Hollywood tells against such an excuse. To my ears, Errol Flynn never lost his Australian twang, yet time and again he was cast as an American and no explanation was offered of his way of speaking. He is only a single name on the list, but there were other imports not on the list, such as Leslie Howard and David Niven, whose accents similarly were unexplained and unsubtitled.

An incidental point made by other commentators is that sound filmmakers sought players with an enunciation comprehensible to the broadest numbers of people – hence extremely marked accents, such as Boston, Brooklyn, or Deep South were seldom heard from the big stars when the role they played had no regional specificity. Clark Gable made no effort to sound particularly "Southern" in *Gone With the Wind*, and neither did Leslie Howard. Vivien Leigh made an attempt at it, and again in *A Streetcar Named Desire*, in which latter she was not followed by Marlon Brando or Kim Hunter.

As with surnames, accents are not especially good or specific indicators of ethnicity, and they muddle actor, star, and role. Furthermore, because accents are rather bland among most of the stars on the list, tending in most cases toward the Midwest-California speech that has emerged as American Standard, they can now be set aside.

Appearance and ethnicity

Before we know a person's name, before we hear them speak, they present an appearance to us. Appearance is a marker of limited use to this discussion. When ethnicity centered around "color," appearances were paramount; blacks, Indians, and Orientals were largely identified by their looks ("visible minorities"). An immediate result of the claim that we are all ethnics now is to displace color as a primary ethnic signifier. Indeed, the bulk of ethnic groupings are to be found within the "white" category. Superstition to the contrary, there is no way of identifying Irish, Italians, Jews, and Scandinavians by appearances. Furthermore, it is rightly thought to be offensive to make any such claim. Without exception, all of the stars on the list are "white" in appearance, especially insofar as the bulk of their films were in black and white, and the combination of that medium and their make-up would ensure that such subtleties as "swarthiness" would be ironed out. In this period there were leading actors who had an ethnically identifiable appearance, but none has entered the selection. In the 1920s, Sessue Hayakawa was a star, one whose appearance and name clearly identified him as Japanese; the same holds true for Anna May Wong as Chinese in the 1930s. And, of course, only a handful of black actors had recognizable names, and perhaps only Paul Robeson and Lena Horne approached star status.[11]

Ethnic profiles

In Table 10.1, and in the preceding text, a distinction has been made concerning the ethnicity of the actor (ethnicity 1), the ethnicity of the star's persona (ethnicity 2), and the ethnicity of the screen roles (ethnicity 3). Emerging profiles can be examined under these three headings.

The actor's ethnicity

Overwhelmingly, actors and actresses are white, Christian, European, native English-speakers, American-born, and highly assimilated. This last feature is important. Even in cases in which actors had a different ethnic trace, it was not emphasized. These were Hollywood actors, not in Yiddish theater or some other ethnic preserve. The choice to pursue success in Hollywood ensured that, as actors, the roles they would be called upon to play, the sorts of off-screen lives they could pursue, would be those possible in the very strange new community that the movie industry was forming on the West Coast. Although odd in the way of other one-industry towns,[12] Hollywood was in fact tolerant of a good deal of the traditional ethnic diversity that was supposed to be dissolved in the melting pot. Religious practice off-screen, for example, might continue regardless of whether it conformed to some WASP norm. Assimilation was also taking place in another domain, the work that actors were able to do. Hollywood participated in the process of assimilating Americans of diverse origin, not by enforcing Norman Rockwell life-styles at home but rather by projecting and promoting a picture of American culture and society more homogenized than true. I would, however, reject Winokur's view that the transformation of William Powell from ethnic roles to romantic hero "reflects the engineered, mechanized transformation of an actor's character actor status to star and leading man status. It is the local version of a fantasy life that film moguls at Paramount and MGM participated in at wider levels when they created out of the Southern California farms and wilderness a version of a city that they controlled and in which they could then feel at home in as founding fathers and natives. They created from the material of the villain, the ethnic, and the revolutionary a romantic protagonist."[13]

Other demographic features of the list pertain to the male–female ratio, longevity, and age. As was noted previously, most of the stars listed were male. Males also stayed on the lists longer. John Wayne held the record, with twenty-five years, but most of his reigning years fall outside the period under discussion. In the present list the leaders were Clark Gable, fifteen years; Gary Cooper and Bing Crosby, twelve years each; Bob Hope, eleven years; and Spencer Tracy, ten years. The leading woman, Betty Grable, also led ten years on the list.

With the exception of the child stars, actors and actresses were of mature age by the time they were declared top box-office attractions. This is rather different from the situation in the silent period, when actresses especially were extremely young, and in the period subsequent to 1951, when the phenomenon of the teenage star became more common. Although the stars invariably played roles that were younger than their chronological ages, their true age and experience enabled them to play their young parts with a maturity and confidence that assisted in fulfillment of the audience's fantasy. The characters might be young, but they operated in the world with a confidence that many viewers wished they had – or had at that age. This connects negatively to ethnicity: individual qualities, not cultural and ethnic background, accounted for who the actor was.

The ethnicity of the star personae

Actors were carriers of something extra, a particular social status we call the "movie star." One way to model this is to think of the star persona as a doppelganger, a shadow self that is always present but not in all respects identical to the actor and hence not the same person as the actor. Another way to think of it is as a living mask that can be taken to be a person, although it in fact conceals another person beneath. The mask analogy is misleading only in that it tempts us to think of the person wearing the mask as real and the mask as appearance. When our topic is stars, the reverse is the case.

A star persona is, sociologically, a real thing.[14] It is a persona as distinct from the roles played as is the actor playing the roles. A star was a persona created, with or without the cooperation of the actor concerned, by the publicity machine of the studio collaborating with the press, other media such as radio, fan clubs, and word of mouth.[15] A crucial instrument was the studio biography of the star in which fact and fiction were mixed into a factoid, perhaps hinting at lowly ethnic origins, or at lofty ones, or at ordinariness, in a manner calculated to match what were thought to be the lines of appeal and enigma that suited the looks, the publicity campaign, the activities, and perhaps, the roles, the star played or was to play.[16]

In an important theoretical discussion of the content of television, Sari Thomas has argued that such material was designed to send the specific message that although there was room at the top, life there was difficult.[17] It could also be said that the star system in general sent those messages. The promise of stardom to white ethnics was that they too could choose to escape the constraints of ethnicity without giving it up in real life by aspiring to become a star. However, the price could be high if there was a tension: the possibility of confusing the off-screen self (ethnicity 1) with the star persona (ethnicity 2) in cases in which these were different.

The ethnicity of the role

Unsurprisingly, and in agreement with the charge of stereotyping so often leveled at Hollywood, most actors and stars most of the time played roles the ethnicity of which conformed to their ethnicity 1 and ethnicity 2. Seldom were their faces and features made up, their accents changed in order to make them change ethnicity. Abbott and Costello always played themselves, and much the same could be said of Bing Crosby, Bob Hope, Shirley Temple, or Sonja Henie, even though they assumed different names in their roles.

There was, then, what the statisticians call good agreement among the ethnicity of the actors, the ethnicity of the star personae they assumed, and the ethnicity of the roles or vehicles in which their star personae were displayed on the screen. Spencer Tracy might play Dr. Jekyll and Mr. Hyde; might play an American flier; might play George Heisler, a German; but in general he did not play Orientals, Italians, blacks, Hispanics, and so on. Much the same was true of Will Rogers, or Clark Gable, or John Wayne. If anything, the male stars in particular seldom strayed far from their ethnic identity (ethnicity 2).

Although its connection to ethnicity is indirect, it may be appropriate here to discuss the frothy nature of so many of the stars' personas and their roles: Shirley Temple, Jane Withers, Hope and Crosby, Mickey Rooney, Abbott and Costello, Esther Williams, Martin and Lewis, and Sonja Henie were famous for performances in material so lightweight that it has gone almost undiscussed in academic film studies. Their films aimed to be light, amusing, harmless, inoffensive, and to conform politically and sexually to the strictest Hays Code standards. The films represented a WASP America that was carefree and inward-looking. When Abbott and Costello and Martin and Lewis appeared in comedies about the armed services, when Hope and Crosby took the road to all manner of exotic locales, without exception all were filmed on back lots and studio sets that bore as much resemblance to the real world as did blackface vaudevillians to Negroes. Both the realities of their own society and the actual look of the rest of the world could be ignored without damage at the box office. The heavy guns of political and deconstructionist criticism have yet to be turned on this material and its popularity.

Notes

1 Max Weber, *Economy and Society* (New York: Bedminster Press, 1968), p. 389.
2 Despite my search for defensible criteria, I suspect that Table 10.1 contains names that some readers will have difficulty placing, for example, Charles Farrell and Jane Withers.
3 Weber, *Economy and Society*, p. 395.
4 For example, *Scarface, The Good Earth, Juarez, The Story of Louis Pasteur,* and *The Life of Emile Zola*.
5 Both Donald and Mickey, especially the former, seem to me to inhabit a Norman Rockwell world, which, I take it, is basically WASP.
6 The rough boundaries of the golden age are the consolidation of sound (around 1929) and the age of gimmickry and television-induced decline (1952–55).
7 Cobbett Steinberg, *Reel Facts: The Movie Book of Records* (New York: Vintage Books, 1982). Doris Day comments: "The ultimate yardstick of achievement in Hollywood has been the annual poll of theatre owners of America. To be voted by them into the top ten is to enter the celluloid sanctum sanctorum," A. E. Hotchner, *Doris Day: Her Own Story* (New York: William Morrow, 1975), p. 143.
8 It may be that the public does not agree with Stanley Cavell: "One remembers how much of the history of film is a history of the firmament of individual women established there. Individual men, even the greatest, with few exceptions are fads or conveniences by comparison," *The World Viewed* (New York: Viking Press, 1971), p. 48.
9 As happens in Mark Winokur's article, "Improbable Ethnic Hero: William Powell and the Transformation of Ethnic Hollywood," where ethnicity is crudely identified with criminality and lower class origins, *Cinema Journal* 27 (Fall 1987): 5–22.
10 Garbo's name change did not alter her ethnicity as a star, which always was Scandinavian, so perhaps it was for euphony.
11 Sidney Poitier was a well-known and successful actor, for example, but did not build, so far as I know, a star persona. Entertainers who also worked in movies – Harry Belafonte and Sammy Davis, Jr. – came from the end of the studio era in which Lena Horne flourished.
12 It is important to refer to Hollywood as a one-industry town, and not to Los Angeles. The latter was not at the time, or in any period since, economically or politically dominated by the movie industry.

13 Winokur, "Improbable Ethnic Hero," p. 11.

14 The concept of the star persona is analyzed thoroughly in Donald Horton and R. R. Wohl, "Mass Communication and Para-Social Interaction," *Psychiatry* 19 (1956): 215–29. Their article was written just as television was making its impact so they were able to contrast the emerging television star personae with the traditional movie star personae. "Para-social" interaction is their term for interaction between star and public that simulates two-way interaction while being in truth one-way.

15 With the decline of the studio system the star system has, in my view, undergone radical change. It no longer centers on movies and movies alone. This in itself licenses the promiscuous usage of, for example, *The National Inquirer*, which will refer to Vanna White or Lisa Bonet or Wayne Newton as "stars." They are not stars in any sense coherent with those being discussed herein, but then there may be none of these people now because the system has changed.

16 See "Publicity" in Christopher Finch and Linda Rosenkrantz, *Gone Hollywood: The Movie Colony in the Golden Age* (New York: Doubleday, 1979); and Peter Valenti, *Errol Flynn: A Bio-Bibliography* (Westport Greenwood Press, 1984).

17 Sari Thomas, "Mass Media and the Social Order" in *Inter/Media Interpersonal Communication in a Media World*, ed. Gary Gumpert and Robert Cathcart (New York: Oxford University Press, 1986), pp. 611–27. Thomas pinpoints the myths "there's room at the top," "anyone can achieve," and "it's not so great at the top."

Hollywood Exoticism

11

SARAH BERRY

> Thirty years ago, no lady ever made up. . . . And now, from the greenish or umber
> sheen of her eyelids to the flame or saffron of her lips and nails, the lady of to-day
> is a subtle and marvelous creation based on the entity that is – Herself.
>
> – *Vogue*, June 1934

Since the early days of the star system, Hollywood femininity has been closely tied in
with the marketing of cosmetics, and one of the most important stylistic vehicles for this
relationship was the glamour of exoticism. The stereotypes of exotic ethnicity deployed
in Hollywood films were both repeated and modified within cosmetics advertising of the
1930s, and numerous female stars endorsed makeup brands. It has been argued that the
use of exoticism in cosmetics advertising has historically "displaced" discourses of race and
gender via a "language of 'color' and 'type.'"[1] This can be seen as a suppression of racial
difference, but commercial discourses have also worked to normalize difference by treating
it euphemistically. For example, in the early 1930s Max Factor began designing cosmetics
to correspond with a range of complexion, hair, and eye colors, and this "personalized" color-
matching system (which was widely adopted by other brands) avoided issues of race by
describing differences in skin tone as aesthetic categories or "complexion types." Cosmetics
advertising of the 1930s certainly utilized stereotypes (popular makeup products used
"Tropical," "Chinese," and "Gypsy" colors), but the advertising was, nevertheless, significant
because it described beauty in terms of multiple points on a spectrum, rather than a single,
monochromatic ideal.

The paleness that many women, both "white" and of color, had struggled for years to
create with bleach creams, arsenic and lead powder, veils, and parasols was, I would argue,
significantly modified by Hollywood's familiarization of the sensual, painted face. This
relativization of beauty norms also resulted from the expansion of a commercial beauty
culture that relied economically on the promotion of new looks, new faces, and new
colors. The 1930s' exotic makeup lines can thus be seen as an early form of commodified
multiculturalism aimed at maximizing cosmetics sales. By mid-decade, most cosmetics
manufacturers had stopped advertising traditional, lily-white facial powder altogether.

By the end of the decade, the cinematic projection of sexuality onto nonwhite women,
typically characterized as dangerous "vampires" or tragic native-girls, had also been modified.

Sensuous and dusky dark-haired sirens like Dolores Del Rio, Dorothy Lamour, Hedy Lamarr, and Rita Hayworth had replaced pale platinum blondes as icons of glamour. It is difficult to interpret such changes in fashion iconography, but what is clear is that in the 1930s a relative increase occurred in the range of beauty types on the American screen and in advertising, suggesting that the dominance of white, monoracial beauty was significantly challenged by previously marginalized female identities.

From their first appearance at the turn of the century, Hollywood's ethnic stereotypes were predicated on the notion that there exists a category of nonethnic whiteness. Even in the late 1930s, when Mendelian genetic theory had disproved the concept of "pure" races with that of the human gene pool differentiated only by temporary geographical isolation, Hollywood perpetuated myths of racial purity and the dangers of "mixed blood." Films and publicity materials continued to refer to racial purity even as genetic theory was becoming popularized in the form of pro-assimilation arguments, which gradually displaced hereditarian and eugenicist racism in mainstream ideology.[2] At the same time, however, Hollywood's constructions of race were visualized in the form of clearly artificial "ethnic simulacra," the cosmetic basis of which was often described by publicity in terms of the wonders of Hollywood makeup illusionism.

These "simulacra" are the material of what Ella Shohat calls Hollywood's "spectacle of difference" – its creation of ethnicity as a consumable pleasure.[3] One of the primary products of this spectacle, the image of exotic beauty, was indispensable to the recuperation of cosmetics. The frequent use of exotic female stars as endorsers of women's beauty products was thus at odds with nativist norms of beauty, just as women's obsession with Rudolph Valentino, Ramon Novarro, and Charles Boyer's passionate sexuality was seen as a rejection of culturally approved but boring WASP masculinity.[4] One way to explore the controversial popularity of "ethnic" beauty is to look closely at the discourses around it, such as the way that racial difference was used in marketing, and the range of readings that such strategies made available.

The artificiality of Hollywood's ethnic categories was visible not only in discourses about cosmetics but also in publicity about nonwhite stars and films that represented hybrid racial identities. Notes from the Production Code Administration's censorship of *Imitation of Life* (1934), for example, are symptomatic in their unease about Peola, the film's mulatta character (played by Fredi Washington). Washington's image on screen clearly undermined the myth of racial "purity," but the Hays office, which coordinated the industry's self-censorship, responded by referring to the character of Peola as "the negro girl appearing as white." The film disturbed the Production Code Administration because it undermined the visual inscription of race as color, as well as implicitly reflecting to the history of miscegenation. The Hays office insisted that the invisibility of Peola's race was "extremely dangerous" to "the industry as a whole" and stipulated that the film script attribute her lightness to an albino-like aberration within "a line of definitely negro strain."[5] The difficulty of inscribing racist essentialism in terms of skin color also emerges in *Photoplay*'s description of Nina Mae McKinney, star of *Hallelujah!* (1929), which begins, "Nina isn't black, she's coppery," and concludes with the comment, "She may be black, but she's got a blonde soul."[6] The visual culture of Hollywood consumerism made it increasingly difficult to assign fixed identities to glamourized racial stereotypes.

Ella Shohat and Robert Stam have pointed out how the "racial politics of casting" in Hollywood effectively "submerged" the multiculturalism that is at the center of American national identity, replacing it with a visually coded racial hierarchy.[7] But the constant publicizing of Hollywood's cosmetic illusionism, along with marketing discourses obsessed with the "makeover," undermined the racial essentialism that required stereotypes to be taken as signs with real-world referents. Hollywood's exoticism of the 1930s was a product of centuries of Eurocentric representations and decades of racist production practices. But these films also popularized a form of exoticism as masquerade within an increasingly diverse market for both Hollywood films and associated goods like cosmetics, subjecting their images to an idiosyncratic process of consumer appropriation.

Western beauty and split femininity

Modern cosmetics have been promoted in terms of a fairly recent concept of "democratic" beauty, based on the proposition that with good grooming and makeup, every woman can be beautiful in her own, unique way. In the early 1930s, beauty columns began to suggest that facial beauty was simply a matter of effort and technique. This concept of beauty as universally attainable was predicated on a sense of the body's malleability and constructedness, and like the notion that one's personality could be endlessly modified through fashion, it supported the requirements of a consumer economy. Within the Judeo-Christian tradition, however, concepts of physical beauty have been even more controversial than debates over the legitimacy of fashion. Beauty as a social value continues to be highly problematic from a range of perspectives, including contemporary feminist ones. But the condemnation of physical beauty has a long history in relation to the moral condemnation of women's sexuality, and a discussion of the rise of commercial beauty culture needs to take account of this.

Christian warnings against "vanity" and the cultivation of physical attractiveness have often clearly articulated anxieties about the expression of female sexuality. Historian Arthur Marwick has traced the discourse of English, European, and American beauty manuals from the sixteenth century onward, arguing that their emphasis on the cultivation of feminine virtue was linked to fears of female physical beauty as a form of power. Until the nineteenth century, many books on beauty were, in fact, written by church officials or professional moralists, and reflect a long-standing European model of split femininity iconically represented by "the Madonna and the whore." Real feminine beauty is said to reflect moral goodness (the beauty of the Madonna), but it can also exist physically in the absence of goodness (the seductiveness of the whore). In Gabriel de Minut's 1587 book *Of Beauty*, for example, the author explains that an attractive woman who is not virtuous is only *seemingly* beautiful, while in fact stimulating "the pollution and contamination of vice and ordure."[8] Beauty is thus a sign whose meaning can only be determined by the feelings it invokes in men: if it stimulates lustful desire, it is not "real" beauty but a sign of the *woman's* immorality. The usefulness of this ideology for inhibiting women's expression of their own sense of attractiveness is clear, given the risk of inspiring the "wrong" kind of appreciation.

In spite of this moralizing split between physical and spiritual beauty, by the late eighteenth century there was a large market for practical advice on techniques of cosmetic self-improvement. As the nineteenth century progressed, the value of beauty for both men and women within a growing capitalist and service economy became obvious, and the recognition of beauty as social capital is evident in its absorption into a feminine work ethic.

Women's cosmetic self-maintenance came to be seen as a process that might not *produce* beauty but could help retain positive attributes and was, therefore, dutiful rather than unethical. This view led to a plethora of beauty guides that originated and circulated in England, France, and the United States. Their authors included "society beauties," professional writers on fashion and etiquette, and purveyors of scientific beauty treatments.

In the nineteenth century a fairly limited range of cosmetic aids were used, however, particularly by comparison with the earlier popularity of cosmetics among social elites in the seventeenth and eighteenth centuries. Bourgeois women limited their use of beauty products to items like refined soap, lotions and astringents for softening the skin, hair oils and tints, and facial powder. In 1866, poisonous white facial powders made from lead or arsenic salts were finally replaced by an oxide of zinc, which was cheap and became available to working-class women.[9] Christian anxieties about physical beauty and cosmetic self-adornment remained powerful, however, until the popularity of cheaper cosmetics after World War I began to mitigate the social stigma of makeup.[10] In the transitional, prewar period, bourgeois women's interest in cosmetics was made morally acceptable by the quasi-spiritual philosophies of "beauty culturists." These were primarily female entrepreneurs who, like Elizabeth Arden and Helena Rubenstein, had some knowledge of dermatology and a lot of marketing skill. They made cosmetics morally acceptable by promoting a philosophy of "Natural Beauty" to be achieved through good health, expensive massage, and "scientific" skin treatments. Their approach combined moralizing about the need for inner perfection with the pleasures of salon pampering: as one advertisement asked, "Is your complexion clear? Does it express the clearness of your life? Are there discolorations or blemishes in the skin – which symbolize imperfections within?"[11]

But this mind–body philosophy, which was carried over from the nineteenth century, also implied that individuals who were less than beautiful could be judged as to their moral interiority, a theory popularized by the pseudoscience of phrenology. In addition, it presumed to set the standards of "Natural Beauty" according to northern European ideals, implying that racial "difference" could be read as both an aesthetic and a moral imperfection. Such theories represented a nativist bias in the United States that became increasingly virulent in response to new patterns of immigration and resulted in the eugenics movement. Eugenics brought together Christian notions that the body was a mirror of the soul, a Darwinist emphasis on heredity, and a pseudoscientific notion of racial purity. It aimed to purify the "white" race by restricting immigration and miscegenation, and by preventing "deviant" bodies from reproducing.[12]

Following World War I, however, nativist claims to physical and aesthetic superiority became increasingly incompatible with the demands of the new consumer economy. Given the requirements for "Natural Beauty" – a WASP pedigree, lots of fresh air, and virtuous thoughts – most American women would have been doomed to an inferior visage. But consumer-marketing professionals needed women to look in the mirror and see potential beauty so that new products could be positioned as a means of self-improvement. The cosmetics industry had also begun to shift from a "class" to a mass market in the nineteenth century, when white-collar women were confronted with the value placed on their personal appearance in the commercial service sector. This market of working- and middle-class women gradually became far more significant to the cosmetics industry than its traditional market of elite female consumers.[13]

The makeover and the Max Factor

The growing presence of women in service-sector work and the entertainment industry throughout the nineteenth century meant that female beauty became increasingly visible as a form of social capital. New women's magazines and self-help literature facilitated the rise of a commercial beauty culture that increasingly looked to actresses to legitimize new modes of self adornment.[14] Throughout the nineteenth century, cosmetics manufacturers had solicited letters of endorsement from reigning theatrical divas to be printed in publications aimed at bourgeois women.[15] In the early twentieth century, however, endorsements by cinema stars began to outnumber those from "legitimate" stage actresses, as popular appeals to a mass market for beauty products displaced reliance on elite consumers.

Helena Rubenstein opened a salon in London in 1908 and by 1916 had begun a chain that included salons in several major U.S. cities. Mainstream American women were still reluctant to adopt her eye shadow, however, and Rubenstein turned to Hollywood for promotional help by designing the Orientalist eye makeup for Theda Bara in A Fool There Was (1915).[16] With their heavy, seductive eyes and "vampire lips," Hollywood silent-film stars like Bara, Nita Naldi, Pola Negri, and Alla Nazimova successfully challenged American norms of childlike beauty epitomized by Dorothy and Lillian Gish and Mary Pickford. Their success can be seen in the popularity of Clara Bow's huge eyes and "bee-stung lips," which were incorporated into the innocent but assertive sexuality of late 1920s flappers like Colleen Moore and Joan Crawford.[17] By 1934, the style pedagogy of Hollywood was metaphorized in a film featuring Thelma Todd as a model who demonstrates the miracle of cosmetics in the window of a beauty emporium, while a simultaneous huge "close-up" image of her face is projected alongside her in the shop window, attracting a crowd of onlookers (in Hips, Hips, Hooray).

Makeup played a significant technical sole in the production of the Hollywood screen image. The use of heavy makeup on film actors was initially necessary to conceal the skin's red corpuscles, which were visible on orthochromatic film; it also hid imperfections exaggerated by the camera and provided a more consistent image for continuity purposes. By the early 1930s, panchromatic film stock allowed the use of a thinner greasepaint, and studio makeup artists began producing a carefully shaded and contoured face for the Hollywood screen – a look that was further stylized by studio lighting and photographic retouching.[18] To maintain the image he had created of Marlene Dietrich, Josef von Sternberg supervised all her studio portraiture: to make Dietrich's nose more aquiline, he once painted a thin silver line from the bridge to the tip of the nose and focused a small spotlight on it, with effective results.[19]

The stars' faces were individualized with a range of signature features: the shape of the mouth and eyebrows, the color and form of the hair, and the amount and style of eye makeup worn. Stars usually maintained a consistent makeup style from film to film, except when playing a "character" role, although they adapted to and modified broader fashions in makeup. Joan Crawford's mouth, for example, was painted inside her natural lip line throughout the 1920s to make her mouth smaller and rounder. In 1932, however, the films Letty Lynton and Rain display a fuller, somewhat overpainted mouth. As one article noted, "The lipstick extended beyond the corner and the mouth was greatly exaggerated in both thickness and length." In spite of the controversy this caused, Crawford's trend setting established what came to be seen as the "natural"-shaped mouth.[20]

The logic of an expanding consumer market for cosmetics helps to account for steady increases in the variety of products available from the early twentieth century onward. In 1931, an article in *Harper's Magazine* commented:

> A quarter of a century ago perfume, rice powder, and "antichap" for the hands constituted the entire paraphernalia of a woman's boudoir table. Now that table looks like a miniature chemist shop. No detail of appearance which can safely be entrusted to artifice is ever left to nature. . . . As a result feminine beauty, once the Creator's business, is now Big Business's.[21]

The article reported that more than two billion dollars were spent each year on beauty products, and that forty thousand beauty shops were scattered across the United States. The marketing strategies that fueled this growth were based on a few key concepts, most of which had also been applied to fashion marketing. These included the cultivation of a personal style chosen from a range of "types," the idea that this style could be changed at will, that an openness to change was necessary for finding or perfecting one's style, and that Hollywood stars represented idealized types for emulation and also demonstrated the effectiveness of cosmetic self-transformation.

Profiles of female stars in Hollywood fan magazines inevitably include a photograph of the star when she had just arrived in Hollywood. Much is made of the quaintness of her appearance in contrast to the astounding beauty she has cultivated since, which is credited to both her drive for self-improvement and the skill of studio makeup artists and designers.[22] In the 1933 article "These Stars Changed Their Faces – And So Can You!" this process is described in terms of facial features that have been "remodeled" by particular stars:

> Though styles may change in dresses and hats, most of us cart about the same old face . . . year in and year out. And sometimes we'd be glad to exchange the old looks for some new ones. But how can it be done? The movie stars are showing you! . . . In the new films, there are many "new faces," which have been remodeled over familiar frames. And something tells us that these new eyebrows, lips and hairlines are going to be as avidly copied by Miss America as the Hollywood clothes styles have been.[23]

Beauty advice columns of the early 1930s focused increasingly on the use of cosmetics, as indicated by the article, "What Any Girl Can Do with Make-Up." The columnist describes a young woman who went from "demure" to sophisticated, thanks to "a new coiffure, a different line in clothes, and most important of all, a new make-up scheme." The column concludes by suggesting, "why don't you try a few changes . . . we girls of 1930 have waked up to make-up!"[24] A Max Factor advertisement in the same issue repeats this narrative in the form of a testimonial by Bessie Love (an MGM star) titled "I Saw a Miracle of Beauty Happen in Hollywood": "She was just like a dozen other girls, but Max Factor, Hollywood's Make-Up Wizard, by the flattering touch of make-up, transformed her into a ravishing beauty . . . Revealing the secret of how every girl may obtain New Beauty and New Personality."[25]

The degree of artifice employed by Hollywood makeup artists was actually played up in beauty articles, and the very artificiality of the made-over face was celebrated as evidence of the democratization of beauty:

There is a corrective formula for everything that is wrong with the feminine face. . . . The miracle men know what that is. They put it to work. And they transform those who are average . . . into individuals whose attraction and charm circle the globe.[26]

The concept of the "makeover" is regularly promoted in Hollywood fan magazines, although the first use I found of the term itself was in January 1939: in a beauty column, several female stars describe their New Year's fashion and beauty resolutions, which articulate concisely the cosmetics marketing strategies noted earlier. Anne Shirley, for example, "feels that only by experimenting can a person discover what's most becoming to her," and Joan Blondell states categorically, "the whole secret of beauty is change. . . . A girl who neglects changing her personality gets stale mentally as well as physically. So I'm going to vary my hair style, my type of make-up, nail-polish, perfume." In this article, constant self-transformation is also described as a source of pleasure rather than just a means to an end. The makeover epitomizes consumer marketing because it is a process that is simultaneously goal-oriented *and* its own reward – it offers the pleasure of potentiality: "If you get bored with yourself at times, let your resolution be to do something about it. Experiment with new make-ups, change your hairstyle and make yourself over into a new person."[27] Advertising for beauty products, however, still emphasized the positive results of their use – like romance or a job – and cinematic makeover sequences often had even more dramatic consequences.

Along with self-transformation and change, the promotion of color was a successful cosmetics-marketing concept. Just as product stylists in the 1920s stimulated the market for household products by designing them in vibrant colors, cosmetics began to be produced in an ever wider range of tones by the end of the 1920s. For cosmetics, the fashion "type" became linked to hair and eye color rather than personality, encouraging women to try a variety of makeup hues to see which ones matched their own coloring. In 1928, Max Factor changed the name of his cosmetics line from "Society MakeUp" to "Color Harmony Make-Up," on the advice of his marketing agency, Sales Builders, Inc. Their research showed that women usually bought cosmetics items in different brands; if the need to buy "harmonized" products was stressed, however, women would buy every article in the same brand. The result was the Max Factor "Color Harmony Prescription Make-Up Chart," which indicated the complementary shades of powder, rouge, and lipstick to be used according to complexion, hair, and eye color. This "harmonizing" concept was part of a widespread technique of marketing women's fashion separates and accessories as complementary "ensembles." Richard Hudnut cosmetics used it successfully in an "eyematched makeup" line, which offered a variety of cosmetics chosen according to eye color, while advertising for "Lady Esther" cosmetics cautioned that "the wrong shade of powder can turn the right man away! . . . so I urge you to try all my shades."[28]

One of the most significant aspects of the use of color to promote the growth of cosmetics was the introduction of new facial powders and rouges that were meant to accommodate a wider range of skin tones. In previous centuries, women had bleached, enameled, and powdered their faces with an array of frequently toxic substances. A gradual change took place, however, as outdoor activities like bicycling and tennis became popular among upper-class women, and working-class women moved from farm to factory labor. Suntanned skin became associated with bourgeois leisure, while pallor represented long hours worked in sunless factories. In addition, beach resorts like the Riviera became meccas for social elites in the 1920s, resulting in a vogue for suntan as a visible sign of upper-class travel; as a writer for *Advertising and Selling* mused,

What inherent urge causes people to paint upon their faces the visible marks of their political or social levels? . . . The outdoor complexion has now met with consumer recognition . . . prompted by the desire to imitate leisure – that leisure which may go to Florida, Bermuda or California and bask in the sun.[29]

Cosmetics manufacturers took notice of the new acceptability of nonwhite skin and began to produce darker powders, as well as artificial bronzing lotions. By 1929, Jean Patou and Coco Chanel had introduced suntan products, and Helena Rubenstein was selling "Valaze Gypsy Tan Foundation." Other cosmetics manufacturers were blending powders to be "creamy," rather than white, and producing "ochre," "dark rachel," and "suntan" shades. Joan Crawford was credited for spreading the trend among Hollywood flappers – in addition to tanning her face, Crawford browned her body and went stockingless, a style that was popular "for sleeveless, backless frocks." Predictably, hosiery soon became available in darker colors as well.[30]

The end of the suntan fad was predicted periodically in early-1930s magazines, and Crawford was reportedly told by MGM to stop tanning because she looked "like a lineal descendent of Sheba," and "contrast[ed] strangely with the pale Nordics in her films."[31] Instead, it became the norm for women to tan in the summer, or even year-round if they lived in a warm climate. Golden Peacock Bleach Cream and other facial bleaches, which were advertised regularly in women's magazines until the late 1920s, appeared only rarely after the early 1930s, although skin lighteners were still marketed to the African American community.[32] But as the racist quips about Crawford's suntan attest, the end of idealized pallor did not mean the end of the color line in American culture. What it accompanied, however, was a period of intensified commercial and cinematic representation of non-Anglo ethnicity, in the form of an appropriable exoticism. But the implication of such marketing was that nonwhite beauty cultures had an increasing influence on the mainstream. The cosmetics industry's maximization of its market through exoticism, in other words, resulted in a diversification of aesthetic ideals rather than the promotion of exclusively nativist, "white" beauty.

Hollywood exoticism and beauty culture

An expanded range of color tones had been introduced into mainstream cosmetics by the late 1930s, but the discourses surrounding this change had a complex history both in Hollywood and in the marketing of cosmetics. Silent-screen "vamps" and the love goddesses who succeeded them were products of Hollywood's participation in a long tradition of project-ing sexual licentiousness and exoticism onto colonized subjects. In the United States, European obsessions with the East were augmented by political and economic designs on Latin America and the South Pacific, giving rise to additional ethnic stereotypes and erotic "others" associated with those cultures. From its beginning, cinema had played a significant role in the popularization of imperialist fantasies and ethnic stereotypes, and the Hollywood studios found that the sexual exoticism associated with these themes was consistently popular.

Hollywood offered a range of nonwhite characterizations throughout the 1930s, from the "Latin Lover" roles of Ramon Novarro and Charles Boyer to the Latin, Asian, and South Seas beauties played by stars like Dolores Del Rio, Lupe Velez, Dorothy Lamour, and Hedy Lamarr. The European stars Greta Garbo, Marlene Dietrich, and Lil Dagover were also "Orientalized" in many films and described as embodying a "pale exoticism." The casting of Euramerican actors in "ethnic" roles was commonplace in Hollywood, and the process of transforming them via elaborate character-makeup techniques was often discussed and illustrated in magazines.[33] Most non-Anglo Hollywood performers had their names anglicized, however, to eliminate any reference to their cultural background. Others were chosen to represent foreignness and rarely allowed to do anything else. On occasions when a star constructed as "ethnic" played a "white" role, it was noteworthy: when the Mexican actress Dolores Del Rio was cast as a French-Canadian lead in *Evangeline* (1929), *Photoplay* noted that "after winning a place on the screen because of her sparkling Spanish beauty and the fire of her performances, [she] now steps into a role that might have been reserved for Lillian Gish. It's a tribute to her versatility."[34]

More frequently, non-Anglo actors played a wide range of exotic roles; Lupe Velez was cast as a Chinese woman in *East Is West* (1930), a Native American in *The Squaw Man* (1931), and a Russian in *Resurrection* (1931). There was an interchangeability between all "ethnic" roles, but movement from "ethnic" typecasting to "white" roles was rare. One of the most notorious cases of casting discrimination in the 1930s took place when MGM asked Anna May Wong to audition for the role of the maid, Lotus, in their 1937 production of *The Good Earth*. The Los Angeles-born Wong had performed successfully on the stage in London and Europe and was the most popular Chinese American performer in Hollywood. In spite of Wong's status, the leading role in *The Good Earth* was given to Austrian actress Luise Ranier. Disgusted, Wong refused to play Lotus, questioning why MGM was asking her to play "the only unsympathetic role" in the film, while non-Chinese Americans played the main characters.[35]

In the United States, these characterizations were screened in the context of a nativist backlash against immigration aimed at both Asians and the "new immigrants" – Jewish, Italian, and Eastern Europeans who arrived in the late nineteenth century. Unlike their Anglo, German, and Nordic predecessors, the "new immigrants" were perceived as being unfit to assimilate into a nativist-defined American identity, which was in danger of being "mongrelized" by their presence. In 1907, Congress established an "Immigration Commission" to look into the impact of the new immigrants on the country; two years later, the report granted Congress broad powers to exclude and deport specific categories of immigrants. According to David Palumbo-Liu, "from 1921 to 1925, nearly thirty thousand people were deported," and over the next five years that number doubled; the Tydings-McDuffie Act of 1934 effectively restricted all Asian immigration.[36] Hollywood's exotic ethnicity of the 1930s thus arose in the context of social anxiety about race but also represented an ongoing attraction and fascination with idealized forms of ethnicity.

Hollywood ethnicity in the 1930s also had hierarchical distinctions, with Castillian Spanish "blood" as the most idealized and assimilable form of nonwhiteness possible. Like the Mediterranean-influenced French and Italians, the Spanish were seen as both exotic and European. Dolores Del Rio was repeatedly described as having an "aristocratic" family in order to distinguish her from mixed-race Mexicans, and the studios' disregard for Spanish-speaking countries' linguistic differences led them to dub films into Castillian Spanish, even when they were set in Mexico, Cuba, or Argentina. Actresses described as Spanish appear to have outnumbered any other "ethnic" category in the late 1920s and early 1930s; in addition to Del Rio and Velez, the performers Raquel Torres, Conchita Montenegro, Arminda, Rosita

Figure 11.1 Dolores del Rio
Courtesy of Photofest, New York

Moreno, Movita Castaneda, Maria Casajuana, and Margo all appeared, for a while at least, on-screen and in the pages of fan magazines. The sex appeal of the "Latin type" is clear from an article noting that Casajuana was discovered when Fox, "on the lookout for sultry types, staged a beauty contest in Spain."[37] Like the "Spanish blood" that redeems Valentino's character in *The Sheik* (1921), Spanishness is often Hollywood's ethnically acceptable alibi for hot-blooded sexuality. It was also used as a racial default-setting for performers who played a range of ethnic roles; a magazine profile of Margo, whose biggest Hollywood role was as a Russian in the Orientalist fantasy *Lost Horizon* (1937), notes, "Margo's exoticism is not an affectation. It is an inheritance bequeathed by her Castillian ancestors."[38]

Nativist ideology had often stressed women's role in maintaining "racial purity": in 1922, feminist Charlotte Perkins Gilman supported the eugenics movement by calling on women to utilize "their racial authority" in order to "cleanse the human race of its worst inheritance by a discriminating refusal of unfit fathers." The same year, the Cable Act declared that any female citizen who married an immigrant who was unable to naturalize would automatically lose her own citizenship. As Palumbo-Liu notes, the only other act for which one's citizenship could be revoked was treason; a woman's conception of a child with an "alien" man was thus seen as the equivalent of treason.[39] Miscegenation was identified as "race suicide," and was included in the Motion Picture Producers and Distributors of America (MPPDA) list of representational prohibitions when Will Hays became president in 1922, removing the possibility that any Hollywood film narrative could include a non-tragic cross-racial romance.[40] Nevertheless, by promoting stars who represented a sophisticated ethnicity designed to be mass marketed internationally, Hollywood utilized "the spectacle of difference" in ways that allowed for anti-essentialist readings.

Hollywood's émigré performers were a crucial part of the film studios' attempts to maximize international distribution, and numerous production decisions about casting, dialogue, and representational issues were also made in relation to the requirements of nondomestic markets.[41] The consideration of different national codes of censorship was a particularly relevant factor, as was the popularity of specific stars overseas. In 1933, *Variety* took stock of the value of Hollywood stars in foreign markets, noting that

> there are some picture stars in the U.S., very popular here, who are even more popular abroad. . . . The foreign stars in the U.S., of course, like Marlene Dietrich, Maurice Chevalier, and Lillian Harvey can be figured on to garner at least as large a harvest outside the American boundaries as within them. Not true of Greta Garbo or Ronald Colman, however, because of the amazing strength both have at home.[42]

The importance of stars as global commodities was highlighted when the studios, attempting to maintain their foreign markets following the transition to sound, tried making multiple foreign-language versions of selected films; in most cases, a completely different cast was used – without the English-speaking star. But when the original star happened to be bilingual (as were Dietrich, Garbo, and Novarro), a foreign-language film could be produced with equal star value, doubling profits.[43] This desire for international appeal accounts for much of Hollywood's consistent poaching of foreign talent. Arguing in support of Hollywood's use of non-American labor in 1937, an attorney for the MPPDA told a congressional committee on Immigration and Naturalization that "[s]ome of the world-wide character and appeal of American motion pictures must be credited to the employment of foreign actors."[44]

Hollywood's use of stars representing "foreignness" can therefore be seen as an attempt to target three distinct audiences: (1) Anglo-American viewers who liked exoticism, even if only in terms of racist stereotypes; (2) an immigrant-American audience interested in multicultural characters; and (3) nondomestic viewers with various linguistic and cultural preferences. The desire to create a global product thus put the studios somewhat at odds with the racist xenophobia of 1930s America. Such a conflict between audiences was also evident in the studios' battles with the Christian Right over what mainstream moral standards were, resulting in stricter Production Code enforcement after 1934. Hollywood's glamorization of racial difference and simultaneous pandering to racist stereotypes can thus be attributed, in part, to marketing conflicts and the desire to create non-Anglo characters that were acceptable both at home and abroad.

The Technicolor face: "jungle madness for cultured lips"

Twentieth-century cosmetics advertising vividly documents the importance of Hollywood exoticism to the construction of a new kind of beauty achievable through a more colorful use of makeup – a discourse linked to Hollywood's gradually increasing use of Technicolor from the mid-1930s onward. Early Technicolor sequences had been used in black-and-white films of the 1920s to highlight spectacular scenes such as fashion shows or elaborately decorated sets, while color simultaneously appeared in consumer product design and advertising graphics. In 1932, however, the Technicolor company developed a three-strip process that, although expensive, was used for big-budget costume and adventure films. Big-budget productions became increasingly popular by mid-decade on the theory that, as David Selznick argued, money could be made during the depression only by producing either a lot of cheap films or a few expensive ones.[45]

The new Technicolor process was first tested in the Disney cartoon *Flowers and Trees* (1932), then in a two-reel short called *La Cucaracha* (1934), and finally in the feature *Becky Sharp* (1935). Three-strip films initially tended, like earlier two-strip sequences, to be in spectacular rather than realist genres because of anxieties that viewers would find the color jarringly stylized when paired with a realist mise-en-scène. Color was thus used in musicals or backstage entertainment/fashion films like *The Dancing Pirate* (1935), *A Star is Born* (1937), *Vogues of 1938* (1937), and *The Goldwyn Follies* (1938); in Westerns such as *Dodge City* (1939), *Drums along the Mohawk* (1939), and *Jesse James* (1939); and in fantasy/costume dramas like *The Garden of Allah* (1936), *Ramona* (1936), *Adventures of Robin Hood* (1938), *Gone with the Wind* (1939), and *The Wizard of Oz* (1939). Selznick International Pictures also produced a successful Technicolor comedy, *Nothing Sacred*, in 1937. The question of whether Technicolor would be accepted by viewers as compatible with Hollywood's realist conventions focused, in particular, on the importance of the face as a privileged signifier. In 1920, a producer warned that Technicolor threatened to overwhelm the screen with visual information, which conflicted with established goals of focusing attention on performers' faces and eyes through lighting and cinematography: "The human being is the center of the drama, not flowers, gardens, and dresses. The face is the center of the human being. And the eyes are the center of the face."[46] Another critic complained of early Technicolor that "when the figures retreat to any distance, it is difficult to distinguish their expression."[47] Anxiety that facial features could not be photographed in color with the same attention-riveting results that had been achieved in black and white became central to the Technicolor firm's research. As David Bordwell has noted, "The firm was at pains to compromise between developing a 'lifelike' rendition of the visible spectrum and developing a treatment of the human face that would accord with classical requisites of beauty and narrative centrality."[48]

One way that the chaos of the Technicolor palette was adapted to Hollywood norms of facial representation and beauty was to use performers whose style could be "naturally" associated with bright colors. Female stars who were "the Technicolor type" had "vivid" features and personalities, which often meant that they were exotically ethnic. When *Motion Picture* ran a profile of the actress Steffi Duna called "Steffi Is a Perfect Type for Color," Natalie Kalmus, Technicolor's production advisor, was asked why Duna had been chosen for the first three-strip films (*La Cucaracha* and *The Dancing Pirate*). She listed Duna's qualifications: "A colorful complexion; a contrasting shade of hair; natural rhythm (color accents a woman's gracefulness you know); a personality vivid enough to counter-balance the most brilliant kind of setting; and she's the type that can wear picturesque clothes." Along with having "natural rhythm," Duna was described as exotic: "Steffi of Hungary . . . and all the bright romance of it sings in her blood. In Budapest, you see, children are weaned on the gypsy music. . . . Steffi could dance to it before she could talk."[49] The description of ethnicity in terms like "vivid," "colorful," and "picturesque" was also commonplace in the promotion of stars like Dolores Del Rio (the "Sparkling Spanish beauty"), Tala Birell ("she's as exotic as a red camellia"), and Anna May Wong ("she brings to the screen . . . the mysterious colors of her ivory-skinned race").[50] But the advent of Technicolor produced even more emphasis on the relationship between color and exotic beauty, with Hollywood stars playing a central role in the promotion and naturalization of "colorful" femininity.

Along with Duna, a new style of tropical exoticism appeared in the mid-1930s that contrasted sharply with Garbo's "pale exoticism."[51] It had been visible in the 1920s' deluge of South Seas island films, which usually featured romance between a white hero and a native woman, since the Production Code Administration considered such couples relatively non-threatening and ruled in 1937 that romance between "white" characters and the "Polynesians and allied races" did not constitute miscegenation.[52] The island girl made a dramatic reappearance in the early 1930s just in time for a major fashion vogue in tropicalism. Balinese batik appeared in beachwear, along with the "Goona-Goona bathing suit" and a general "Javanese Influence." In 1935, an advertisement for brassieres declared that "Women of the Isle of Bali have always had the most beautiful breasts in the world," and a Tahitian-style bathing suit advertisement noted that "it all started in the Riviera. Smart women . . . adopted the daring costumes and colors of primitive islanders." *Vogue* concluded that "it's smart, this year, to look like a Balinese maiden when you have the figure for it," and also advised:

> If you are wearing a swathed Oriental evening frock . . . your make-up should be as glamorous as possible – deep, mysterious eye shadows, with perhaps a touch of gold or silver. This is the moment to use mascara on your lashes, and even indulge in kohl, and to make yourself, in general, as exotic as you possibly can.[53]

The following year, Dorothy Lamour made her sarong debut in *Jungle Princess* (1936) and became synonymous with the tropical look in subsequent films, like *The Hurricane* (1937), *Her Jungle Love* (1938), *Tropic Holiday* (1938), and others. By 1938, Lamour's long dark hair, sultry brown eyes, and prominent red mouth were being emulated widely, as an advertisement for lipstick in "a wicked new shade" indicates: "Jungle madness for cultured lips . . . the sublime madness of a moon-kissed jungle night . . . the most exotic color ever put into a lipstick."[54] Also available was "tropic beauty for your fingertips," with nail polish in shades like "Congo," "Cabaña," and "Spice."[55]

The Lamour "type" was a boon to the cosmetics industry, as well as to Technicolor, because her dark hair and skin tone could accommodate a wide range of cosmetics. The perfect expression of this type appeared in 1938 when Hedy Lamarr caused a sensation with her appearance in *Algiers*. While Lamour was called "untamed and torrid," Lamarr was a "red-lipped, tawny-eyed, black-haired girl" whose "lush, exciting beauty" combined sensuousness with an aloof glamour.[56] The Max Factor company was central to the promotion of sultry new stars like Lamarr, Ann Sheridan, and Rita Cansino (soon to be Hayworth), using them to endorse the new, multicolored approach to cosmetics. One Max Factor advertisement, featuring a photograph of Lamarr, stated: "Beauty's secret attraction is color . . . for it is color that has an exciting emotional appeal." Soon older stars followed the new "brunette trend"; Joan Bennett switched from blonde to raven hair and even duplicated Lamarr's long bob with a center part, her distinctive, downward-curving eyebrows, and wide, red lips. Bennett noted that with her new coloring, she could tan her face and wear stronger shades of makeup and heavier, "more Oriental" perfumes.[57]

Max Factor had been commissioned to devise an improved makeup foundation for use with Technicolor, one that could be layered in different shades without being too thick or reflective. The result was "Pan-Cake" makeup, which made its official debut in Walter Wanger's *Vogues of 1938*. According to reviews of the film, the goal of Technicolor realism had been reached with a "natural" rendering of facial tones and features. One critic devoted most of his review to a discussion of the new makeup, while another wrote that the actresses "were so lifelike . . . it seemed like they would step down from the screen into the audience at any minute."[58] Once Technicolor and cosmetics manufacturers had established both the beauty advantages of color and the naturalism of the new representational palette, it remained for Pan-Cake makeup techniques to be promoted to consumers. Referred to as "shaded" or "corrective" makeup, it was said to give Dietrich "that lovely exotic high-cheek-boned look" and to disguise numerous structural imperfections in other stars' faces. Contoured makeup could, in effect, give anyone high cheekbones, a "new nose," or "larger eyes." Most important of all, the process required the use of more than one foundation color – potentially doubling sales of facial powder. To make cheekbones stand out, they could be powdered with a light shade, while a darker "shadow" was applied underneath. If, like Dietrich, one applied the shadow in a triangle shape, the results would be "positively Oriental."[59]

Technicolor makeup techniques were thus said to increase the transformative qualities of makeup and the range of complexions and colors located within the new norms of natural-looking beauty. A *Photoplay* beauty column of 1938 was devoted to a discussion of the "Technicolor . . . school of beauty"; in addition to exoticism, the Technicolor face is said to represent the full range of different complexion and coloring types among women. Using *The Goldwyn Follies* as an example, the writer suggests that there are at least thirteen different "variations of coloring" represented by women in the film, offering female viewers the opportunity to find their own "color harmony" among the many facial shades available. In addition, she points out that film stars now wear different make-ups for different color gowns, so that the whole ensemble is a perfect blending of color." The column is essentially an advertorial for the Max Factor company's "personalized color palette," system, even incorporating the company's slogan of "color harmony" into the text. But it also demonstrates the way that the growth of the cosmetics industry was predicated on women's use of an ever greater range of products and colors on their faces.[60]

Hollywood exoticism was thus central to discourses that fueled the renaissance in cosmetics, as were Technicolor and the desire for export-market appeal. The high point of Hollywood's vivid exoticism was reached in the 1940s with the Technicolor figure of Carmen

Miranda. "Good Neighbor" films like The Gang's All Here (1943) presented not only the archetype of the Hollywood Latina (with huge eyelashes, red lips, and a multicolored "tutti-fruity hat") but also a pro-Latin American sensibility designed to foster Pan-American solidarity against the Axis powers. Miranda's first Hollywood film, Down Argentine Way (1940), features a musical number in which the blond-haired Betty Grable emulates Miranda's look, wearing vivid makeup, an ornamented turban, costume jewelry, and a ruffled, off-the-shoulder gown. Grable represents the consumerist assimilation being promoted by such films, in which Latin American style is domesticated via music and comedy. Soon numerous American women would also emulate Miranda by wrapping their hair in colorful floral scarves for factory work and using bright red lipstick and costume jewelry to make their rationed outfits more exotic.

Notes

1 Kathy Peiss, "Making Faces: The Cosmetics Industry and the Cultural Construction of Gender, 1890–1930," Genders 7 (spring 1990): 164.

2 David Palurnbo-Liu, "The Bitter Tea of Frank Capra," positions 3, 3 (1995): 782.

3 Ella Shohat, "Gender and Culture of Empire: Toward a Feminist Ethnography of the Cinema," Quarterly Review of Film and Video 13, 1–3 (1991): 63.

4 Cf. Gaylyn Studlar, This Mad Masquerade: Stardom and Masculinity in the Jazz Age (New York: Columbia University Press, 1996).

5 Feature film entry for Imitation of Life, The AFI Catalog of Motion Pictures Produced in the U.S.: Feature Films, 1931–1940, exec. ed. Patricia King Hanson, assoc. ed. Alan Gevinson (Berkeley, Calif.: University of California Press, 1993), 1013; Susan Courtney, "(De)Coding Hollywood's Fantasy of Miscegenanon," paper given at the Society for Cinema Studies Conference, Dallas, Tex., Mar. 1996.

6 McKinney's mother is also described as a woman "of light skin, who might have Spanish blood"; Herbert Howe, "A Jungle Lorelei," Photoplay 36, 1 (June 1929): 118–19.

7 Ella Shohat and Robert Stam, Unthinking Eurocentrism: Multiculturalism and the Media (London: Routledge, 1994), 189, 224, 220.

8 Arthur Marwick, Beauty in History: Society, Politics, and Personal Appearance c. 1500 to the Present (London: Thames and Hudson, 1988), 70.

9 Gilbert Vail, A History of Cosmetics in America (New York: Toilet Goods Association, 1947), 77–78, 87, 98–99; Kate de Castelbajac, The Face of the Century: One Hundred Years of Makeup and Style (New York: Rizzoli, 1995), 12.

10 De Castelbajac, The Face of the Century, 46.

11 Peiss, "Making Faces," 147; Lois Banner, American Beauty: A Social History through Two Centuries of the American Idea, Ideal, and Image of the Beautiful Woman (New York: Knopf, 1983), 214.

12 Mark H. Haller, Eugenics: Hereditarian Attitudes in American Thought (New Brunswick, N.J.: Rutgers University Press, 1963), 153.

13 Marwick, Beauty in History, 245; Banner, American Beauty, 207, 217.

14 Fenja Gunn, The Artificial Face: A History of Cosmetics (Newton Abbot: David and Charles, 1973), 123, 139; Lillian Russell, "Beauty as a Factor in Success on the Stage," Woman Beautiful 4 (Apr. 1910): 39.

15 Vail, A History of Cosmetics in America, 102.

16 Helena Rubenstein, *My Life for Beauty* (London: Bodley, Head, 1964), 58–59.

17 Fred E. Basten with Robert Salvatore and Paul A. Kaufman, *Max Factor's Hollywood: Glamour, Movies, Make-Up* (Santa Monica, Calif.: General Publishing Group, 1995), 34, 90.

18 Alicia Annas, "The Photogenic Formula: Hairstyles and Makeup in Historical Films," in *Hollywood and History: Costume Design in Film* (London: Thames and Hudson; Los Angeles County Museum of Art, 1987), 55–56.

19 De Castelbajac, *The Face of the Century*, 75.

20 Ruth Biery, "The New 'Shady Dames' of the Screen," *Photoplay* 42, 3 (Aug. 1932): 28; in letters to the editor, fans reportedly "liked 'Letty Lynton' but wished Joan wouldn't use so much eye and mouth make-up"; "The Audience Talks Back," *Photoplay* 42, 3 (Aug. 1932): 6–7.

21 Jeanette Eaton; "The Cosmetic Urge," *Harper's Magazine* 162 (Feb. 1931): 323.

22 Cf. Carolyn van Wyck, "Photoplay's Own Beauty Shop," *Photoplay* 41, 5 (Apr. 1932): 55.

23 Dorothy Manners, "These Stars Changed Their Faces – And So Can You!" *Motion Picture* 45, 5 (June 1933): 32–33.

24 Carolyn van Wyck, "Friendly Advice on Girls' Problems: What Any Girl Can Do with Make-Up," *Photoplay* 38, 3 (Aug. 1930): 18, 116.

25 Max Factor advertisement, *Photoplay* 38, 3 (Aug. 1930): 101.

26 Adele Whitely Fletcher, "Miracle Men at Work to Make You Lovelier." *Photoplay* 53, 7 (July 1939): 26.

27 Carolyn van Wyck "Photoplay's Own Beauty Shop," *Photoplay* 53, 1 (Jan. 1939): 66.

28 Basten, *Max Factor's Hollywood*, 80; Roland Marchand, *Advertising the American Dream: Making Way for Modernity*, 1920–1940 (Berkeley: University of California Press, 1985), 132–40; advertisement, *Photoplay* 53, 9 (Sept. 1939): 77.

29 Marie du. Bois, "What Is Sun-Tan Doing to Cosmetics?" *Advertising and Selling* 13, 4 (June 12, 1929): 19.

30 De Castelbajac, *The Face of the Century*, 44; advertisement in *Photoplay* 36, 1 (June 1929): 76; advertisement, *Photoplay* 36, 3 (Aug. 1929): 105.

31 Dorothy Spensley, "The Most Copied Girl in the World," *Motion Picture* 53, 4 (May 1937): 30–31.

32 Peiss, "Making Faces," 160.

33 In her early career, Myrna Loy's heavy-lidded eyes and round face inspired producers to cast her in a series of "native" roles, including Chinese, Malay, Hindu, Egyptian, and French African women. In 1936, however, a *Photoplay* caption noted that whereas "[s]he used to play slant-eyed Oriental seductress roles, today she is the ideal screen wife."

34 Photograph caption, *Photoplay* 36, 2 (July 1929): 22.

35 Edward Sakamoto, "Anna May Wong and the Dragon-Lady Syndrome," *Los Angeles Times*, July 12. 1987: n.p.

36 Palumbo-Liu, "The Bitter Tea of Frank Capra," 761.

37 "New Pictures," *Photoplay* 35, 6 (May 1929): 21.

38 Denise Caine, "Beauty Is Kin Deep!" *Motion Picture* 54, 2 (Sept. 1937): 51.

39 Cited in Studlar, *This Mad Masquerade*. 163: Palumbo-Liu. "The Bitter Tea of Frank Capra," 761.

40 Thomas Cripps, *Slow Fade to Black: The Negro in American Film*, 1900–1942 (New York: Oxford University Press, 1977), 94.

41 Ruth Vasey, "Foreign Parts: Hollywood's Global Distribution and the Representation of Ethnicity," *American Quarterly* 44, 4 (Dec. 1992): 625.

42 "U.S.' Overseas Panickers," Variety 112, 3 (Sept. 26, 1933): 3.

43 Kristin Thompson, Exporting Entertainment: America in the World Film Market 1907–34 (London: BFI Publishing, 1985), 162.

44 Vasey, "Foreign Parts," 625.

45 David Selznick is said to have run Selznick International Pictures on this premise; Thomas Schatz, The Genius of the System: Hollywood Filmmaking in the Studio Era (New York: Pantheon, 1988), 178.

46 Cited in David Bordwell, Janet Staiger, and Kristin Thompson, The Classical Hollywood Cinema: Film Style and Mode of Production to 1960 (New York: Columbia University Press, 1985), 355.

47 Cited in Fred Basten, Glorious Technicolor (New York: A. S. Barnes, 1980), 27.

48 Bordwell, Staiger, and Thompson, The Classical Hollywood Cinema, 356.

49 Virginia T. Lane, "Steffi Is a Perfect Type for Color;" Motion Picture 52, 1 (Aug. 1936): 43.

50 Photograph caption, Photoplay 36, 1 (June 1929): 22; "Two New Exotics," Photoplay 41, 6 (May 1932): 74; photograph caption, Motion Picture 27, 3 (Apr. 1924): 21.

51 Madame Sylvia, "Garbo's Glamor . . . Mystery or Misery?" Photoplay 50, 6 (Dec. 1936): 56–57.

52 Vasey, "Foreign Parts," 629.

53 Advertisement in Vogue, Dec. 1, 1932: 3; "The Javanese Influence," Vogue, Jan. 1, 1933: 28; advertisement in Vogue, Dec. 1, 1934: 117; advertisement in Vogue, Jan. 1, 1935: 79; Vogue, June 1, 1935: 44.

54 Advertisement in Photoplay 48, 7 (Dec. 1935): 110.

55 Advertisement in Photoplay 52, 10 (Oct. 1938): 90.

56 Ruth Waterbury, "Close Ups and Long Shots," Photoplay 52, 6 (June 1938): 13; Sara Hamilton, "Hedy Wine," Photoplay 52, 10 (Oct. 1938): 21.

57 Advertisement in Photoplay 52, 10 (Oct. 1938): 21; Basten, Max Factor's Hollywood, 139, 163; advertisement in Photoplay 52, 9 (Sept. 1938): 77; Carolyn van Wyck, "Photoplay's Beauty Shop," Photoplay 53, 11 (Nov. 1939): 10–11; Barbara Hayes, "Hedy Lamarr vs. Joan Bennett," Photoplay 53, 11 (Nov. 1939): 18–19.

58 Basten, Max Factor's Hollywood, 147.

59 Jan Fisher, "If You Want to Be a Glamorous Beauty," Photoplay 51, 11 (Nov. 1937): 5; Carolyn van Wyck, "Photoplay's Beauty Shop," Photoplay 52, 3 (Mar. 1938): 8.

60 The marketing strategy of encouraging women to buy different lipsticks to match their dresses began in 1931. Cf. Carolyn van Wyck. "Friendly Advice of Girls' Problems: New Make-Up Theory," Photoplay 40, 4 (Sept. 1931): 16: Carolyn van Wyck. "Photoplay's Beauty Shop," Photoplay 52, 1 (Jan. 1938): 60.

Paul Robeson

12

Crossing over

RICHARD DYER

> One ever feels his twoness – an American, a Negro; two souls, two thoughts, two
> unreconciled strivings, two warring ideals in one dark body, whose dogged strength
> alone keeps it from being torn asunder.
>
> – W. E. B. DuBois, *The Souls of Black Folk*

In the jargon of the contemporary pop music business, a cross-over star is one who appeals to more than one musical subculture; one who, though rooted in a particular tradition of music with a particular audience, somehow manages to appeal, and sell, beyond the confines of that audience. Dolly Parton, Gladys Knight, Paul McCartney are recognisably country, soul and rock performers respectively, but they have a following among people who are not especially into those kinds of music. While having this wider appeal, they are still rooted in the particular musical subculture that defines them – in crossing over, they don't lose their original following. Or not too much of it.

The term cross-over, in this sense, did not exist when Paul Robeson was a major star, but, at least between 1924 and 1945, he was very definitely an example of it. His image insisted on his blackness – musically, in his primary association with Negro folk music, especially spirituals; in the theatre and films, in the recurrence of Africa as a motif; and in general in the way his image is so bound up with notions of racial character, the nature of black folks, the Negro essence, and so on. Yet he was a star equally popular with black and white audiences. There were other black singing stars as, if not more, popular than he in the twenties and thirties – Louis Armstrong, Bessie Smith, Ethel Waters, Cab Calloway, Billie Holiday – but none of these quite established the emblematic or charismatic position, for blacks and whites, and in more than one medium, that Robeson did. How did he manage this?

Some would argue that his achievements were so unarguably outstanding that he had to be recognised. Certainly there is no gainsaying those achievements – a brilliant academic record at Rutgers University (1915–19), where he was the only black student at the time and only the third ever to have been admitted, and at Columbia graduate law school (1920–1) where he was again the only black student; a great football player, the first black player ever selected to play for the national team (the All-Americans) from the university teams, all the more remarkable, according to Murray Kempton, for being from Rutgers, a less prestigious university (Kempton, 1955, p. 238); certainly the best known and most successful male singer of Negro spirituals, in concert and on record, and always highly acclaimed critically; the performer of what has been called the definitive Othello of his generation ("The best remembered Othello of recent decades", wrote Marvin Rosenberg in 1961 (p. 151)) and in the longest running Shakespeare production in Broadway history (1943–4); one of those performers who has made one of the standards of the show business repertoire, Old Man River, wholly identified with him, so much so that he was himself often referred to as Old Man River; singer of the hugely successful patriotic Ballad for Americans (1939) that the Republican party adopted for their National Convention in 1940; rapturously received in the theatre, particularly in The Emperor Jones (New York, 1924; London, 1926; Berlin, 1929), All God's Chillun Got Wings (New York, 1924; London, 1933), Show Boat (London, 1928; New York, 1932) as well as Othello (London, 1930; New York and US tour, 1943–5; Stratford-on-Avon, 1959); and if nothing in his film career quite matches up to all that, still he was big enough to be billed outside a London cinema for the première of Song of Freedom (1936) as 'GREATEST SINGING STAR OF THE AGE' and worked with the most important black film-maker of the time, Oscar Micheaux (in Body and Soul, 1924), with the avant-garde group surrounding the magazine Close-Up (Borderline, 1930), in a lavish Hollywood musical (Show Boat, 1935) and in a series of popular and, shall we say, for the most part decent British films of the thirties, as well as narrating a number of documentaries, including Native Land (1941) by Frontier Films and, outside our period, Song of the Rivers (1954) by Joris Ivens.

Yet such a list of achievements does not really explain his stardom. Whilst I don't want to diminish his talent or effort, this list is for the most part a statement of the fact that he was highly acclaimed, very popular, in other words, a star. But why were these achievements of so much interest to so many people? How were his remarkable qualities also star qualities? How and why were these the qualities of the first major black star?

We need to get the question right. How did the period permit black stardom? What were the qualities this black person could be taken to embody, that could catch on in a society where there had never been a black star of this magnitude? What was the fit between the parameters of what black images the society could tolerate and the particular qualities Robeson could be taken to embody? Where was the give in the ideological system?

Yet another way of putting it might be – what was the price that had to be paid for a black person to become such a star? Harold Cruse, the subtlest critic of both Robeson and the Harlem Renaissance with which he was associated, argues that from the perspective of black politics and black consciousness the price was too high. He finds Robeson too integrationist, too concerned with adapting himself to white cultural norms, too far removed from the real cultural concerns of black people, and too little aware that cultural development is not a thing of the spirit alone but is rooted in material conditions, the necessities of funding and support usually absent in black communities (Cruse, 1969, 1978). Likewise, Jim Pines (1975, p. 32) suggests that Robeson's work is a 'largely individualist and generally mystifying protest . . . [that] seems to substantiate the ineffectualness of individualist forms of protest against cultural exploitation by the media'; and Donald Bogle (1974, p. 98) even argues that Robeson was not only individualist in Pines' sense of an isolated individual but in the sense of self-seeking – 'No matter how much producers tried to make Robeson a symbol of black humanity, he always came across as a man more interested in himself than anyone else'.

The figure of Robeson still sets off argument about images of black peoples, and there is still a striking disparity in the different ways he is perceived. I am confining myself to the period in which Robeson was a cross-over and major star, roughly 1924–45, when the politics are less explicit and explosive than afterwards. What particularly interests me is the way that Robeson's image takes on different meanings in this period when read through different contemporary black and white perspectives on the world. There are different, white and black, ways of looking at or making sense of Robeson, but it would be a mistake to think that the white view is the one that stresses achievement, the black the one that stresses selling out. To set against Cruse, Pines, Bogle and the other black writers, there is *Paul Robeson: The Great Forerunner*, a book of articles and tributes, produced by the radical black magazine *Freedomways* (*Freedomways* editors, 1978), as well as countless celebrations of Robeson by black people throughout his career. Likewise, one can find – less easily, it is true – white writers quick enough to point to his artistic limitations or, like Murray Kempton (1955, p. 259), to deny his significance as an embodiment of black people: 'There was absolutely nothing between him and the people for whom he affected to speak'.

Equally, in speaking of different, white and black perspectives, I don't imply that black people saw him one way and whites the other. What I want to show is that there are discourses developed by whites in white culture and by blacks in black culture which made a different sense of the same phenomenon, Paul Robeson. There is a consistency in the statements, images and texts, produced on the one hand by blacks and on the other by whites, that makes it reasonable to refer to black and white discourses, even while accepting that there may have been blacks who have thought and felt largely through whites discourses and vice versa.

The difficulty of this argument is not so much theoretical as discerning the difference between black and white discourses in relation to Robeson. The difference is not obvious in the texts, and that is part of the explanation of how Robeson's cross-over star position was possible. For much of the time it could seem that the black and white discourses of the period were saying the same thing, because they were using the same words and looking at the same things. Robeson was taken to embody a set of specifically black qualities – naturalness, primitiveness, simplicity and others – that were equally valued and similarly evoked, but for different reasons, by whites and blacks. It is because he could appeal on these different fronts that he could achieve star status.

All the same, Robeson was working, particularly in theatre and films, in forms that had been developed, used and understood in predominantly white ways. In appearing in white plays and films, Robeson already brought with him the complex struggle of white and black meanings that his image condensed – but what happened to those meanings? Just by being in the plays and films, some of those black meanings are registered – but they are part of a broadly white handling of him, and this is significant not so much at the level of script and dialogue, as at the level of various affective devices that work to contain and defuse those black meanings, to offer the viewer the pathos of a beautiful, passive racial emblem.

The strategies of the white media worked to contain Robeson, but only *worked* to. How he was handled by the media is conceptually distinct from how audiences perceived him. By so doing the media might reinforce white discourses that intended to contain what was dangerous about black images in general, but by registering the black meanings in his image they also made these widely available, for use by black people. There is plenty of evidence of the impact that Robeson had on black audiences, but James Baldwin's notion of the way that Robeson (and other black stars) could work against the grain of his films suggests, at least, how a black viewer could see it that way, and with the force of 'reality' and 'truth':

It is scarcely possible to think of a black American actor who has not been misused: not one that has ever been seriously challenged to deliver the best that is in him . . . What the black actor has managed to give are moments, created, miraculously, beyond the confines of the script; hints of reality, smuggled like contraband into a maudlin tale, and with enough force, if unleashed, to shatter the tale to fragments . . . There is truth to be found in . . . Robeson in everything I saw him do.

(Baldwin, 1978, pp. 103–5)

It is the range of potential reading, black and white, in the context of an overall white media handling of Robeson that is the subject of this essay.

Body and Soul

Before examining the strategies of the white media for handling Robeson, and as both a prelude to that and a recapitulation of what has been said so far, I want to look in some detail at a film that is differently placed in relation to these problems and yet is profoundly caught up in them. This is *Body and Soul*. It is in a different position from the rest of Robeson's stage and film work partly by virtue of its early date, 1924, when Robeson was only just becoming established as a star, and partly because it was written, directed and produced by the black film-maker Oscar Micheaux. I am not claiming that because a film-maker is black (or a woman, or gay) his or her work will necessarily be more truly expressive of black (or female, or gay) experience much less of progressive views of that experience. But it is likely to be couched in specifically black (or female, or gay) subcultural discourses, to be in at least a negotiated relationship to mainstream discourses. Not inevitably, but likely; and, as Thomas Cripps (1977, p. 193) observes, *Body and Soul* is remarkable because it does bring together 'alternative life-models', specific to black American existence, 'close-packed upon each other in competition'. In other words, Cripps suggests it has an inwardness with the different contradictory ways (images and practices) that black people had of making sense of their situation to a degree no white made film ever did.

Body and Soul is not a film that is easy to get to see. Cripps suggests that there were two versions, the one that Micheaux originally made, and a revised version made under pressure from the New York censor board, whose objections according to Cripps, were 'much the same (as) the NAACP would have given' (ibid., p. 192), namely, its rather lascivious depiction of ghetto low life. The version preserved at George Eastman House in Rochester, New York is presumably the latter, although it bears only some resemblance to Cripp's account of the film. This version, and the fact that Micheaux had to adapt his film to white ideas, itself encapsulates the dilemma of constructing such a film. It does not just register, as in Cripps's reading, the alternative life-styles of ghetto society itself but also the problems of how to represent that society, and in particular how to represent black sexual mores.

This is also the problem in Paul Robeson's image at this stage. It is quite clear that he was thought to have 'sex-appeal'. Some found it in his voice.

The best description I ever heard of Robeson's voice was from Norman Haire – but unfortunately it is unprintable, since sexual imagery in this country is *verboten*, in spite of the fact that sex is life, and all art sexual.

(Mannin, 1930, p. 158)

Figure 12.1 Paul Robeson
Courtesy of Photofest, New York

Eslanda Goode Robeson's 1930 biography also stresses how much women found her husband sexually attractive. This is never so powerfully expressed in later references, but in addition to the brute/rape motif, the idea of a less aggressive, but still potent, sex appeal was enough to make the Art Alliance of Philadelphia return their commissioned nude statue of Robeson to the artist, Antonio Salemme. It is interesting to note the differences in the costume designs for Robeson's three Othellos, all working within the all-purpose, Tudor-theatrical style. The 1930 version has him in tights, with sensuous tops of fur and flowing velvet or puff-sleeved brocade; legs and inner thighs (if not exactly crotch) are revealed below, chest and arms amplified above. In the 1943 production, on the other hand, he is in flowing robes that wholly conceal the shape of the body, or leave only the arms bare in the murder scene. The same is true of the 1959 Stratford production. There is too a difference in the overall feeling conveyed by him in production photos. In 1930, he is glowering, smouldering; in 1943, troubled; in 1959, anguished, angry. Though it would be wrong to read him in the 1930 photos as just sexual, sexuality is present there to a degree not true of the others.

In the context of Robeson's functioning within white discourses, the gradual elimination of this sexuality from his image can be understood as a further aspect of the need to deactivate, lessen the threat of, his image. *Body and Soul*, however, suggests that there is a tension surrounding this within black discourses too. There is a central dilemma in most black thought of the period, especially that coming out of the Harlem Renaissance – is celebrating black sensuality insisting on an alternative to white culture or, on the contrary, playing into the hands of white culture, where such sensuality could be labelled as a sign of irrational inferiority and more grossly read as genital eroticism, as 'sexuality'? In *Body and Soul* this dilemma is worked through the figure of Robeson, who, in the available archive version anyway, plays two roles, both sexually ambiguous.

One role is Isiah. An opening shot of a newspaper item announces the escape of a prisoner posing as a preacher; there is then a cut to Isiah/Robeson seen from behind. From the start then the film gives the audience a position of knowledge in relation to Isiah – we know he is bad but his parishioners do not. The major narrative of the film concerns Isiah's misuse of his position and the adoration of his congregation to get free liquor and access to Isabelle, the daughter of one of his most loyal admirers, Martha Jane. His rape of Isabelle and her flight in shame to Atlanta, where Martha Jane finds her and learns the truth, lead to Isabelle's denunciation of him in church and the congregation hounding him out of town.

Martha Jane and Isabelle represent the familiar melodrama values of poor-but-honest, toiling and God-fearing folk. This is established in the very first shot of them, the one in bed, the other ironing, which is cross-cut with shots of Isiah talking with the local liquor salesman, threatening to preach against drink if the salesman doesn't keep him supplied with it. This elaborated use of editing is characteristic of the film's method. A later example occurs in the scene between Martha Jane and Isabelle in Atlanta; Isabelle is explaining what kind of man Isiah really is, and this is done through a series of flashbacks. In one, Isabelle has been left by Martha Jane with Isiah, ostensibly so that Isiah can persuade her to give up her wish to marry the man she loves, Sylvester. Isiah attempts first to rape/seduce Isabelle (not for the first time), and then gets her to produce the family Bible (which we already know is where Martha Jane keeps their savings). Three close-ups follow, one of dollars in Isiahs hand, the next of Martha Jane ironing, the third of her picking cotton. This is followed by the title 'Blood Money'. The editing no less than the story is generically classic melodrama, a stark opposition of good and bad, the pure women at the mercy of the heartless villain, the honest poor abused by the greed of the strong.

Yet this is complicated by the fact of Isiah/Robeson's sex appeal. It is not just that Robeson had it, or that, in Cripps's words (ibid., p. 192), 'Robeson fairly oozed . . . sexuality', but that we are repeatedly encouraged by the film to feel that sex appeal. Cripps (ibid.) refers to 'tight close-ups that tilted up to capture a virility long missing from black figures'. In the rape scene – presented as Isabelle's first memory/flashback to her mother in Atlanta – we are placed with Isabelle, and although the purpose of the flashback is to reveal Isiah's dastardly duplicity, it greatly emphasises the sensuality of the experience. Isiah and Isabelle are hiding in a shack after their horse has broken loose from their buggy during a storm. Isiah leaves the room (exiting screen left) so that Isabelle can undress for bed. There follows a sequence of cross-cutting of Isabelle's bare head and shoulders and his feet walking slowly forward (rightwards) in the passage. We have the eroticism of her undressing and nudity, and the tension of his making his way towards her. As we see her in full light, in a classic 'beauty' pose, and see only his active feet, we might seem to have here a standard identification with the male hero in his quest to get the beautiful female object of desire. Certainly we can easily place ourselves thus in relation to the events; but we are invited to place ourselves with Isabelle – it is her flashback – and the final shot, when Isiah enters and before the discreet fade, is a shot of him smiling at her/the camera, *not* of her cowering or responding to him/the camera. Moreover, this shot of him emphasises his flesh by his shirt being opened at the neck (the only time in the film) and by the fact that it is in an iris, a form of framing that often connotes 'the loved one' in silent films (an analogy with the shape of nineteenth-century pocket portrait photographs – compare D. W. Griffith's use of this in relation to Elsie/Lillian Gish in *Birth of a Nation*).

One could not really construe the film as saying that Isabelle wanted to be raped. Her virtue and his evil are quite clear in the narrative context; but the immediate treatment of him in the scene yields to the notion of his sexual attractiveness, even in a rape context. His attractiveness is anyway clearly marked at the beginning of the film. He is the only good-looking male character (bar one significant one) in the film. The first scenes show him with a businessman, who has luridly made-up lips and bright, dirty Jim Dandy clothes, and with a character called Yellow Curley, whose face looks as if it has been plastered with chalk. Both these characters look as corrupt as they are. Beside them, Isiah/ Robeson looks the strikingly handsome man he was. He also looks blacker than they do. The businessman's lips suggest an attempt to alter their shape to conform closer to white norms, while Yellow Curley looks a classic stereotype mulatto. Isiah/ Robeson is not only blacker in feature, but is not trying to look white either.

We have then in Isiah a character who is unquestionably bad, and yet very attractive because he is so black. It was the lot of black women stars to become known for their beauty only to the degree that they were fair. This is true of several of Robeson's co-stars, including the actress playing Isabelle in *Body and Soul*, as well as Fredi Washington (*Black Boy*, *The Emperor Jones* (film)), Nina Mae McKinney (*Sanders of the River*), Elizabeth Welch (*Song of Freedom*, *Big Fella*) – and, most notoriously, Lena Horne. This has not been true of black male stars, although between Robeson in *Body and Soul* and the appearance of stars such as Jim Brown, Richard Roundtree and Billy Dee Williams, there are only two black leading men stars, Harry Belafonte and Sidney Poitier. The question of the sexuality of their image, as of the blackness of it, is a vexed one, but neither were allowed the kind of directly, smoulderingly sexual appeal of Isiah/Robeson or of Brown, Roundtree and Williams.

One further element of *Body and Soul* raises, and confuses, the fact that Isiah/Robeson can be taken as attractive: the only other attractive man in the film, Sylvester, the man Isabelle wishes to marry, is also played by Robeson. Sylvester/ Robeson is a much less developed character. We are first introduced to him in an iris shot, walking through woods; this is a cut from a close-up of Isabelle, indicating not what she is looking at but what she is thinking of. (It may even be an important convention that male objects of female desire are introduced this way, thus making the desire more distant and spiritual; compare the introduction of Ahmed/Rudolph Valentino as the object of Yasmin/Vilma Banky's thoughts in *The Son of the Sheik* (see Dyer, 1982a, p. 2512).) This shot/thought occurs in a scene at Martha Jane's home, while she and Isiah are talking – but no title indicates who this is (the title may be lost, of course). For all we know, it could be Isabelle thinking of having seen Isiah romantically: the confusion of finding Isiah/Robeson attractive has set in. Sylvester/Robeson only occurs a few times in the rest of the film, chiefly as a brief reminder of who Isabelle really loves. Only at the end does he come into his own. He has invented something (it is not clear what), his invention has been accepted, he has enough money to marry Isabelle – the two of them and Martha Jane are grouped before a portrait of Booker T. Washington, the apostle of just such a black enterprise as Sylvester/Robeson represents. Isiah/Robeson's power was his sex appeal; Sylvester/Robeson's is his respectability.

But there is one further twist. Just before this final scene, there has been a climax to the Isiah story. Fleeing from his congregation, he finds himself in the forest, pursued by a small boy. He turns on him and begins to beat him with a stick. Cut to Martha Jane starting awake in her chair, and the title 'For it was all a dream', at which point Isabelle and Sylvester enter. Isiah then presumably never existed; he was a figment of Martha Jane's dream. Easy enough to read this as psychologically motivated – a mother's fears about the man her daughter loves. But it also represents the wider dilemma the films presents, as did Robeson at that point – the difficulty of stating black sexual appeal. In Martha Jane's dream Sylvester/Robeson's absent sexuality becomes Isiah/Robeson's disturbingly present, attractive, duplicitous, aggressive sexuality.

The rest of Robeson's work, especially in film, works to banish that image even as a spectre in a dream; but it is worth registering how powerfully, disturbingly present it could be. At least a black film-maker, torn apart by the contradictions posed for black culture and politics by the image of an active black male sexuality, registers the problem of handling the image. The later work perhaps handles it all too efficiently, to the point that one might not notice it was there.

Passivity and pathos

There was no conscious strategy to handle Robeson a certain way. However, even the most progressive white uses of Robeson, such as the avant-garde *Close-Up* group that was behind *Borderline* or the Labour Party-identified group behind *The Proud Valley*, were caught in white discourses that had a way of handling the representation of black people so as to keep those represented in their place. The basic strategy of these discourses might be termed deactivation. Black people's qualities could be praised to the skies, but they must not be shown to be effective qualities active in the world. Even when portrayed at their most vivid and vibrant, they must not be shown to do anything, except perhaps to be destructive in a random sort of way. If narratives, even the residual narratives of songs and photographs, are models of history, then blacks in white narratives may be the colouring of history and the object of history, but not its subject, never what makes it happen.

In this regard, the treatment of blacks bears many resemblances to the patriarchal treatment of women. In addition, the cinematic treatment of Robeson is, with a few exceptions, striking for the degree to which the films deactivate any role that their star may have, in the narrative or even simply in his presence on the screen. As a result there is a contained power about his appearance, a quality that many have found the most moving thing about him.

The most sustained use of Robeson in such a way is seen in *Borderline*. Here the emblematic approach meshes with the theoretical position that informs the film, derived from Soviet theories of montage. *Borderline*'s use of Robeson might even be the same as Sergei Eisenstein's would have been, had they made a film together as they planned. Vladimir Nizhny's description of how Eisenstein spoke in his classes of using Robeson suggests an essentially emblematic function. He showed the class photographs of Robeson, and referred to his 'rich temperament . . . physique and marvellous face' (1962, p. 27), and then talked about a scene in which Dessalines storms a castle. In discussing how to achieve maximum impact, Robeson, the performer, becomes a plastic element, important for his 'temperament' and emblematic blackness –

> when . . . a candelabrum, with lighted candles to boot, sparks blazing and flickering from its pendants, is raised by a man of gigantic stature, with dark face and flashing eyes and teeth (remember Paul Robeson), this will be not only effective, but a veritable climax to Dessalines' indignation.
>
> (ibid., p. 58)

The ideological–aesthetic justifications for this emblematic use of performers are well known – the desire to make crowds not individuals the hero of the (hi)story, the use of individual performers as types representative of social groups. In the context of *Black Majesty*, where all performance might have been approached in this way, this might not have made Robeson's appearance in the film different or passive (– though Eisenstein's words do suggest the frisson of the white contemplation of the huge black man). In *Borderline*, the same approach is more problematic.

Borderline was written and directed by Kenneth Macpherson, a member of the avant-garde group associated with the film journal *Close-Up* which had links with the Harlem Renaissance (producing a special issue on blacks and film), the literary and quasi-feminist avant-garde (H.D., Marianne Moore, Gertrude Stein, Dorothy Richardson), psychoanalysis (Barbara Low, Mary Chadwick, Hans Sachs and Freud himself), as well as formalist film theory (publishing the first translations of Eisenstein among others). (For a full account of this see Friedberg, 1980–1.)

Although constructed more insistently through the chains of association and rhythmic effects of its montage, *Borderline* does have a plot, concerning a white couple, Thorne and Astrid, and a black couple, Adah and Pete (Eslanda and Paul Robeson), all of whom live in the same inn in a small village. There is an implication that Thorne and Adah have been sleeping together. Astrid and Thorne fight, over his infidelity perhaps but also out of the jadedness of their relationship. Thorne stabs Astrid. The racial prejudice of the other villagers mounts; Adah goes away, leaving Pete a note saying it is all her fault. Pete is ordered out of the town by the mayor, but before he goes. Thorne, who has been acquitted of murdering Astrid, comes to the station to say good-bye. This bare outline of a deliberately elliptical plot already suggests how little an active role the Paul Robeson character has in the narrative. The highly complex use of montage only reinforces this inactivity.

The film is organised around the basic anatomy or black and white at every level, aesthetic, metaphorical, ethical, ethnic. The photography exploits black and white stock for dynamic visual effects, effects, that is, based on an aesthetic of contrast or clash between dark and light areas and shapes. Equally the film sees black and white people antithetically. The traditional Western moral dichotomy of black and white is also maintained, but reversed in its conflation with race – that is, in *Borderline* racially black equals morally white and vice versa. These antinomies are further expressed in other elements of film style – black characters are shot still and in repose, in visually simple compositions; white characters are shot in frenzied movement and gesticulation, in complex compositions. As a result, black performers (the Robesons) do not do anything, whereas white performers, especially H.D. as Astrid, are constantly, albeit destructively, active. All this recalls the white alienation versus blackfolks spirituality opposition that runs through discourses on blackness in the twenties and thirties.

A good example of *Borderline's* method occurs early in the film. Thorne and Astrid are in their room, bored and tetchy; Pete is in his, just there. The cuts in the Thorne–Astrid scene focus on jagged, quick movements, Astrid clutching at her fluttering tea-gown, Thorne playing with a knife. The cuts in the Pete scene are a series of close-ups of Pete/Robeson's body in repose – his profile, his hands, his body stretched out on the bed. Neither scene is primarily concerned with narrative, rather they contrast the feeling of the black and white temperaments.

Shots of Paul Robeson throughout further emphasise his passive, emblematic beauty – his dark, smiling face contrasting with bulbous white clouds; shots of him motionless on a hillside intercut very fast with a tumbling waterfall (this, again, being also a cutting between a predominantly black and still and predominantly white and fast image); a close-up of him laughing, with a white flower in his ear, and so on.

In addition to the racial and aesthetic significance of this photography, there is an implicit sexual dimension. Although hardly an explicitly gay film, the construction of the narrative and the emphasis on Robeson/Pete's passive beauty both suggest that he functions as an object of desire in the film. There are touches of gay subcultural iconography – the dyke style of the innkeeper and her woman friend, for instance, and the piano player with the photo of Pete/Robeson on his piano. More importantly, the last scene in the film with any emotional weight is that between Thorne and Pete, looking at each other and, in extreme close-up, shaking hands. At one level this suggests friendship transcending race, but it is also a friendship transcending adultery and death.

After it we have a shot of the flower Pete/Robeson was wearing in the bar, dead in its glass, and a shot of Thorne sitting alone beneath a cherry tree on the mountain. The flower imagery evokes love and the death of love between the two men.

Borderline's use of Robeson can be seen as a product of aesthetic theory, blackfolks ideology and gay sensibility. It is different from the use made of him in other films, but it is still broadly within the general discourse that deactivates the black person even while lauding her or him.

The only exception to this kind of treatment is Robeson's roles in left theatre. As Toussaint l'Ouverture (1935) and John Henry (1940), in the plays of C.L.R. James and Robert Roark respectively, he played the traditional active hero of a narrative. Two socialist plays, *Stevedore* and *Plant in the Sun*, developed a different kind of protagonist–narrative relationship. Neither play was written with Robeson in mind, and he appeared not in their original US productions but in those by the Unity Theatre in Britain. Both are concerned with racial questions, but their emphasis is on the need to sink racial differences in the recognition of class identity, neither black nor white but workers.

In each case Robeson plays a worker who is both an organiser of his fellows and a victim of discrimination because of it. In *Stevedore* (London, 1935), a wrongful accusation of rape against the Robeson character, Lonnie, is used as an excuse for attempting to lynch him and so curb his union activities; in *Plant in the Sun* (London, 1938), his character, Peewee, is fired for such activities. In both cases his treatment is what galvanises his fellow workers, white as well as black, into action in support of him. *Plant in the Sun*, a lighter play with much humour in it, ends with the action of Peewee's immediate mates, a sit-down strike, inspiring the whole works to join in, thus promoting the tactic of the sit-down strike that had been so success-fully used at General Motors in 1936 (see Goldstein, 1974, pp. 184–5). Accounts of the play suggest that Robeson/Peewee gives the initial impetus for what happens by articulating the politics of action and by being the occasion of it; thereafter his role is as one of the group. In the London production, this was echoed in the way that he was not given star billing but simply treated as one of the company – the mode of production of the play embodied the ideal represented by the play.

Stevedore, a more sombre piece, ends with Robeson/Lonnie shot by the leader of the white lynch mob, an action which leads first to the blacks turning on the lynch mob rather than taking the quietist stance that many have been urging up to that point, and then by Robeson/Lonnie's fellow white workers joining in and routing the lynch mob. In Karen Malpede Taylor's (1972, p. 77) description: 'The curtain falls on a tableau like the Pietà: Ruby holds Lonnie's lifeless body in her lap'. As with *Plant in the Sun*, the Robeson character both articulates the socialist and racial consciousness of the play and is the occasion for realising that consciousness in action. Taylor argues that although each of *Stevedore's* three acts ends 'with a moment of pathos', Lonnie dragged away to be lynched, another character shot, Lonnie murdered, 'the crux of each act, the moment of conflict which determines in which direction the future action will go, occurs as the black community confronts its white oppressors . . . The defeat and deaths of individuals provide three emotional endings. Yet this . . . domestic tragedy is undercut by an epic movement which . . . [represents] a nation struggling to be born' (ibid., pp. 77–8). The Robeson character is active in the narrative, but ultimately this action is taken up into the broader sweep of collective action. Whereas the mainstream plays and films render the Robeson character passive and ineffective, the left-wing plays show his individual action as part of collective action in history. Yet it is interesting that *Stevedore* should end on a Pietà – the resonance of the pathos of the kind of black male image that Robeson was elsewhere taken to embody in his singing and person is still drawn on here, perhaps only as a universalising touch, but maybe as a lingering register of the 'romantic realism' of the left.

The image of the heroic Robeson/Lonnie dead at the end of *Stevedore* may also have had a peculiarly powerful pathos because it reworks a certain kind of feeling that is often proposed in Robeson's work. This is the contrast between his terrific potential for action and the fact that it is either curbed or not used; it is the pathos of strength checked, of power withheld, of the beast caged.

Robeson's given physical power was always evident. His sheer size is emphasised time and again, as is the strength presumed to go with it. *Song of Freedom* early on has him picking up a crate single-handed that his white workmates can't manage; when he starts singing, someone says. 'Where did you hear that?' He replies, 'It's been at the back of my head ever since I was a little fella', to which comes the retort, 'When was you ever a little fella?' His size is evoked in the title of *Big Fella*, and used for wry visual humour in the scene where he first meets the tiny Phyllis in *The Proud Valley*. The crate lifting in *Song of Freedom* is like a strong man's turn, as are shifting the boulder in *King Solomon's Mines* or the fallen timbers in *The Proud Valley*. Size and strength were complemented by the power of his voice, its deep, resonant quality. The critic of the *Hartford Daily Times'* description of Robeson's suitability for his role in *Black Boy* sums up the sense of power of Robeson's physical make-up, though the final reference to 'mobility of expression' is interesting as a reference to something more often, as I've argued, curbed in most productions:

> Mr Robeson's equipment for this role is well-nigh perfect; a physical giant with a voice so deep and rich and powerful, both in speech and song, that it would make a dramatic appeal even without the aid of a mask of extraordinary mobility of expression.
>
> (ibid., 12.9.26; quoted by Schlosser, 1970, p. 92)

Yet this power was often contained, by being turned into the spectacle of passive beauty, by becoming a turn, by the editing techniques I've discussed, or by the contrast between it and the subject matter Robeson was performing. Here was this big man singing songs that were taken to express sorrow, resignation, humility. Here was this giant playing men humiliated – by their own superstition (*The Emperor Jones*), by their love for a worthless white woman (*All God's Chillun Got Wings*), by schoolmasterly white superiority (*Sanders of the River*). Above all, there was the contrast between the potential bodily power and his actual stillness and, most movingly, between the potential vocal power and his soft, gentle, careful actual delivery of speech and song.

This is very clear in Robeson's earliest recordings, made in 1925 and 1926 and reissued in 1972 by RCA as *Songs of My People*. The voice here, as later, is capable of great power; some phrases and passages are delivered with a full-throated energy; there are already the deep, resonant, sustained notes so characteristic of the sound of Robeson in popular memory. These heavy, forceful qualities are lightened here by a number of factors: a wider vocal range, so that he can move into the tenor register easily and soaringly, without the (exciting) sense of effort he required later; greater use of grace notes, making the overall effect more elegant but also less direct; the choice of as many fast and exultant numbers as slow and mournful ones, sung with an astonishing brilliance, rapid phrases tripping off the tongue in a manner not generally associated with bass singing. At the end of *Get On Board, Little Children*, he sings the refrain once through straight and strong, but then softens his voice (and Lawrence Brown self-pedals the piano) so that the final statement of the refrain is not loud and firm, but muted and delicate. For the last phrase 'many a more', his voice takes on the plummy, rounded sound of parlour balladry on 'many a' and then just fades gracefully on the long-held final note on 'more'. The kind of rousing, affirmative feeling that is usual with this song (and in some of Robeson's later performances of it) is modified by a gentleness and quietness which could also be called damping and restrained.

Many listeners sought phrases that would capture something of this remarkable quality:

G. B. Stern said to me that Rebecca West had described Robeson's voice as 'black velvet', but that Van Druten defined the shade as 'mulberry', which did I think the better adjective?

(Mannin, 1930, p. 157)

He combined with a rich and mellow voice a dramatic restraint and power that seemed to *hold* unheard *thunder* behind each song.

(unnamed article quoted by Ovington, 1927, p. 213; my emphasis)

Some tones were so deep that they suggested the elemental sound of thunder; others were strangely clear, high, sweet and gentle.

(Seton, 1958, p. 50)

Cicely Hamilton's description of Robeson in the London production of *The Emperor Jones* articulates the kind of affect produced by this contained, restrained, withheld power:

Something of Mr Robeson's success is due, no doubt, to his personality; to his voice, which is soft as well as resonant, to his racial intonation and his size. Above all to his size; there was pathos almost unbearable in the humbling of so mighty a man.

(*Time and Tide*, vol.6, no.39, September 1925, pp. 938–9;
quoted by Schlosser, 1970, p. 79)

Similarly, Marie Seton's (1958) description of his singing *Sometimes I Feel Like a Motherless Child* in concert:

There was something almost painful about this massive man with strong, forceful features speaking in song with such infinitely tender and sorrowful yearning.

It makes a difference what the source of humbling is – whether contained by the compositional or narrative structures of the text he appears in or held back by his own performance technique – but the fact of it, the moving affect of it, may be the emotional heart of Robeson's cross-over appeal.

At the end of the film version of *Old Man River* (which Robeson recorded close to the microphone, hence softly, not boomingly), there is an extreme close-up of Joe/Robeson. He finishes singing, and then looks ahead for a few moments – neutrally? sadly? bitterly? – before gradually forcing a smile through his face, so that the shot and number can fade on a sambo grin. It is the kind of moment John Ellis (1982) refers to as something we search out in star performances, that meaningful flicker of expression that we think we see when we have mentally cleared away all the hype and production.

It looks like Robeson the performer having to make Joe the character smile, being forced to play Sambo. It is 'unbearably moving' because it is the humbling of a great singer in the service of a demeaning stereotype. Obviously, what I am offering here is my own reaction as evidence of a possible reaction, but it is of a piece with Hamilton and Seton, quoted above, and many others. It is a response that needs a critique, for it puts me in the position of agonising exquisitely over the fate of a black man, getting off emotionally on the humiliation of a people. That is the kind of price being a cross-over star may involve with some audiences.

In any event, when Robeson no longer played the part of power withheld and became more vigorous and harsh in his vocal delivery as well as his opinions, he ceased to be a cross-over star.

References

Baldwin, James (1978) *The Devil Finds Work* (London: Pan; Michael Joseph 1976).

Berghahn, Marion (1977) *Images of Africa in Black American Literature* (Totawa NJ: Rowman & Littlefield).

Bogle, Donald (1974) *Toms, Coons, Mulattoes, Mammies and Bucks* (New York: Bantam; Viking, 1973).

Cripps, Thomas (1970) 'Paul Robeson and Black Identity in American Movies', *Massachusetts Review*, vol. 11, no.3, Summer 1970, pp. 468–85.

Cripps, Thomas (1977) *Slow Fade to Black* (Oxford: Oxford University Press).

Cruse, Harold (1969) *The Crisis of the Negro Intellectual* (London: W.H. Allen).

Cruse, Harold (1978) 'The Creative and Performing Arts and the Struggle for Identity and Credibility', in Harry A. Johnson (ed.) *Negotiating the Mainstream* (Chicago: American Library Association).

DuBois, W. E. B. (1969) *The Souls of Black Folk* (New York: New American Library).

Dyer, Richard (1982a) 'The Son of the Sheik', *The Movie*, no. 126, pp. 2512–13.

Ellis, John (1982) 'Star/Industry/Image', in BFI Education, *Star Signs* (London: British Film Institute) pp. 1–12.

Freedomways Editors (eds) (1978) *Paul Robeson: The Great Forerunner* (New York: Dodd, Head).

Friedberg, Anne (1980–1) 'Approaching *Borderline*', *Millennium*, nos. 7/8/9, Fall/Winter 1980–1, pp. 130–9.

Goldstein, Malcolm (1974) *The Political Stage* (New York: Oxford University Press).

Harrington, Ollie (1978) 'Our Beloved Pauli', in *Freedomways* Editors, qv, pp. 100–6.

Mannin, Ethel (1930) *Confessions and Impressions* (New York: Doubleday, Doran) pp. 157–61 ('Paul Robeson: Portrait of a Great Artist').

Nizhny, Vladimir (1962) *Lessons with Eisenstein*, trans. Ivor Montague and Jay Leyda (London: Allen & Unwin).

Ovington, Mary White (1927) *Portraits in Color* (New York: Viking) pp. 205–15.

Pines, Jim (1975) *Blacks in Films* (London: Studio Vista).

Robeson, Eslanda Goode (1930) *Paul Robeson, Negro* (New York: Harper & Bros).

Robeson, Paul (1978) 'The Culture of the Negro', in *Freedomways* Editors q.v. pp. 65–7 (originally published in *The Spectator*, 15 June 1934, vol. 152, pp. 916–17).

Rosenberg, Marvin (1961) *The Masks of Othello* (Berkeley and Los Angeles: University of California Press).

Schlosser, Anatol I. (1970) 'Paul Robeson, His Career in the Theatre, in Motion Pictures, and on the Concert Stage', unpublished PhD. dissertation, New York University.

Seton, Marie (1958) *Paul Robeson* (London: Dennis Dobson).

Taylor, Karen Malpede (1972) *People's Theatre in America* (New York: Drama Book Specialists).

Opera, Folklore, and Ethnicity

The case of Mario Lanza

13

MARCIA LANDY

Heavenly Creatures (1994) prominently features Mario Lanza's movie image and his operatic and ballad singing. His star persona is central to the film's exploration of the problematic connections between everyday life and fantasy. The two young women in the film, Juliet Hulme (Kate Winslet) and Pauline Parker (Melanie Lynskey), brutally murder Pauline's mother and are forever separated from each other as a consequence. For them, Mario Lanza's music is associated with romance, creativity, and freedom from the restraints of education, familial discipline, and sexual repression associated with the materialism, pragmatism, and snobbery of Anglophile New Zealand culture. The film plays with movie stars as fetishes (e.g., Mario Lanza, James Mason, and Orson Welles) configured in the clay figures created by the young women's imagination. These life-sized effigies of the stars and the young women occupy the fourth world where they engage in a frightening drama expressive of the double-edged character of fantasy.

Because of their powerful hold on the imagination of audiences in determining national and, in many instances, local standards of beauty, sexuality, work, social comportment, and talent, the narratives of stardom embed a number of elements that comprise the star as a powerful cultural commodity. The material and historical conditions of their production are inherent to star narratives, both biographical and cinematic, textual and extra-textual. The economy of stardom is never completely effaced. In its operations, it exposes how the commodity is produced, how it circulates, and how it rises and falls in value according to its moment in time. The biographical and cinematic texts of and with stars expose the interventions of entrepreneurs, agents, managers, and patrons in directing the career of the performer both in the narratives of discovery and in the subsequent shaping of the trajectory of the star's career. But acknowledging the material dimensions of stardom does not yield the secret of its seemingly mystical and protean power. In this essay, I examine the production of Mario Lanza's star persona in the 1950s and its current fate. Lanza was still part of the myth-making apparatus of Hollywood that persisted into the post-World War II era, and I discuss how his appearance in the films he made in the 1950s unabashedly reveals and celebrates his exchange value as a star. I identify the terms and conditions of his rise to stardom within the social and cultural milieu of that earlier time in Hollywood as a prelude to assessing the status of his image at the present time. After half a century Lanza's persona continues to circulate in a fashion relevant to the culture and politics of the 1990s. Lanza offers an exemplary instance of how myths of earlier Hollywood stars have altered to suit new economic and cultural exigencies. These myths have not disappeared but have entered into a realm of fantasy – a fourth world – and into other permutations of commodity fetishism.

Lanza in the mythic world of Hollywood stardom

From his first to his last films (from 1949 to 1959), from the height of his adulation to the more negative assessments of his talents, Lanza's image was tailored by the studios and by the press to conform to the conditions of stardom with its value-creating apparatus. The value-laden aspect of the production of stars involves the expenditure of time and money to produce wealth – presumably for the star but more for the studios and recording companies. The Lanza myth was built on familiar Hollywood ingredients – his social class, his Italian-American identity, and his combination of good looks and exceptional singing talent. In the narratives of his films with their familiar scenario of "poor boy makes good," he is identified first with humble working-class origins, then, by virtue of his unique and powerful voice, is transformed into a star.

His labor is evident through his performances on film, recordings, and personal appearances. Signs of his labor are also evident through the operations of studio publicity, the press, and audience reception reflected in box office receipts. Labor was also evident in his off-screen behavior and publicized by the press. Contemporary accounts of his life reveal the work expended in producing the portrait of a tormented man, insecure and unable to meet the demands of fame in managing his income, his personal affairs, and the obligations of his contract. His personal struggles with the studio, his weight, the law, and an adverse press became part of the star image. The tenuousness of success was a necessary ingredient of stardom and testifies to its competitive dimensions as well as to a constant effort on the star's part to refashion his image according to the dictates of the studio. Lanza's biography and the conflicts portrayed in his films involve the role of the press first in predicting his success and then in capitalizing on his personal and legal problems. Publicity plays a key role in the projection of Lanza's image in its transformation from a simple celebration of talent to a portrait of cynicism.

These extra-cinematic demands are not divorced from economic considerations. They are essential to the production of value, since stardom must capture the imagination of audiences who pay with their time, bodies, and money for sharing in the melodrama of creating the persona of the star. Lanza's narrative is not merely a case of failure to meet the demands of fame but a revelation that the specter of defeat is inevitably part of the star scenario. George Custen has indicated how competition and the threat of non-acceptance are inherent to the process.[1] The value of the star is not merely his or her success but the inevitability of defeat due to internal conflict, ambition, illness, and death.

Lanza's cinematic persona was established in his first two films, *That Midnight Kiss* (1949) and *The Toast of New Orleans* (1950), in which he starred with Kathryn Grayson. In these films as in the two that followed (*The Great Caruso* [1951] and *Serenade* [1956]) he was cast as a worker (e.g., truck driver, shrimp fisherman, street singer, and peasant worker in the vineyards). The melodrama focused on a well-worn and successful Hollywood myth: would success in the form of love for upper-class women, wealth, and recognition for a lower-class man spoil vitality and musical talent? Lanza's ethnic identity bore traces of an earlier Hollywood tradition in its neglect of specificity regarding Latin ethnicities.[2] Italian and Mexican-American stars were often called upon to play Mediterranean and Latin-American roles interchangeably. However, Lanza's Italian origins would ultimately play a different role in the consolidation of his stardom. This difference is evident when his image is compared to Rudolph Valentino, a major Hollywood star of the 1920s who was also Italian. Valentino was associated with an aura of exoticism. He was identified with Otherness of the immigrant and invested with the mantle of the Latin lover. The taint of Mediterranean ethnicity, particularly effeminacy, was primary to his image. Miriam Hansen writes that

> Valentino . . . bore the stigma of the first generation, non-Anglo-Saxon immigrant – and was cast accordingly. He began his career as a seducer/villain of dark complexion. When female audiences adopted him, despite the moral/racist injunction, he developed the persona of the Latin lover, marketed as a blend of sexual vitality and romantic courtship.[3]

In the late 1940s cinema, the Italian-American graduated from Latin seducer, dancer, gangster and prizefighter to musical personality with certain corresponding changes in the mythology of masculinity and ethnicity. The popularity of Frank Sinatra, Dean Martin, and Frankie Laine among others was a mark of this transformation, and Lanza was exemplary of the move from Latin exotic other to a mainstream national figure. Although, like these legendary vocalists, Lanza was rebellious, tough, and ambitious, his popularity and his brand of masculinity were also connected to the opera (mainly Italian opera and particularly to the arias of Verdi, Puccini, Bellini, and Giordano), an art form not conventionally identified in Hollywood with major male stars.

From the outset of his rise to stardom, the film narratives in which he appeared paralleled his own life. Lanza, born Alfredo Arnold Cocozza, was from a working-class family of Italian immigrant parents in South Philadelphia. According to biographies and reminiscences, he was intractable, unwilling to be disciplined, a feature often repeated in his film characters and a major aspect of his off-screen persona according to the press. Prior to his arrival in Hollywood, he made a name for himself on the concert stage. When he performed at a Hollywood Bowl concert, he was "discovered" by Louis B. Mayer. (Actually Mayer had already heard Lanza on a recording and was impressed with his voice, but the overwhelmingly enthusiastic response to the concert was the evidence Mayer needed that Lanza had star potential.)

A screen test followed and Lanza's movie career was launched. With the aid of the publicity department at MGM, he was to become a "singing Clark Gable," combining good looks and a powerful voice.[4] While the specific comparison with Gable was not part of Lanza image-making, reviews acknowledged that Lanza combined handsomeness with musical ability. Reviews for *That Midnight Kiss* were extremely laudatory about both his looks and his singing talent. In a review of "Toast of the Town," *Newsweek* proclaimed that "Lanza's first picture was too big a hit to keep him under wraps any longer."[5] The *Christian Century* praised the second film, *The Toast of New Orleans*, for "Its excellence of musical portions that compensates for stereotyped plot and situations."[6] The Lanza myth was consolidated through comparisons between Lanza and the Italian tenor Enrico Caruso as a preliminary to his starring in Caruso's biopic, and the identification with Caruso was to follow him in life and continue after his death. Lanza was skeptical about the comparison, but, as Derek Mannering asserts, "the attention lavished on Mario and the numerous comparisons resulted in the reawakening of the Caruso legend. With the introduction of the LP [format] in 1949, more of Caruso's recordings were sold after 1950 than for many years before."[7]

The cloning of Caruso as Lanza was to remain a constant feature in Lanza's publicity and in his films where he is constantly referred to as "Caruso." His film performances gave every indication of a grand career paralleling "grand opera." Fan mail rolled in, and reviews were by and large enthusiastic. Money followed, though shortage of funds was to dog him for the rest of his life. *Newsweek* commented that *The Great Caruso* was a "Technicolor natural for exploiting the sudden and tremendous popularity of Mario Lanza who taught himself to sing by playing Caruso's records over and over."[8] The review praised his "natural and remarkably powerful voice."[9] *Time* found that the "film is weak in fact and weaker on fiction," but that "Lanza is in fine voice."[10] Repeatedly, reviews of his films offered snippets of Lanza's biography, praised his voice, but found the plots banal.

Lanza's myth relies heavily on his working-class origin. His overcoming of the limitations of his social class are linked to changing conceptions of masculinity and ethnicity. In *That Midnight Kiss* (1949), Italian-American Johnny Donetti (Lanza) owns a truck for hauling. He is discovered by Prudence (Kathryn Grayson), granddaughter of a Philadelphia socialite, Abigail Trent Budell (Ethel Barrymore), when he sits down at the piano he has delivered to the Budell mansion and sings, thinking that no one is at home. His presence is fortunate for Prudence, since she, also an aspiring opera singer, balks against singing with imperious fat Italian tenor Guido Betelli, played by Thomas Gomez. Betelli is a familiar movie stereotype of the opera singer that will in the film as well as in the culture of the 1950s be erased by Lanza's image. Lanza/Johnny's combination of brashness, musical talent, and good looks are more to Prudence's liking. The Italian-American wins out against the Italian Betelli, and Johnny, after many misunderstandings and obstacles to a romantic union with Prudence, is assimilated into Philadelphia Main Line society. His family too is elevated in status.

In *The Toast of New Orleans* (1950), his class identity is again responsible for the formation of his musical and acting persona, and one that he forgets at his peril. He has to learn the social graces and to smooth over the more exuberant aspects of his public demeanor; that is, he cannot speak too loudly or appear too enthusiastic and his clothing must be less flamboyant and he strains against conforming to the new exigencies of his social life as an opera singer. The uncouth, even vulgar, aspects of his character become a burden to his manager and his operatic co-star as he is rudely initiated into the social manners and values befitting a successful opera star. He progressively succumbs to gentrification at the hands of his managers and co-star only to learn that he has lost his virility in the process. Only when he is reminded that his ethnic and working-class identity are the source of his power as a performer is he able to make contact with the emotional wellspring of his talent and thus reassert his masculinity. He does not revert to his earlier forms of behavior, but, in his work as a performer, he is able to combine his new mannerly behavior with the "passion" of the worker.

The motif of embattled masculinity in *The Toast of New Orleans* is shared thematically with other films – biopics, social problem films, musicals, and melodramas of the 1950s. In keeping with the terms and conditions of stardom, Lanza's persona had to offer both familiar and unique properties. His singular gift was his voice and his dramatic delivery. Lanza's contribution to popular cinema was his ability to endow the male opera singer with an attractive and accessible identity. He was one of the first prominent movie stars to make opera respectable and profitable on screen, though male and female opera singers had long appeared in the movies. Prior to Lanza, the opera singer in Hollywood of the studio years was not a major drawing card, though there are films that star such divas as Lily Pons and Grace Moore. In contrast to Lanza, singers such as Lauritz Melchior and Leo Slezak (who appeared often with Deanna Durbin), are seen not as divos but as father figures, or, as a *Saturday Review* article describes:

> Great tenor voices come in rather unpresentable male packages . . . When a great tenor moves from opera house to movie screen his character is adjusted to accord with the visual rather than the acoustic image. And so Lauritz Melchior ceased to be Siegfried and became Foxy Grandpa as Leo Slezak before him turned from high tragedy to low comedy.[11]

In the 1950s, Lanza was to make the image of the opera singer romantic, glamorous, and profitable, and his popularity signals the disappearance of the stigma of effeminacy usually associated in Hollywood with the image of the operatic singer. His assuming the role of Enrico Caruso in *The Great Caruso* (despite Dore Schary's, the head of MGM, resistance to him as too young and too uncultivated)[12] was a landmark in Lanza's career, helping to consolidate an image of him as a musical prodigy and as heir to the genius of Caruso. The film was important for establishing his dramatic talent – as well as helping to eradicate the image of stodginess typically associated with opera singers. *The Great Caruso* drew huge crowds, becoming MGM's biggest money-maker for 1951. Reviews of the film were generally favorable though there was some dissent on the part of critics who complained about the simplistic narrative and unfavorable comparisons between Lanza and Met singers.

The folklore of Lanza's greatness and his popularity do not rest solely on the many opera arias he sang in films. His repertoire, like that of "the three great tenors" popular today – Pavarotti, Carreras, and Domingo – also contained popular songs, in particular Neapolitan street songs. In *The Great Caruso*, Lanza not only sings arias from *Aida*, *Il trovatore*, *Rigoletto*, *La bohème*, *Cavalleria rusticana*, *Tosca*, and *Lucia di Lammermoor* in conjunction with Metropolitan opera divas Dorothy Kirsten, Blanche Thebom, and Lucine Amara, but he also sings such popular songs as "Marecchiare," "Funiculi funicula," and "A vuchela." His combination of opera and popular music not only identified him as a versatile performer, but offered an image of the Italian-American as more than a Mafioso, prizefighter, and failure.

In Cold War America, the Lanza persona was an expression of the power of "people's capitalism" touted in ads of the time, an embodiment of the myths that were forged in post-World War II culture and politics. Lanza offered an image of a clean-cut, naive, and unaffected young man as opposed to the image of the "alien" often identified with Communist subversion, anti-capitalism, and Jewishness. "[F]ar from the caricatured opera tenor, he is a nice-looking youngster of the average American boy school,"[13] said one review.

Another aspect of the Lanza myth that circulated was his generosity to those in need. The story of his contribution to many causes is recounted by Roland Besette: "Though the press wrote them off as cheap publicity stunts, Lanza performed good deeds for no purpose beyond the pleasure he derived from them."[14] Besette lists Lanza's contributions to charitable organizations and describes the star's donating his time willingly to telephone hospitalized people. Biographies recount the story of a young girl, Raphaela Fasano, dying of leukemia, whose mother phoned and asked Lanza to sing to her daughter. According to the story, Lanza phoned the ten-year-old, and then invited her at his expense to visit at his home in Los Angeles. He gave her a silver medal with which she was buried.[15]

Unfortunately, Lanza was often conned by agents, lawyers, and hangers-on. Exploitation by unscrupulous individuals eager to take advantage of the newly found success of the star and of his inability to handle sudden wealth is also part of the mythology of stardom. These dramas circulate in the ubiquitous biographies and press reviews that capitalize on the trials and tribulations of personalities and in the content of biopics and musicals that focus on the various crises in the birth, rise to fame and fortune, and decline of the star, a reminder that melodrama reigns in myths of stardom. Stardom and melodrama are companions: both thrive on adversity, and Lanza's career was increasingly to become a public melodrama.

The Lanza love affair with the critics and the public took a rapid downward turn. The press began to circulate critical reviews of his personality and of his film career. In a cover story of the tenor in 1951, *Time* was one of the first to predict failure. From this review and others to follow, another dimension of the Lanza myth was forged. The negative reviews attacked his lack of training and discipline, and his popularization of opera as a form of vulgarization. A persistent myth about Lanza is that the powerful voice attributed to him was merely the consequence of electronic manipulation. *Time* described him as having a voice of

> natural power and quality, though not of training and polish, a voice that many experts rank with the titans of opera. The voice sells Lanza, but Lanza also sells the voice with curly-haired good looks and a paradoxical combination of beaming boyishness and hairy-chested animal magnetism. He is at once the delight of bobby-soxers, song lovers, and the despair of musical highbrows who believe that a great singer's goal should be the Metropolitan, not Metro-Goldwyn-Mayer.[16]

The article further depicts the "onetime street wise guy who never did a day's work until he was 21" as a "Dead-end Kid" from South Philadelphia, and as gorging himself to the point that he once weighed 300 pounds and with as large an ego, constantly referring to him condescendingly as "Freddy" (Americanized Alfredo). The article ends with a discussion of Lanza as "another American tragedy." He is presented as a classic instance of an artist squandering his gifts, as a performer for whom Hollywood has "been his Frankenstein."[17] (This article was written well before the trouble that arose between Lanza and Dore Schary [who by then had replaced Louis B. Mayer as head of MGM] and before the events that were to cause the suspension of his contract and keep him from acting in *The Student Prince*, though he was featured on the musical soundtrack).

Lanza's career at this point once again reveals that the economic and cultural scenario of stardom is not seamless and untroubled. The performer must constantly compete with others and with himself to maintain his popularity. The test of the star's value resides in overcoming (like the stock market) the possibility of a crash. He must constantly live up to the greatness of his reputation and, in the case of Lanza, to the comparison with Caruso. He must not only prove himself "after a series of hard trials, earned through hard work or apprenticeship,"[18] but he must continue to repeat his triumphs. Equally important to the star persona is the validation of his greatness by a reigning figure, one who assists the newcomer in gaining recognition. Yet the star cannot rest on his past triumphs. The star's value is always threatened – on screen and off – by his own refusal to conform to expectations (as for example in *Serenade*, a film that did less well at the box office).

By 1956, Lanza's star image had undergone alteration. *Newsweek*, in a news report entitled, "The New Lanza," wrote

> Right after the entertainment halls resounded with his vocal derring-do in "Because You're Mine," Mario Lanza's career started downhill and traveled fast. His great popularity in 1952 gave him a big head, which made him difficult on the set (when he deigned to show up on the set) and a big tummy (nearly 300 pounds). About the only thing Hollywood considered him for was another lawsuit.[19]

The most problematic aspect of Lanza's screen presence became, as this review indicates, his physical appearance. He was threatening to recapitulate the caricatured portrait of the fat Italian opera singer in *That Midnight Kiss*. While his physical appearance remained "boyish," "unaffected," and "ruggedly handsome," his body weight began to fluctuate in ways unacceptable to the studio with its insistence on slimness. Having been hired to present a new streamlined image of the opera star, his increased weight threatened to undermine that image and to expose the behind-the-scenes and unglamorous aspects of the production of stardom. Since the body is the manifest sign of the cultural economy of stardom and slimness, an index to the star's exchange value, the battle over Lanza's weight exposed how little control the star has over his or her body. His weight became most troublesome to the studio after the filming of *Because You're Mine* (1952) and was to constitute an ideological battleground between Lanza and his employers. In his resistance to controlling his weight, he was challenging the studio system's insistence on absolute power over every aspect of a star's persona.

Lanza's appearance in the film ranges awkwardly from shots of his bulging, corseted figure, to those in which he is considerably slimmer. The film stars Lanza as an army draftee, Rinaldo, who is accorded special favors (e.g., leaves and release from strenuous activities) by his sergeant, Batterson (James Whitmore). Batterson is a fan of the opera singer, but the sergeant is also eager to help his sister, Bridget (Doretta Morrow) forge a career in opera. At first Batterson indulges the recruit but then turns on Rinaldo when he assumes that the singer has manipulated him merely to get a leave to sing in a concert. In this film, the singer's ability to perform is never in question. Rather the film capitalizes on the protagonist's personality, whether he is an opportunist or genuinely eager to advance Bridget's career, and whether he experiences true affection for her.

Lanza's weight had risen to 250 pounds and he had to go on a crash diet (one of many to come) to get down finally to 160 pounds in preparation for his filming of *The Student Prince*. At the same time, his relationship with Schary, who had replaced Mayer as head of production at MGM, was one of constant antagonism. A businessman with a concern for keeping production costs down, Schary did not handle the star with kid gloves and was quite overt in his disdain of Lanza. Lanza's situation at the studio reached a climax with *The Student Prince* (1954). His weight soared dramatically and the film was delayed while he was supposed to bring it down. He had already recorded the score. When a slimmer Lanza appeared on the set, his troubles were not over. New difficulties arose when the film's director, Curtis Bernhardt, found fault with the star's acting style. Again the film was postponed and again Lanza's weight soared. Upon finally returning to the set, he and Schary again quarreled and Lanza walked out of the studio. He was sued by the studio and prohibited from singing publicly. He was replaced by a British actor, Edmund Purdom, who mimed Lanza's singing.

Figure 13.1 Mario Lanza
Courtesy of bfi Stills, London

The absence of the star and the appropriation of his voice by another is obvious to the viewer. One expects to see the Lanza image that corresponds with the recognizable voice and instead finds a more urbane, sophisticated star, the image of the prince but with a powerful voice that signals a different personality one that is more vital, more supple than the visual image. Certainly, the absence (or the off-screen presence) of Lanza carries other associations for those who are fans of the star or knowledgeable about his struggles. Even more, what might be concluded from this unnatural superimposition is the question of property (who owns the voice) and of the enigma of the star's representation.

This substitution of Purdom for Lanza was publicized broadly and attributed to Lanza's difficulties not only with the studio but with his overeating, his own problems with controlling his image. Since the star is a complex union of visual as well as aural properties, Lanza was shorn of a major source of his appeal – his engaging physical presence. Several reviews (mainly mixed about the film's virtues), comment adversely on the merging of Lanza's voice with Purdom's acting. For example, Moira Walsh in a review of the film for *America* commented on the "disparity between off-screen voice and on-screen personality . . . disconcertingly evident every time he [Purdom] opens his mouth to sing."[20]

Newsweek also complained that "Although Lanza's voice is dubbed in expertly, there is, nevertheless, a jarring contrast between his flamboyant tenor and Purdom's more conservative style."[21] Purdom had this to say about acting to Lanza's voice: "His voice was an absolutely tremendous experience . . . It was enough to make you sweat, just listening to the voice, particularly at a very high level."[22] The substitution of Purdom for Lanza mitigates a major dimension of Lanza's contribution to the cinema. The star's body is revealed as expendable, an indication of the magic of cinema and of the power of the studios, and even as a prolepsis for the ultimate disappearance of Lanza. Two years were to pass before Lanza made another film – *Serenade* (1956). During this time, he did a minor amount of recording and fell back into the habit of drinking and heavily overeating. He appeared on a live television broadcast, sponsored by Chrysler, which was to be the source of another scandal, since he mouthed recordings made a couple of years earlier. The press detected this cover-up, and rumors began to circulate that the tenor had lost his voice. He appeared in a second Chrysler show and revealed that, though physically overweight, his voice was intact, the rumors of his failing talent unfounded. His failure to meet an obligation to appear in Las Vegas set off another round of speculations about his reliability and even talent as a performer.

Serenade (based on the James M. Cain novel) was a Warner Bros. production in which Lanza again portrays a worker becoming an opera star as he did in *The Toast of New Orleans* and *The Great Caruso*. *Serenade* opens when Damon Vincenti, played by Lanza, is performing his last day's work in a California vineyard. He is on his way to audition in an Italian restaurant in San Francisco. A wealthy patroness of the arts, *femme fatale* Kendall Hale (played by Joan Fontaine), accompanied by another Italian-American, Marco (Vince Edwards), loses her way on the road, and encounters Damon when the couple stop for directions. Damon directs the couple to the right road. The looks exchanged between Kendall and Damon foreshadow his amorous desires and subjugation to her fatal charm.

Damon and Kendall meet again at Damon's premiere at the San Francisco restaurant, where she and an impresario, Charles Winthrop (Vincent Price), happen to be in the audience and, after hearing Damon sing, they offer to assist his career. Kendall abandons her prize-fighter and begins a relationship with Damon. Unable to balance his attraction for her and his desire for a career, the remainder of the melodrama portrays Damon's fatal (and masochistic) attraction to Kendall and its effects on his artistry and masculinity. Distraught over her acquisition of a new lover, a sculptor this time, Damon walks off stage during the last scene of a performance of Verdi's *Otello*. He tries to retrieve his career but, during an audition for the role of Don Ottavio in *Don Giovanni*, he discovers himself blocked and unable to perform. He travels to Mexico, and almost destroys himself with drink until he is saved by a Mexican woman, Juana (Santa Montiel). They fall in love, and she aids him in recovering his wounded masculinity so that he can return to the opera stage. The narrative sets up an analogy between Damon and Juana's father, a bullfighter who was fatally gored, having been disappointed in love, but through Juana's nurturance Damon is saved from a similar fate.

The following year, Lanza went to Italy, where he was to make only two more films before his untimely death – *The Seven Hills of Rome* (1957) and *For the First Time* (1959). *The Seven Hills of Rome* portrays him as a singer who comes to Rome not for his career but to win back the love of an American heiress (Peggy Castle). He befriends a young Italian woman, Rafaella (Marisa Allasio), who has no place to stay in the city, joins forces with his cousin, and forges a career for himself and his cousin, Carlo (Renato Rascel), in Rome. He almost ruins his cousin's and his own career in his quest for romance, however. Finally he abandons his love for the socialite in favor of Rafaella. The reviewers of the film were more taken with the "topography" of Marisa Allasio (the reviewer's euphemism for her shapely body) than with Lanza's performance, and with helicopter shots of Rome which one critic described as "fascinating . . . the viewer gets some wonderful views of the hills of Rome," though Lanza is described in less complimentary terms: "As the man gets fatter, the voice gets thinner."[23] The reviewer commented though that Lanza's acting "shows . . . considerable improvement." References to Lanza's weight had by now become an essential ingredient of most reviews.

Two episodes in *Seven Hills of Rome* are exemplary of other aspects of Lanza's stardom. Twice in the film, he performs spontaneously; as befitting the musical, life is made to appear as a stage. First, he appears on a Rome street with a child (an actual street singer) who sings for passers-by, and he considerably enlarges her profits for the day. Consistently, in his films, he is portrayed as offering his talents freely, often in opposition to his managers. Second, he performs for a group of young people jitterbugging on the street, doing impersonations for them of other Italian American and African-American singers, namely Dean Martin, Perry Como, Frankie Laine, and Nat King Cole. This episode illustrates Lanza's talent, namely, as a comedian and mimic, situating him in the company of popular vocalists.

Lanza's persona is thus "one of the guys." Whether he is playing as the Great Caruso or as the shrimp fisherman in *The Toast of New Orleans*, he is portrayed as generous, with his gifts singing on the street, in restaurants, at festivals, or outside the concert hall – proffered for free. *The Great Caruso* identifies Caruso and Lanza by extension as appealing to the masses and expressing their bond with their audiences by performing spontaneously without charge. Thus, like the musical form generally and like Lanza's legend, episodes like these set up a distinction: the familiar and mystified connection between use value and exchange value where, in the final analysis, exchange masquerades as use value. That is, the wealth and profit derived from Lanza's off-screen performance are presented on-screen as having intrinsic value derived from its seeming naturalness and usefulness. Lanza's performance is the product of labor and his performance is a commodity exchanged for money. His labor appears to be given voluntarily without regard for compensation and bearing no sign of its monetary value.

For the First Time was a melodrama that appears strikingly different from his earlier films, both in the transformation of his earlier exuberant persona to a subdued if not worldly performer and in the obvious bid to a young audience as reflected by the on-screen teenage audience. In this film, which also stars Zsa Zsa Gabor, he has the reputation of an irresponsible performer, one who does not meet his obligations. Lanza is no longer a worker to be discovered but a disgruntled celebrity hiding from his public – though not completely hardened to the pleas of fans, especially young people. His irresponsibility is supposed to be due to an excess of love for his audience, especially for those who cannot get tickets to his performances, but his behavior is also consistent with rebelliousness. As the audience waits for him to appear inside the Vienna opera house, he stands outside and sings to those who have been turned away, causing the opera to be canceled. A young deaf woman, Christa (Johanna Von Koszian), with whom he falls in love, restores his belief in performance by giving him a goal for which to strive: to earn the money through appearing in concerts in Europe to pay the medical expenses for restoring her hearing. A melodrama, the film has the familiar fifties thematic of troubled masculinity expressed in Lanza's changed star image. That the object of his love is unable to hear allows the film to play with Lanza's restored screen image and of his voice as the instrument of restoration. Similar to *The Seven Hills of Rome*, *For the First Time* shifts the emphasis from his appeal to older and upper-class audiences to youth: an appeal based on changing audience demographics. Hence, the emphasis on opera is more restrained.

Re-animating Lanza

Lanza's films capitalized on the melodramatic nature of star mythology: the incompatibility of career and personal satisfaction, the seductive but cynical and opportunistic role of managers and patrons and the impossibility of a successful resolution to these dilemmas except in the realm of folklore and fairy-tale. His films increasingly capitalized on Lanza's growing reputation as a troubled and an unpredictable performer a star whose body was out of control, an ageing performer who came late to performances or did not appear at all, a man who had slipped from the dazzling heights of fame. Lanza's star biography thus encompassed the full melodramatic trajectory of stardom, beginning in promise, realizing an exceptional talent, being the center of adulation, and then inevitably slipping from the pinnacle of success through self-destructive behavior or through natural causes – alcoholism, psychic instability, illness, and ageing. The underside of success can also be a source of value and after the star's death become part of the regeneration of his or her image in the realm of the fourth world.

Lanza's death of a heart attack produced predictable hysteria on the part of his fans, though not as great as that expressed by fans for either Valentino's death or later Elvis's. Lanza's funeral which took place in Los Angeles where he was buried, was attended by co-stars from his films and admirers. Death is not alien to the fourth world of fantasy. In Wheeler Winston Dixon's view, "What the cinema does, what photography and popular culture hope to accomplish . . . is nothing less than the retrieval of the dead and the reentry of their phantom presences in the realm of the living."[24] Almost immediately, the fantasy grew that Lanza's death was the consequence of a Mafia vendetta, since he had been friendly with Mafia figures, though this was never documented. Another fantasy that circulated was that he had committed suicide. Despite medical reports that attribute his death to heart failure, neither of these fantasies has been laid to rest.

In 1962, three years after his death, the Mario Lanza Institute was formed, and it has continued to grow since then. The Institute is located in the same building in South Philadelphia that also houses the Mario Lanza Museum, containing artifacts from the singer's life and career. The Institute sponsors competitions for young singers, an annual Spring concert, an annual ball, a scholarship fund, and a web site (http://www.mariolanza-institute.org). The web site contains a number of Mario Lanza fan clubs active in the US and throughout Europe, and especially in Britain, Australia, Italy, the Netherlands, and Germany. Anecdotes, appreciations, and information on Lanza's life and work can be downloaded from the web and several book-length biographies are available for purchase; the two most recent are Derek Mannering's Mario Lanza (1996) and Roland Besette's Mario Lanza: Tenor in Exile (1999).

In the last decade, Lanza's singing has undergone reevaluation in the testimonials of opera stars such as Richard Leech and Placido Domingo, who have acknowledged Lanza's influence on their careers in opera. These testimonials have countered the prevailing view that Lanza was no opera singer and that he made no impact at all on the world of opera. For example, Leech has stated that "it was Mario Lanza's voice booming from my parents' hi-fi, that was my first exposure not only to opera but to the tenor voice itself."[25] Lanza's name also appears among responses to an Opera News questionnaire addressed to prominent opera singers, "What Is the Greatest Voice You Ever Heard?" Leech asserted, "His passion became the reason I sing. Because of The Great Caruso, he became a role model, not only for me but for countless American kids."[26] And Eric Meyer writes:

> When a voice becomes recognizable enough to be used on the soundtracks of Mercedes-Benz commercials, it is truly consecrated. Mario Lanza reached that exalted status last summer. Fifty years after the fact, consumers are hip to what Lanza fans have known since his heyday in the '50s: the troubled but gifted Italian-American tenor was, simply and indisputably, one of the century's greatest vocal phenomena.[27]

Some of the praise for Lanza is associated nostalgically with the 1950s as a contrast to the present time where, in Florence King's words, "We have carried egalitarianism to such a maniacal extreme that we regard beauty as an affront." According to her,

> Lanza's success began in the hearts of teenage girls but it went straight to the heart of something much deeper. As a music critic of the time put it: "Mario Lanza is the symbol of America's cultural democracy." Because of him, anyone who was in high school in the early Fifties stands an excellent chance of being an opera lover regardless of background or education.[28]

King's comments offer one explanation for Lanza's return in the 1990s; namely, that the 1950s have come to represent a watershed, the last gasp of an innocent and uncomplicated world, a black-and-white world that the film Pleasantville satirizes as repressive and bigoted. A large share of the current encomium for Lanza is devoted to the influence of his voice on opera and popular culture. The appearance of Lanza impersonators – though not to the same extent as Elvis impersonators – is testimony to the vitality and endurance of Lanza's persona. Victor Lanza claims to be the star's son, to the dismay of the family, and has made a career out of performing the Lanza repertoire. Charles GaVoian has gathered admirers for the effectiveness of his Lanza singing style and mode of performance.

For many social critics and filmmakers, Lanza's star image, like those of other popular film and recording artists, has become part of a contemporary fascination with revisiting the past. In this moment of "postmodernity," the Lanza phenomenon for many entrepreneurs serves to reinvigorate the value of the star as a commodity through new technologies and through the reissuing of films on video and DVD and re-recordings of music. A glance at current releases suggests that the Lanza revival has not peaked. CDs by BMG of *Mario Lanza in Hollywood* and Victor's *Mario Lanza: Opera Arias and Duets* and *Mario Lanza at His Best* contain selections from his film soundtracks, from earlier records of his operatic arias as well as his singing of many Neapolitan and operetta songs. These reissues of Lanza's recordings also contribute to restoring the sagging reputation of opera for a new generation of audiences.

Lanza's never totally forgotten but now reinvigorated star image is not a unique phenomenon in the 1990s: it unites commodities and profit to an inordinate investment in the past – what Jacques Derrida has called archive fever.[29] However, the dizzying replication of images, the resurrection of these images in new technical forms, calls attention to the need to rethink the notion of history as it is being rapidly transformed through the contemporary electronic world of speed, instantaneity, and reproduction. The new technologies will ensure that his biography, his films, and his recordings – as well as the world of the 1950s in which they are embedded – will be circulated at a dizzying pace and to ever-larger audiences and to ever-increasing testimonials to his greatness. They do so, however, to an emptying of critical meaning and analysis and, hence, to a reconfiguration of the fourth world of fantasy.

The growing interest in, vitality of, and presence of stars from the past such as Lanza (through remakes and morphing) can be traced to a large body of critical writing on the role of stardom that seeks to rethink ethnicity, masculinity and femininity, sexuality, and the role of memory as a means of altering cultural values. According to these studies, stars "personalize social meanings and ideologies" and stardom is implicated "in the critique of individualism, consumerism, and social stereotyping."[30] While these studies add important psychological and sociological insights on the nature of the star image in relation to its impact on gendered, racial, sexual, and class oppression, they often fall short in neglecting to provide a broader theoretical analysis of value formation. They fail to grasp the slippery and elusive form of the star commodity as it, like the mythical creature, Proteus, changes forms through production, circulation, and consumption, and it is not merely the different forms that the star commodity expresses, but the more fundamental (and abstract) character of how value is assigned. In this context, value belongs to another realm where the seemingly concrete nature of the commodity reveals itself as illusory. The fourth world does not give up its secrets easily.

Heavenly Creatures is a tantalizing text to explore the character of this fourth world and its relation to the phenomenon of stardom and value, particularly since it is an important current evocation of Lanza's stardom. Moreover, the film is significant for its return to the 1950s (as in *Pleasantville*). The film's recourse to the 1950s is evidence of unfinished cultural business (again as in *Pleasantville*), where Cold War conceptions of family, social class, gender, and sexuality are revealed to be in crisis. This period of time is portrayed not as an idyllic black-and-white world without conflict but as a source of antagonisms that cannot be contained. The film's focus on two young women's love for each other and on the forces that ultimately separate them – parents, class differences, and the white, snobbish, Anglophile New Zealand world – are revealing of antagonistic forces that cannot be constrained by parental authority and the disciplining dimensions of education, religion, and psychotherapy.

In contrast to films of social realism that focus on "problems" generated by social non-conformity (e.g. youthful delinquency, sexual promiscuity, aggressive behavior, etc.), *Heavenly*

Creatures adopts an anti-naturalistic style, comprised of contrasting sequences between the everyday world and the world of imagination associated with music, cinema, monochrome and colored episodes, and the dissolving of the natural landscape into a brilliantly colored paradisal panorama. This style enables the spectator to move between the grotesque character of the "real" world that the girls inhabit and a fantasy world that offers other, affect-laden gratification as they conflict with their everyday world. The music of Mario Lanza, so popular with female teenagers in the 1950s, particularly his recording of *The Student Prince*, is associated with an enigmatic fourth world. In contrast to the other movie icons invoked in the film – James Mason and Orson Welles – Lanza's image, identified with working-class and with ethnic identifications, is radically other to the strait-laced British heritage in the 1950s world in which the young women lived.[31]

Heavenly Creatures shares with many other films of the nineties a concern with the past and with rewriting history to include the role of cinema and popular culture, specifically as it raises the issue of lesbian love and associates it with the fourth world. The flights of fantasy in the film invite a meditation on how cinema has shaped the spectator's understanding and experience of the world in order to make socially disallowed desires appear comprehensible and manageable. Unlike the geographical and cultural designation of First, Second, and Third Worlds, the fourth world belongs to the realms of myth, religion (the hymn-singing in the film), and fetishism (the kingdom of Borovnia) where it becomes abstract and ahistorical, seemingly independent of labor and the state.

In their study of the two women, Parker and Hulme, Glamuzina and Laurie provide a gloss on the fourth world that connects it to Maori beliefs. Summarizing a discussion with a Maori Tohunga, they write that "He said that the saints [expressed through the invocation of the movie stars] and the use of the numbers seven and ten could be interpreted as gatekeepers to the fourth world."[32] This view of the fourth world is identified with spiritual forces that stand in stark opposition to the legalistic and restrictive apparatus of the state predicated on normative conceptions of sexuality. While not negating the force of this interpretation, my use of the fourth world proceeds in another direction.

I identify the fourth world with desire and need, with what can be called "affective value," a form of value that is normally considered outside the circuits of capital. However, I regard the fourth world as containing the possibility of exposing the false dichotomy between desire and economic production and its relation to the state. In this context, the cinematic commodity of the star appears to hold the key to a demystification of what Marx called commodity fetishism, "where the products of the human brain appear as autonomous figures endowed with a life of their own."[33] The enigma of stardom has continued to challenge film critics who regard the cinema's creation of "heavenly creatures" as a key to open a door to the perennial fascination with the affective power of the human face and body and with prevailing norms of belief and action.[34] Relations between myth, folklore, and the misty realms of religion are not direct, since, as Marx has written, value has never had "its description branded on its forehead."[35]

The heyday of star mythology in the pre-World War II world and in the decade to follow had powerful currency. It conveyed an appearance of naturalness and functioned as an object of value closely aligned with the social and material forces from which it emerged. The mythology of stardom was saturated with belief in the world that produced it. In the 1950s, Hollywood cultural and political mythmaking via the manufacture of the star capitalized on pressing anxieties linked to the Cold War and to the threat of nuclear disaster. Inherent to these myths was the refashioning of images of masculinity, ethnicity, and social mobility to suit new circumstances. Lanza's persona belongs to this labor to reinvigorate belief in an America of opportunity, an enterprise that was not seamless and transparent but that exposed, if often indirectly, the antagonistic conditions that underpin this cultural capital. Lanza's star commodity is no longer identified in terms of the labor of creating, adhering to, and emulating a myth of power and singularity: it now belongs to a fourth world of fantasy uprooted from its earlier context in the world of the 1950s. Lanza's star appeal in the 1990s belongs to the fourth world, a seemingly impenetrable region. In it, the commodity is evident as commodity; its value is more blatantly translated into monetary terms and into accumulation. The quest to unite the material object to the world of imagination, affect, and belief is yet another form of alchemy, of transforming base metals into gold. The commodity and imagination cannot be reconciled, since one negates the other. The recognition of the antagonism between the economic production of the commodity and its personalized consumption saturated with affect suggests that, instead of seeking reconciliation between the two, the critic of stardom should focus on their incompatibility.

Instead of finding a psychological or anthropological origin for the desire generated by the star, one might better acknowledge that stardom functions in the absence of concreteness, commensurability, and meaning. It survives on its memory and on its commercial viability which it now blatantly and opportunistically announces through the everexpanding media. Thus, unraveling the mysteries of the fourth world leads in two directions. One direction leads to escape, vicarious pleasure, immersion in the power of the commodity itself to the annihilation of the external world. Another, more difficult direction leads to critical reflection on the sources for the antagonism between desire and realization, its mode of construction, its ephemeral and insubstantial character through the media.

Cinema and television continue to refashion folklore, but this folklore is now recognized – as in the case of the circulation of Lanza's image and voice – as a form of nostalgia, a nostalgia that denies the present and any possibility of belief in the world. In Gilles Deleuze's words:

> There are no longer grounds for talking about a real or possible extension capable of constituting an external world: we have ceased to believe in it, and the image is cut off from the external world. But the internalization or integration of self-awareness in a whole has no less disappeared.[36]

Thus Lanza's image offers a meditation on the vanity of trying any longer to connect the star to the affective dimensions of identification and belief that belong to a vanished world. In the fourth world of today, stardom has a different life. Shorn of myth, its virtue and its profitability lie in the power of memory and repetition, in the "fourth world," where fantasies can be transmitted and consumed electronically and otherwise.

Notes

1 George Custen, Bio/Pics: How Hollywood Constructed Public History (New Brunswick, NJ: Rutgers University Press, 1992), 72–73.
2 Chon Noriega, "Internal Others: Hollywood Narratives 'About' Mexican-Americans," in

John King, Ana M. López and Manuel Alvarado, eds, *Mediating Two Worlds: Cinematic Encounters in the Americas* (London: British Film Institute, 1993), 52–66.

3 Miriam Hansen, "Pleasure, Ambivalence, Identification: Valentino and Female Spectatorship," in Jeremy Buder, ed., *Star Texts: Image and Performance in Film and Television* (Detroit: Wayne State University Press, 1991), 287–288.

4 Roland L. Besette, *Mario Lanza: Tenor in Exile* (Portland, OR: Amadeus Press, 1999), 68.

5 *Newsweek* 37 (March 5, 1951), 84.

6 *The Christian Century* 69 (December 29, 1950), 1439.

7 Mannering, *Mario Lanza*, 99.

8 *Newsweek* (May 14, 1951), 98.

9 Ibid.

10 *Time* 57 (May 21, 1951), 116.

11 *Saturday Review* 39 (September 29, 1956), 34.

12 Besette, *Mario Lanza*, 102.

13 Ibid., 80.

14 Ibid., 115.

15 Ibid., 115.

16 *Time* (August 5, 1951), 60.

17 Ibid., 60.

18 Custen, *Bio/Pics*, 67.

19 *Newsweek* 47 (April 9, 1956), 116.

20 Moira Walsh, "Films," *America* 91 (June 12, 1954), 306.

21 *Newsweek* 43 (72) (June 18, 1954), 73.

22 Derek Mannering, *Mario Lanza: A Biography* (London: Robert Hale, 1996), 81.

23 *Time* 71 (80) (February 3, 1958), 80.

24 Wheeler Winston Dixon, *Disaster and Memory: Celebrity Culture and the Crisis of Memory* (New York: Columbia University Press, 1999), 27.

25 Ralph Blumenthal, "50 Years Later, Lanza Booms Forth," *New York Times* (June 23, 1998), E5.

26 *Opera News* 64 (3) (September, 1999), 58.

27 Eric Meyer, *Opera News* 63 (9) (March, 1999), 38.

28 Florence King, "The Misanthrope's Corner," *National Review* 47 (20) (October 23, 1995), 68.

29 Jacques Derrida, *Archive Fever* (Chicago: University of Chicago Press, 1999).

30 Christine Gledhill, "Introduction," in Christine Gledhill, ed., *Stardom: Industry of Desire* (London: Routledge, 1991), xiv.

31 For a detailed discussion of the social and historical circumstances of Parker and Hulme, see Julie Glamuzina and Alison J. Laurie, *Parker and Hulme: A Lesbian Impression* (Ithaca, NY: Firebrand Press, 1991).

32 Ibid., 148.

33 Karl Marx, *Capital*, vol. 1 (New York: Vintage Books, 1977), 165.

34 See Richard Dyer, *Stars* (London: Bridsh Film Institute, 1986); Buder, ed., *Star Texts*, Gledhill, ed., *Stardom*; Gaylyn Studlar, *This Mad Masquerade: Stardom and Masculinity in the Jazz Age* (New York: Columbia University Press, 1996).

35 Marx, *Capital*, 167.

36 Gilles Deleuze, *Cinema 2* (Minneapolis: University of Minnesota Press, 1989), 277.

PART FIVE

THE NETWORK TELEVISION STAR

Introduction

This final section explores the transmogrification of stardom through television and other electronic media and offers an overview of the changing conceptions of celebrity. While none of the essays which follow configures television as the cultural villain, they do reveal significant differences between the television and movie star. In ways quite different from the studio system and closer to the broader cultural focus on personality, television has created stars in abundance – from Lucille Ball and Milton Berle to Jerry Seinfeld and Sarah Jessica Parker, from producers to talk show hosts, from sports commentators to soap opera divas. The strict censorship controls and constraints that governed the stars of the pre-World War II television world have relaxed, if not disappeared. The television star of today – often with much less longevity than earlier celebrities – is minutely scanned, described, and valued for signs of transgression and calamity. Much like the excessive soap opera characters that some television stars play, they are often valued for the very outrageous qualities that the movie studios sought to suppress in the golden age of cinema. The character of celebrity has also been altered in the context of a television medium that is constantly hungry for news and breaking disasters – creating different, more ephemeral forms of the personality cult.

Comedienne Roseanne (whose name has been attached to the surnames of Barr and Arnold) is the creation of the televisual medium – in contrast to stars who have crossed over from film to television (like Ida Lupino or Loretta Young). Kathleen Rowe, in her study "The Unruly Woman: Gender and the Genres of Laughter," explores the character that brought fame to Roseanne. Tracing the ways in which Roseanne's disruptiveness has functioned in the media, Rowe stresses her unconventional control "over men, financial power, celebrity power, [and] sexual power." Tracing Roseanne's career from Denver in the 1980s to her appearance on major networks in the late 1980s and 1990s, Rowe reminds the reader that stardom for Roseanne has not, in Richard Dyer's terms, "resolved contradictions," but has only made contradictions more visible through her outrageousness, crudeness, and grotesque body. Contrasting Roseanne's ironic Domestic Goddess to earlier small screen sitcom heroines (of *I Love Lucy*, *The Donna Reed Show*, *Leave it to Beaver*, and *All in the Family*), Rowe reveals changes in the medium that enable Roseanne to develop a persona suited to the postmodern character of contemporary television. Beyond this, in her program, woman is freed from "the ideology of the self-sacrificing wife and mother" to forge a new comic paradigm which invokes "the contradictions of women's lives."

The talk show has played a key role in television, producing new celebrities and one of the most powerful of these is Oprah Winfrey. In "C'mon, Girl: Oprah Winfrey and the Discourse of Feminine Talk," Gloria-Jean Masciarotte examines the format and dynamics of the talk show through an analysis of the media success of Winfrey. Specifically, Masciarotte asserts that Winfrey's talk show (in contradistinction to an early articulation of the genre by Phil Donahue) "consolidates the spectacle of the talking woman" – making this type of show "more emotional and less issue-oriented" while encouraging a "more vulgar, graphic, voyeuristic, or sensationalist [mode of] exchange."

Winfrey's show does not work to fix stable identities but produces shifting subjectivity, creating a plurality of positions and emphasizing fragmentations of subject positions. Furthermore, the show does not offer facile solace but "irritation," as its host routinely talks about "her life as abuse victim, substance abuser, black person, single working woman, and girlfriend of [the recalcitrant] Steadman." Her shows rely on stories that stress the importance of everyday life, the impossibility of reconciling conflicts, the centrality of multiple points of view, and a heightened sense of affect bordering on the operatic. Finally, her discourse marks a racial difference as she "slide[s] from standard speech to street-inflected talk" – a style "offered up as evidence of the obvious contradiction of her own dominant presence in a system that works to erase it."

Wheeler Winston Dixon in "The Moving Image in Crisis" explores the complexity of celebrity status, its imbrication in the information systems produced by television, the Internet, and media conglomerates. In particular, he focuses upon the public's fascination with scenarios of disaster and the implication this has for a quotidian world of sameness. He asserts that the classic Hollywood narrative model has been exhausted through overuse of dramatic closure, reliance on excessive spectacle and hypertechnical soundtracks, to the point that the contemporary cinema has become simply a memory of itself, a replaying of old roles and outmoded plotlines, all fueled by the inexorability of a "star system that manufactures then discards the protagonists of this phantom automatism." On the other hand, the media fascination with the real-life death of Princess Diana was shaped like a fictional melodrama of popular appeal – starring a poor rich little princess, a rejected then enraged wife, a divorcee, a seeker of love and "happiness." Her narrative was a scenario of disaster, a prime fixation of late twentieth-century media. But the event that was to make television and cultural history was the breaking news of the car crash that killed her, then the reclaiming of her body, the day-long televised funeral, the mountains of written material speculating on her life and death, the controversies of whether the media was to blame for her fate, and the made-for-TV movies and documentaries about her life. In this sense, her life and death can be considered not only as a "creation" of television but as a further permutation of postmodern stardom.

Roseanne

The unruly woman as domestic goddess

KATHLEEN ROWE KARLYN

14

Sometime after I was born in Salt Lake City, Utah, all the little babies were sleeping soundly in the nursery except for me, who would scream at the top of my lungs, trying to shove my whole fist into my mouth, wearing all the skin off on the end of my nose. I was put in a tiny restraining jacket. . . . My mother is fond of this story because to her it illustrates what she regards as my gargantuan appetites and excess anger. I think I was probably just bored.

                            – Roseanne Barr (Arnold) (*Roseanne* 3)

Last week, America's patience snapped. With a single voice the nation thundered, "Intolerable!" We are a people slow to anger but fierce when galvanized, as by Pearl Harbor or, as last week, by Roseanne Barr's rendition of "The Star Spangled Banner." Barr is a star and a slob. She is a star because the country has a robust appetite for slob television, the theme of which is: Crude is cute. Up to a point. There are limits.

                            – George Will ("Cities Gleam with Gunfire")

In July 1990, Roseanne Barr Arnold, star of the top-rated ABC sitcom Roseanne, was invited to sing the national anthem at a double-header between the Cincinnati Reds and the San Diego Padres. Tom Werner, co-producer of the TV show and owner of the Padres, thought that the fat and noisy comedian would give a boost to his losing team. It was Working Women's Night at the San Diego stadium, and Arnold was nationally known for her depiction of working-class family life in *Roseanne*. With thirty-thousand fans in the stands, Arnold screeched out the song, grabbed her crotch, spit on the ground and made an obscene gesture to the booing crowd. Werner had been right; the team won its next two games. But the performance intended as a parody of baseball rituals, unleashed a firestorm in the press. CNN broadcast the story with interviews of outraged "people on the street." In one segment, baseball fans drove a steamroller over a boom box containing a tape of her voice. Angry calls flooded the switchboards at ABC. On national television, President George Bush called her performance "disgraceful." Arnold received threats on her life.

    The incident boosted media coverage of the already controversial Arnold from the tabloids to the establishment press and from the gossip columns to Page One. Headlines joked about "the fat lady singing" or the "Barr-mangled banner," while the tabloid *Star* more graphically exclaimed "Barrf!" and then listed "Her 10 most gross moments." From sports writers to political commentators, all felt compelled to say something about the incident. William C. Rhoden wrote in the *New York Times*: "Barr is merely the symptom of the excesses of greed in American sports. . . . One gets what one pays for" (B9). Opera singer Robert Merrill, who had sung the anthem at Yankee Stadium for eighteen years, spoke of "this woman, who obviously has no taste at all. . . . It was like, 'Here I am, and to hell with you.' . . . I almost upchucked my dinner. . . . I don't know if I've ever felt so angry" (quoted in Georgatos A4). Perhaps the most virulent reaction was that of conservative columnist George Will. Leading his column with quotations from five news stories about children killed or critically injured that summer by gunfire in New York City, he linked Arnold's performance not only to the horrors of American cities in decay but to the sneak attack on the nation by the Japanese at Pearl Harbor. What seemed to distress him most was that, in his view, she was feeding the nation's fatal appetite for "slob television." First paraphrasing the American epic poet Walt Whitman ("I hear American bullets singing"), he then lamented the "alabaster cities" of "America the Beautiful" which no longer "gleam, undimmed by human tears!" (A15).

Obviously Arnold had struck a nerve. Other singers have been criticized for their highly stylized renditions of "The Star Spangled Banner" – among them Jose Feliciano, Bobby McFerrin, Marvin Gaye, and Willie Nelson. And one could argue that Arnold, as a comedian, was doing nothing more than they had, shaping the performance according to her own comedic artistry. But none provoked a reaction comparable to this one. Arnold jested about it – "I must be the greatest singer. My voice can stop a fucking nation." But a year later she said more reflectively:

> It's because I'm a woman. And I was making fun of men and, you know, we have to remember, that's really dangerous. It still is. I really thought I was to that point in my career where I had broken all those barriers down, and it served to remind me that it's still dangerous to be a woman who makes fun of men, or a woman who is funny, or a woman who does any social criticism, or a woman who has a brain, or a woman who has anything to say, or, you know, a woman, period. . . . It's dangerous and frightening.
>
> (Arnold, Interview)[1]

In other words, as Will insists, there are indeed limits or barriers, especially for women who behave as Arnold does. His description of her as a "star and a slob" only dimly suggests the powerful and contradictory status she has achieved by whining, wisecracking, munching, mooning, screeching, and spitting her way into the national consciousness. If it is dangerous "to be a woman, period," it is especially so to be an *unruly* woman, and Arnold's performance in San Diego that summer confirmed her status as such.

Women rarely have the opportunity to claim the kind of public space that Arnold did that day, and her experience offers abundant lessons about the relation between social power and public visibility. Invisibility helps constrain women's social power; as long as women are not seen in the public sphere, they do not exist. Arnold heightened her visibility by forcing herself from one – less visible – category of popular discourse into another usually unavailable to women – from "soft news" to "hard news." Soft news includes gossip, the tabloids, *People* magazine, lifestyle and entertainment sections of the newspaper; hard news covers events clearly in the public sphere and appears on the front pages and op-ed pages of newspapers

and at the beginning of newscasts. If sports is not exactly hard news, it's not soft either, because of its particular status in masculine culture. When Arnold walked into that stadium, she made herself the subject of hard news, subject to those voices that had never touched her when she was safely contained in a place marked "sitcom" or "HBO Comedy Special," or in the feminized discourse of gossip columns and tabloids.

Implicit in the unruly woman's heightened visibility is her potential to bring about a process Erving Goffman describes as "breaking frame." Goffman suggests that social life is an "endless negotiation" about which cultural frame should surround, and thereby give meaning to, various events and bits of behavior. He argues that the meaning of a social situation can be radically altered by changing the frame in which it is perceived and that frames are most vulnerable at their margins. Because she is dangerously situated in the margins of social life, the unruly woman enjoys heightened "frame-busting" power.

Arnold entered a space that day already defined as liminal or sacred in patriarchal culture. Baseball is not merely a game, something that is played, but a collective, public, and masculine ritual, a quasi-religious reaffirmation of patriarchy, patriotism, and the myth of our nation's Edenic history. Unlike football, its rival in the national mythology of sports (at least until the rise of basketball in the past twenty years), baseball, with its grace and decorum, is the game of choice for intellectuals and the upwardly mobile. It is George Will's favorite sport. Free of the narrative constraints of her television series, Arnold staged a joke that refrained that ritual event and turned it into something else – a carnivalized moment of leveling, mockery, and inversion. By exceeding the limits of play tolerated on that diamond, parodying the gestures of the Boys of Summer, and singing the national anthem less than reverentially – in effect, by being who she was, a comedian, joke-maker, and unruly woman – she violated the space of that ritual and, indeed, the national airwaves that had been given over to its celebration. What might have been a harmless spoof of the tropes of masculinity and patriotism became a threat to the sanctity of all American institutions, invoking that "perilous realm of possibility," in Victor Turner's words, where "'anything *may* go'" (41).

According to Turner, at times of dramatic social change, sacred symbols – such as baseball, the national anthem, and the flag – burst into the public arena to mobilize people to defend their cultures. In the summer of 1990, the U.S. government was laying the groundwork for its showdown with Saddam Hussein and preparing to deploy sixty thousand troops in Kuwait. Flag-burning had become a controversial issue, with proposals in Congress for a constitutional ban against it. Arnold's performance made her vulnerable to the official voices of masculine authority, the voices of news and government from George Will to George Bush, which projected onto her all perceived threats to the dominant culture. Indeed, Will's near loss of control over his own rhetoric exposed his column's subtext – the range of repressed fears this disorderly fat woman released about racial threats to the nation's "alabaster" cities, about mass culture with its "slob" values encroaching on the tidy domain of those who know Walt Whitman's poetry well enough to paraphrase it.[2]

Not only in this incident but throughout her career Arnold has used the semiotics of unruliness to break frame, to disrupt, to expose the gap between, on the one hand, the New Left and the women's movement of the late 1960s and early 1970s, and on the other, the realities of working-class family life two decades later. On one level, of course, Arnold's joke backfired. On another and more important one, however, it succeeded as a powerful demonstration of the disruptive power of the unruly woman. Even as fans were booing her in the stadium, others were cheering.[3] As Arnold's career has unfolded, her fat, unruly body – and her noisy, angry, funny persona – have shape-shifted into forms that might appear less transgressive than the ones that first defined her. A new history shaped by her disclosures of incest, a new body shaped by dieting and cosmetic surgery, and even a new name when she dropped Barr for Arnold have created what might be considered a new Roseanne, whose power to continually re-create herself as a boundary breaker remains to be seen. [. . .] I wish to emphasize how she created her definitive persona (re-created nightly on syndicated reruns of *Roseanne*) through an inspired use of the semiotics of unruliness. Throughout this discussion, I use "Arnold" to refer to Roseanne Barr Arnold not as a "real" person but in Richard Dyer's sense, as a sign created by her various public roles, performances, and interviews and by the commentaries about them. I reserve "Roseanne" to refer more narrowly to the character she plays by that name. Together, these elements evoke an ambivalence that has both produced and threatened her popularity.

In the press: "Roseanne – Yea!" "Roseanne – Nay!"

The cover of the December 1990 issue of *Vanity Fair* – headlined "Roseanne on Top" – shows Arnold holding the wrists of her husband Tom Arnold to pin him beneath her. Her mouth is open in what appears to be a laugh. She is wearing a low-cut red dress, a strawberry-blonde wig, diamonds, and a white fox fur, a look that parodically recalls the blonde bombshells and gold diggers of early classical Hollywood film. The photograph, a medium shot, centers on Arnold's massive cleavage. Tom Arnold's face, looking at the camera and registering little emotion, is upside down.

The words and images of the cover suggest that Arnold wields power in multiple dimensions – power over men, financial power, celebrity power, sexual power. These words and images also acknowledge that she has achieved that power by cultivating a particular persona defined by gender inversion. Inside, more photographs give Arnold's outrageous-ness, vulgarity, and excesses the validation of high style. Shots of her mud wrestling with Tom Arnold in playful, sexually suggestive poses literalize her "earthiness." One photo-graph, captioned "filthy rich," shows the couple covered with mud and bathed in golden light. It brilliantly displays the ambivalence and danger – the "dirt" – represented by the convergence of money and sexuality in the person of the unruly woman. Beneath the "Roseanne on Top" cover headline, however, is a smaller subhead asking, "But Who's the Boss?" While recognizing, and even celebrating, Arnold's status as one of television's highest-paid performers, the magazine still has trouble fully granting that this monumental figure is indeed the boss.

Arnold's rise to such success began in Denver in the early 1980s, when she worked first as a wisecracking cocktail waitress and then as a performer in local comedy clubs. After auditioning for the Comedy Store in Los Angeles, she was invited to perform on *The Tonight Show*. A concert tour followed, and her national career took off. Here, briefly, are some of her personal and professional milestones of the next few years.

Arnold produced her first HBO special, "The Roseanne Barr Show," in 1987, and in January 1988 signed on with producers Marcy Carsey and Tom Werner. Carsey/Werner, who had developed the top-rated sitcom *The Cosby Show* (1984–1992) out of Bill Cosby's standup comedy act, hired Matt Williams as executive producer, but almost immediately Williams and Arnold started battling over artistic control of the show. According to Arnold, he wanted

to name it *Life and Stuff* so that it would not become a star vehicle for her. The show made its debut in October of that year as *Roseanne* and became one of the top three television series of the year. In January 1989, Williams was forced off the show and two weeks later it hit number one. That spring, the tabloid press pried open confidential records and identified a daughter Arnold had given up for adoption eighteen years earlier. In July she filed to divorce her first husband, Bill Pentland. In September, she published her autobiography, *Roseanne: My Life as a Woman*, which became a best-seller. In December, she made her film debut in Susan Seidelman's *She-Devil*, also starring Meryl Streep. The film was a critical and box-office failure.

In January 1990 Arnold married her longtime friend, standup comedian Tom Arnold. (The *New York Times* noted that he was six years younger than she.) Meanwhile, the turmoil on the *Roseanne* set continued. In March Jeff Harris, the executive producer who had replaced Williams, resigned, taking out an ad in *Variety* about leaving for a vacation "in the relative peace and quiet of Beirut." On July 25, Arnold touched off a national scandal by her rendition of "The Star Spangled Banner." In September, *Little Rosey*, an animated Saturday-morning children's show, made its debut, with Arnold providing the voice for the show's main character. She described the cartoon show as the only one on television with a girl hero, no violence, and no sexism. The show lasted only one season because she refused to comply with the network's insistence that more boy characters be added.[4] In December, Amy Heckerling's film *Look Who's Talking Too* was released, with Arnold providing the voice of the wise-cracking girl.

Arnold's second HBO special, "Roseanne Barr: Live from Trump Castle," was aired in January 1991. In June, she and Tom Arnold settled a $35-million lawsuit against the *National Enquirer* and the *Star*, the terms of which were not disclosed. Tom Arnold converted to Judaism, the couple renewed their vows in a religious ceremony, and Roseanne Barr changed her name to Roseanne Arnold. In September, she announced that she was an incest survivor at a conference in Denver attended by 1,100 people. *Backfield in Motion*, a made-for-TV movie starring Roseanne and Tom Arnold, was broadcast in November of that year, and her third HBO comedy special, "Roseanne Arnold," in June 1992. By 1992, *Roseanne* had reached number one in the United Kingdom, a sign of the international success Arnold had achieved, and she was now one of the highest-paid performers on television, earning about $100,000 per episode. In 1992 she and Tom Arnold completed a deal with ABC, which included the series *The Jackie Thomas Show* for him. When *Roseanne* finished its fourth season in 1992, it went into syndication, reportedly earning Arnold at least $30 million (Hirschberg 186), while continuing to run at or near the top of the ratings in prime time.

Despite this record, Arnold's success has not generated universal enthusiasm, as the national-anthem incident made clear. Nor was that incident an isolated event, but merely the most provocative in a series of episodes that included dropping her pants at other public events, cracking jokes about menstruation on national television, and generally "making a spectacle of herself." Many people find Arnold's persona deeply offensive, and controversy has followed her up almost every rung of the ladder to success. She and her series have been trashed by the tabloids, snubbed by the Emmies, and condescended to by media critics.[5] At the same time, her fans have been loyal and numerous enough to propel her to, and sustain, her success. In a *People* magazine poll, readers voted her their favorite female television star and the one most likely to have a flourishing career in the year 2000. The August 1989 issue of *Esquire*, on its favorite (and least favorite) women, concisely displayed this ambivalence, or difficulty in placing her, by running two stories by two men, side by side – one called "Roseanne – Yea," and the other, "Roseanne – Nay."

While this ambivalence cuts across media and class lines, the supermarket tabloids have perhaps played the largest role in creating and popularizing Arnold's unruly persona. The tabloids are the carnivalesque of the popular print media, giving heightened representations of the kinds of "weirdness or disjunction" their readers experience in everyday life (Fiske 114). They are popular with the same demographic group targeted by Arnold's show, women aged 18–34, or, as comedian Alan King more colorfully describes them, "the hopeless underclass of the female sex. The polyester-clad overweight occupants of the slow track. Fast-food waitresses, factory workers, housewives – members of the invisible pink-collar army. The despised, the jilted, the underpaid." "In other words," as Arnold replies, "the coolest people" (both quoted in O'Connor B27). Arnold shares with the tabloids a taste for the self-consciously excessive, vulgar, and sensational. Both Arnold and the tabloids carnivalize, invert, and mock the norms of bourgeois taste.

Consider this description of Arnold's wedding to Tom Arnold:

> Hilarious five-page photo album – ROSEANNE'S SHOTGUN "WEDDING FROM HELL" – Dad refuses to give pregnant bride away – "Don't wed that druggie bum!" Maids of honor are lesbians – best man is groom's detox pal. Ex-hubby makes last-ditch bid to block ceremony. Rosie and Tom wolf 2 out of 3 tiers of wedding cake.
>
> ("Roseanne's Shotgun 'Wedding from Hell'")

The headlines cover a simulated photo of her tossing her bridal bouquet. With her tongue protruding, she is grotesquely shot from below to exaggerate her size. Other tabloid headlines proclaim additional atrocities: "ROSEANNE TELLS KIDS 'DROP OUT OF SCHOOL.'" "ROSEANNE BEAT UP HER HUSBAND – AND HAD AFFAIRS WITH SIX MEN (She often ignored her children, leaving it up to Bill to fix the youngsters' meals and wash their clothes)." "ROSEANNE INVESTIGATED FOR CHILD ABUSE." "STAR-SPANGLED SICKO ROSEANNE: 'DON'T SEND ME BACK TO THE PSYCHO WARD'." "ROSEANNE'S DISGRACE! THE REAL REASON TV'S STAR IS MAKING AMERICA HATE HER." "ONE OF THE MOST HATED WOMEN IN AMERICA." "BEFORE, HER ADVISERS WOULDN'T LET HER GO OVER THE BORDER OF DECENCY, BUT WITH TOM THERE ARE NO BORDERS!"

It is hard not to see much of Arnold's treatment by the tabloids as tongue-in-cheek, as in the remarkable list of taboos called up by the description of her "wedding from hell," or the inversion of the classical wife-beating story that elicits sympathy for her husband as victim (for having to "fix the youngsters' meals and wash their clothes"). However, that tone often conveys a scarcely concealed condescension. Granted that the tabloids are *about* excess and about showing celebrities in revealing or compromising poses, there is an edge of cruelty to their treatment of Arnold, especially in photographs that exaggerate her fatness and her willingness to show her anger or to ignore the conventional standards of female beauty. The media have betrayed the same mixed bag of emotions toward a group of wealthy, aging women (among them, Imelda Marcos, Leona Helmsley, Tammy Faye Bakker, Elizabeth Taylor, and Zsa Zsa Gabor) who have shared the tabloid covers and gossip columns with Arnold.

The tabloids can be cruel to everyone, but when that cruelty is directed against the transgressive older woman it often takes the form of comedy, turning her into a grotesque clown. For example, Zsa Zsa Gabor's advancing age has increased her unruly standing. Her circus-like trial (at the age of seventy-two) for slapping a Beverly Hills police officer coincided

with Arnold's anthem episode and made her a rival for coverage in the gossip columns. After her trial, she was booed and called a floozy when she rode her horse in a parade. The case of Leona Helmsley is even more suggestive since, unlike Gabor, she does not work in show business and so would seem protected from the excesses of publicity associated with stardom. *Newsweek* brought considerable criticism on itself for the tone of its cover story about the 69-year-old billionaire when she was charged with tax evasion. The story used her age and sex to ridicule her. Headlined on the magazine's cover with "Rhymes with Rich" and written as a take-off on *Alice's Adventures in Wonderland*, the article described "Leona-bashing" as "summer's most fashionable sport" (Waters et al. 46). The story elicited angry letters from women complaining that powerful male figures charged and convicted of much more serious crimes are never trivialized in such a manner. As sociologist Jack Leven said in the article, "Here's this abrasive, aggressive, stubborn, wealthy person who happens to be a woman. If Donald Trump behaved in the same way, people would overlook it or might even admire it" (51).

In Arnold's case, especially in the early years of her career, the tabloids displayed an effort to wrest her definition of herself from comedy – where she asserts her power to be the subject of laughter – and transfer it to melodrama, where she becomes an object, a victim. When Tom Arnold gets the "credit" for Roseanne's transgressions, she becomes a victim of her own powerlessness, simply a woman out of control. Melodrama, unlike much comedy, punishes the unruly woman for asserting her desire. Such parodies of melodrama make the unruly woman the target of *our* laughter, while denying her the power and pleasure of her own.

Arnold hardly fared better among more sophisticated commentators. In an early review of *Roseanne*, Elvis Mitchell noted in the *Village Voice* how "startled" he was to see "this kind of arrogance so early in the run of a TV series" (47). He criticized the general lack of "class" or "taste" in television viewers and reviewers, describing her show as the "1040 EZ, low-income, no deductions" version of *The Cosby Show*. And according to Joyce Maynard, Exeter- and Yale-educated author of the syndicated column "Domestic Affairs," Arnold was "obnoxious and insulting to the average American wife/mother and homemaker" (C1). Both commentators displayed certain recurring problems in contemporary cultural criticism – the left's difficulties with gender, and middle-class feminism's with class. While Mitchell appreciated the "tastelessness" of *Married With Children*, finding the show a hip send-up of working-class family life, *Roseanne*, with its strong female character and feminist content, was "arrogant." Maynard's difficulty in understanding Arnold's appeal began with her unthinking assurance that she could speak for the "average American wife/mother and homemaker," despite the class privileges that she enjoys.[6]

One explanation for the contradictions that have characterized Arnold's reception in U.S. culture lies in the phenomenon of stardom itself. As Dyer has explained (*Stars*), people become stars because their images play on – and magically resolve – ideological contra-dictions of their times. In Arnold's case, her copious body could be seen as a site which makes visible, and reconciles, the conflicts women experience in a culture that says consume (food) but look as if you don't. Or it makes visible the conflict any member of the working class might experience in a culture that says consume (goods – conspicuously and lavishly) but don't expect a job that provides you with the means to do so. This explanation is apt, but it doesn't fully explain the extreme ambivalence that has marked Arnold's career from its outset.

Such an explanation, I believe, would locate Arnold in the historical and theoretical context of female unruliness. In an article on the op-ed page of the *New York Times* ("What Am I, a

Zoo?"), Arnold describes her own awareness of the carnivalesque heterogeneity of her image by enumerating the groups she has been associated with – the regular housewife, the mother, the postfeminist, the "Little Guy," fat people, the "Queen of Tabloid America," the "body politic," sex, "angry womankind herself," "the notorious and sensationalistic La Luna madness of an ovulating Abzugian woman run wild" – and so on. All are valid, she believes, although many people insist on reducing this multivalence to a single truth:

> Some people, they look at me, and they'll see a real person that's "down," you know, earthy or (what are some of the nasty things they say about me?) "crude." They'll say that. And it is there. And then other people will see that there's some spiritual or deeper meaning, and they'll see that. Some people will just see one and then other people will see both of them, because I think that what I'm really trying to do is project both of them at the same time, because I think they are equally here and equally valid and equally human.
>
> (Arnold, Interview)

She projects both that "crudeness" and that "deeper meaning" most exuberantly and defiantly by inscribing across her body the signifiers of female unruliness.

Arnold's carnivalesque body

Arnold's unruliness is more clearly paradigmatic than syntagmatic, less visible in the stories her series dramatizes than in the image cultivated around her body: Roseanne Arnold-the-person who tattooed her buttocks and mooned her fans, Roseanne Conner-the-character for whom farting and nose-picking are as much a reality as dirty dishes and obnoxious boy bosses. It is Arnold's *fatness*, however, and the *looseness* or lack of personal restraint her fatness implies, that most powerfully define her and convey her opposition to middle-class and feminine standards of decorum and beauty. Indeed, the very appearance of a 200-plus-pound woman on a weekly prime-time sitcom is significant. More than anything, I believe, her fatness is the source of the hostility directed against her. Even if a fat woman says or does nothing, her very appearance, especially in public space, can give offense. Fatness has carried more positive implications for women in other historical periods and among other ethnic and racial groups, but in white, late-twentieth-century America, it signifies a disturbing unresponsiveness to social control.

As Michel Foucault has shown, social groups exercise control over their members by inscribing standards of beauty and perfection, of social and sexual "normalcy" on their bodies. At the same time, the body serves as a vehicle for communication from subject to social world – a nonverbal communication that is often hidden by the social privileging of speech (Douglas, *Implicit Meanings* 87). Body language conveys the individual's relation to the social group along a continuum of control, from strong to weak, from total relaxation to total self-control. Among the socially powerful, relaxation signifies "ease." Among those deemed in need of social control, it signifies "looseness" or "sloppiness." The body that "refuses to be aestheticized," that does not control its "grotesque, offensive, dirty aspects," can thus communicate resistance to social discipline (Fiske 97). George Will could find no better way to express his reaction to Arnold's rebelliousness than by describing her as a "slob."

Arnold's body epitomizes the grotesque body Bakhtin described, an affinity that is clear from the first paragraph of *Roseanne: My Life as a Woman* (Barr), where her description of her "gargantuan appetites" even as a newborn baby brings to mind Bakhtin's study of Rabelais. Arnold compounds her famess with a looseness of body language and speech. She sprawls, slouches, and flops on furniture; her speech – even apart from its content – is loose, its enunciation and grammar "sloppy," and its tone and volume "excessive."

In twentieth-century U.S. culture, these qualities have long lost the positive charges they might have carried in the cultures Bakhtin described. Our culture stigmatizes all fat people by psychologizing or moralizing their obesity.[7] For *women*, body size and bearing are governed by especially far-reaching standards of normalization and aestheticization, which forbid both looseness and fatness. Women of ill-repute, whether fat or thin, are described as "loose," their bodies, especially their sexuality, seen as out of control. Similarly, fat women are seen as having "let themselves go." To protect themselves against the threat of rape, violence, come-ons, and offensive male vulgarity, poor women, especially women of color, may assume a bearing that is "stiff" and "ladylike." Anita Hill displayed extreme dignity and reserve during the 1991 Senate hearings on the appointment of Supreme Court Justice Clarence Thomas, although that bearing did not protect her from sexual innuendoes by men or charges of "aloofness" by women.

The cult of thinness is among the most insidious means of disciplining the female body in contemporary U.S. culture. Because a woman's social well-being is largely dependent on her appearance, heavy women suffer more than heavy men from the culture's tendency to stigmatize fat people.

Comedians make fat jokes about Arnold but they usually spare John Goodman, the equally fat actor who plays her husband on her sitcom. While other cultures have considered round and fleshy women as sensuous and feminine, our culture considers them unfeminine, rebellious, and sexually deviant, either undersexed or oversexed. In her studies of women's relation to food (*Fat is a Feminist Issue* and *Hunger Strike*), Susie Orbach has described anorexia as the "metaphor of our times," an expression of the extreme contradictions women experience when they are socialized to tend to the needs of others but deny their own. Femininity is gauged by how little space women take up; women who are too fat or move too loosely appropriate too much space, obtruding upon proper boundaries (Henley 38). It is no coincidence, Orbach writes, that since the 1960s, when women accelerated their demands for more space in the public world, the female body ideal has become smaller and ever more unattainable. At the same time, the incidence of anorexia has sharply increased. The anorectic takes the imperative to deny her desire and "aestheticize" her body beyond healthful limits, her emaciated form becoming a grotesque exposure of the norms that seek to control women's appetites in all areas of their lives.

The transgressive, round female body is also the maternal body, and maternity ties women to the process of generation and aging. As a result, the figure of the grotesque old woman often bears a masculinist culture's projected fears of aging and death. While Arnold is hardly an old woman and the media do not attempt to portray her as such, fatness and age are closely related because both foreground the materiality of the body. Warning against a misogyny she finds in camp aesthetics and certain postmodern tendencies in general, Tania Modleski argues that the "disembodiment" or "body without organs" celebrated by some theorists of postmodernism (such as Gilles Deleuze and Felix Guattari) remains a uniquely *male* body. The "essentially 80s figure of masculinity," she writes, is Pee Wee Herman,

Figure 14.1 Roseanne
Courtesy of Photofest, New York

who remains pre-adult and pre-sexual while the "fat lady" and "aging actress," stock figures in the camp aesthetics Pee Wee draws on, must get old, get fat, and die (*Feminism Without Women* 99–103).

Women are expected to keep not only their bodies but their utterances unobtrusive. As Henley notes, voices in any culture that are not meant to be heard are perceived as loud when they do speak, regardless of their decibel level. The description of feminists as "shrill" – with voices that are too loud and too high-pitched – quickly became a cliché in accounts of the women's movement. Dominant cultures characterize minorities among them as loud – Americans in Europe, Japanese in the United States. In white U.S. culture, the voices of blacks are characterized as not only "loud" but "unclear," "slurred," and "lazy" – in other words, loose. Farting, belching, and nose-picking convey a similar failure – or refusal – to restrain the body. While boys and men can make controlled use of such "uncontrollable" bodily functions to rebel against authority, such an avenue of revolt is generally not available to women. But, as Henley suggests, "if it should ever come into women's repertoire, it will carry great power, since it directly undermines the sacredness of women's bodies" (91).

Expanding that repertoire of revolt is entirely consistent with Arnold's professed mission. She writes of wanting "to break every social norm . . . and see that it is laughed at. I chuckle with glee if I know I have offended someone, because the people I intend to insult offend me horribly" (Barr, *Roseanne* 50). Arnold describes how Matt Williams, the producer she eventually fired from her show, tried to get *her* fired: "He compiled a list of every offensive thing I did. And I do offensive things. . . . That's who I am. That's my act. So Matt was in his office making a list of how gross I was, how many times I farted and belched – taking it to the network to show I was out of control" (quoted in Jerome 85–86). Of course she was out of control – *his* control.

By being fat, loud, and ever willing to "do offensive things," the star persona "Roseanne Arnold" displays, above all, a supreme ease with her body – an ease which triggers much of the unease surrounding her because it diminishes the power of others to control her. Pierre Bourdieu describes such a manner as an "indifference to the objectifying gaze of others which neutralizes its powers . . . [and] appropriates its appropriation" (208). It marks her rebellion against not only the codes of gender but those of class, for a culture's norms of beauty or the "legitimate" body – fit and trim – are accepted across class boundaries while the ability to achieve them is not. Ease with one's body is the prerogative of the upper classes. For the working classes, the body is more likely to be a source of embarrassment, timidity, and alienation.

While her body bears the coding of the working-class woman's "alienated" body, Arnold rejects what that coding signifies. Her indifference to conventional readings of her body exposes the ideology underlying them. Concerning her fatness, she resists any efforts to define and judge her by her weight. Publicly celebrating the pleasures of eating, she argues that women need to take up more space in the world, not less. She similarly attacks the "legitimate" female body, which conceals any traces of its reproductive processes. On national television she announced that she had "cramps that could kill a horse" and described the special pleasure she took from the fact that she and her sister were "on their period" – unclean, according to Orthodox Jewish law – when they carried their grandmother's coffin. And in her autobiography she writes about putting a woman, a mother – her – in the White House: "My campaign motto will be 'Let's vote for Rosie and put some new blood in the White House – every twenty-eight days'" (Barr, *Roseanne* 117).

A woman's relation to cultural standards of female beauty, Arnold suggests, is complex, created from an interplay between her internalized body image and her external resources. Arnold often appears in public and on her series fashionably dressed and immaculately groomed, and in her second HBO special, "Roseanne Barr: Live from Trump Castle," she parodies glamorous stars by appearing convincingly glamorous herself. Yet in the more typical style of the Domestic Goddess, her basic character, she also shows why the overworked housewife may not have the time or money to spend on the regime of personal beauty required by a patriarchal consumer culture. She rejects the barrage of ads that tell women they can never be young, thin, or beautiful enough and that their houses – an extension of their bodies – can never be immaculate enough. She denies the pollution taboos that foster silence and self-hatred in women by urging them to keep their bodies, like their bathroom fixtures and kitchen appliances, deodorized, anticepticized, and "April fresh." Instead, she reveals the social causes of female fatness, irritability, and messiness in the strains on working-class family life. For "Roseanne Conner," junk food late at night may be a sensible choice for comfort after a day punching out plastic forks on an assembly line.

Roseanne: the domestic goddess and the sitcom

Despite television's interest in a female audience, the male point of view informs most classics of the domestic sitcom genre, from I *Love Lucy* and *Leave It to Beaver* (1957–1963) to *All in the Family* (1971–1979). And while the domestic sitcom is founded on male/female conflict, the degree of female unruliness each series allows is tempered by the ethnic, class, and racial differences it attempts to negotiate. Sitcoms set in middle-class WASP families (*Leave It to Beaver; The Donna Reed Show* [1958–1966], *My Three Sons* [1960–1972], *The Brady Bunch* [1969–1974], and *Father Knows Best* [1954–1960]) tend to leave the authority of the husband/father largely unchallenged. The same is true of *The Cosby Show*, which replicates many of the values of the WASP upper-middle-class family. Tolerance for a wife/mother's disruptiveness tends to increase when a sitcom plays across ethnic or class difference. A husband's authority can be tested more boldly when he is non-WASP, like the Cuban Desi Arnaz or the Jewish George Burns, or if, like Darren in *Bewitched*, his wife makes use of extrahuman sources or power. The working-class sitcom also opens up more room to demystify the idealized WASP family and to mock the male, but in its best-known examples, *The Honeymooners* (1955–1956) and *All in the Family*, it has still supported masculine authority in the home and conveyed that "male point of view coming out of women's mouths." Edith may be the moral center of *All in the Family* and she gains stature and respect in later seasons – but we remember her as the "dingbat."[8]

Arnold wanted something different. In expressing a *woman's* point of view on the family, *Roseanne* acknowledges the frustrations of the wife and mother but also affirms her strength and commitment to her husband and children: "I'm not Lucy trying to hide 20 bucks from Ricky, or June Cleaver gliding around in a dust proof house in pearls and heels. I'm a woman who works hard and loves her family, but they can drive her *nuts*" (quoted in Hicks 4). One episode explicitly alludes to *Leave It to Beaver* by playing its theme music and switching to black and white when Aunt Jackie, who has been a substitute wife and mother to the Conner family during Roseanne's absence, hands the children their lunches and books with a beatific smile as they skip out the door on their way to school. While *Roseanne* is often praised for seeming more "real" than most other television sitcoms, the world of the Conners, like that of the Ricardos and Cleavers, is, of course, a fiction as well – but one based on an explicitly feminist and working-class point of view. In Arnold's vision of family life, the children talk back, the house is a mess, money is always in short supply. The Conners, a blue-collar family, live in a tract of bungalows in the mill town of Lanford, Illinois. Dan works in construction and eventually starts up a small cycle business. Roseanne moves from one pink-collar job to another and is often out of work. The series has followed goody-goody Becky and tomboy Darlene through their rebellious adolescence, with DJ, the little brother, mostly staying out of the way. Deviating from the television norm (evident in such recent examples as *Wonder Years*

[1988–1993], *Doogie Howser, M.D.* [1989–1993], and *Brooklyn Bridge* [1991–1993]), *Roseanne* gives greater attention to the stories of the daughters than to those of the son.

In its first season, the show presented its dramatic conflicts starkly, relying primarily on one-liners and blunt confrontations between its characters ("That's why some animals eat their young") for its humor and its bite. By the fourth season (1991–1992), the Conners had acquired a lengthy history, and the show approached the emotional range of the domestic drama or soap opera. For example, in an early episode, fifteen-year-old Darlene appears in a funk, and she remains that way for most of the season, dressed in black, lying on the couch, radiating gloom. The series did not attempt quickly to explain or remedy her depression.

As in the soap opera, the wife/mother in *Roseanne* is ultimately responsible for the emotional well-being of the family, and in the title sequence (which changes only slightly in the series' fifth and sixth seasons), family life is shown to be a circle which literally begins and ends on her. Roseanne sits at a cluttered kitchen table with her husband, children, and sister Jackie. The group is playing cards. The camera begins on Roseanne, then moves around the table, until it finally returns to Roseanne and stops. Meanwhile, the show's folksy theme song plays. Roseanne wins the hand, appears to burst out laughing, and sweeps up her earnings, clearly delighted to be the "woman on top." As the music fades into silence, its sound is replaced by her exuberant laughter, which continues a few moments longer. The sequence provides a backdrop of resilient, uncomplicated laughter for the more sardonic laughter that usually follows in each episode.

Jackie, played by Laurie Metcalf, holds a special place in that family circle. Husbands and wives typically discuss family issues together in a sitcom, and *Roseanne* is no exception. But Jackie provides Roseanne with a *female* confidante and ongoing opportunities for "girl talk." The series motivates Jackie's casual, regular presence in the household with the simple fact of dirty laundry; she drops in to use the Conners' washer and dryer. As a character in her own right – the thirty-something single woman who can't find any track, never mind a fast track – she provides interest and comedy through her efforts to find "meaningful" relationships with men and "rewarding" jobs primarily in male-dominated fields, first as a cop, then as a truck driver. Through her presence, the series examines the ambivalences of sisters' relationships with each other in adult life. Most important, Roseanne's regular conversations with Jackie allow her to address her audience as women, and to continually provide female-to-female commentaries on the events that unfold in the series.

While the Conners' social circle is casually integrated, *Roseanne* leaves the issues of race, ethnicity, and its own whiteness unexamined. Instead, it mines the terrain of class and gender, showing how the Conners' class position affects their lives at home and in the workplace. Home life deteriorates when Roseanne is out of work; the family suffers financially and emotionally from her anxiety and loss of self-esteem. Home life also suffers when she *does* have a job, since most of the ones available to her make no allowances for her needs to tend to her family. Every visit to school when a child is in trouble means time off without pay and an angry boss. In one of the strongest episodes about the oppression of working-class women, Roseanne confronts her threatening and patronizing new boss at Wellman Plastics, where she has worked on an assembly line for eleven years. He has increased the quota of piecework beyond what the workers can do. He resents Roseanne's refusal to be intimidated by him and when she asks him privately to lower the quota, he agrees, as long as she displays a new, subservient attitude toward him. For a while, she goes along with his public humiliations but then he raises the quota anyway, teaching her that it was not productivity he wanted but power. She saves her self-respect by quitting the job.

That episode ends with a triumphant celebration at the Lobo Bar. But subsequent episodes trace the trials of Roseanne's unemployment and her demoralizing search for a new job, continually interweaving the politics of gender and class. Roseanne enters the pink-collar ghetto of phone sales and fast food. She is disqualified from one appealing job because she hasn't learned to use a computer. Her boss at a fast-food restaurant is a spoiled and arrogant teenage boy. Her search ends for a while when she takes a job at a beauty shop sweeping the floor, answering the phone and making coffee. The job is not ideal; she must walk Mrs. Wellman's dog and pick up her dry cleaning – even though after eleven years Mrs. Wellman still calls her "Roxanne Conway." "The work is degrading," she tells Dan after he makes an insensitive joke about the triviality of being a "shampoo girl," "but nobody there makes me feel like it is. That is *your* job." Her female boss, on the other hand, treats her with respect and appreciation. "I like the people, they like me; and that makes sweepin' hair not so bad." By the fourth season, the series has muted its treatment of worker/management conflict by creating her new boss, a gay man, as a sympathetic character.[9] Whether at Chicken Divine or Rodbell's Coffee Shop, however, these are Roseanne's "jobs," which she distinguishes from her career – the work she does at home raising her family. One episode focuses on exposing the hidden work of that career. When Dan is invited to discuss his work on Career Day at Darlene's school, Roseanne protests that she wasn't also invited to discuss hers. She then takes Darlene's home economics class on a field trip to the grocery store, showing them how to juggle limited money and time to produce a meal for five between errands and loads of laundry.

Roseanne treats gender and issues related to the female body with particular candor, wit, and poignancy. In one Halloween episode (and Halloween seems to hold a special place in the series), the holiday's invitation to masquerade and transgression becomes the means for commentary on the social construction of gender. The episode combines one story line about DJ's insistence on dressing as a witch with another based on Roseanne's disguise as a man. DJ's costume distresses the normally easygoing Dan, who urges him to be a warlock or wizard – a "guy witch" – instead, and to carry a fire poker instead of a broom. Roseanne reminds Dan that he thought Darlene was cute when she dressed up as a pirate for three years. Later, when Roseanne's car breaks down, she stops at the Lobo Bar in costume. In her beard, scruffy hat, overalls, and bulky jacket, she infiltrates the male culture of the bar, exposing the tropes of masculinity by exaggeration and direct challenge. She swaggers, struts, grunts, and mocks the sexual tall tales men tell each other.

In the course of its first four seasons (1988–1992), the series followed the Conner girls from late childhood to the brink of adulthood, and it gave a degree of attention unusual in American popular culture to female rites of passage. An episode about Darlene's first period acknowledges her fears about growing up and losing the easy equality she has had with boys before either have moved into their adult heterosexual roles. Her first period makes her angry, sad, and afraid that she will take up the detested feminine traits of her older sister. Dan doesn't help when he congratulates her with an awkward "Good job." "My life is over and he congratulated me," Darlene tells Roseanne, when the two talk together in Darlene's room. Yet the episode uses this occasion to make a powerfully positive statement about femininity. Roseanne, conscious of the negative feelings her own mother conveyed to her about her body, tells her, "It's not a disease. It's something to celebrate. You've become a full-fledged member of the Woman Race." Darlene is not convinced. "I'm probably going to start throwing like a girl, anyway." Roseanne answers: "Definitely. And since you got your period, you're going to be throwing a lot *farther*. . . . Now you get to be part of the whole cycle of things."

The Conners rarely convey their love for each other directly, but here Roseanne comes close when she ties her own participation in "the cycle of things" with having Darlene as a daughter. The episode is a favorite of Arnold's, and she has been thanked for it by mothers who have used it in conversations with their own daughters. In another episode, Becky asks her mother for birth-control pills. Roseanne agrees, but with extreme reluctance. By the end of the episode, Roseanne learns that Becky has already had sex with her boyfriend. She gives her a long hug, Becky says, "Mom, let go," and Roseanne answers, "In a couple of years." The moment captures the complexity of a mother's feelings about the eventual, inevitable separation between parent and grown child.

In other episodes the series looks at PMS and false-pregnancy alarms. In one, PMS motivates Roseanne's transformation into a demonic, husband-terrorizing woman on top. The episode, which recycles material from her standup routine, is told from Dan's point of view in a takeoff on the film *Apocalypse Now* (1979). Its opening allusion to the film also calls up film noir, with its evocations of macho toughness and angst. In a point-of-view shot from Dan on the bed, we see a ceiling fan and its shadows (which in the film become the blades of a helicopter). In a voice-over, Dan describes the house in terms of a combat or war zone. "Today's the day. Twenty-four hours of hell. I must get out of the house. Far from ground zero." He then looks into the camera: "The horror! The horror!" In another episode, Roseanne fears that she is pregnant. The family reacts selfishly. The girls complain about the extra work they'll have to do and the money they won't be able to spend on themselves. Dan blames her for getting pregnant. At the end, the test results are negative. The children are delighted. Roseanne, however, is not so sure. While relieved, she also feels a sense of loss, which she conveys when she flatly tells Dan the names she had picked out for the baby.

One unusually stylized episode ("Sweet Dreams") warrants a more detailed look because it so effectively defines Roseanne's unruliness against its opposite, the ideology of the self-sacrificing wife and mother. It depicts this clashing of discourses by playing three styles against each other: a realist sitcom style for working-class family life; a surreal dream sequence for female unruliness; and a musical sequence within the dream to reconcile the "real" with the unruly. Dream sequences invariably signal the eruption of unconscious desire, and in this episode, the dream is linked with the eruption of female desire, the defining mark of the unruly woman.

The episode begins as the show does every week, in the normal Conner world of broken plumbing, incessant demands, job troubles. Roseanne wants ten minutes alone in a hot bath after what she describes as "the worst week in her life" (she just quit her job at the Wellman factory). But between Dan and her kids, she can't get into the bathroom, and she falls asleep waiting. At this point, all the marks of the sitcom disappear. The music and lighting tell us we are in a dream. Roseanne walks into her bathroom, but it's been transformed into an opulent, Romanesque pleasure spa where she is pampered by two bare-chested male attendants ("the pec twins," Dan later calls them). She's become a redhead. Even within this dream, however, she's haunted by her family and the law that stands behind it.[10] One by one, the members of her family appear and continue to nag her for attention and interfere with her bath. And one by one, without hesitation, she kills them off with tidy and appropriate means. (In one instance, she twitches her nose before working her magic, alluding to the 1960s sitcom *Bewitched*). As *A Question of Silence* suggests, revenge and revenge fantasies are a staple of the feminist imagination. In this case, Roseanne murders not for revenge but for a bath.

Roseanne's unruliness is further challenged, ideology reasserts itself and the dream threatens to become a nightmare when she is arrested for murder and brought to court. We learn that her family really *isn't* dead, and, along with her friends, they testify against her, implying that because of her shortcomings as a wife and mother she's been murdering them all along. Crystal says: "She's loud, she's bossy, she talks with her mouth full. She feeds her kids frozen fish sticks and high-calorie sodas. She doesn't have proper grooming habits." And she doesn't treat her husband right, even though, as Roseanne explains, "The only way to keep a man happy is to treat him like dirt once in a while." The trial, like the dream itself, dramatizes a struggle over interpretation of the frame story that preceded it: The court judges her desire for the bath as narcissistic and hedonistic and her barely suppressed frustration as murderous. Such desires are taboo for good self-sacrificing mothers. For Roseanne, the bath (and the "murders" it *requires*) are quite pleasurable, for reasons both sensuous and righteous: Everyone gets what they deserve.[11] (Coincidentally, during this episode ABC was running ads for the docudrama *Small Sacrifices*, aired November 12–14, 1989, about a real mother, Diane Downs, who murdered one of her children and tried to kill the other two.)

Barely into the trial, it becomes apparent that Roseanne severely strains the court's power to impose its order on her. The rigid oppositions it tries to enforce begin to blur and alliances shift. Roseanne defends her children when the judge – Judge Wapner from *People's Court* – yells at them. Roseanne, defended by her sister, turns the tables on the children and they repent for the pain they've caused her. With Dan's abrupt change from prosecutor to crooner and character witness, the courtroom becomes the stage for a musical. Dan breaks into song, and soon the judge, jury, and entire cast are dancing and singing Roseanne's praises in a bizarre production number. Female desire *isn't* monstrous; acting on it "ain't misbehavin'," her friend Vanda sings. Even though this celebration of Roseanne in effect vindicates her, the judge remains unconvinced, finding her not only guilty but in contempt of court. Dream work done, she awakens, the sound of the judge's gavel becoming Dan's hammer on the plumbing. Dan's job is over too, but the kids still want her attention. Dan jokes that there's no place like home, but Roseanne answers "Bull." On her way, at last, to her bath, she closes the door to the bathroom to the echoes of the chorus singing "We Love Roseanne."

The requirements for bringing this fantasy to an end are important. First, what ultimately satisfies Roseanne isn't an escape from her family but an acknowledgment from them of *her* needs and an expression of their feeling for her – "We love you, Roseanne." I'm not suggesting that *Roseanne* represents a miraculous transcendence of the limitations of primetime television. To a certain degree this ending does represent a sentimental co-opting of her power, a shift from the potentially radical (what if Roseanne woke up and walked out?) to the liberal. But it also indicates a willingness to engage with the contradictions of women's lives. Much of Roseanne's appeal lies in the delicate balance she maintains between individual and institution and in the impersonal nature of her anger and humor, which are targeted not so much at the people she lives with as at what makes them the way they are. What Roseanne *really* murders here is the ideology of "perfect wife and mother," which she reveals to be murderous itself.

The structuring – and limits – of Roseanne's vindication are equally significant. Although the law is made ludicrous, it retains its power and remains ultimately indifferent and immovable. As usual (whether at Wellman Plastics or even at the Padres game), Roseanne's "contempt" seems ultimately her greatest crime. More important, whatever vindication she does enjoy can happen only within a dream. It cannot be sustained in real life. The realism of the frame story inevitably reasserts itself. And even within the dream, the reconciliation between unruly fantasy and ideology can be brought about only by deploying the heavy artillery of the musical. Few forms embody the utopian impulse of popular culture more insistently than the musical, and within musicals, contradictions difficult to resolve otherwise are acted out in production numbers (see Altman; Feuer).

That is what happens here. The production number gives a fleeting resolution to the problem Arnold has typically played with in her tumultuous career, the problem of representing what in our culture still remains largely unrepresentable: a fat woman who is sexually "normal"; a sloppy housewife who is also a good mother; a loose woman who is tidy, who hates matrimony but loves her husband, and who can mock the ideology of true womanhood yet consider herself a Domestic Goddess.

Notes

1 I interviewed Roseanne Arnold on June 20, 1991. Earlier in her career, Arnold was known as Roseanne Barr. She took the name of her husband, Tom Arnold, in 1991, when they renewed their wedding vows and he converted to Judaism. These comments came in response to my question about whether she had had any new thoughts, almost a year later, about the national-anthem incident.

2 As Arnold herself noted, the reaction to her performance, not the performance itself, carried the more alarming message. As for Bush, she says, he "should have been paying attention to Kuwait" (quoted in Hirschberg 224).

3 Later that year, the incident appeared in an episode of the courtroom drama series, L.A. Law, where it was rewritten as a conflict between a sympathetically portrayed, heavy black male blues singer and a team owner, whose stuffiness was shown to be un-American.

4 In May 1991 ABC also canceled the Saturday-morning show New Kids on the Block, a favorite of girls, and Saturday morning TV became exclusively boy oriented. Network executives noted that only girls were watching New Kids on the Block and that while girls will watch shows with male heroes, boys won't watch shows with female heroes.

5 In July 1991, she beat four male competitors – Dan Quayle, Saddam Hussein, U.S. Senator Jesse Helms, and developer Donald Trump – to win the first annual "Sitting Duck" award given by the National Society of Newspaper Columnists ("People" 2A).

6 After being deluged with letters from her readers, Maynard later acknowledged that she had felt threatened by a woman who discarded so many of the super-woman expectations that she had placed on herself. Subsequently Maynard described the breakup of her own marriage and ended her column. Arnold has criticized the middle-class biases of popular U.S. feminism: "I feel bad when I read Ms. magazine and they have a whole article about, like Tracey Ullman and Carol Burnett and Bette Midler, and don't mention me – I mean, as a woman who did the first show about how women really live. And then I go, it's classism. It's even more insidious than any sort of sexism . . . Because I'm of a

working-class background. I mean, I get every kind of ism that there is. And they're all ugly" (quoted in Hirschberg 231).

7 Marcia Millman writes that fat people arouse "horror, loathing, speculation, repugnance, and avoidance" (71). In the working class, fatness becomes a sign of a failure to achieve upward mobility. She also notes that some men hold a secret attraction to fat women.

8 See Wexman for a Bakhtinian analysis of the carnivalesque fat man Jackie Gleason. Like Arnold, Gleason was snubbed by the Emmies; he did not receive an honorary award even after his death. And like *All in the Family*, M*A*S*H eventually tempers the clownishness of its main female character, turning Hot Lips into Margaret.

9 *Roseanne*'s attention to homosexuality has continued into its fifth and sixth seasons, with regular appearances by Sandra Bernhard as Nancy, a family friend who comes out as a lesbian.

10 The law is a common motif for patriarchy in feminist work (e.g., A *Question of Silence*) and provides a familiar site for female disruption in mainstream work (e.g., the 1953 film *Gentlemen Prefer Blondes*). Note also how Leona Helmsley, Zsa Zsa Gabor, Imelda Marcos, and Tammy Faye Bakker have all been recently involved in highly publicized trials.

11 As Phyllis Chesler might have testified, women's space in contemporary American culture is so freely violated that many women surrender their "privacy, life space, sanity and selves . . . in order not to commit violence" (quoted in Henley 39). Here, a "room of her own," to borrow from Virginia Woolf, becomes a bathroom.

References

Altman, Rick. *The American Film Musical*. Bloomington: Indiana University Press, 1987.

Arnold, Roseanne. Interview with Kathleen Rowe, June 20, 1991.

Bakhtin, Mikhail. *The Dialogic Imagination*. Ed. by Michael Holquist. Trans. Caryl Emerson and Michael Holquist. Austin: University of Texas Press, 1981.

Barr, Roseanne. *Roseanne: My Life as a Woman*. New York: Harper and Row, 1989.

Bourdieu, Pierre. *Distinction: A Social Critique of the Judgement of Taste*. Trans. Richard Nice. Cambridge, MA: Harvard University Press, 1984.

Douglas, Mary. *Implicit Meanings: Essays in Anthropology*. Boston: Routledge & Kegan Paul, 1975.

Dyer, Richard. *Stars*. London: British Film Institute, 1979.

Fiske, John. *Understanding Popular Culture*. Boston: Unwin Hyman, 1989.

Georgatos, Dennis. "When the Fat Lady Sings . . . Some San Diego Padre Fans are Glad When It's Over." *Eugene [Oregon] Register-Guard*, July 27, 1991: A1, A4.

Goffman, Erving. *Frame Analysis: An Essay on the Organization of Experience*. Boston: Northeastern University Press, 1986.

Henley, Nancy M. *Body Politics: Power, Sex and Non-Verbal Communication*. EngleWood Cliffs, NJ: Prentice-Hall, 1977.

Hicks, Jack. "No Holds Barred." *TV Guide*, January 28, 1989: 2–5.

Hirschberg, Lynn. "Don't Hate Me Because I'm Beautiful." *Vanity Fair*, December 1990: 182–186.

Jerome, Jim. "Roseanne Unchained." *People*, October 9, 1989: 84–98.

Maynard, Joyce. "Domestic Affairs." *The Oregonian*, February 11, 1989: C1.

Millman, Marcia. *Such a Pretty Face: Being Fat in America*. New York: W. W.Norton, 1980.

Mitchell, Elvis. "Smug Trafficking." *The Village Voice*, April 25, 1989: 47–48.

Modleski, Tania. *Feminism Without Women: Culture and Criticism in a "Postfeminist" Age*. New York: Routledge, 1991.

O'Connor, John J. "By Any Name, Roseanne is Roseanne is Roseanne." *New York Times*, August 18, 1991: B1, B27.

Orbach, Susie. *Fat is a Feminist Issue* II. London: Arrow, 1982.

Orbach, Susie. *Hunger Strike: The Anorectic's Struggle as a Metaphor for Our Age*. New York: W. W. Norton, 1986.

"People." *Eugene [Oregon] Register-Guard*, July 1, 1991: A2.

Rhoden, William C. "Sports of the Times: In the Land of the Free." *New York Times* (national ed.), July 31, 1990: B9.

"Roseanne's Shotgun 'Wedding from Hell'; Pregnant Roseanne's Wedding Shambles Goes Off With 101 Hitches." *Star*, February 6, 1990: 10–14.

Turner, Victor. "Frame, Flow and Reflection; Ritual and Drama as Public Liminality." In *Performance in Postmodern Culture*, edited by Michel Benamou and Charles Caramello, pp. 33–55. Milwaukee: University of Wisconsin–Milwaukee Press, 1977.

Waters, Harry F., with Steven Waldman, Daniel Glick, and Kim Fararo. "Rhymes With Rich: A Queen on Trial." *Newsweek*, August 21, 1989: 46–51.

Will, George. "Cities Gleam with Gunfire." Syndicated column in *Eugene [Oregon] Register-Guard*, August 1, 1990: A15.

C'mon, Girl

15

Oprah Winfrey and the discourse of feminine talk

GLORIA-JEAN MASCIAROTTE

By all critical accounts, the 1980s saw the consolidation of a media economy which operated in the ever-widening and whirl-pooling exchange between a hyper reproduction and an endless consumption of images, representations, simulations, fabrications, fabulations, sound bytes, and so on. But perhaps "exchange" does not quite delineate the axiomatic operation of this economy. For instance, Jean Baudrillard, the foremost theorist of the media economy, characterizes the relationship more in terms of a passive consumption, or, really more in terms of an inverted, vampirelike consumption where the media economy consumes or engulfs its spectator subject in the gigantic black hole of wildly reproducing simulations of mass culture.

However, one gesture of the media economy frequently indicted as a major device in the flattening out of cultural currency hardly seems a passive operation – the television talk show. In fact, the television talk show seems almost extravagantly participatory what with a panel of guests sharing their experiences; a group of invited specialists interpreting the proffered experiences; a studio audience commenting on all that is said on stage; viewers calling in to share or comment; the preachings or proddings of the talk show host him/herself; and the tabloid spin on the lives of those hosts. The talk show aggressively promotes discursive participation through the telling of the painful experience or the uncured activity in full view of that ubiquitous television audience of "millions of people." [. . .]

Yet, there are very few articles that pay close attention to the structure of the talk on these shows: Who gets to talk? About what can/do they talk? How do they talk? Why? [. . .]

A place to start an examination of the seeming challenge of the television talk show's participatory chaos, spectacular emotionalism, and "dangerous" attention to surface (rather than depth) experience is at the talk show's most ubiquitous sign: Oprah Winfrey. In fact, some people say that Oprah Winfrey, herself, defined, charted, embodied, and mobilized this evacuation of the individual by mass culture.

While Oprah Winfrey's show consolidates the spectacle of the talking woman, first there was Phil Donahue's show, which is generally credited with shifting the political issues of the day to the everyday. In fact, recently "Lifetime" channel talk show host Jane Wallace celebrated Phil Donahue's twentieth-year anniversary show by noting, "Phil is the reason we're all here today[1] and he made the issues, the guests." This originary position is supported by the fact that Phil Donahue's first show aired in 1968.

Oprah could have only come after Phil. But in coming after Phil, Oprah reconstructs the ontology of talk. Of course, a large black woman who is indexed as rich, well liked, smart, and glamorous would have to reconstruct the ontology of talk in order to talk.[2] For the most part, the significance of her difference has been noted in the following condemnatory generalizations: (1) Oprah Winfrey has made the talk show more emotional and less issue-oriented; (2) Oprah Winfrey's personality has eclipsed the talk shows caring, informative, "genuine" function; and (3) Oprah Winfrey has encouraged a more vulgar, graphic, voyeuristic, or sensationalist exchange.[3] I am not about to disagree with these descriptions, just their negative evaluation. But first let me note what may be at the heart of these condemnations: the insistence on discussing Oprah Winfrey as an individual. The cultural importance of "The Oprah Winfrey Show" for the viewer is not in being Oprah or in being like Oprah but in being subject to Oprah. In other words, one can only understand Oprah Winfrey as a determinant media image in the structure in which she is mobilized and mobilizes. Oprah Winfrey is not a powerful individual per se; she is powerful in terms of the narrative structure of the talk show and its cultural-political negotiations of the disenfranchised voices. Therefore, in order to re-evaluate the structures of emotionalism, personality, and sensationalism and delineate structural constraints and conjectural possibilities "The Oprah Winfrey Show" affords by its mobilization of these "offending" structures, I will separate Oprah Winfrey into two distinct but overlapping mechanisms: the narrative structure of the talk on her show, and the media operation of representing Oprah Winfrey.

Case study as story: subject of/to: victim of/in

The narrative structure on "The Oprah Winfrey Show" fully realizes the irritated I with its irritatingly repetitive chorus of ME . . . ME . . . ME . . . ME. This talk show best articulates the deconstruction of the promise of liberal democracy and its necessary hierarchy of enunciation. [. . .] One of the most noticeable ways in which the show manifests the baroquely privi-leged I is evident in the fact that Oprah Winfrey's host function is consumed by the story function. She too performs as talker, as a storied subject among a host of storied subjects. Oprah routinely talks about her life as abuse victim, substance abuser, black person, single working woman, and girlfriend of Steadman. Her recent show on her own weight loss is right in keeping with the show's excessive narrative function; she was always already one of her own guests. Her frequent lapse into black street rhetoric and street posturing is part of the privileging of the story function.

Oprah's storytelling consists of the inclusion of her everyday life: her best friend Gail's mother is mentioned constantly and was featured on a show about children picking dates for their parents; her battle with controlling her weight crops up endlessly on a myriad of shows, including one on body image where she invited the woman at her gym whose body she most idolizes; the feminine "problem" of looking good and feeling good was discussed on a show about make-overs which included as a featured guest the poorly dressed security guard at Harpo Studio that Oprah confronts each morning. This storytelling on the part of the host is a significant difference between her and Donahue. Donahue constantly refuses to discuss his "personal" life and looks embarrassed whenever the audience or featured discussants bring it up. In this way Phil Donahue keeps up the important bourgeois distinction of private and public. His lack of storied life insures that there is a device to read and place the others' stories into an appropriate space of social, generic trends.[4] But Oprah Winfrey's personal stories show no bourgeois modesty and respect no such split. But of course Oprah Winfrey is a "full-figured" black woman and Phil Donahue is a gray-haired white man: Which body is the private and which the public in U.S. society today?

The importance of Oprah Winfrey's storytelling as a denial of the classical subjective split and an operation specifically of an African American subject in/to contemporary patriarchal consumer society is best understood in relation to the problematic of the African American voice that Henry Louis Gates, Jr., delineates in *The Signifying Monkey: A Theory of African-American Literary Criticism*, specifically in his analysis of the works of Zora Neale Hurston. In Hurston's original use of free indirect discourse alongside the expected use of crafted poetic discourse, Gates notes that "signifyin(g)" correlates to the traditional black oral narration with its "profound attempt to remove the distinction between repeated speech and represented events. Here the discourse is not distinct from events . . . [therefore] subject and object dissolve into each other. Representation which guaranteed the distance between them is in danger."[5] Thus, in the traditional African American sense of the "talking book" or the "speakerly text," signifyin(g) means to show off through the telling of a dramatic/comic story of victimization in which the object antithetically becomes a subject through a reversal of fortune, or through a witty remark (back talk) that assesses the inherent misuse of power in the given situation. Gates's discussion of Hurston's powerful algebra of speakerly and writerly texts suggests that the speakerly tradition underlines the performative or narrative as an analytical gesture. The storied voice contextualizes within the lived experiences of power and the specific differences of race, gender, and class. Importantly for the talk show and Oprah Winfrey's transformative function, Gates also recalls that in *Mules and Men*, where Hurston worked to represent the ritual of "signifyin(g)," she demonstrated that "women most certainly can and do Signify upon men" to develop their consciousness of black and female in a white and male society.[6]

Oprah's show-off stories as well as her slide from standard speech to street-inflected talk and her use of local markers of class and race – "Girl, you ain't gonna find these men at the Jewel!" (The Jewel is a ubiquitous supermarket in less well heeled Chicago neighborhoods, while the Treasure Island chain is the opposing yuppie supermarket) – are offered up as evidence of the obvious contradiction of her own dominant presence in a system that works to erase it. Her stories are a necessary part of the spiralling process of narrative as self-consciousness and a narrative as a contextualizing structure that defines individual pain as systemic malfunction or even systemic violence. These stories function as her mark of difference, her complication, her catch in the social field that allows her to talk. It is important to note that the stories are motivated by the catch. As such, they are neither essentialist gestures of biological details nor egoist gestures of emergent "self-hood." The mechanism of her privilege operates from the difference, the complication, the catch of her subjectivity in relief, and so it initiates for the show's immediate audience, the featured guests, and the viewing audience a process to read yourself and read yourself in terms of systemic construction.

Oprah Winfrey's further rejection of Phil Donahue's sociological discourse manifests itself in her organization of issues beyond classical debate structures. On "The Oprah Winfrey Show" the debate operates from specific to coalition, which worries both parts of discussion along the line of sure fixed system building. One of the common responses to this move is that it confuses the issues at hand. This may be one of its strengths if one considers that the confusion is only confusion along a classical axis of debate that privileges generic oppositions, resolving them in a new transcendental thesis. "The Oprah Winfrey Show" refuses this resolution by refusing to limit differential strategies which exacerbate the storied function beyond consensus. On one level, Oprah's panels consist of more racially and more class-defined subjects insuring ground zero of difference. But even this important demographic pluralism could be reconciled in a "family of man" consensus. However, on a given topic her panels exceed all possibility of resolution by including narratively different voices, like victim and victimizer (an unremorseful father who sexually abused all his daughters, and the daughters) and discursively different voices, like represented, imposed, desired, and debunking positions (an actress who plays popular bitches on soap operas; a woman who believes herself a bitch; a woman called a bitch by others; a woman who refuses the term *bitch*; and a woman who would like to be a bitch). Given these participants there is no way to reconcile the topic into a trend or even to contain it in a single gesture. For example, on the show about bitches, the variety of positions from self-identified bitches to woman who plays bitches mobilizes a free-floating discussion about power (economic and sexual); desire (consumer and sexual); aggression; femininity; masculinity; masculine fear; the disadvantages of gender markers for success and self-esteem; and the use of social narratives for pleasure and power. By the end of the show, the term *bitch* was not reclaimed, as much as it was scattered.

Obviously, her panels seem composed more of different narrative positions rather than differing political or social positions, pointing out that the fictions we watch are the fictions we live. While part of the pleasure of these confused panels is certainly the hegemonic gesture of defining normal boundaries that result from being distanced by the excessively perverted guest, Oprah Winfrey's baroquely panelled discussions operate on identification of the normal as perverse (and not Phil's operation of the perverse as normal). Recalling Freud's strategy in *Three Essays on a Theory of Sexuality*, this labor of creating endless categories of perversity forces the narrative of the self into a critique of the self. These multiple stories speak of discrete identities that stand in for an analysis of difference and power, all of which operates against the bourgeois belief in the transparency of language and the liberal empowerment strategy of identity politics. Here one can see explicitly how the talk show's necessary privilege of the middle instead of the end of narration plays on the hypernarrative's discursive gesture of the I caught, complicated by difference. By discursively extricating the caught I from the common citizenry but not the social matrix, Oprah Winfrey's show privileges the grain of the voice against the mirror of the eye. The determinate difference of this storied subjectivity, the confrontation of I to I to I, exacerbates the contradictions within the curative oppositions of family/individual, good girl/bad girl, older/younger generation, etc. In her falling away from Phil's liberal political discourse of talk for an emotionalism or affective talk, she reveals what is hidden: the dysfunction of the subject's labor as production and function of labor as constitutive. This is the moment of the malaise: the difficult labor of subjectivity.

The third way in which Oprah Winfrey's storytelling significantly changes the talk show is its reliance on the heightened emotionalism of the talk show. It would be too easy to read this move to the emotional discourse under Oprah Winfrey's tutelage as an emptying out of the issues. Oprah Winfrey's use of emotionalism moves Donahue's original practice of making the issues of the day everyday issues to its furthest extent by making issues of the everyday. In a sense, then, on "The Oprah Winfrey Show" there is no area of politics that is not personal and no space where the personal is exempt from politics. In an essay in the

Village Voice, Emily Prager likened Oprah's show to opera: the effusion of sound, the extreme narrative, the baroque enunciator.[7] Prager notes that the emotions, the opera of Winfrey's approach to talk, stem from her absolute insistence on the graphic gestures of lived experience and so refuse the catharsis of sentimentalism. Prager explains this analytical or resistant emotionalism in a reading of the program where Oprah goes to a white racist town which had a civic committee titled "Committee to Keep Forsyth County White." After giving an all-white audience of self-proclaimed and quite proud racists an hour-long platform, Oprah addresses the problem of the sympathetic ear which colludes with the speaker in some form of "understanding." In the final moments of the show Oprah points out that some people may say she has "turned white" by lending her ear to this audience, but with "eyes widening in a mixture of anger, pride, and amazement, said to the crowd, 'I'm black, you know.'" Here the crescendo of emotion is simultaneously extended, inflamed, and punctuated by the statement of her difference and so the emotional refuses the whitewash of sympathy. In this scene the force of specific and contentious emotionalism is more akin to the evangelical practice of the fire and brimstone Puritan than the sentimentality of the "three-hanky" writers. Prager notes, "Oprah's refrain seems more powerful. She thunders against secrets, against skeletons in the closet, against putting a good face on things. In a one woman crusade against hypocrisy she acquaints us and reacquaints us with the hidden corruption in so-called normal family life." Thus, Winfrey's emotional stories reject the sociological discourse that normalizes and denies the difficult specifics of lived experience.

The force of the specific and the urgency it gives to the contextualization of narrative are evident further in the operation of her constant tag line, "C'mon" – a comment that acts as mock disbelief or cajoling question. It is a tag that asks for a more graphic or "real" story. One of the best examples of her promotion of narrative, operatic excess is a program on sex addiction in which the guest was recalling her history in the language of ego psychology, the language of cured addict, the language of case study, not story. Oprah was unsatisfied with this recounting and prodded the woman into telling the graphic details of her addictive behavior instead of speaking from the generic rhetoric of her cure. Oprah extracted from the cured voice stories of compulsive, hourly sex, sex with a mentally handicapped boy, stories of sexual betrayal of a husband on a honeymoon, making a spectacle of the individual caught in a narcissistic blackout and dramatizing a systemic lack of self-esteem. In soliciting a painful story of the abject feminine (individuals without power and recourse to power), after the rehearsal of these details Oprah made this woman cry and the audience squirm. Then the audience began to confess their addictions too: One man told the story of his shoplifting addiction after invoking the line "I understand. My experience is just like yours." The similarity of shoplifting and sexual addiction may seem odd at first, but in the course of her story the sex addict had noted that she called her afternoon attempts to get a sex partner "shopping" as she cruised the men's department of better stores.

These two stories point out the connection on which the subjective coalition is formed: powerlessness in a capitalist, consumer culture and the all-too-ready subjective violence even when exercising the proper way of alleviating it – acting on your freedom of "consumptive" choice. Here was the "truth," and it was in the telling of the specific, graphic details of "my story" rather than in the collective historical structure of the cured subject. Oprah initiated an exchange that produced stories, identities in the stories, and a coalition of those identities in the pain rather than the cure. Though her stated message may advocate cure, her investigative method denies the importance of cure. She wants us to recognize the pain that comes from the tension of the individual in society, in what Jacques Lacan calls the fixing of the subject and what Louis Althusser calls the hailing of the subject.

On a larger stage, the effect of this irritated storytelling implies a configuration of the subject and subject identity realized in contradiction. Oprah Winfrey's operatic storied voice privileges the feminine that has no Other and so denies that the move into language is an assumption that functions by substitution; that is, the mechanism the male subject is afforded when he substitutes the distance from the Other for the pain of the split subject. Read in this way, talking suggests that the movement into language is the body's "twists and vicissitudes" within the system the language supports and our discontent is the recognition of that irritation of this voice in that system.[8] Oprah Winfrey's denial of the cure, the denaturalization of the subject position, and the fascinating displeasure are marked tellingly in the talk show's own construction of its object: the psychosocial problems of modern living, that is, women who love too much; married cross-dressers; victims of incest, of child abuse, of spousal abuse, of substance abuse, of racial prejudice, of "bad relationships," of distant fathers, of over-bearing mothers, of sibling order, of too much or too little sexual desire, on so on.

The conceptual needs which talking fills are many, but starting from the discursive pleasure in displeasure one must look to another practice of subjectivity, one not so bound by the hale, hearty, healthy, and whole body. I suggest that talking as an enunciative category is the critical, mass secularization – not the schematic popularization – of Freud's radical project of/on/from femininity. Thus, the victim on the talk show is the slide of marked body into voiced body. And with that slide there is a significant disruption of the easy assumption of/to the subject position.[9] The significance of the disrupting effect of this slide to the voiced body is that it moves the feminine away from the essentialist, and even culturalist, strategies of speaking from margins and/or under repression. The disruption moves the gesture of the speak-ing from the feminine toward the voiced body as the speaking detail; that is, the marked body as the object of power/knowledge/pleasure systems, or the site or the lever of the systemic mapping of subjectivity. The talking subject indicts the system from which it speaks.

The talk show's speaking subject is constituted in the speaking of its subjection to a system(s), of its struggle with the necessary determinants of subjectivity. The talk show subject is known only in the instance of speaking its struggle with the system(s) that represents it. It is the resistance of the voice silenced and so the construction or the asym-metrical construction of the subject as critique of the very systems that claim to know it. It is not coincidental that this displacement comes as the therapeutic discourse moves into the mass culture subjectivity. The move from individual to mass exposes the necessary bourgeois illusion of the distinction between public and private and so admits of a complicity between the subject and the system in the structuring mechanism of discontent. Given the scandal position of the feminine in representation, it is also no coincidence that this move occurs alongside the articulation of a feminine subject, a public feminine authority.[10] The coordination and reconfiguration of that move say that the healthy, the nonvictim speak from a position of denial. They deny the violence of the systemic fixing of the subject.[11]

Seen in this light, the operations of pain and struggle on "The Oprah Winfrey Show" suggest that it is not just the classical dialectic of subject/object but the interpellation of subject identity and privilege through the denial of the generic body, the mindful body, the in-different subject.[12] Thus the nerve-wracking constellation of story, information, communication, mass-produced subject is held in contentious relationship at the site of difference; in other words, the problem with the talk show is that it is all about *her* getting to speak about whatever *she* wants to whomever *she* wants. It is said that the talk show's obvious disturbance is a realignment of the important oppositions of fact/fiction, information/entertainment, objectivity/subjectivity. But that opposition has been site of other struggles (one such would be the debates that surrounded the rise of the novel). What makes this realignment more telling is Oprah Winfrey's confusion of issue and story. Talk shows have renegotiated the kind of information that constitutes issues and have reconstructed the way those issues are presented for resolution, which implies the site of the feminine body, the struggling subjectivity, is the place of that confusion of issue and story. It is the discursive use of narrative and emotion as information and issue that then places the talk show within the resistant economy of another speaking body and its feminine authority.[13]

Cultural Oprah-tion: tongue-twisting and the gendered body

In a *New York Times Sunday Magazine* article, "The Importance of Being Oprah," Barbara Grizzuti Harrison assesses the phenomenon of Oprah Winfrey in terms of the profaned development of a single, individuated self. She reads Oprah Winfrey and her show as a robber baron and "his" parasitical industrial expansion in terms of the democratic, capitalistic trajectory of Horatio Alger. The title of Grizzuti Harrison's article best states the ironic tone, the confused awe, and the none-too-subtle critical read that results from this characteristically individualistic focus on Oprah Winfrey.[14] Harrison suggests that Winfrey embodies and utilizes a false earnestness along with rampant individual ambition that at best depoliticizes this excessively successful black woman and at worst makes her a dangerously conservative role model for those still disenfranchised. From her first paragraph, Harrison's defining question, "How does one make a self?" parallels the worried focus of the article in the *San Francisco Chronicle*. In fact, for most media critics the set of directions inherent in Oprah Winfrey's hobby model kit of the self displaces the sacrosanct structures and guaranteed boundaries of the bourgeois individual: family, friends, and therapy. In their quick glance and expletivelike analysis, Winfrey and her show and herself constitute the emptying out of the individual, the flattening out, the surface mapping of the self.

But shouldn't the "self" Winfrey's show exploits be one different from the Horatio Alger or Dr. Feelgood narratives into which cultural critics confusedly force it? The almost expletivelike use of these narratives to condemn the talk show and Oprah Winfrey before close analysis makes it necessary to recall a few important concepts in those supposedly parallel stories. First, the Horatio Alger narrative is the nineteenth-century Protestant work ethic wedded to the seventeenth-century Protestant concept of the elect, which understood the individual in terms of external, proprietary marks of successful domination of the environment. Second, the signifying end of this narrative was extended in the late nineteenth century through a manifestation of the logical extreme of its patriarchal axiom by replacing simple capitalist accumulation with early consumer display in the necessary creation of the lady of leisure. And third, the Dr. Feelgood narrative was a bastardization of Herbert Marcuse and Sigmund Freud to articulate the middle class or, again, proprietary narcissism and isolationism of American's counterculture "rebels" where there was no other than the transcendental subject of ego pleasure. Many historians of the youth culture and its radical politics credit the abuses of this transcendental middle-class, white, and patriarchal ego as one of the primary factors that gave rise to the contemporary women's movement in the United States. Given these often-noted problematics and structural logics, Oprah Winfrey and the talk show would have to contradict, if not necessarily deny, the subjective heroics of these hegemonic narratives.

Perhaps a better "success" story or bildungsroman for reading the Oprah Winfrey phenomenon would be found in Henry Louis Gates, Jr.'s delineation of the successful African American writer as the double-voiced sign "which manifests the problematic of representation between what is represented and what represents." The doubling of the sign of the different subject articulates the fact that in order to speak she has to represent her similarity to the dominant order and to represent the material effects or history of her difference within that order – the legacy of slavery and the determinations of racism. She has to speak first "to demonstrate his or her own membership in the human community and then to demonstrate her resistance to that community."[15] Therefore, the conflicting and confusing evaluation of Oprah Winfrey's "person" depends on her necessarily double-voice public identity as a large black woman: the matriarch of difference, the phallic mother, the sign of negativity in bourgeois, white patriarchy; *and* at the same time as a rich, glamorous television producer/star: the patriarch of representation, the Law, the signifier of transcendental capitalist subject. It is important to note that the sign of Oprah Winfrey traverses not only race and gender but also declines these determinates within the cultural politics of body and presence.[16] She is a sign squared so her media sign cannot deny the inherent abjection of her differences. The result of her overdetermined subjectivity is manifest in the televisual and media gossip that delights in her battles with food, her troublesome relationship with a good-looking guy that foregrounds and (according to the common wisdom of white patriarchal aesthetics) contradicts her own more "mammylike" appearance and function, and her fluctuating hairstyles and fashion choices.[17] In other words, her inappropriate appetites for success, power, and a feminine voice are an integral part of the spin she gives the talk show and its production of subject. In fact, I would suggest that the jokes on Carson, Letterman, and so on and the relentless tabloid interest in Oprah Winfrey's visible differences are what inflamed the national cult of the talk show as "abusable" object, profane object, object of television's lowest common denominator.[18]

Is it a coincidence then that the critical and theoretical slurs against consumer and media culture choose to focus on Oprah Winfrey? If one recalls Andreas Huyssen's "As Culture as Woman: Modernism's Other" and Tania Modleski's "Femininity as Mas(s)querade," where they critique high theory's cultural critics in general, and Baudrillard specifically, for their frequently apocalyptic model of criticism in response to popular culture, media economy of reproduction, and consumer culture which hides an antifeminist and antiwoman bias that indicates the real threat of cultural change for these writers is the decentering of phallic identity.[19] Given Huyssen's and Modleski's analyses, I too think the talk show's cultural work *is best defined* by Oprah Winfrey in that she is a large (or noticeable seesaw-size), outspoken, aggressive, and successful black woman. Obviously, then, this culturally abject (threatening and seductive) subject position must not be understood, cannot be not understood in terms of the paradigmatic individual, or the misrecognized, mirrored back fiction of the complete self.

Oprah Winfrey's "meteoric" rise to media stardom gave rise to the discourse of sensationalism not only because she changed the talk show format but because she was "so there." Her overdetermined or too well-marked presence provides a historical possibility in terms of an irritation, a dissonance in the hegemonic chorus that allows Others to talk. In this

Figure 15.1 Oprah Winfrey
Courtesy of Photofest, New York

way she functions culturally quite like the analyst in Jacques Lacan's notion of transference, where the analysand aggressively takes on (takes over) the presence of the analyst (identifies with the "supposed" signifying position of the analyst in a love/hate relationship) to negotiate her own subjective resistance. Oprah Winfrey's presence, literally her body (big, black, feminine) is too marked in the specular exchange to be a conduit of objective debate, social truth seeking. Her specular resistance to dominant aesthetics makes her the cultural point of resistance. Is it transference or resistance of what toward what, or who toward whom: an individual toward an individual (a single viewer toward a single discussant or Oprah herself, alone); an individual toward an isolated group experience (the single viewer toward the spectacle of a single show); or a group onto a group experience (the viewing audience at large toward the spectacle of the generic experience of the show)? I think it is all of these relations. Thus, the connection between talk shows, sensationalism, and the feminine as speaking body carries with it significant strategies about whose story and what stories are privileged and how those stories are told. This is a move to material body politics instead of brute or natural bodies.

The embarrassed pleasure of talk: the irritated subject

The sensationalist tag and its attendant aesthetic disclaimers of the voyeuristic excess and graphic horror that surround Oprah Winfrey's celebrity function is that she *speaks* from the position of that which is abjected by culture. Popular culture constructs Oprah Winfrey as what Julia Kristeva calls the abject. The abject is a struggle: "a violent, clumsy breaking away, with the constant risk of falling back"; a "confrontation with our personal archeology"; and "a condition of precariously casting out of primal repression which marks the emergence of the signifying subject." In the traditional aesthetics of subjectivity, the abject is a necessary Symbolic category for the interpellation of the subject into the dominant social political exchange, but a necessarily expelled category usually located on the borders of acceptable signification and in the details of difference. It is not the margin or the center but the ground on which aesthetic boundaries are built. The conjectural opportunities of Oprah Winfrey is her re-inscription of the abject in the Symbolic register. The potentially radical power of her reinscription rests on its representation of resistance or negativity: the abject articulated.[20] As noted above, the talk show does not offer a moment of consolidation of the subject but an operation that irritates the subject by recalling the system's expelled details of the material conditions of reproducing subjectivity, that is, from the body; in an oscillation of similarity and difference; and out of/into a system of other bodies. Oprah Winfrey produces the spectacle of abjection by refusing the essentialist algebra of hegemonic acceptance: black + woman = Mammy = M/Other = the absolutely Othered = the Other of us all. Thus, the key to Oprah Winfrey's abject position – the talk show's abjection – is its reliance on the process of narrative, instead of the mechanisms of individuality, personality, or character.[21]

Consolidated around the sensationalized issues of gender and race which are declined by the issues of weight and body, the effect of Oprah Winfrey's confused celebrity is delineated as the hinge in an operation of negative subjective; that is, as the bad M/Other, the Object who refuses the child's projections and force feeds the child its own subjective malaise. A guest on an Oprah Winfrey show on shopping addicts makes this operation of negative subjectivity clear when she interrupts the flow of discussion to protest, "I didn't say that . . . I said . . . I guess I did say that . . . (laugh) Mother warned me . . . You put words in my mouth . . . My mother said Oprah'd put words in my mouth and I'd say things that'll embarrass the family." As viewers we can only ask: What *did* this woman say that was so embarrassing? What did Oprah make this woman say? What horror did Oprah put in her mouth? And how did it get there? Well, let's see, the guest said that she had a knack for putting together outfits, pulling together natty ensembles that she could really coordinate. Where is the transgression in that confession? Certainly most mothers in this consumer economy hope their daughters can coordinate. In this often repeated scenario, one can see Oprah Winfrey's double-voiced sign in that while she does not fulfill the hegemonic sign of the "mammy" in that she is silent mirror of the dominant order, she fills hegemonic sign of the "mammy" by exposing the labor of M/Othering that upholds the economic, racial, and gender oppression. Obviously, the horror is not the specific story or fact to which the speaker confessed. The horror is the act of speaking itself, and that horror is linked implicitly to Oprah Winfrey's use of the M/Otherly mechanism.

The negative aesthetic evaluation of Oprah Winfrey is at its most powerful and telling signification in that it indexes her as the initiation of a kind of speaking that cannot be translated away from its material conditions. Oprah Winfrey's talking can never be figured as the beautiful mystical ejaculations of Lacan's Saint Teresa, the site that provides a vehicle for the spectator to transcend the limits of his fixed subject. Oprah Winfrey's "idle gossip or mere verbiage" is the abject gesture: the doubled voice of a woman speaking against and within the grain of the representational Law of the Father.[22] To return to that woman who could coordinate so well, it is important to remark now that the abject gesture of speaking or talking is not in any way parallel to the confessional gesture. In fact, the abject status of this talking subject is its structure as laborer. Its subjectivity is determined in the labor of splitting and in the resistance necessary to tell a story different from the hegemonic story. This is not the pre-Oedipal or semiotic subject which is constructed in the gaps and margins of the hegemonic narrative. And, again, it is not the fragmenting process pure and simple – like the biological function of cell division or the physical operation of desire – but fragmentation as it signifies the catch or the stress of contradictions of the social field. The subject under the sign of Oprah Winfrey is constructed at the point of narrative irritation, complication, catch. It is the subject as an intervention at the site where contradictions pull at the threads of the dominant narrative. It is a subject clearly located in the Symbolic register who is structured in and by the gravitational pull and push in the stories we have to tell ourselves.

Given this insistence on resistance, resistance to the dominant, curative, normalizing narrative, as the moment of subjective consolidation, perhaps the most important part of Oprah Winfrey as cultural sign is its participation in the reorganization of the representation of social success over personal adversity and of the reinterpretation of the marginal object into powerful subject. The possibility present in Oprah Winfrey's operation of oxymoronic subjectivity is that it opens a space for the social to be "unsocialized" or "asocialized" in terms of hegemonic culture and specifies a historically different subject from the traditionally disenfranchised object in the modern capitalist state: The traditionally disenfranchised subject is really the object, that is, the individual denied individual status because his or her subjectivity is marked singularly or in combination by one of the traditionally sociological object or other categories of the American bureaucratic liberal late-capitalist system – women, working or lower class, and people of color. Any person who falls into one or several of those object categories is read under/by the system of interventionist state organization as a mass subject instead of as a middle-class, individuated subject. In other words, those individuals who are marked by social differences are Othered by being made mass subject in the sociological gaze. But Winfrey gives voices to this mass subject, showing the struggle, the necessary resistance, the catch on the level of the everyday. Thus the lady who coordinates so well is not embarrassed because she reveals a secret fact or because she speaks in a proud narcissistic gesture. She is embarrassed and troubled by the necessary labor in a system that catches and alienates her labor through its in-different subjective gesture.[23]

Notes

1   A sentiment echoed by Sally Jesse Raphael on her recent show also celebrating the twentieth-year anniversary of "The Phil Donahue Show."

2   James R. Walker, "More than Meets the Ear: A Factor Analysis of Student Impressions of Television Talk Show Hosts," unpublished paper delivered at Speech, Communication Association Conference, November 1987.

3   The frequent critical connection of vulgar and graphic representation and the term *sensationalist* is most illuminating. Antonio Gramsci explains that ideology is a product of sensationalism and that Freud and Marx were that last great Sensationalist. Gramsci's categorical connection of Freud and Marx defines sensationalism then as the analytical formula of the subject known in it subjection to various systems. In defining the category as such he foregrounds it as the representation, the analysis of the material relations/productions of "ideas." This suggests that sensationalism articulates the subject as a system, a practice in a determinate relation to its historical moment. Therefore, this signifying body is not fleshy, not essentialist, but a cross-sectioned map of Cornel West's "structural constraints and conjectural possibilities." Thus, Sensationalism narrates from the different body in which a signifying specificity of difference articulates a systemic reordering of truth, knowledge, masculine, feminine, and so on. The body is the practice, the ritual of talk, and its shock is to the generic I and its natural truth. Winfrey's difference, its spectacular difference, articulates a body or a material presence articulated in and through discourse. In this sense, Sensationalism as an aesthetic and philosophical category helps to define her "semiotic politics." See Antonio Gramsci, "The concept of 'Ideology,'" in *Communications and Class Struggle: 1. Capitalism, Imperialism*, ed. Armand Mattelart and Seth Siegelaub (New York: International General, 1979), 99–100.

4   The importance of gender in the determination of the operation of talk on talk shows was again evident when on a recent show on the tragedy of infertility Geraldo included his wife and himself on the panel. But even when he positioned himself as a guest, Geraldo never talked simply as a guest. In a performance that suggested a comedy routine of self-reflexivity or split personality, he would step back and ask his wife and even himself questions in the omniscient, third person voice as Geraldo-investigative-reporter-and-talk-show-host, then literally turn around and give answers in the pained first person voice as Geraldo-part-of-an-infertile-couple. The masculine voice never just talks, it is always positioned in the classical paradigm of subject/object.

5   Henry Louis Gates, Jr., *The Signifying Monkey: A Theory of African-American Literary Criticism* (New York, Oxford: Oxford University Press, 1988), 182.

6   Ibid., 196.

7   Emily Prager, "Oprah's Opera," *Village Voice*, March 10, 1987, 45, 48.

8   See Jacqueline Rose, "Feminism and the Psychic," in *Sexuality in the Field of Vision* (London: Verso, 1986), 15. "It does seem to me however, that it is precisely because of what psychoanalysis throws into question at just this level that feminism too, which has centered sexuality on the political stage, often about turns of psychoanalysis when faced with the twists and vicissitudes which psychoanalysis exposes at the heart of sexuality itself."

9   Recently, Jesse Jackson, 1988 presidential candidate and great liberal hope, announced that he will host a syndicated talk show to discuss the important issues and give voice to

the disenfranchised. He sees this move as a political venture, not as entertainment. It is this acknowledgement of the talk show format that indicates its potential as popular political site of resistance in the Gramscian sense.

10 See *Newsweek*, March 13, 1989, "How Women Are Changing TV: New Power On and Off the Screen." This cover story is the popular articulation of the flip side, a renegotiation of the talk show's subject as victim phenomenon, but a side that could only have come after Oprah and the talk show put women as a subject category on TV. I think it is interesting that the epitome of this trend is located in Murphy Brown, a TV journalist, the respectable version of Oprah – white, WASP, thin, and seriously minded in the information industry. Here is the Fiskeian claw-back effect which is operative also in the "sitcomitization" of this storied subjectivity. In the sitcom, women whine, act aggressively, and speak from "bad PMS" about the shit that they take from society and get applauded for their feisty personalities. The applause comes because the sitcom provides episodic or fictive closure for the feminine displeasure; it provides a structure to read the grain of that disruptive voice away. Diane English, executive producer of "Murphy Brown" notes that "TV's new women aren't trying to please other people. Saying what's on your mind is in. Not being afraid of what people think of you is in. You have to have *edges* to work today." I believe the irritating woman is applauded in this format because the sitcom closes down the resistant interpellation in that it moves the process of subject recognition back along the axis of narcissistic identification, character identification: thus, "We are represented, so I do not need to be represented." These shows operate through a misrecognition in which the struggles of feminine subjectivity are resolved and the good woman is identified at the end of each episode.

11 In her defense of psychoanalysis as a feminist practice, Jacqueline Rose notes that "only the concept of subjectivity at odds with itself gives back to women the right to an impasse at the point of sexual identity with no nostalgia whatsoever for its possible future integration into a norm." In suggesting the epistemological and political links between psychoanalysis and feminism, Rose constructs the necessity of another process of subjectivity. She reads this different process of the feminine from Freud's comments on femininity and his larger, more radical project (the Lacanian Freud of the split subject), where he notes the exacerbated struggle of the feminine subject the incomplete struggle of the feminine subject, and, so, the feminine subject as the privileged subject as object for tracing the trace of ideological discontent of the subject. Rose, "Feminism and the Psychic," 15.

12 It is this configuration of the feminine's/victim's/struggling subject's story that indicates that the best prop for this discursive victim – the privilege to speak – might be that of the analysand. However, feminist theory has figured the analysand as the always-already spoken, that the feminine, especially in the therapeutic gesture, has no access to language. But in Jacques Lacan's re-turn to transference he agrees with this position, then dissents. He opens up a space for the articulation of the subject in the moment of negative transference when the analysand rejects the analyst's analysis, when the analysand resists not analysis, not articulation, but that specific articulation. Lacan remarks that the constitution of the subject is a dialectical process in which the determinate moment is not the synthesis but the negative transference. In negative transference the analysand acts from a resistance that is not a leaving behind the activity of analysis but a blurring the line between the positions in of subject/object, subject/Other, analyst/analysand, and

so creating a space for her to speak her story. While this subject formed through negative transference is not cured, obviously, it is not the "cure" as ego psychology would have it.

13 This redefinition of issues was clear in the just completed presidential race in which the candidates fielded questions like "What would you do if your wife was raped?" These questions ask for a narrative position, an unfolding of the subject in a story, rather than a policy statement.

14 Barbara Grizzuti Harrison, "The Importance of Being Oprah," *New York Times Magazine*, June 11, 1989, 91–98.

15 Gates, Jr., *The Signifying Monkey*, 127–130.

16 One of the best examples of Oprah Winfrey's overdetermined position was the media brouhaha over TV *Guides'* August 20–September 1, 1989, cover. The cover story was: "Oprah! The richest woman on TV? How she amassed her $250 million fortune." But it was the accompanying illustration that had Oprah Winfrey's head on Ann Margaret's (tanned? colorized?) body glamorously dressed in a revealing and sparkling frock seductively perched on a pile of money. The composite drawing drew much comment ranging from continued attacks on Oprah's weight and her greed to TV *Guide's* loss of its "reputation." But the image indicates well the multiple discourses the sign of Oprah Winfrey traverses, for example, (1) class, both the Horatio Alger success story of democratically guaranteed upward mobility and the post modern success story of consumer fulfillment and media labor; (2) body, both the story of celebrity glamour and the story of abject feminine; (3) race, both the story of "passing" and the story of identity politics; and so on. The only sure message the collage states is that it is impossible to render Oprah Winfrey – her difference denies authenticity and "natural" representation. In fact, the double operation includes Oprah Winfrey herself. In interviews with the *New York Times* and MS. magazine, she presents herself in terms of the human success story refusing to be identified as an African American woman. In those texts, race and gender are barriers to be overcome by the strong in spirit. On the other hand, Oprah Winfrey uses her very real power over production in the media industry (Harpo industries) to insist on racially mixed panels on her talk show; to make even the most innocuous talk show programs racially conscious (like the clichéd talk show program on the makeover where she spent a good part of the show on the myths and problems of black hair, skin care, and cosmetic products); and to produce in the popular media (TV movie of the week, sitcoms, and so on) primarily projects with a strong cultural significance to the African American voice. In fact, her first dramatic project – a TV movie adaptation of Gloria Naylor's "Women of Brewster Place" – was so stridently black and feminist that African American and white men's groups complained of the gender bias and forced the softening of the narrative when the movie became a series. I think it is her overdetermined difference that has allowed her the space to succeed in commanding cultural attention. It is this kind of difference that makes her space on the talk show circuit so powerful that in a little over three years she has become a household word and substantial media power. But the doubling operation of her subjectivity makes her a media star more of awe than adoration especially because her racial difference is combined with a strident gender difference.

17 In 1984 she became the host of a then ratings-floundering show "A.M. Chicago" after a successful stint of reporting and anchoring on a local news program, then graduating to co-hosting a local talk show, "People Are Talking", on ABC's Baltimore affiliate. The year her Chicago show went national – 1986 – she won three Daytime Emmys. She also became

the focus of tabloid scandal and comedic attention befitting major media stardom and developed her own production company to develop dramatic series and specials of her own choosing (all distinctly African American projects to date).

18 The tabloid and the intertextual interest in Oprah as the site of discursive disturbance in the vision of television were equal, if not greater than the recent use of Geraldo Rivera, Morton Downy, and Maury Povitch. Of course, the talk show's threat to civilization was only registered when the masculine speaking subject become involved in this "body politic" of information and debate. Before the men dived and danced into the (cess)pool, the talk show, as Oprah defined it, was a joke, a disturbance, a mere eruption of the repressed, a mere slip of the tongue.

19 Andreas Huyssen, "Mass Culture as Woman," in Tania Modleski and Kathleen Woodward (eds) *Studies in Entertainment: Critical Approaches to Mass Culture* (Bloomington: Indiana University Press, 1986). Tania Modleski, "Femininity as Mas(s)querade: A Feminist Approach to Mass Culture," in Colin McCabe *et al.* (eds) *High Theory, Low Culture* (Manchester: Manchester University Press, 1986).

20 I am taking this notion of the abject as the hinge of the Symbolic system that manifests the specific, graphic detailing of difference(s) from a combination of Julia Kristeva's theory of abjection in *Powers of Horror: An Essay on Abjection* (New York: Columbia University Press, 1982), specifically chapters 2–4: and Naomi Schor's theory of the feminization of the detail in Western representation in *Reading in Detail: Aesthetics and the Feminine* (New York: Methuen, 1987).

21 As Freud, Lacan, Barthes, Eco, and so on have noted, narrative is inherently Symbolic. In fact, in *Three Essays on Sexuality* (New York: Basic Books, 1975), and *Image-Music-Text* (trans. Stephen Heath, New York: Hill and Wang, *c.* 1977), Freud and Barthes, respectively, suggest that it may be the first symbolic act on the part of the child as subject: as a childish investigator into the theories of birth, and as the subject rewriting the family romance in order to accept the rule of the Law.

22 I am taking this concept of the negatively structured subject from Kaja Silverman's *The Acoustic Mirror: The Female Voice in Psychoanalysis and Cinema* (Bloomington: Indiana University Press, 1988), where she attempts to reread the Maternal space as a space of symbolic resistance and negatively constructed subjectivity. Silverman's suggestion that the space of the M/Other structures a speaking subject in resistance makes sense of Oprah Winfrey's negative appeal. And, then, it is no coincidence that the guest quoted above creates an awkward opposition between her good mother and Oprah, now situated as the bad mother. In the light of Silverman's argument Oprah Winfrey signifying relationship to her guests, the media, and the audience indicate clearly how the different body is necessarily negotiated within the Symbolic register. Silverman's analysis of maternity as necessarily within the Symbolic economy, points out that "body" or the marks of difference may be abjected but they still function within systems of discourse and representation. They do not fall outside representation, outside language. This redrawn feminine body privileges of the labor of mouth (speaking) and ears (hearing), instead of the labor of the natural orifice of birth (uterus/vagina).

23 I would like to thank Lynne Joyrich, Hilary Radner, and Denise Witzig for their listening to and talking through important issues in this essay.

The Moving Image in Crisis   16

Disaster and memory

WHEELER WINSTON DIXON

First of all, we must understand that we are living in the final years of the twentieth century. The numerous technological, social, political, and epidemiological changes during the past one hundred years – even from the midcentury mark – are both striking and curiously cyclical. The Internet and the web, both in their infancy, roughly parallel the development of the cinematograph almost exactly a century ago. AIDS and HIV infections, once the stuff of science fiction, have become routine markers of mortality. "Information" is tightly controlled, channeled, and manipulated by a few giant conglomerates; what we receive at the end of the "news filter" is a precensored, predigested diet of titillation and gossip, lacking both the style and substance of empirical factual reportage.

Yet certain alternative voices creep through the dominant superstructure of the news media. Sometimes these stories are buried in national newspapers, far from the front page, and occasionally they appear in antiestablishment journals. Chat rooms on the Internet offer a variety of wild speculation and gossip, all of it infected with a tossed-off flavor of instantaneous composition and dissemination. But as we crest on the wave of the twentieth century, slouching uneasily toward the millennium (whether it starts in the year 2000 or 2001 is itself a matter of contentious debate), the public discourse of our century's conclusion is framed by a series of disturbing polarities: the embrace of spectatorial violence versus the search for political and social peace; the desire for escapist entertainment, coupled with a near-prurient absorption in the most private details of the lives of total strangers; the denial of the body in what is undoubtedly the opening decades of an unforeseeably protracted battle against a series of worldwide epidemics, as augured by HIV and AIDS; and a desire to sacrifice personal freedom for an antiseptic fantasyland of manufactured domestic tranquillity, as typified by the move toward "gated" communities, or compounds like the Disney Corporation's "instant town," Celebration, U.S.A.

At the same time, televisual media mini-conglomerates have sprung up in the late 1990s which aggressively and shamelessly cross-plug each other, not surprisingly since they are often owned by the same parent organization: NBC's *Dateline* plugs *People* magazine as part of its ostensible news programming, to better publicize both corporate entities; MSNBC cannibalizes the stock news footage from NBC's library into an ultra-cheap retrospective show entitled *Now and Then*; Ted Turner's various networks (CNN, Headline News, TNT, the Cartoon Network, and Turner Classic Movies) relentlessly promote each other's interests in crossover advertisements. But it goes much further than this. Turner was acquired in the late 1990s by Time Warner, which owns the cable networks HBO, Cinemax, and other cable providers (it also has a share in Court TV, Comedy Central, and Black Entertainment Television). This, of course, is in addition to its publishing and motion picture production interests, in which it competes with Disney/ABC and Viacom/MTV, two other giants in the cable industry. The Viacom/MTV bloc owns Nickelodeon, VH1, MTV, Showtime, The Movie Channel (TMC), TV Land, and M2, in addition to a 50 percent stake in the USA and Sci-Fi Channel networks. Disney/ABC controls not only the ABC network and its various on-line progeny (all the individual cable and broadcast networks mentioned above maintain a significant web presence) but also the Disney Channel, 80 percent of ESPN1 and ESPN2, 50 percent of Lifetime, and 37.5 percent of A&E and the History Channel (*see* Dempsey, 1). This in itself explains why these particular cable networks dominate the current programming fare offered by most cable operators (such as Falcon Cable and Cablevision); they're all various "narrowcasting" elements of the same organization.

But even this is only a fragment of the overall televisual and theatrical motion picture landscape. While CBS/Westinghouse scrambles to get its own cable network off the ground, paying a reported $1.55 billion in stock for ownership of the Nashville Network and Country Music Television (CMT) (Dempsey, 1), cable suppliers such as TCI also own an interest in the various channels they provide to the public, including a stake in all the previously mentioned Time Warner services, plus "The Discovery Channel, The Learning Channel, The Family Channel, E! Entertainment Television, Court TV, Encore and Starz" (Dempsey, 84). Thus distribution and production of programming are vertically integrated in the style of late nineties' production, distribution, and exhibition all owned by a few major players who control the overwhelming majority of home televisual programming, whether disseminated by a cable operator or supplier, or through a direct satellite broadcast (dish) system. No matter which system the viewer chooses, the "choices" are the same: slices of the same monolithic visual block, each channel relentlessly counterpromoting the other.

Packages of new channels are thus spun off from existing channels by the major conglomerates and parceled out with previously existing cable channels in a presold set of offerings that are often forced upon cable suppliers in a "take it or leave it" manner, thus mimicking the nearly century-old theatrical distribution practices of *block booking* and/or *blind bidding*, in which theater owners were forced to take a series of inferior films from a major studio in order to obtain rights to one or two blockbuster releases (block booking), often without even seeing the product they were being sold (blind bidding). When Ted Turner purchased Metro-Goldwyn-Mayer, he quickly sold the physical assets of the company (real estate, buildings, and the like), but retained control of MGM's most important asset: a motion picture library of more than five hundred feature films, plus numerous shorts, cartoons, one-reelers, and promotional films, all of which he programmed first on his TNT network (with commercials) and later on TCM (Turner Classic Movies) without sponsor interruptions.

This explains why American Movie Classics (AMC), which is primarily (75 percent) owned by the cable supplier Cablevision, but which currently owns none of the films it programs, is looking at the back inventory of both Columbia and Universal as potential acquisitions, in return for a percentage of AMC (Dempsey, 84). The most important property for these cable channels is product programming – which they can cycle and recycle in various packages, specials, documentaries, and clip compilations to their subscribers. The former MGM building is a repository only of memories; the real property of MGM (as well as of

Universal, Paramount, Twentieth Century Fox, Columbia, Warner Brothers, and the other Hollywood studios) is their back library of theatrical motion pictures, which Turner now owns.

Similarly, in theatrical motion pictures, we are witnessing the same cross-plugging and conglomerate practices which now dominate our viewing at home. It makes sense; motion picture production is now a ruinously costly affair, with films like James Cameron's *Titanic* approaching the $200 million mark by many estimates, simply for its negative cost, before any exhibition, distribution, or promotion expenses are added in. *Titanic* (1997) is essentially a remake of Roy Ward Baker's *A Night to Remember* (1958). Unlike Baker's film (and the ones that preceded it, including Werner Klingler and Herbert Selpin's 1943 Nazi version, and Jean Negulesco's 1953 Hollywood film, both also simply called *Titanic*), Cameron's *Titanic* offers spectacle in the place of substance and cynically attempts to capture the audience's attention through the use of an archetypal Romeo and Juliet "star cross'd lovers" conceit. Contemporary teen idol Leonardo DiCaprio appears in the film as the fictive Jack Dawson, an American sketch artist who wins two tickets to the *Titanic*'s maiden voyage in a last-minute poker game, while Kate Winslet portrays rich heiress Rose DeWitt Bukater, another passenger on the ill-fated ship, who falls into Dawson's arms to escape an arranged marriage with one Cal Hockley (Billy Zane). The entire story is told in flashback, narrated by a very elderly Rose (Gloria Stuart), who survives the disaster through a series of fortuitous circumstances; Jack Dawson perishes in a suitably heroic manner.

Titanic strives to live up to its tide, and indeed, in budget, length (195 minutes), and sheer aural/visual spectacle, it certainly does so, but Cameron simultaneously reduces the human element of the tragedy to a series of schematic caricatures. Jack is entirely true and brave; Rose is a misunderstood rich girl who adores Picasso and Monet; Cal is a ruthless, sneering villain, straight out of a Victorian melodrama. The music cues relentlessly attempt to manipulate our emotions (now you should cry; now you're scared), the dialogue is astonishingly wooden (when the *Titanic* first hits the iceberg, Jack declares solemnly, "This is bad"), and every other character in the film (with the possible exception of Kathy Bates as Molly Brown) is marginalized in a foredoomed attempt to focus our attentions solely on the young lovers, to the expense of all the other passengers.

In contrast, *A Night to Remember* views the *Titanic* disaster as a series of interlocking human tragedies, in which each character is given an equal amount of screen time, and no one story overwhelms the others. Further, Baker's film, while quite convincingly brutal in its final sequences of the disaster, never allows the spectacle to overpower the human aspect of the drama. Thus, *A Night to Remember* emerges as a profoundly moving and emotional tragedy on all levels, rather than a mammoth disaster spectacle masquerading as a heterotopic teenage love story, aimed primarily at PG-13 audiences. In addition, the budget for *A Night to Remember* was also much smaller than that of the 1997 *Titanic* – slightly over $1,000,000.

Indeed, at the midcentury point a major studio release could be whipped up for as little as $210,000 (Eugene Lourie's *The Beast from 20,000 Fathoms*, 1953), utilizing a series of back-projection plates, a papier-mâché dinosaur left over from *Bringing Up Baby*, and Ray Harryhausen's then state-of-the-art stop-motion special effects. Lourie shot the film in a mere twelve days; the film was then sold outright to Warner Brothers for $450,000, launched with a media campaign costing less than $100,000 and released to a gross of $5 million (Lourie, 234–41). The $210,000 figure included, incidentally, the rights to Ray Bradbury's short story, "The Fog Horn," which served as the basic narrative backdrop for the piece. Similarly, in 1956 Ray Harryhausen provided a series of spectacular special effects depicting the destruction of Washington, D.C., by a fleet of alien spacecraft in Fred F. Sears's *Earth vs. the Flying Saucers*, completed in less than two weeks for slightly less than $200,000, which also opened to respectable box office figures and later served as the template for Roland Emmerich's mega-budgeted remake *Independence Day* (1996), a film costing nearly $100 million to create and promote. As of this writing, the average budget of a theatrical motion picture for the negative cost alone is approximately $50 million – plus the expenses for prints, advertising, and promotion; nearly fifty years ago American International could produce such films as Roger Corman's *The Pit and the Pendulum* (1961) in Panavision and Pathécolor for a mere $300,000, a figure that seems risible today. Numerous other disaster films of the fifties, sixties, and seventies brought about the destruction of cities, countries, and even entire civilizations in a compellingly low-budget manner. Maurice Yacowar cites a series of basic "types" of conventional generic disaster films in his excellent essay "The Bug in the Rug: Notes on the Disaster Genre," detailing a group of "Natural Attack," "Ship of Fools," "The City Fails," Monster, Survival, War, Historical and Comic Disaster films, in which women and men face disaster and usually escape without serious consequences, except in the more ambitious examples of the genre. Thus John Guillermin and Irwin Allen's *The Towering Inferno* (1974) becomes roughly equivalent to Fritz Lang's *Metropolis* (1926); in each film, the hub of a gigantic city collapses (in Guillermin and Allen's film an enormous skyscraper, in Lang's an underground worker's city) while frantic efforts are made by various figures of authority to reestablish order. In all these films, as Yacowar notes, a series of conventions or archetypes are at work, including the use of various cast members to dramatize racial and/or social inequities, and the fact that the genre disaster film isolates its characters in order to place them in a position of peril, in which "all systems fail" inexorably, one after the other (see Yacowar, 261–79). All these films were created for comparatively little money; almost without exception. their special effects (the "disaster" sequences, specifically, or their very reason for existing as cinema entertainments) have become dated and unconvincing with the passage of time, and the increasing reliance on digital special effects. But though technology continues to evolve, the disaster film continues to thrive in ever-more-rarified territory, the cost of production driven up into the $50–90 million range through the demands of increased star salaries, lavish sequences of destruction, and international ad campaigns which routinely launch a film in thousands of theaters simultaneously.

As costs have risen, so have the concomitant risks of production, resulting in a spate of big-budgeted sequels (hardly a new practice, of course: consider the *Bowery Boys / East Side Kids / Dead End Kids* films of the thirties through the fifties, or the *Sherlock Holmes*, *Blondie*, *Henry Aldrich*, *Andy Hardy*, *Hopalong Cassidy*, *Charlie Chan*, or the *Whistler* series from the same approximate era). But where the modest genre films of an earlier era were content to support an A feature of greater artistic and aesthetic ambition on the bottom half of a double bill, today's genre films have become the main attraction, the dominant force in motion picture production and exploitation, because (as with all genre films and/or sequels), they are to a large extent a presold, pretested quantity whose qualities and limitations are known to the audience before they enter the theater, or see a trailer, or view a promo clip on television during an interview with one of the film's star commodities.

An excellent example of this is Les Mayfield's 1997 remake of Robert Stevenson's *The Absent-Minded Professor* (1961), this time around simply titled *Flubber*, after the gooey, endlessly elastic substance accidentally created by a befuddled, lovable college professor working at home in his basement laboratory. The original film, modestly budgeted, shot in black and white with Fred MacMurray as the star, has been transmogrified in the 1997 version into a multimillion-dollar digital special effects festival, starring Robin Williams as the absent-minded Professor Philip Brainard, and featuring a host of technical tricks which become the sole focus of the film's narrative thrust and/or aesthetic ambition. Both films, the original and the remake, are primitive genre entertainment, but the new version lacks the virtue of any originality (it is merely a carbon copy of the first film, with increased technical wizardry and a robot sidekick Weebo, to hype up the action), and, unlike the original film, exists in a cinematic landscape where nearly every other major studio release is a genre film as well (Rogers 1997a). In addition, Disney is shrewdly banking on baby boomers' memories of the first film to bring parents to the sequel with their offspring, in a psychic construct which thus ensures a return to the past for the adult viewer, and a presold customer in the child viewer, who is thus primed for the numerous sequels which usually follow a major studio genre release, sequels which now bypass the theatrical marketplace altogether and are released, in mass quantities, as straight-to-tape home videos. After Disney successfully released Aladdin in theaters in 1992, Honey, I Shrunk the Kids in 1989, and Beauty and the Beast in 1991, subsequent sequels were simply released to home video, having been sufficiently presold to both parents and their children by virtue of the initial theatrical outing.

Indeed, it is the sameness of these films that assures audiences that they will not be challenged, confused, or surprised in anything other than the most elementary manner. The classical Hollywood cinema model has been exhausted through overuse of narrative closure, reliance on excess of spectacle, hypertechnic sound tracks, and the like, to the point that the contemporary cinema has become simply a memory of itself, a replaying of old roles and outmoded plotlines, all fueled by the inexorability of a "star" system that manufactures and then discards the protagonists of this phantom automatism. Thus Masayuki Sao's 1997 film Shall We Dance? – a Japanese production clearly targeted directly at Western audiences – exudes a sense of forced Orientalism with each succeedingly calculated frame, or Nick Cassavetes' 1997 She's So Lovely emulates the work of his late father without adding any element of true risk or experimentation to the proceedings. Anthony Minghella recycles the spectacle of David Lean's ultracolonialist Lawrence of Arabia (1962), a 222-minute blockbuster from the era of The Sound of Music (1965) and Mary Poppins (1964) in his 1996 film The English Patient, a conflation, as Jonathan Miller suggested to me, of Barbara Cartland's novels and the character of "Biggles," the 1940s aviator-hero featured as the central protagonist in a series of books that captured the imagination of British schoolboys in post-World War II Britain (Dixon interview). The commercial and mainstream critical success of this Best Picture Oscar-winner should thus come as no surprise because the film itself was designed and marketed precisely for the purpose of providing the public with a simplistic romantic adventure, complete with a "sympathetic" Nazi as the film's ostensible hero, and bodice-ripping scenes straight from the back cover jacket blurb of a Harlequin romance novel. Similarly, Steven Spielberg's Schindler's List (1993), clocking in at a mammoth 195 minutes, uses black-and-white cinematography merely for effect in its disturbingly sanitized retelling of the Holocaust, commercially but not aesthetically eclipsing either Alain Resnais's Night and Fog (Nuit et Brouillard, 1955), a short film that nevertheless brings the carnal brutality of the Nazi regime into sharper and more clinical focus than Spielberg's work, or Claude Lanzmann's Shoah (1985), a 570-minute film that relentlessly documents the testimony of both victims and perpetrators of the Holocaust with a carefully considered, meditational camera eye.

For *The Scarlet Letter* (1996), Roland Joffe reworked Hawthorne's novel so that it now incorporates a generically acceptable narrative closure; Richard Attenborough's *Gandhi* (1982) reduces a curiously complex character to the one-dimensionality of a cardboard religious icon; Alan Parker's *Mississippi Burning* (1988) reframes the civil rights conflict through the eyes of two white FBI agents, Gene Hackman and Willem Dafoe; Sydney Pollack's *Out of Africa* (1985) romanticizes the early days of Kenyan colonialist domination by the British empire; Randal Kleiser's *It's My Party* (1996) turns a fatal AIDS infection into an excuse for a series of maudlin farewells and a two-day, Capraesque party in which the protagonist is reconciled with his estranged lover and extended family before committing suicide with an overdose of barbiturates; Jonathan Demme's *Philadelphia* (1993) similarly manages to snare audience sympathy through a series of clichés and stereotypes in its tale of a gay attorney, Andrew Beckett (Tom Hanks), fired from his job at a high-powered law firm because he has contracted the AIDS virus.

Beckett's eventual courtroom victory and martyr's death are eerily mirrored by Irwin Winkler's artificially upbeat conclusion to *Guilty by Suspicion* (1991), Winkler's revisionist take on the Hollywood blacklist of the late 1940s and early 1950s. When Robert De Niro defies the House Committee on Un-American Activities (HUAC) against the advice and counsel of his associates in the final scene of the film (just as Woody Allen did in Martin Ritt's 1976 film *The Front*), we are participating in a cathartic yet completely unrealistic fantasy of the supposedly inevitable triumph of good over the machinations of criminal governments or the intractable exigencies of disease. Bob Fosse's 1974 *Lenny* sanitizes the brilliant scatology of the late comic; Tim Burton's 1994 *Ed Wood* creates a happy ending in which Wood's film *Plan Nine from Outer Space* (1959) is released to an enthusiastic public reception; in fact, the film received a few desultory theatrical bookings before being dumped unceremoniously into television syndication in the early 1960s – even failure becomes a resounding success in the Hollywood genre machine.

Compare these films to Alfred Hitchcock's *Psycho* (1960) or *Vertigo* (1958), Blake Edwards's *Breakfast at Tiffany's* (1961), Robert Aldrich's *Kiss Me Deadly* (1955), Billy Wilder's *Some Like It Hot* (1959), Richard Brooks's *Cat On a Hot Tin Roof* (1958), Mike Nichols's *Who's Afraid of Virginia Woolf?* (1966), Howard Hawks's *Scarface* (1932), Leo McCarey's *Duck Soup* (1933), Frank Capra's *It Happened One Night* (1934), Fritz Lang's *Fury* (1936), William Wellman's *Public Enemy* (1931), Tod Browning's *Freaks* (1932), W. S. Van Dyke's *The Thin Man* (1934), or any other of several thousand possible examples from the first seventy-five years of the Dominant Hollywood cinema, and the vacuousness of the current product becomes instantly and painfully apparent.

With the current pervasive utilization of computer-generated image technology, which arguably reaches its contemporary zenith in the digital creature effects of Phil Tippett in Paul Verhoeven's *Starship Troopers* (1997), the theatrical motion picture has become the repository of spectacle above all other considerations. But even the brilliantly digitized arachnid warriors of Verhoeven's film can't disguise its essential emptiness; although Verhoeven acknowledges the film's various stylistic and thematic debts to Capra's *Why We Fight* series and Leni Riefenstahl's Nazi propaganda films, he has basically created a film in which the updated nightmare insects (reminiscent of Gordon Douglas's *Them!*, 1954) meet the cast of the teleseries *Baywatch*. Casper Van Dien, Dina Meyer, and Denise Richards are perfect icons for a new cinema age: plastic, perfect, endlessly interchangeable action figures without depth and/or emotion.

Nor is Verhoeven shy in annotating his various cinematic homages in the film. In an interview he noted directly that "the first shot [in the film] is taken from [Riefenstahl's] *Triumph of the Will* (1935) . . . when the soldiers look at the camera and say, 'I'm doing my part!' That's from Riefenstahl. We copied it" (Svetkey, 8). As to the profusion of Nazi-styled uniforms, insignias, giant eagles, and other paraphernalia sprinkled throughout the film's visual design, *Starship Troopers'* screenwriter, Edward Neumeier, explained that "the reason for all the German uniforms and everything is because the Germans made the best-looking stuff. Art directors love it" (Svetkey, 8). Verhoeven avows that his underlying purpose in making the film was to "use subversive imagery to make a point about society. I tried to seduce the audience to join [the futuristic] society, but then ask, 'What are you really joining up for?'" (Svetkey, 9). Yet the protofascist imagery, and the equally lockstep ideology propounded by both the film and Robert Heinlein's 1959 source novel of the same name is so enthusiastically triumphant that one can see why the film generated more than $22 million on its opening weekend; once again, it makes fascism chic.

This desire for control, community, and a commonality of shared experience has been exemplified on a global scale by the media frenzy over the violent death of Diana Spencer in the aftermath of an automobile accident in Paris on Sunday, August 31, 1997. Salman Rushdie was perhaps the first writer to draw the comparison between the death of Diana and the public's fascination with spectacles of violent vehicular carnage as presented in David Cronenberg's film *Crash* (1996). But as Rushdie himself admitted, the connection is an obvious one. Noted Rushdie: "It is one of the darker ironies of a dark event that the themes and ideas explored by [J. G.] Ballard [British author of the novel *Crash*, on which the film was based] and Cronenberg, themes and ideas that many in Britain have called pornographic, should have been lethally acted out in the car accident that killed Diana, Princess of Wales, Dodi Fayed, and their drunken driver" (Rushdie, 68).

Rushdie goes on to argue that the public's desire to possess Diana through the lens of the camera, to possess the simulacrum of her silver gelatin image printed on the page, in conjunction with the relentless pursuit of what are now being termed the "Stalkerazzi," together conspired to bring about the circumstances leading up to Diana's death. "In Diana's fatal crash, the camera (both as reporter and lover) is joined to the automobile and the star, and the cocktail of death and desire becomes even more powerful than the one in Ballard's book" (38). Rushdie then goes on to suggest that, in view of the Windsors' treatment of Diana during her marriage to Prince Charles, "the Royal Family itself . . . may just possibly be on the way out" (69), dethroned by an outraged public who at long last have had enough with the inequitable rule of a capricious monarchy, one that grows increasingly unpopular (or so it would seem) with the British public day by day.

Other commentators, most notably Christopher Hitchens, are far less sympathetic to Diana's posthumous celebrity and far more suspicious of her motives. Even the otherwise laudatory Rushdie admits that Diana had learned how to use the media to create a suitable image of herself for public consumption:

Diana, Princess of Wales, became skillful at constructing the images of herself that she wanted people to see. I recall a British newspaper editor's telling me how Diana composed the famous shot in which she sat, alone and lovelorn, in front of the world's greatest monument to love, the Taj Mahal. She knew, he said, exactly how the public would "read" this photograph. It would bring her great sympathy, and make people think (even) less well of the Prince of Wales than before. Diana was not given to using words like "semiotics," but she was a capable semiotician of herself. With increasing confidence, she gave us the signs by which we might know her as she wished to be known.

(Rushdie, 68)

Picking up on this, Hitchens argues that Diana's ultimate triumph of construction was not only her image as a "lovelorn" mother of two, cast aside by the unfeeling members of the Royal Family. Comparing Diana with Agnes Bojaxhiu, or Mother Teresa, Hitchens commented that "both had spent their careers in the service and the pursuit of the rich and powerful. Both had used poor and sick people as 'accessories' in their campaigns. And both had succeeded in pulling off the number-one triumph offered by the celebrity culture – the achievement of a status where actions are judged by reputation and not the other way around" (Hitchens, 7). Indeed, Diana's carefully managed photo ops in service of the poor and the afflicted are reminiscent of the staged newsreels in John Schlesinger's *Darling* (1965), in which Diana Scott (Julie Christie) becomes "Princess Diana" when she marries an Italian prince. Princess Diana Spencer's own later public appearances were themselves mini-masterpieces of press manipulation. Staged for the mutual benefit of a press corps (and its public) that couldn't get enough of her visage (she was on the cover of *People* magazine an astounding forty-three times), and for Diana's personal benefit as a young divorcée fighting to hang on to the trappings of power and wealth with feverish intensity, they served everyone's purposes admirably. Hitchens notes that "by her embrace of the Fayed family, [Diana made it clear] what

Figure 16.1 Charles and Diana, Prince and Princess of Wales
Courtesy of Photofest, New York

sort of company and society she considered desirable. Nonetheless, it seemed that every person in Britain believed she cared for them individually and would be at her happiest when dining in a homeless shelter" (7). In the event itself, the mass media coverage in the aftermath of the death of Diana Spencer was remarkable not only for its quantity but also for the overwhelming uncritical sentimentality that characterized its appearance in newspapers, television, and on various web sites and Internet chat groups around the world.

As Jacqueline Sharkey noted in her essay, "The Diana Aftermath," news coverage for the week of August 31 to September 6, 1997, could aptly be summarized with the phrase "All Diana, All the Time." In that week CBS, NBC, and ABC devoted a total of 197 minutes on their main evening broadcasts alone to Diana's violent death and a seemingly endless recapitulation of her life, complete with video clips of her marriage to Prince Charles, footage of the Princess and her sons on vacation, images of scandal and ceremony commingled into a continuous stream of almost unceasing media coverage. E! Entertainment Television broadcast the funeral of Diana live, as did CNN, CNBC, MSNBC, and numerous other cable services around the world. MSNBC and several other cable and/or broadcast networks replayed a video of the wedding of Diana and Prince Charles intact (except for commercial interruptions) the day after her death, for added horrific contrast.

In the days following the fatal accident, Diana became the ultimate medieval consumerist icon, the sign that far from abandoning the idea of the British Royal Family, the world audience, to say nothing of the British public, demanded not only a monarchy but its continuation, as Diana's two young sons now stand directly in line for accession to the throne. Even the tabloid press rushed to consecrate Diana in death. While the *National Enquirer*'s headline the week before her death had shrieked "Di Goes Sex-Mad – 'I Can't Get Enough!'" (Sharkey, 21), in the ensuing weeks the *Enquirer* and other supermarket tabloids would serve up a newly minted Diana for public consumption, a thirty-six-year-old humanitarian cut down in the prime of her life by the unwanted attentions of an irresponsible press corps that refused to leave her alone. The more respectable journals profited as well: *Time* sold 850,000 issues on the nation's newsstands the week of Diana's death, about "650,000 [issues] more than normal" (20).

A week later, a commemorative issue of *Time* magazine devoted exclusively to Diana sold an astounding 1.2 million copies, "the two largest sellers in the history of the magazine, according to Managing Editor Walter Isaacson" (Sharkey, 20). Fifteen million people watched a special edition of *60 Minutes* covering Diana's life and death on August 31, 1997, an hour-long show hastily assembled on the very day of her death (Sharkey, 20). Nor did the media viewing frenzy abate within a few days, or even a week; "the week of September 15 – two weeks after Diana died – broadcast networks devoted more time to the Princess and the British Monarchy than any other story" (Sharkey, 20). Compare these figures to the sixteen minutes of nightly network news time Mother Teresa received when she died on Friday, September 5, less than a week after the accident that claimed Diana's life; in that same week, Diana dominated the nightly network news airtime by nearly a ten-to-one ratio.

Diana's companion in death, Emad Mohamed "Dodi" al-Fayed, received almost no coverage at all; his father, the Egyptian tycoon Mohamed al-Fayed, owner of the department store institution Harrods and an unsuccessful suitor for British citizenship, arranged for an immediate burial, which was discreetly carried out away from the glare of news cameras and their attendant publicity. Clearly, the death of Diana Spencer dominated the public consciousness during the first weeks of September 1997 as no other story had previously been able to do. What was it about Princess Diana's troubled life and violent death that so riveted the readers and viewers of the world, some essence that other supposedly newsworthy spectacles lacked? Why was Diana's death more keenly felt, more adroitly exploited, more avidly consumed than the deaths of John or Robert Kennedy, Martin Luther King, the space shuttle Challenger disaster, Pearl Harbor, or, to be concise, any other violent celebrity death and / or international catastrophe of the entire preceding century?

In part, the answer lies in the sheer profusion of the news media available to disseminate Diana's image-in-death. One of the last images we have of Diana, perhaps the absolute last, is her ghostly presence as she exits from the Ritz Hotel through a revolving door, captured for one last time on a hotel surveillance camera. Diana's image has been cropped, scanned, digitized and reconstructed in literally hundreds of thousands of photographs, miles of film and videotape, and then sluiced out to a waiting, eager public through magazines, newspapers, web sites, cable networks, broadcast networks, local television stations, academic journals, CD-ROMs, DVDs, home video cassettes, not to mention (particularly after her death) postage stamps, coffee mugs, place mats, dish towels, commemorative dinner plates, porcelain dolls, memorial "coins" custom-stamped by various private mints, and various and sundry other items.

No wonder that on December 1, 1997, a group of attorneys filed a petition in London on behalf of the Diana, Princess of Wales Memorial Fund to have Diana's face certified as a trademark with Britain's patent office, in the hope of controlling the flood of exploitational materials created to merchandise her image. Indeed, as late as mid-December 1997, a site existed on the World Wide Web offering two "nude" photographs of Diana for public consumption, free for anyone to download without cost of any kind. A Princess Di look-alike still offers her services on the web for "TV, film and photo opportunities, corporate and commercial advertising, corporate and commercial entertaining ('meet and greet'), promotional and charity work, personal appearances, [and] modeling," although the person whose image she resembles has passed from the realm of the living into the shared sarcophagus of collective visual memory. And a transcript of the parodic "Top Ten Surprises in the Princess Diana Interview" from *The Late Show with David Letterman* for November 21, 1995, is still archived on the web, including the fictitious claims that "[it] turns out she's Mexican" and "[she] works nights at Euro-Hooters."

But can we blame the social parodists? In life, Diana was the subject of at least four TV movies, including Peter Levin's *The Royal Romance of Charles and Diana* (1982), starring Christopher Baines as Prince Charles and Catherine Oxenberg as Diana; James Goldstone's *Charles and Diana: A Royal Love Story* (1982), with David Robb and Caroline Bliss as Charles and Diana; John Powers's *Charles and Diana: Unhappily Ever After* (1992), with Roger Rees as Charles and Catherine Oxenberg reprising her role from *The Royal Romance of Charles and Diana*; and Kevin Connor's *Diana: Her True Story* (1993), featuring Serena Scott Thomas and David Threlfall in the key roles. Across the decade of these fictional representations of Diana's life, we can trace not only the "romance novel" narratives imperative of the two 1982 films but also the final images of Hollywood royalty busily engaged in bringing the fictive Diana's story to flickering life. Olivia de Havilland (as the Queen Mother), Dana Wynter (Queen Elizabeth), Stewart Granger (Prince Philip), and Ray Milland all appeared in *Royal Romance*; Christopher Lee (Prince Philip), Rod Taylor (Edward Adeane), and Charles Gray (Earl Spencer) graced *A Royal Love Story*. Interestingly, in the 1982 *Royal Love Story*, both Andrew Parker-Bowles (former "Chad and Jeremy" rock star Jeremy Clyde) and Camilla Parker-Bowles (Jo Ross) are presented as friends of the couple, wishing them all the best; by 1992's *Unhappily Ever After*, Jane How's Camilla is seen as an implacable adversary bent on wrenching the Royal marriage asunder.

By the time of 1993's *Diana: Her True Story*, Camilla's role (now played by Elizabeth Garvie) has been so enlarged as to render her third in a cast of more than twenty-five principal players, and the public revision of Diana's life in the Royal Family has come full circle. Based on Andrew Morton's book of the same title, *Diana: Her True Story* presents Diana as a victim of cruelty and careless indifference, in stark contrast to the happy newlyweds of the 1982 film. But which version are we to regard as authoritative? None of them. All are fictions, disguised as docudramas, created with an intended audience uppermost in the producer's mind. The first two films promised romance, pageantry, and medieval splendor; the second pair of films promised scandal, decadence, and insider information. In all four cases, the films are merely constructs, designed to merchandise and exploit Diana Spencer's image without her direct participation in the project.

You can have Diana's image without actually having Diana's image in these films, which offer at length the Baudrillardian conceit of a copy without an original, based as they are on a public persona manufactured by Diana and her advisers with skill, marketing sense, and an omnipresent eye for the public's appetite for spectacle. During the sixteen years of Diana's relationship with the House of Windsor, Diana mastered the art of presenting to the public exactly the image she wished them to have of her, precisely the impression that she sought to leave with the press and public who were her real courtiers in the world of the public's view.

And yet, Diana's entire childhood and early schooling seemed to prepare her for such a destiny. Born on July 1, 1961, at Park House near Sandringham, in Norfolk, into a family of considerable means, Diana's early life was one of pleasure and power, commingled with the usual domestic entanglements that shape one's interior landscape. Her mother, the Viscountess Althorp, was only twenty-five when Diana was born; her father, Viscount Althorp, was thirty-seven. She had two older sisters, Jane and Sarah, and Diana's birth was followed by that of her younger brother, Charles. The family lived in a palatial house on the Queen's Estate at Sandringham, and at Althorp House, the family estate, in the English Midlands. Diana never felt particularly at home in the vast, museumlike precincts of Althorp House, and much preferred Park House, which was both more intimate and more modern. Nevertheless, Diana's life was one of privilege and power, in close proximity to members of the Royal Family, with Princes Andrew and Edward as occasional afternoon guests, and invitations to "the Queen's winter home" (Morton, 14). But tensions between Diana's mother and father were exacerbated by a series of medical tests Lady Althorp was forced into by her husband after the birth of the couple's son John in 1959, who was born badly deformed, and "survived for only ten hours" (Morton, 10). In 1967 the couple separated, throwing the entire family ménage into psychic chaos. A bitter divorce followed, scattering the children into a variety of boarding schools and temporary living arrangements. Diana's father won custody of the children, and Lady Althorp subsequently married Peter Shand Kydd, a wealthy young entrepreneur (Morton, 16–18). Diana would immerse herself in the romantic novels of Barbara Cartland, her step-grandmother, while a succession of wildly variable "nannies" did little to compensate for the loss of her mother as a result of the divorce (Morton, 19).

Diana was an avid TV viewer, preferring shows like the pop music review *Top of the Pops* and *Coronation Street*, one of the longest-running soap operas in British television history. Indeed, Diana's fascination with soap operas did not diminish with the passage of time. As she entered the Royal Family, she still kept abreast of the plotlines of the most popular British soaps, so that she could discuss them with her constituents as an immediate shared common interest (Morton, 28). She also took ballet lessons, and attended the Riddlesworth Hall preparatory school in Norfolk, moving on to the West Heath School in Kent in 1974. Her formal education was completed at a finishing school in Rougemont, Switzerland. In 1977, Diana first met Prince Charles during a day of outdoor shooting "in the middle of a ploughed field near Nobottle Wood on the Althorp estate" (Morton, 35). Diana was hardly the center of the prince's attention on this occasion, for Prince Charles was at the time involved in a brief flirtation with Diana's sister, Sarah.

But as the relationship between Charles and Sarah diminished, Charles's interest in Diana grew, and she was invited to the prince's thirtieth birthday party at Buckingham Palace in November 1978 (Morton, 37). By the winter of 1979, Diana was moving closer to a relationship with Charles. Charles himself was already deeply involved in a friendship with Camilla Parker-Bowles, who was happy to accompany the prince on his various outdoor sporting trips, while the British public as a whole wanted Prince Charles to settle down and produce an heir to the throne (Morton, 48). In July 1980, Diana and Charles were thrown together during a weekend barbecue at the house of Commander Robert de Pass and exchanged confidences surrounding the Earl of Mountbatten's death and the ensuing funeral procession in Westminster Abbey. Diana expressed great sympathy for Charles's sadness on that occasion, and from that moment on Charles began to aggressively court Diana Spencer (Morton, 49).

By September, Charles asked Diana to join him at Balmoral Castle, for the weekend of the Braemar games (Morton, 51). That weekend she got her first taste of what her hypersurveillant future as a member of the Royal Family would be like when two photographers and a newspaper reporter spotted her fishing with Prince Charles in the Dee River (Morton, 51). Within days Diana was stalked outside her apartment by a bevy of paparazzi, who forced her to pose for photographs at a moment's notice and followed her to the Young England Kindergarten School, where she was working as a teacher. From the moment her connection with Prince Charles was discovered, her private identity and any claim she may have once had to anonymity were finished. On Friday, February 6, 1981, Prince Charles formally proposed to Diana Spencer (Morton, 56). The engagement was announced on February 24, 1981, and Princess Diana left her own flat for the last time. By now, she had an armed bodyguard from Scotland Yard who accompanied her everywhere. As she left her apartment, the body-guard told Diana, "I just want you to know that this is the last night of freedom in your life, so make the most of it" (Morton, 58). After that, Diana belonged more to the public, and to the press, than to herself.

Diana Spencer thus passed from a somewhat unstable and calamitous, if privileged, upbringing into the glaring spotlight of unceasing international celebrity within a matter of a few years. From the moment she entered the prince's orbit, her life was no longer her own. In rapid succession she gave birth to two sons, Princes William (born July 21, 1982) and Harry (born September 15, 1984). Private and public life commingled into a continual dialogue with the public, which often overshadowed her increasingly formal relationship with her husband. In 1982, in a somewhat bizarre quirk of fate, Diana traveled to Monaco to represent the queen at the funeral of Princess Grace, who had died in an automobile accident on September 14. The two women had met before Diana's marriage to Prince Charles at a social event at London's Goldsmith Hall on March 9, 1981, and were photographed chatting amiably amidst their star-studded surroundings.

As many other observers have noted, Grace and Diana's lives had, sadly, a great deal of commonality. Diana died after her Mercedes slammed into a wall in a tunnel under the Place de l'Alma trying to escape a pursuing flock of paparazzi; although she remained conscious for several hours following the accident, her wounds were so severe that she could not possibly have survived. Princess Grace died when her car went off the road on a steep thoroughfare outside of Monaco, hurtled down a precipice, and landed in a culvert. Both Diana and Grace were "commoners" who had married royalty; neither was particularly happy in her marriage. As Diana attended Grace's funeral, she could not possibly have imagined that as a consequence of her own fame, she, too, would die in a violent automobile accident fifteen years later. As an observer noted, "Both princesses felt betrayed in their marriages. But Diana, at least, looked as though she was starting a new life. For Grace, it was already too late" (August, 5A).

In 1983, Diana and Charles toured New Zealand and Australia on a formal visit, and soon official visits (with her two sons in tow) to Brazil, South Korea, Nigeria, Canada, Portugal, Cameroon, Japan, Spain, and other countries followed. By this time, too, Diana was already deeply involved in the charity work that would consume much of the rest of her life, particularly on behalf of persons with HIV/AIDS, and the international abolition of land mines. After her separation from Charles in December of 1992, and their subsequent divorce in August 1996, this work increased, as Diana took on an increasingly demanding schedule of lectures, fund-raising events, and public appearances.

On September 12, 1996, Diana attended the thirtieth anniversary meeting of the International Leprosy Association in London; also in September she attended various charity events for breast cancer. In early January 1997, Diana visited the Diana Red Cross Handicap Hospital in Angola and shortly thereafter turned her attentions to Bosnia, where her campaign against the use of antipersonnel land mines continued in earnest. While in Angola, she also visited various hospitals in Luanda, the capital city, and on January 17, 1997, she attended a meeting of the Red Cross in Washington, again to discuss the issue of land mines as a negative force in maintaining international territorial domains. Diana auctioned off many of her dresses collected over the years at a gala event at Christie's; she comforted Elton John after fashion designer Gianni Versace was senselessly shot to death in front of his house in July 1997. By this time, Diana had evolved into a highly accomplished public speaker and could easily hold the podium, as she did in a series of cancer research fund-raising events in June 1997 in Chicago, Washington, D.C., and London. And as all this charitable work progressed, as Diana was firmly involved in establishing both a new public and private persona for herself, she met Dodi al-Fayed, much to the general disapproval of the press and public, who regarded Mohamed al-Fayed and his son as interlopers in British society, who attempted to buy their respective ways into public favor.

Yet Mohamed Fayed had known Diana "since childhood" (Spoto, 149), before her involvement with the Royal Family, and so Diana's vacation with the Fayed family could easily be seen as an extension of her financially comfortable yet emotionally tempestuous childhood. Gradually, Diana and the younger Fayed became more deeply involved, although Diana remained uncertain about the true nature of her relationship with Dodi. As she told one confidant in the last month of her life, "I haven't taken such a long time to get out of one poor marriage in order to get into another one" (Spoto, 165). Dodi Fayed indeed had something of a reputation as an international playboy and had produced or served as coproducer on such films as Hugh Hudson's *Chariots of Fire* (1981), George Roy Hill's *The World*

According to Garp (1982), and Steven Spielberg's *Hook* (1991). Fayed, a billionaire's son, was thus no stranger to power and celebrity. At the time of his involvement with Diana, the forty-two-year-old sometime film producer, who partied in a series of lavish rented mansions in Beverly Hills at a reported cost of $20,000 to $35,000 a month, was already noted for his high-living, extravagant lifestyle. Dodi Fayed was an inveterate partygiver, whose guests included Ryan O'Neal, Robert Downey, Jr., Brooke Shields, Tony Curtis, and other Hollywood celebrities. A graduate of Sandhurst Military Academy and a junior officer in London for the United Arab Emirates, Fayed would drift from house to house, party to party, often traveling in the company of his father on their multimillion-dollar yacht. Dodi Fayed's life, then, was also a life of power and wealth, and many social observers saw in Diana's relationship with Dodi Fayed a parallel between Jackie Kennedy's romance and subsequent marriage to multi-millionaire shipping entrepreneur Aristotle Onassis.

Diana herself professed to be uneasy with the lavish presents that Dodi pressed upon her: "I don't want to be bought. I have everything I want. I just want someone to be there for me, to make me feel safe and secure," she told a friend (Spoto, 165). But within days, all these concerns would be swept aside by the simple yet unalterable fact that Diana herself had ceased to exist altogether. When she left the Ritz Hotel at 12:15 A.M. on the night of August 31, 1997, and was seen drifting ethereally through the revolving doors of the hotel for one final public moment before her departure from this world, how could she have known that, within a matter of minutes, the black 1994 Mercedes S-280 she and her companions were traveling in would be reduced to a hunk of scrap metal? "The front end [of the car was] telescoped into the engine, which was forced almost through the driver's seat. Inside the pile of rubble, Henri Paul and Dodi al-Fayed were dead, their bodies hideously mangled. [The driver] Trevor Rees-Jones was seriously injured [and] Diana, Princess of Wales was near death. It was 12:24 [A.M.]" (Spoto, 176). Extricated from the wreck, Diana and Rees-Jones were rushed to the Hôpital de la Pitié Salpêtrière, but due to the difficulty in retrieving them from the wrecked automobile, they were not admitted until two in the morning. Despite intensive labors by a medical team that worked feverishly to bring Diana back to life, Diana went into cardiac arrest and died at 4 A.M. on August 31, 1997 (Spoto, 177).

And thus, it was all over, except for the memorial tributes that would soon follow her death and, in a peculiar manner, eclipse and perhaps even transcend the public reception she had been afforded in life. . . .

And now, in death, she has become, along with James Dean, Marilyn Monroe, and a select few others, a legendary pop culture icon. We are right to be suspect of the maudlin outpouring of grief that attended Diana's death, even if it was genuine. For in her violent death, Diana ultimately sacrificed herself on the altar of celebrity martyrdom, thus fulfilling the public's darkest need to witness both the fairy tale beginning, and the tragic conclusion, of a very short and very public life.

References

August, Marilyn. 1997. "Grace, Diana Had Much in Common," *Lincoln* (*Neb.*) *Journal Star*, September 2, p. 5A.

Baudrillard, Jean. 1994. "Crash." In *Simulacra and Simulation*, III–19. Translated by Shelia Faria Glaser. Ann Arbor: University of Michigan Press.

Dempsey, John. 1997. "Cable Ops Caught in Nets." *Variety*, February 17–23, pp. 1, 84.

Dixon, Wheeler Winston. Forthcoming. "When I'm 63: an Interview with Jonathan Miller." *Popular Culture Review*.

Hitchens, Christopher. 1997. "Throne and Altar," *The Nation*, September 29, p. 7.

Lourie, Eugene. 1985. *My Work in Films*. New York: Harcourt Brace Jovanovich.

Morton, Andrew. 1992. *Diana: Her True Story*. New York: Simon and Schuster.

Rogers, Pauline. 1997. "Making Goo: Dean Cundey, ASC, Brings *Flubber* to Life." *International Photographer* (December): 38–43, 55.

Rushdie, Salman. 1997. "Crash." *The New Yorker*, September 15, pp. 68–69.

Sharkey, Jacqueline. 1997. "The Diana Aftermath." *American Journalism Review* (November): 19–25.

Spoto, Donald. 1997. *Diana: The Last Year*. New York: Harmony.

Svetkey, Benjamin, with Chris Nashawaty. 1997. "The Reich Stuff." *Entertainment Weekly*, November 21, pp. 8–9.

Yacowar, Maurice. 1995. "The Bug in the Rug: Notes on the Disaster Genre." In Barry Keith Grant, ed., *Film Genre Reader* II, 261–79. Austin: University of Texas Press.

Bibliography

Affron, Charles. *Cinema and Sentiment*. Chicago and London: University of Chicago Press, 1982.

Anger, Kenneth. *Hollywood Babylon*. New York: Bantam/Doubleday/Dell, 1981.

—— *Hollywood Babylon* II. New York: Dutton, 1984.

Babington, Bruce. *British Stars and Stardom: From Alma Taylor to Sean Connery*. Manchester: Manchester University Press, 2001.

Bálaázs, Béla. "The Face of Man" in Braudy, Leo and Cohen, Marshall. *Film Theory and Criticism: Introductory Readings*. Fifth Edition. New York: Oxford University Press, 1999, 306–311.

Barthes, Roland. *Mythologies*. Trans. Annette Lavers. New York: Hill and Wang, 1972.

—— "The Face of Garbo" in Braudy, Leo and Cohen, Marshall. *Film Theory and Criticism: Introductory Readings*. Fifth Edition. New York and Oxford: Oxford University Press, 1999, 536–538.

Benayoun, Robert. *The Look of Buster Keaton*. Trans. Randall Conrad. New York: St. Martin's Press, 1983.

Bogle, Donald. *Toms, Coons, Mulattoes, Mammies, and Bucks*. New York: Continuum, 1989.

Braudy, Leo. *The Frenzy of Renown: Fame and its History*. New York: Vintage Books, 1997.

Bruno, Michael. *Venus in Hollywood: The Continental Enchantress from Garbo to Loren*. New York: Charles Stuart, 1970.

Butler, Jeremy. *Star Texts: Image and Performance in Film and Television*. Detroit: Wayne State University Press, 1991.

Carroll, Noel. *An In-Depth Analysis of Buster Keaton's The General*. New York University, 1976.

Cohan, Steven. *Masked Men: Masculinity and the Movies in the Fifties*. Bloomington: Indiana University Press, 1997.

Cohan, Steven and Hark, Ina Rae. *Screening the Male: Exploring Masculinities in Hollywood Cinema*. London and New York: Routledge, 1993.

Cohen, Daniel and Cohen, Susan *Hollywood Hunks and Heroes*. New York: Exeter Books, 1985.

Crawford, Christina. *Mommie Dearest*. New York: William Morrow, 1978.

Custen, George F. *Bio/Pics: How Hollywood Constructed Public History*. New Brunswick: Rutgers University Press, 1992.

Da, Lottie and Alexander, Jan. *Bad Girls of the Silver Screen*. New York: Carroll and Graf, 1989.

Damico, James. "Ingrid from Lorraine to Stromboli: Analyzing the Public's Perception of a Film Star" in Butler, Jeremy G. *Star Texts: Image and Performance in Film and Television*. Detroit: Wayne State University Press, 1991.

Deleuze, Gilles. *Masochism: An Interpretation of Coldness and Cruelty*. Trans. Jean McNeil. New York: Brazillerr, 1971.

—— *Cinema: The Movement Image, Volume I*. Minneapolis: University of Minnesota Press, 1990.

Dyer, Richard. *Stars*. London: British Film Institute, 1979.

—— *Heavenly Bodies: Film Stars and Society*. London: British Film Institute, 1987.

Ebert, Roger. "Final Fantasy: The Spirits Within" [Film Review]. *The Chicago Sun-Times* (11 July 2001).

Eckert, Charles. "The Carole Lombard in Macy's Window" in Gaines, Jane and Herzog, Charlotte. *Fabrications: Costume and the Female Body*. New York and London: Routledge, 1990, 100–121.

Gaines, Jane. "Costume and Narrative: How Dress Tells the Woman's Story" in Gaines, Jane and Herzog, Charlotte. *Fabrications: Costume and the Female Body*. New York and London: Routledge, 1990, 180–211.

Gaines, Jane and Herzog, Charlotte. *Fabrications: Costume and the Female Body*. New York and London: Routledge, 1990.

Gemson, Joshua. *Claims to Fame: Celebrity in Contemporary America*. Berkeley: University of California Press, 1994.

Gledhill, Christine, ed. *Stardom: Industry of Desire*. New York: Routledge, 1991.

Griffith, Richard. *The Movie Stars*. Garden City, NY: Doubleday, 1970.

Guiles, Fred. *Legend: The Life and Death of Marilyn Monroe*. New York: Stern and Day, 1984.

Gundle, Stephen. "Fame, Fashion, and Style: The Italian Star System," in *Italian Cultural Studies*. Eds. David Foegacs and Robert Lumley. Oxford: Oxford University Press, 1996.

Hake, Sabine. *Popular Cinema of the Third Reich*. Austin: University of Texas Press, 2001.

Hansen, Miriam. *Babel and Babylon: Spectatorship in American Silent Film*. Cambridge, MA: Harvard University Press, 1991.

James, Caryn. "And Now, the 16th Minute of Fame," *The New York Times* (13 March 2002) B1, 8.

Juran, Robert A. *Old Familiar Faces: The Great Character Actors and Actresses of Hollywood's Golden Era*. Sarasota, FL: Movie Memories Publishers, 1995.

King, John, Lopez, Ana M. and Alvarado, Manuel. *Mediating Two Worlds: Cinematic Encounters in the Americas*. New York: BFI Institute, 1993.

Lamparski, Richard. *Whatever Became Of?* New York: Crown, 1986.

Landy, Marcia. "The Folklore of Femininity and Stardom," *Italian Film*. New York: Cambridge University Press, 2001, 261–309.

Logan, Joshua. *Movie Stars, People, and Me*. New York: Delacorte, 1978.

López, Ana and Noriega, Chon A., eds. *The Ethnic Eye: Latino Media Arts*. Minneapolis: University of Minnesota Press, 1996.

MacCann, Richard Dyer. *Stars Appear*. Metuchen, NJ: Scarecrow Press; Iowa City: Image and Idea, 1992.

McDonald, Paul. *The Star System: Hollywood's Construction of Popular Identities*. London: Wallflower, 2000.

McLean, Adrienne L. and Cook, David A., eds. *Hollywood Headline: A Century of Film Scandal*. New Brunswick, NJ and London: Rutgers University Press, 2001.

Macnab, Geoffrey. *Searching for Stars: Stardom and Screen Acting in British Cinema*. London: New York: Cassell, 2000.

Maland, Charles. *Chaplin and American Culture: The Evolution of a Star Image*. Princeton: Princeton University Press, 1989.

Mailer, Norman. *Marilyn*. New York: Grosset and Dunlap, 1973.

Mellen, Joan. "The Mae West Nobody Knows" in Braudy, Leo and Cohen, Marshall. *Film Theory and Criticism: Introductory Readings*. Fifth Edition. New York and Oxford: Oxford University Press, 1999, 576–583.

Morin, Edgar. *The Stars*. Trans. Richard Howard. New York: Grove Press, 1960.

Naremore, James. *Acting in the Cinema*. Berkeley: University of California Press, 1988.

Oates, Joyce Carol. *Blonde*. New York: Harper Collins, 2000.

Parris, Barry. *Garbo*. New York: Alfred Knopf, 1995.

Pearson, Roberta E. *Eloquent Gestures: The Transformation of Performance Style in the Griffith Biograph Films*. Berkeley: University of California Press, 1992.

Peary, Danny. *Cult Movie Stars*. New York: Simon and Schuster, 1991.

Plantinga, Carl and Smith, Greg M. *Passionate Views: Film, Cognition, and Emotion*. Baltimore: Johns Hopkins University Press, 1999.

Powdermaker, Hortense. *Hollywood, The Dream Factory: An Anthropologist Looks at the Movie-Makers*. Boston: Little, Brown, 1950.

Quinlan, David. *Wicked Women of the Screen*. New York: St. Martin's Press, 1987.

Rigaut, Jacques. "Mae Murray" in Hammond, Paul, ed. *The Shadow and its Shadow: Surrealist Writings on Cinema*. London: British Film Institute, 1978.

Riva, Maria. *Marlene Dietrich*. New York: Knopf, 1993.

Roberts, Shari. "Seeing Stars: Feminine Spectacle, Female Spectators, and World War II Hollywood Musicals." Thesis: University of Chicago, 1993.

Robertson, Pamela. *Guilty Pleasures: Feminist Camp from Mae West to Madonna*. Durham, NC: Duke University Press, 1996.

Shipman, David. *The Great Movie Stars: The Golden Years*. New York: Hill and Wang, 1979.

—— *The Great Movie Stars: The Independent Years*. London: Macdonald, 1991.

Sklar, Robert. *City Boys: Cagney, Bogart, Garfield*. Princeton, NJ: Princeton University Press, 1992.

Stacey, Jackie. *Star-Gazing: Hollywood Cinema and Female Spectatorship*. London and New York: Routledge, 1994.

Staiger, Janet. *Interpreting Films: Studies in the Historical Reception of American Cinema*. Princeton, NJ: Princeton University Press, 1992.

—— *Perverse Spectators: The Practice of Film Reception*. New York and London: New York University Press, 2000.

Steinem, Gloria. *Marilyn*. New York: Henry Holt, 1986.

Studlar, Gaylyn. *This Mad Masquerade: Stardom and Masculinity in the Jazz Age*. New York: Columbia University Press, 1996.

Summers, Anthony. *Goddess: The Secret Lives of Marilyn Monroe*. New York: Macmillan, 1985.

Turim, Maureen. "Designing Women: The Emergence of the New Sweetheart Line" in Gaines, Jane and Herzog, Charlotte. *Fabrications: Costume and the Female Body*. New York and London: Routledge, 1990, 212–228.

Tyler, Parker. *The Hollywood Hallucination*. New York: Creative Age Press, 1944.

—— *Magic and Myth of the Movies*. New York: H. Holt, 1947.

Tynan, Kenneth. "Three Individualists: Garbo" in *Curtains: Selections from the Drama Criticism and Related Writings*. New York: Atheneum, 1961, 347–352.

Vasudev, Aruna. *Frames of Mind: Reflections on Indian Cinema*. New Delhi: UBS Publishers' Distributors, 1995.

Vincendeau, Ginette. *Stars and Stardom in French Cinema*. London: Continuum, 2000.

Wagenknecht, Edward. *Stars of the Silents*. Metuchen, NJ: Scarecrow Press, 1987.

Walker, Alexander. *Stardom: The Hollywood Phenomenon*. New York: Stein and Day, 1970.

Index

Note: page numbers in italics denote illustrations